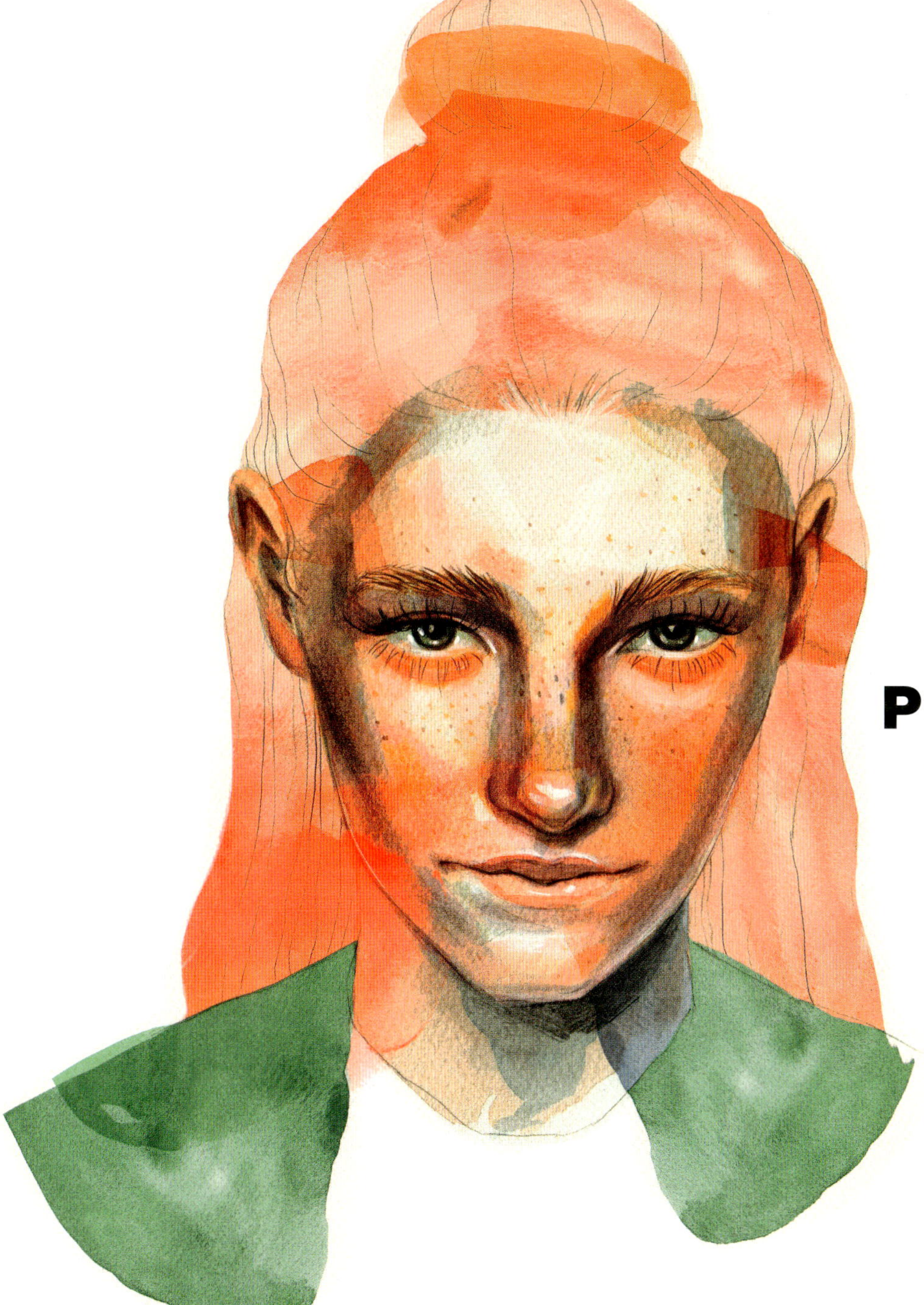

CREATIVE PORTRAITS
IN WATERCOLOR

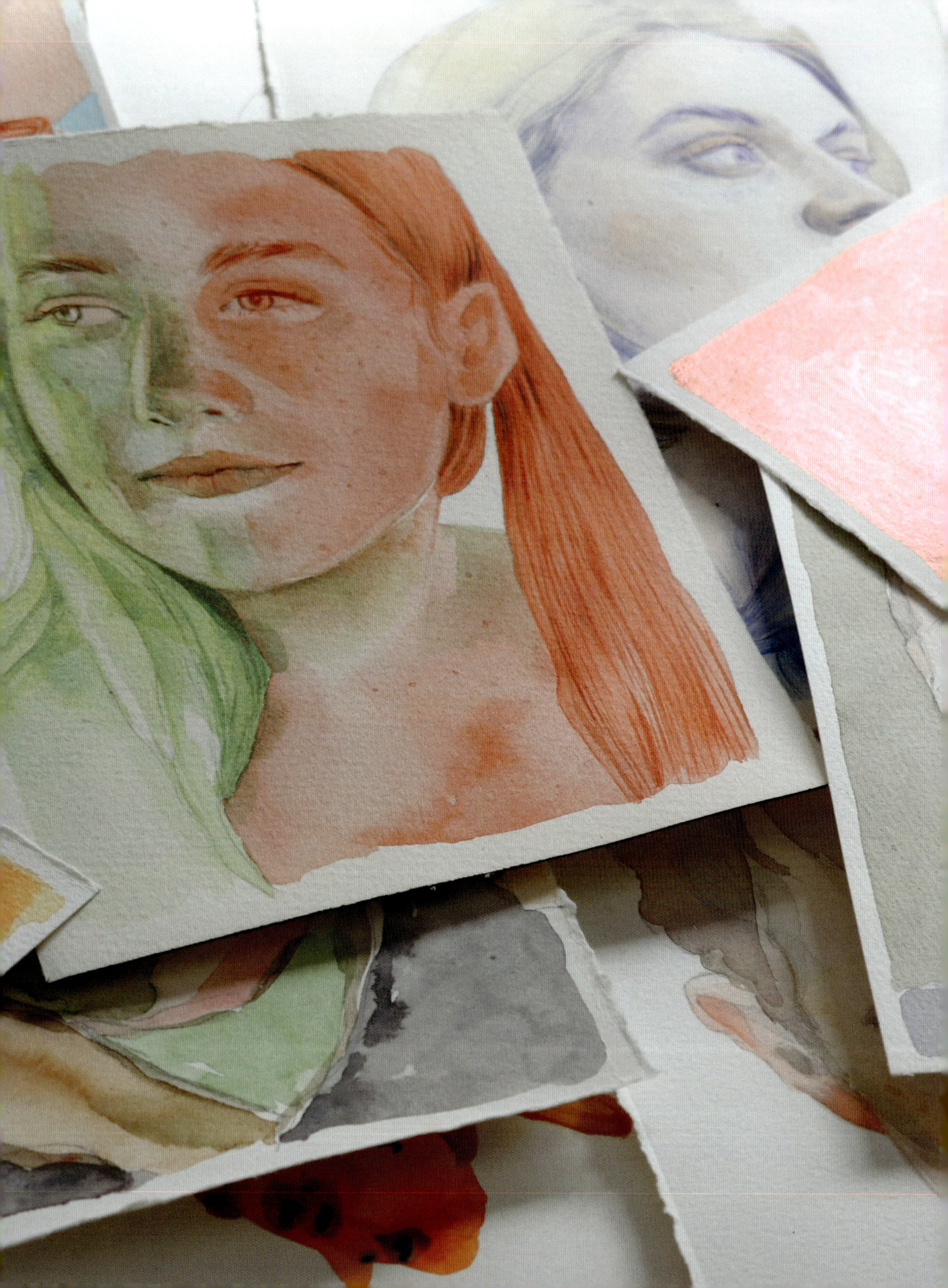

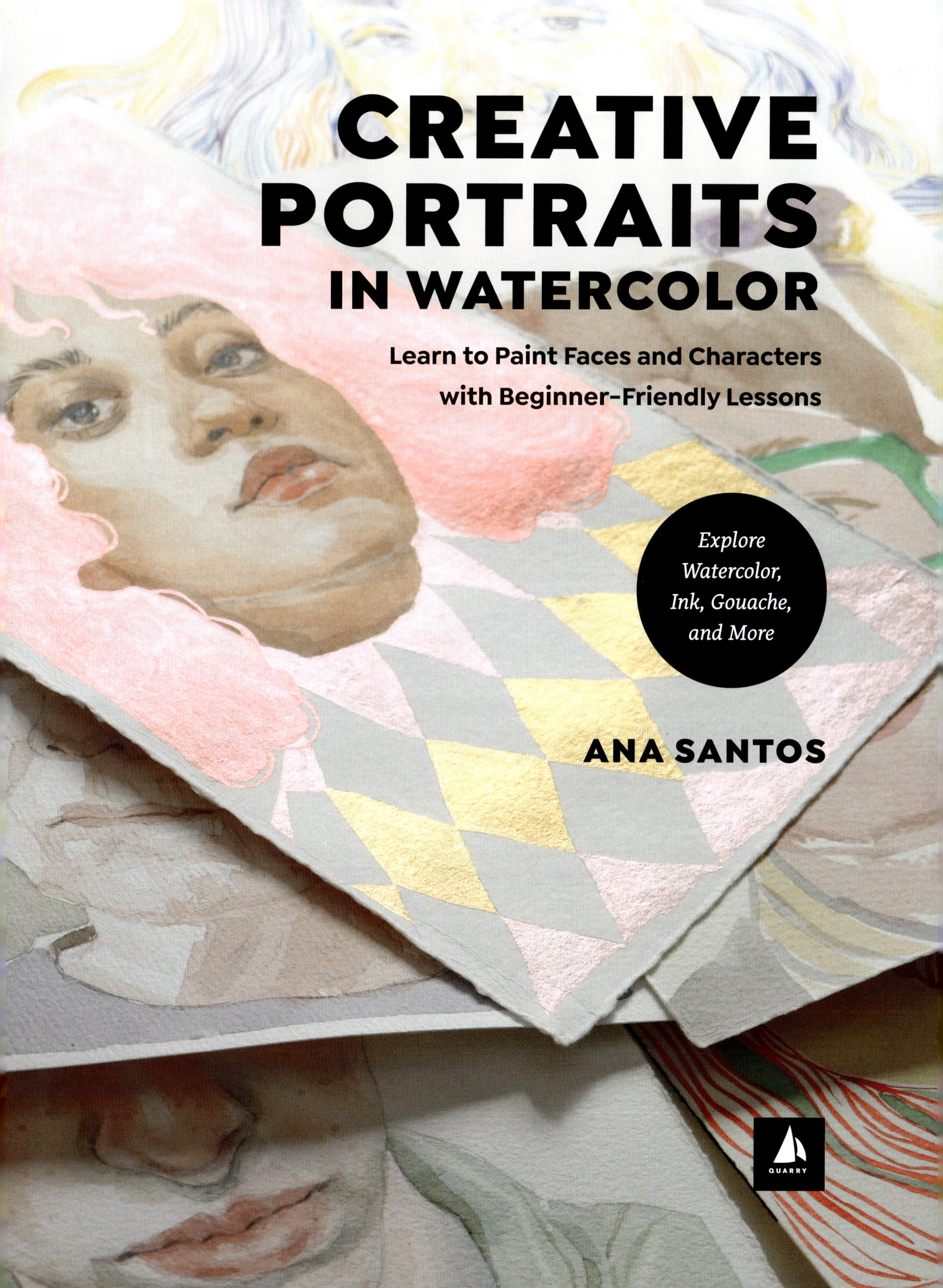

CREATIVE PORTRAITS IN WATERCOLOR

Learn to Paint Faces and Characters with Beginner-Friendly Lessons

Explore Watercolor, Ink, Gouache, and More

ANA SANTOS

QUARRY

CONTENTS

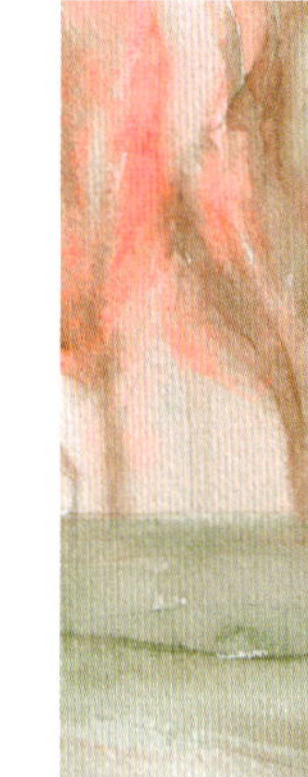

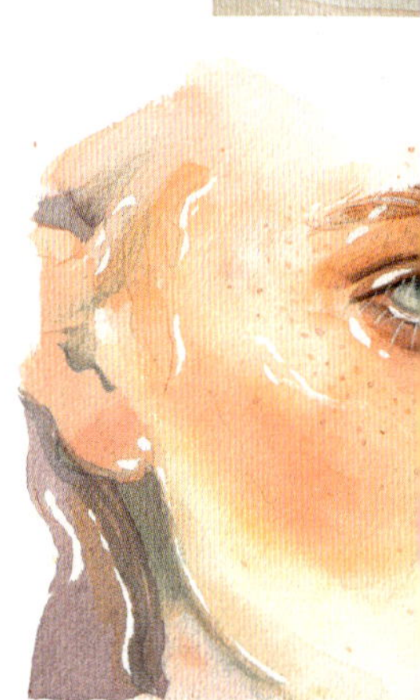

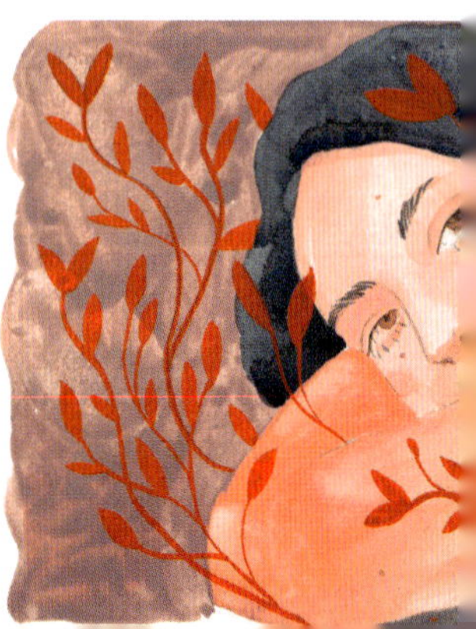

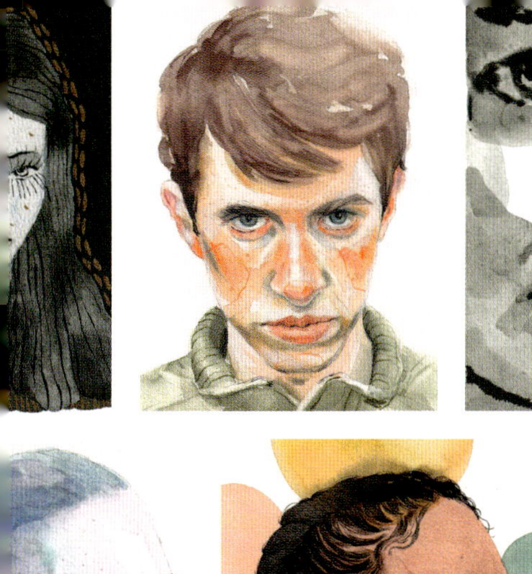
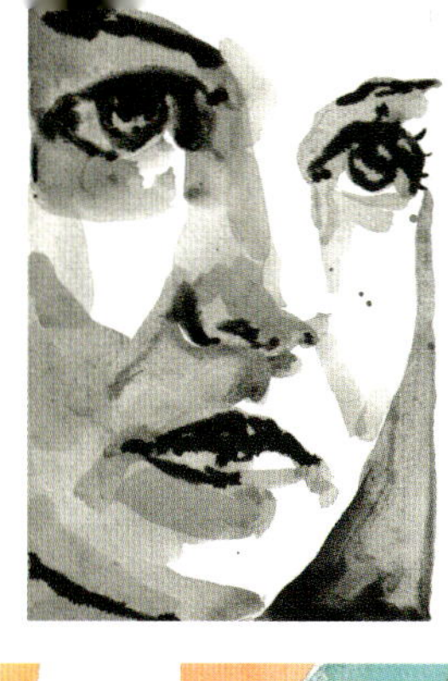
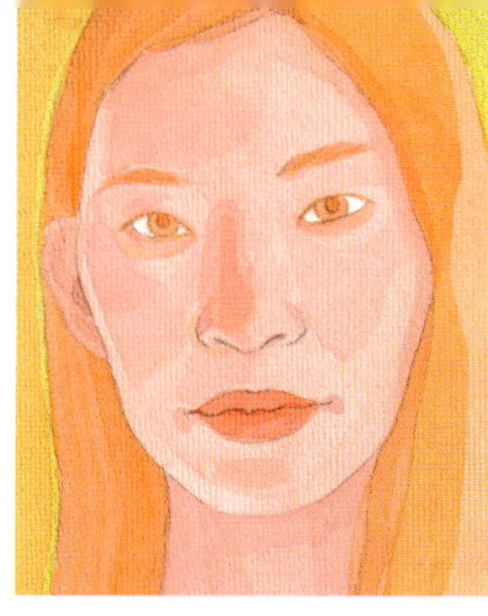
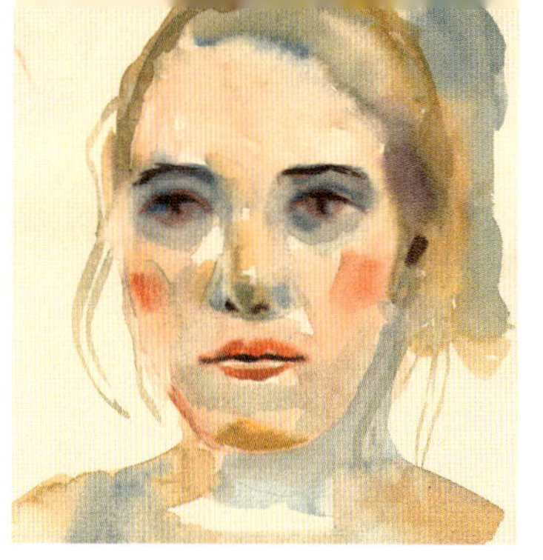
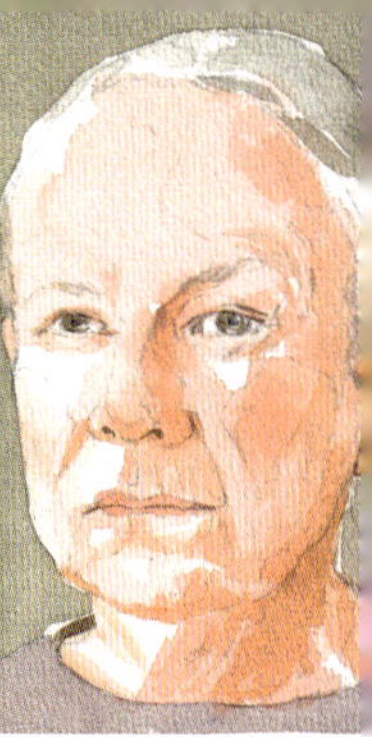
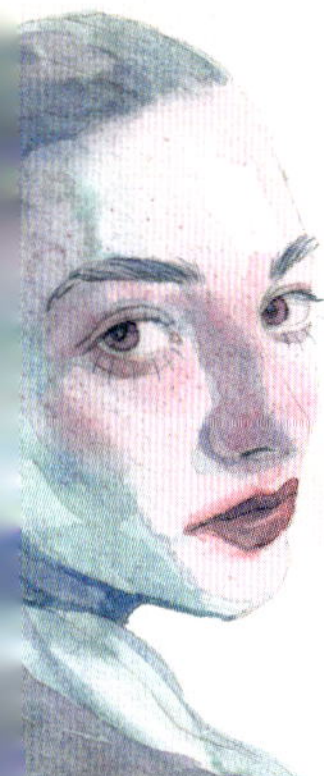
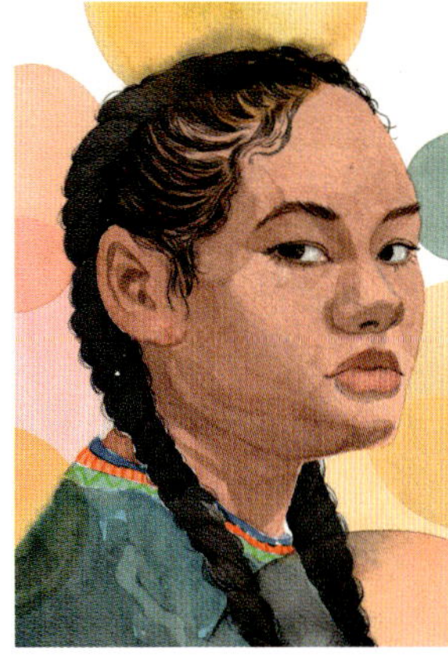
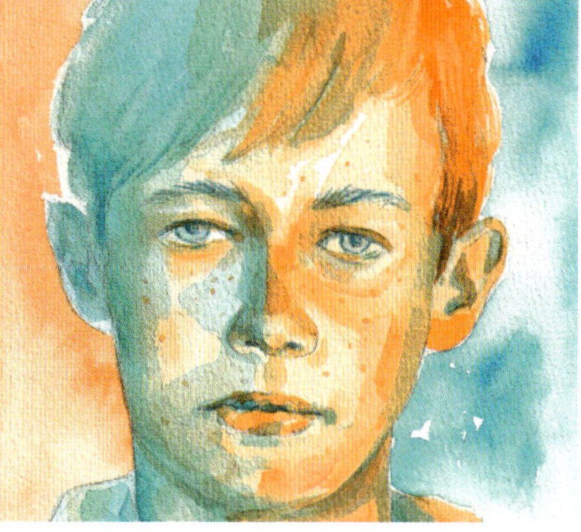
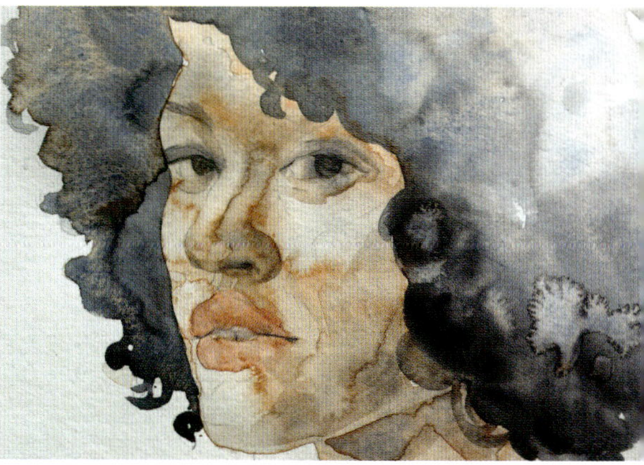
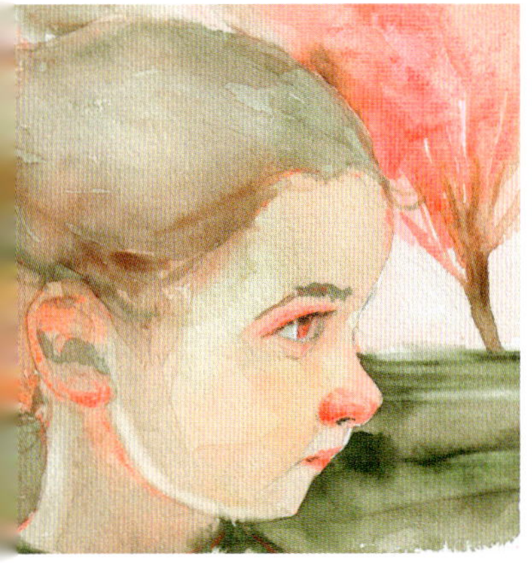
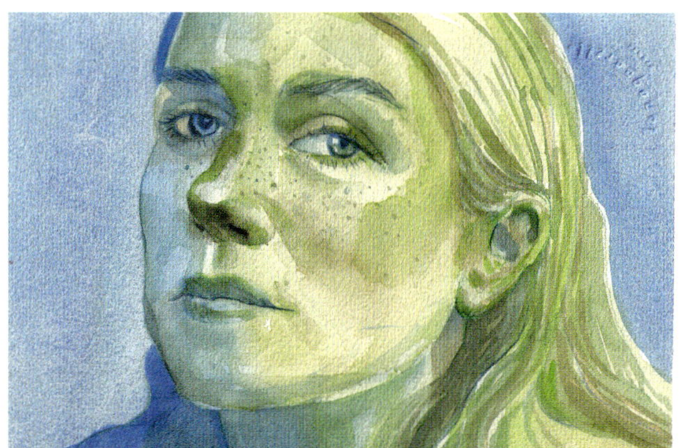
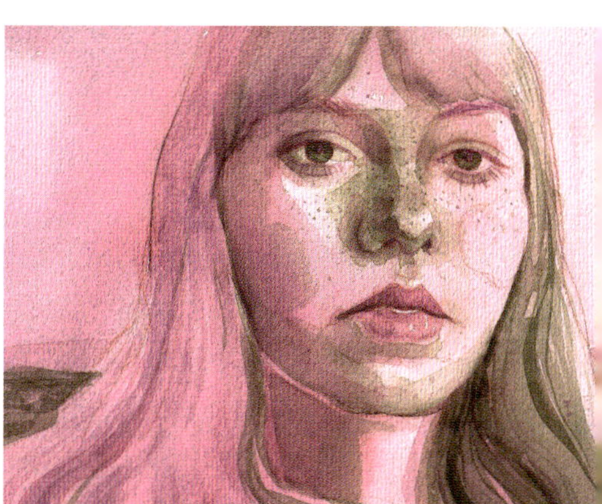
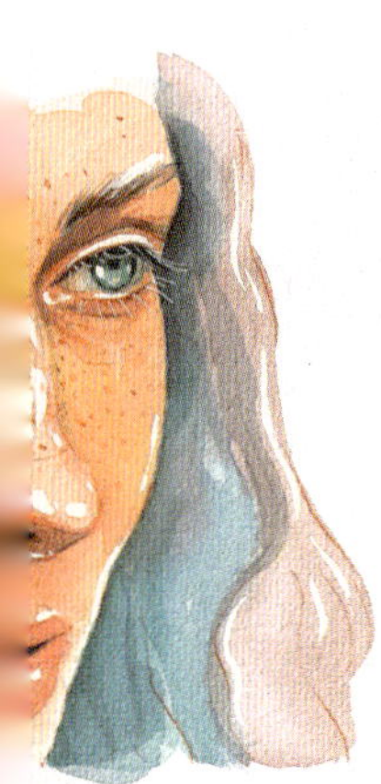
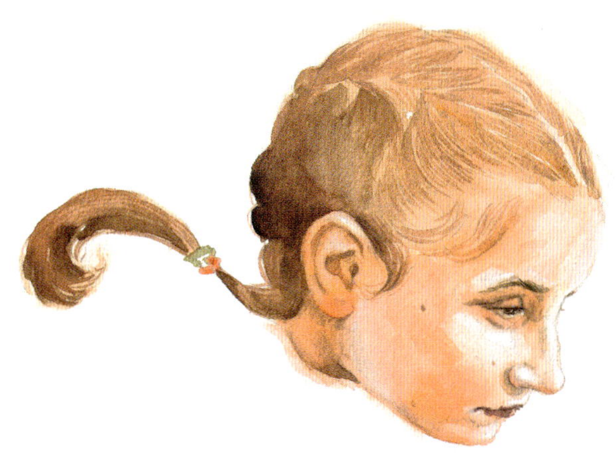
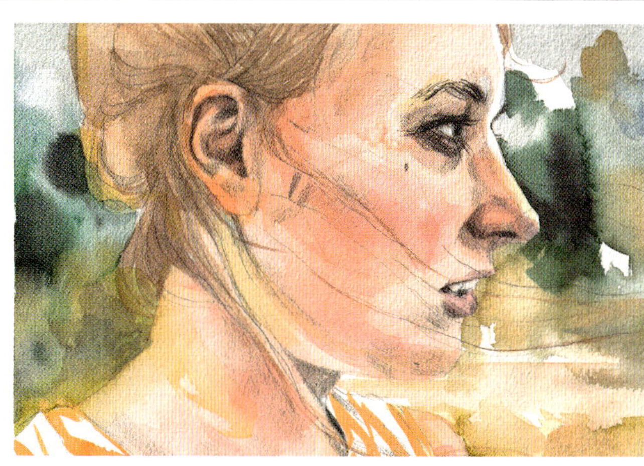
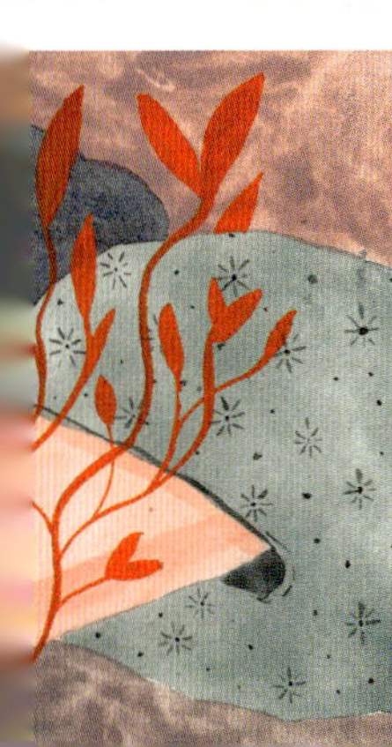
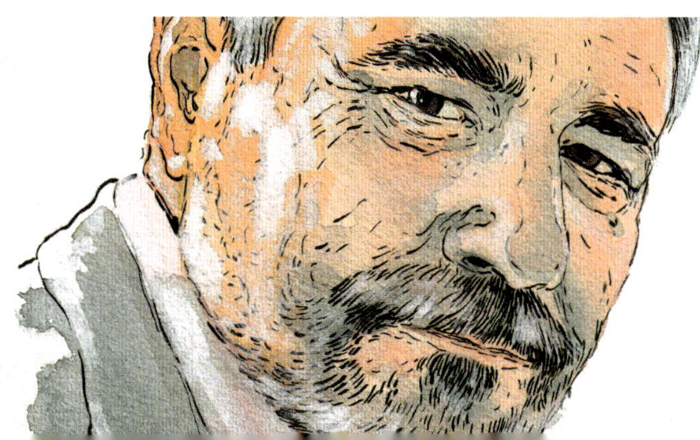
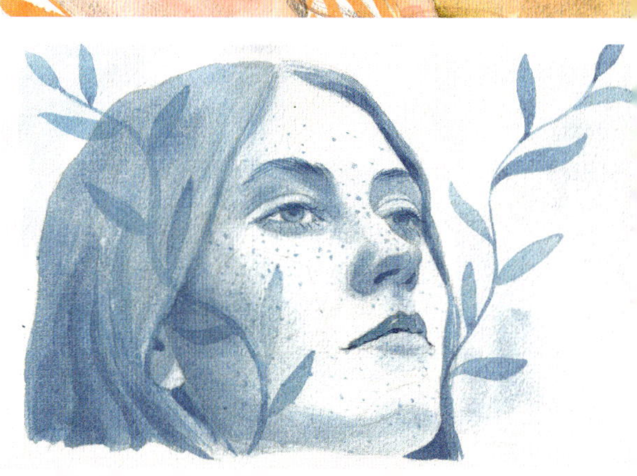

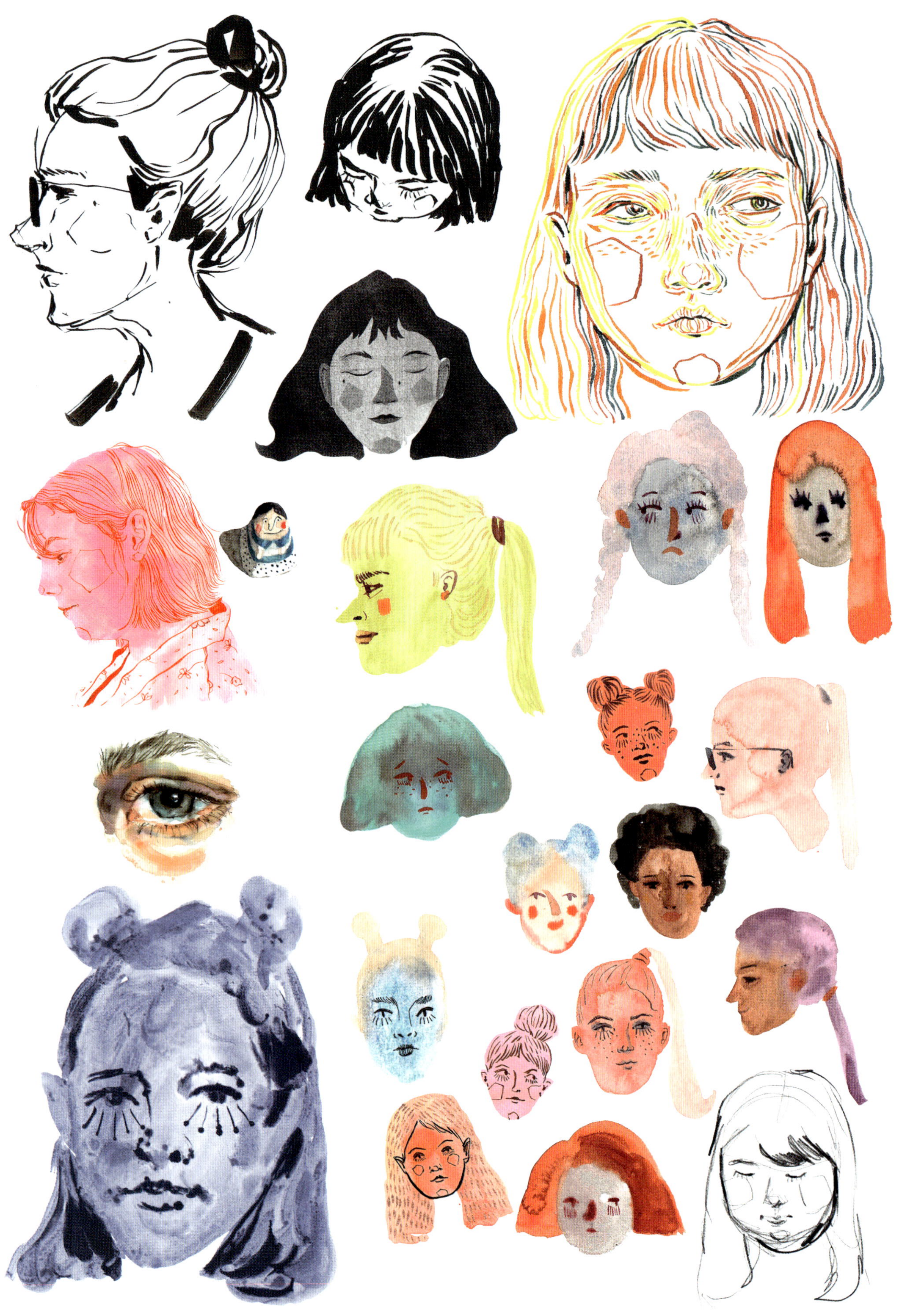

INTRODUCTION

Drawing has been one of my favorite activities ever since I was a girl. It's always been a refuge where I can find calm. Portraits have especially always fascinated me. What I liked the most was inventing faces and giving them a particular personality.

I discovered watercolor in school, and it's been with me ever since. It was when I finished my studies in fine arts that I began to understand watercolor more deeply and became interested in the diverse techniques it offers.

What fascinates me most about this medium is that despite seeming simple, paint plus water, you can create endless effects, textures, and varied strokes, depending on how you combine those two things. It's one of the techniques best suited for combining with other methods and materials, and that makes it even more versatile. Using different types of paper gives you even more possibilities.

For me, watercolor is pure surprise. It's magic and chance, and that's what makes it so special. To let the water flow and adjust itself on its own, to surprise yourself with the result, to have patience during the drying, to discover new effects and finishes—I believe that with watercolor, you never stop learning and surprising yourself.

Play and experimentation are fundamental to my work. Learning new techniques, trying different finishes, and above all, enjoying myself and having fun during the process—I believe these are most important when it comes to choosing watercolor painting as a recreational activity. I like to paint with other types of materials, such as oils, acrylics, and so on, but watercolor has that random and surprising magic that always makes me come back.

In this book, I want to share some of the things that I've learned over the years. I didn't want a very complex book, so I've tried to be brief and introduce simple techniques so you can get to know this mysterious friend watercolor little by little. Even though this book is about portraiture, you can apply what you learn here to whatever you desire—and remember, above all, to have fun and enjoy the process.

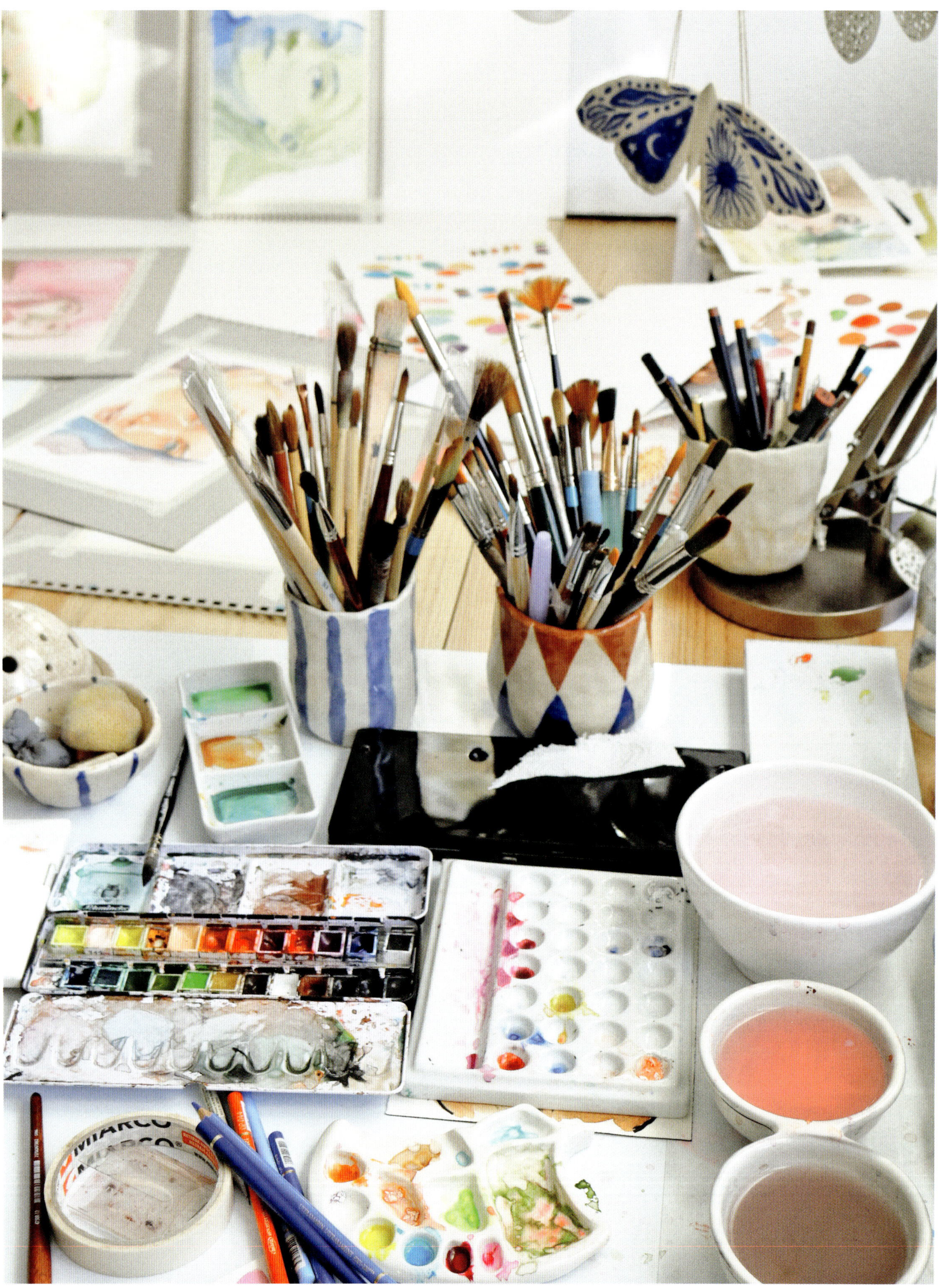

1

ESSENTIAL MATERIALS AND TECHNIQUES

Watercolor is a technique that's easy to combine with a variety of mediums. We'll see some of those later in this book, but to start, let's not get too complicated. It's a good idea to first get familiar with watercolor and its possibilities, and once you've learned the techniques, we can introduce new materials.

TYPES OF WATERCOLORS

Currently, you can find several different varieties of watercolors for sale. There are pan watercolors, tube watercolors, and liquid watercolors, as well as watercolor pencils and markers. What you choose depends on personal taste and what works best for you. Personally, I have all types of watercolors, and I combine them to achieve different effects and results.

PAN WATERCOLORS

Pan watercolors are the best known and most practical type of watercolor paint, especially for painting outdoors or traveling. You can buy a set with basic colors (some brands offer special edition sets with different color palettes), or you can buy a metal watercolor tin, and as you use up colors, you can replace them or add the colors that you like most to your set. For me, this is a really nice option. The tins last a very long time if you take good care of them and keep them clean. Pan watercolor paints also last a long time, and they're activated by wetting the paint with water.

TUBE WATERCOLORS

Tube watercolors have a creamy texture and can be made more transparent or more opaque, depending on the amount of water you mix with them. Some colors are more pigmented in their tube formulation than in pan watercolors.

If you want to create large quantities of color, broad washes, more saturated colors, or more highly pigmented colors, tube watercolors are an excellent option. For these types of paints, it's also a good idea to make yourself a palette to save the colors you want to use. The best choice for this is a metal box where you deposit the color and save what's left to reactivate with water for another time. This is a good option if you know you won't use tubes again for a while. If you open the tubes and don't use them up quickly, they usually dry out. If this happens, you can cut open the tube with a box cutter and use it like a pan watercolor.

Tube watercolors are a good choice if you want more "special" colors. Some colors that come in tubes have unique effects once they dry, such as different textures.

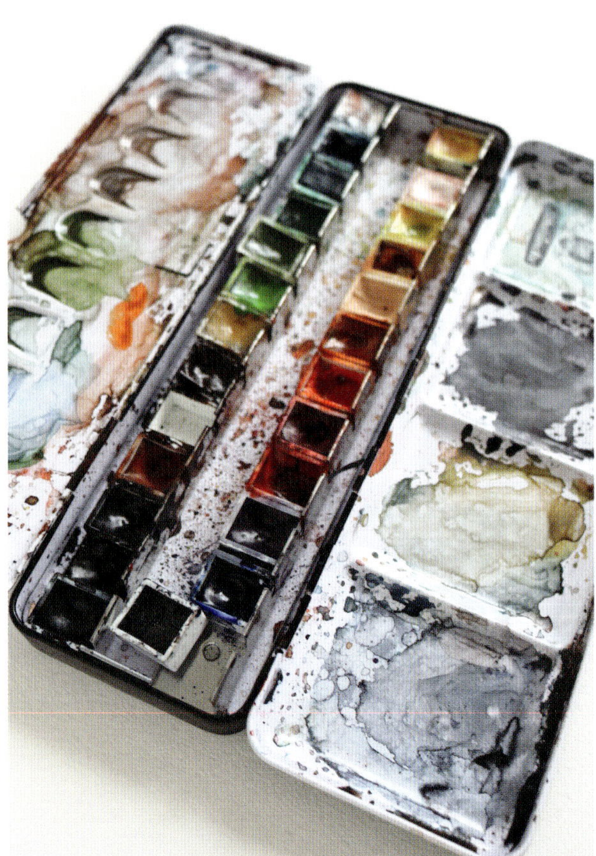

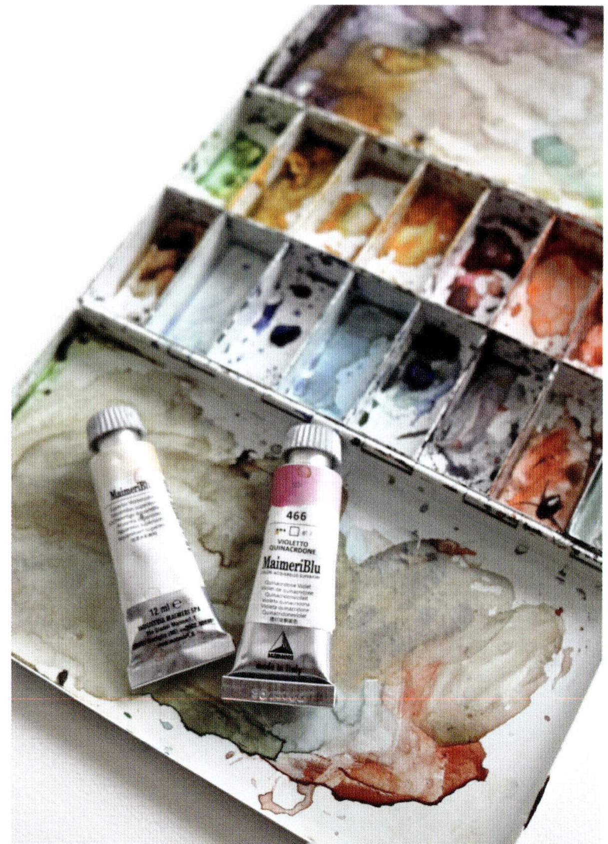

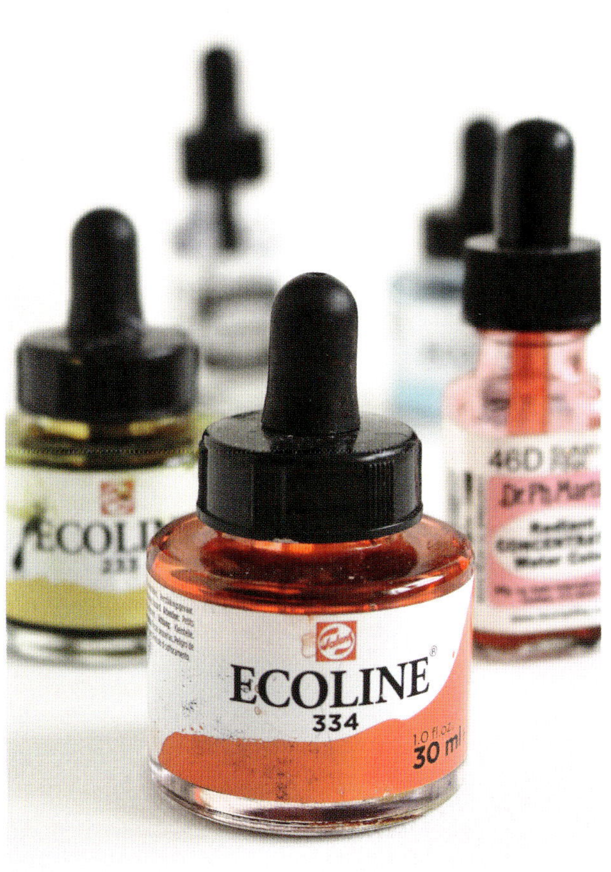

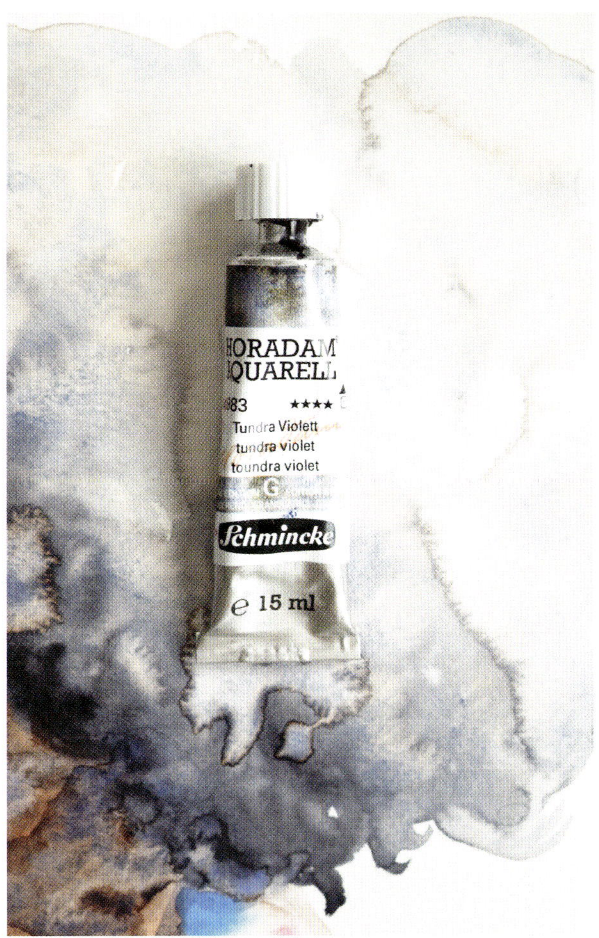

LIQUID WATERCOLORS

Liquid watercolors usually come in plastic or glass bottles with a pipette dropper to facilitate using them without wasting them. What makes these watercolor paints different is the type of pigment they're made of. Since they are a dye, we can make bright and fluorescent colors, and we can obtain more saturated colors than when using pan watercolors.

You can use liquid watercolors directly on paper. Because they're already liquid, they don't necessarily need water. When applied directly, the color will be pure and very concentrated. There is always the option to add some water to increase the transparency or decrease the saturation.

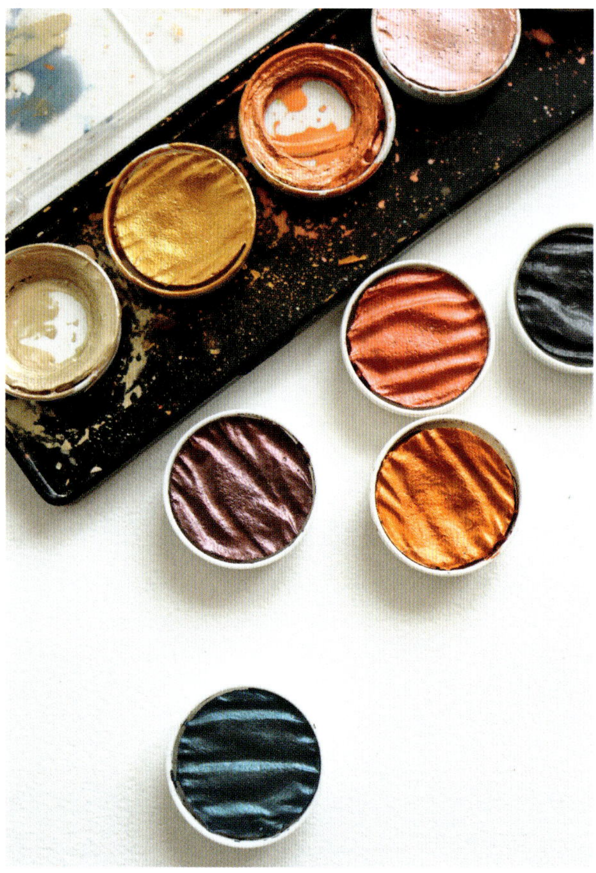

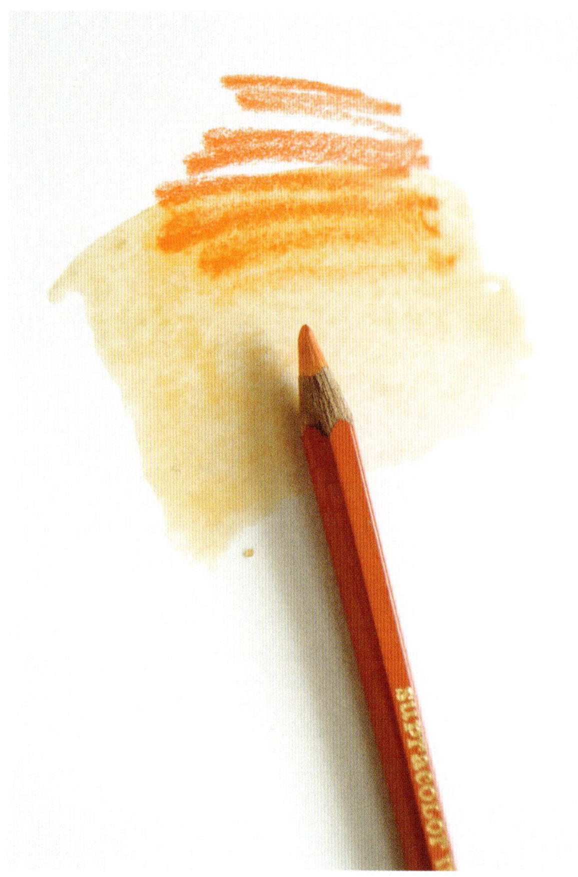

OTHER OPTIONS

Another attractive type of watercolor paints is **metallic watercolors**. If you want a different or shiny finish, metallic watercolors can give you very interesting results.

There are also watercolor crayons, markers, and pencils.

CHOOSING AND USING PAINTS

It's important when you're just beginning to learn any new technique to choose a low-cost material so that you can practice without messing up expensive products. A lot of times when we buy more professional or more costly material, we're afraid to use it or we leave it for "special" occasions. This limits us when it comes time to practice. We don't go that one step farther and instead stay with what we already know how to do. We don't give ourselves the freedom to experiment and see other possibilities.

While it's true that opting for quality material will give better results, sometimes, it also depends on individual skill and the ability to get the most out of the supplies that are available. In my case, I choose not to underestimate any material, and I believe that interesting things can be created even with materials intended for students.

My advice is to take the time to experiment with a material to see what opportunities it can offer you and how it makes you feel while you use it. With time, you'll eliminate some materials and ultimately choose your favorite ones to work with. I like to use and blend the three main watercolor paint options since each one gives a different result. When you combine them, the array of possible outcomes becomes much larger. But no matter what you end up selecting, when you're first starting out, don't invest in the most expensive supplies.

HELPFUL TIPS FOR WORKING WITH WATERCOLOR PAINT

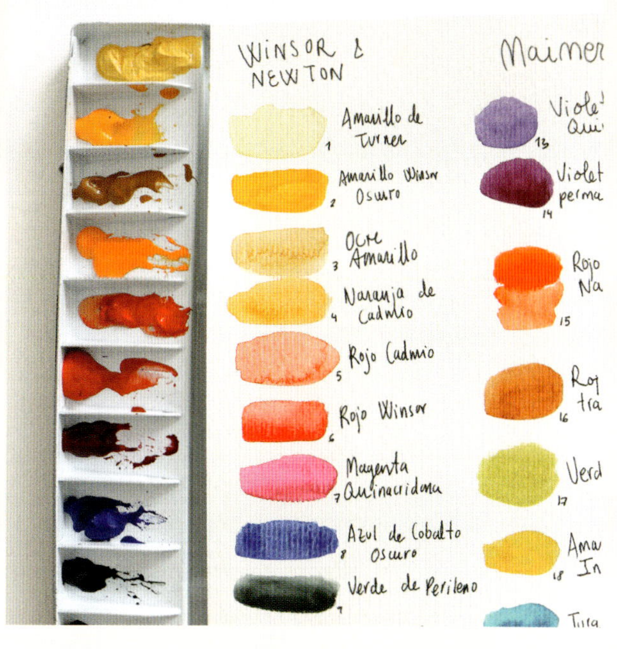

- Don't leave your materials in the sun. Put them away while you're not using them. The same goes for your paintings! With time, the sun will bleach the colors.
- Use a small syringe or pipette dropper to bring a large quantity of water to your palette—it will save you time.
- Before starting to paint, make color palettes to learn the true color of the paints. How colors look in the package is very different from how they look on paper.
- Keep a piece of scrap paper to test a color before painting it on the paper you'll use in the final project.

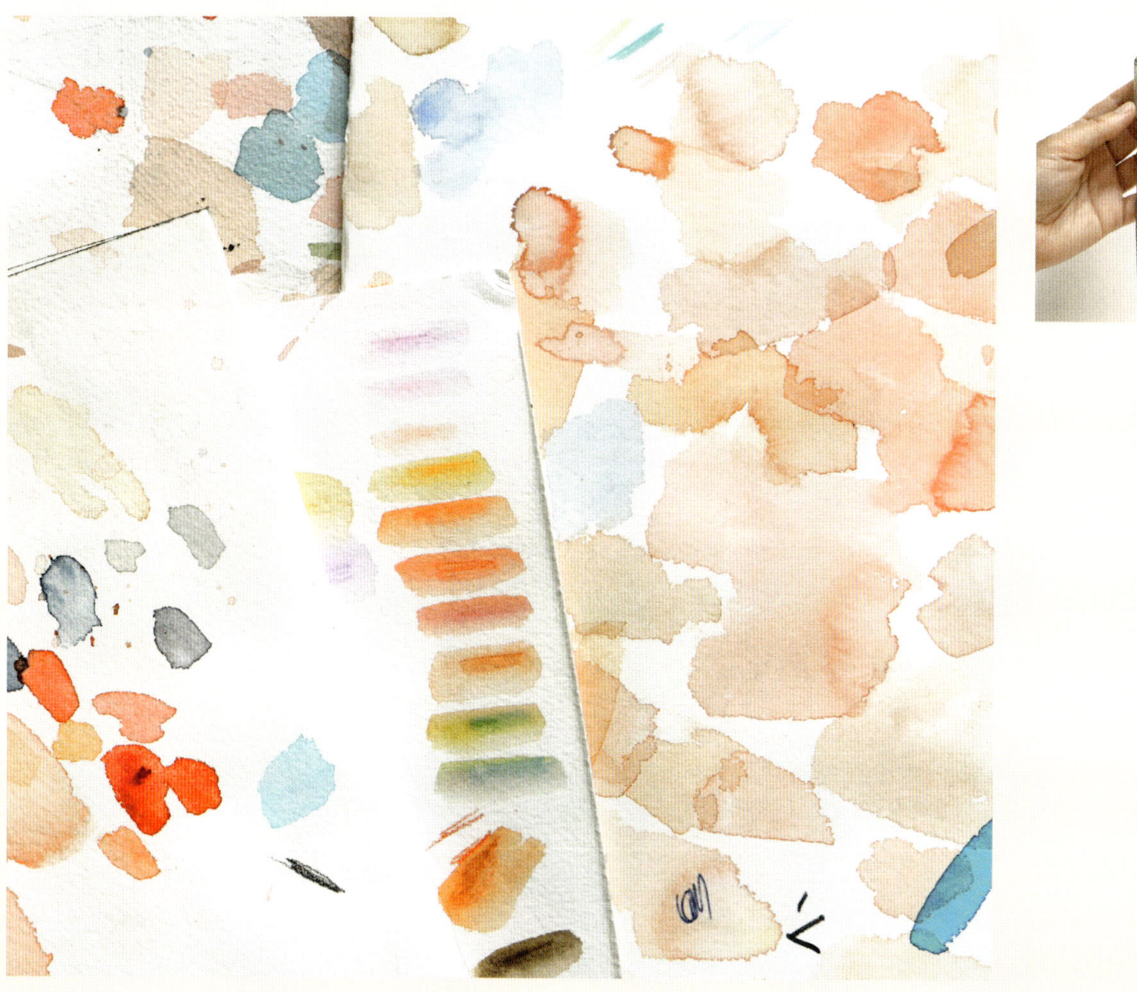

PAPER

Choosing **a good paper is paramount**. Paints are important, but in watercolor, the paper is crucial when it comes to getting a desirable result, since it's the main support for our work.

When people begin with watercolors, they often choose inexpensive paper, and the results sometimes aren't very satisfying. This can be frustrating, and you might start thinking you'll never be good at using watercolors. But by simply changing the quality of the paper, you can often see better results. Fine arts supplies tend to be expensive, so if you need to economize, choose to spend more of your budget on the paper.

There are many different kinds of paper that vary in size, configuration, such as looseleaf or in pads, textures, and weights. There's a huge range of paper available, and it's interesting to try them all—each one will give you a different result!

The paper you choose is very important because it needs to be able to support specific quantities of water and paint. Knowing the weight of the paper is fundamental. The lower the weight of the paper, the fewer layers of water it can handle. I always recommend a minimum weight of 300 grams per square meter (140 pounds), which lets you make paintings using multiple layers of watercolor.

If you do use lower weight paper, be sure not to use too much water or save it for simple works with one layer. I usually use lower weight paper to make simple textures of one layer, for color tests, or for simple sketches when I want to test and experiment before using a more expensive paper.

Paper size and format is a very personal choice.

There are looseleaf, large format papers available that you can cut to your desired size with the help of a paper folder. Or you can use pads of paper. The good thing with pads is that they are usually bound, which keeps the paper tense during the process of painting so it doesn't get wavy. Once it's dry, the paper stays very smooth and then you can tear it from the pad. This is an excellent option, but you can't tear the paper from the pad until your painting is finished. That's why it's good to have a supply of other pads or loose papers if you have a higher volume of work.

Another important quality of paper is **texture**. There are glossy finishes (hot press), as well as fine grained and rough grained (cold pressed) finishes.

Glossy paper is a smooth paper that's pressed through hot rollers that create the smooth texture. This paper is preferred by professional illustrators because it allows for details and finishes that are more defined, delicate, and "clean." When it comes to scanning the image, the details can be better appreciated, and the paper's texture isn't visible in the scan.

Papers with rough grain are cold pressed. These papers usually have more texture, and you can create different types of effects, textures, and brushstrokes. Normally, these papers are used by professionals who paint landscapes, still life paintings, or paint plein-air because they add a lot more character and consistency than a glossy paper does. Visually and to the touch, they have a finish that's most recognizably watercolor for their degree of roughness.

Personally, I like to work with all kinds of paper, and which one I choose depends on the project that I'm going to work on. The same method of painting creates very different results depending on the paper you use.

Allow yourself to test things out and experiment! In the end, we're like chefs—we can use the same materials and paints, but each one of us adds our own personal touch.

Keep in mind that each company has its own way of manufacturing paper. One brand of fine-grained 300 grams per square meter (140 pounds) paper can be very different from another even though they are described in the same way. Personally, I always opt for trying different products whenever I can, and I keep track of the ones that work best for me. Like the entire process, it's all very subjective!

BRUSHES

The choice of brushes is also something very personal. Sometimes, we may go overboard and feel that we need to own as many different types of brushes as possible. But I can tell you that I still have a round-tipped No. 24 paintbrush that I bought for my first fine arts class. I've used it in numerous projects. It's allowed me to work both detail and large washes. It's the only paintbrush I used for all five years of my studies.

This is all to say that a single good-quality brush was enough, and it's still just like new. As long as you take good care of them, brushes tend to be very durable! If you can, treat yourself to good-quality brushes.

It's not necessary to buy every size or shape of brush if that's not realistic for you. Although each kind of brush can give you a different finish or help you sketch out certain things differently, when you're just starting out, it's not essential.

There are both synthetic and natural brushes on the market. Which you choose depends a lot on personal taste. There are certainly very high-quality synthetic brushes.

Brushes are available in all different sizes or numbers. There are round brushes, flat brushes, cat's-tongue brushes, mop brushes, fan brushes, liner brushes, and more. To begin with, it's enough to have just two round brushes: a No. 6 or No. 12 for small details and a No. 20 or No. 24 for large washes. Adding a high-numbered flat brush will also allow you to do large washes.

Personally, my favorites are Japanese (or Japanese-style) brushes. Some have a round tip with a very fine point. They are excellent both for large washes and brushstrokes, since these brushes can hold a lot of water.

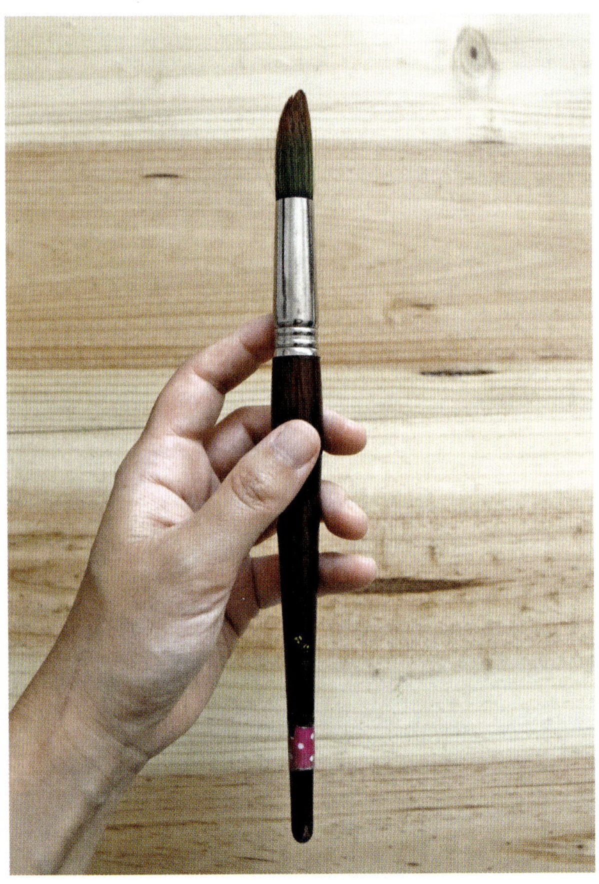

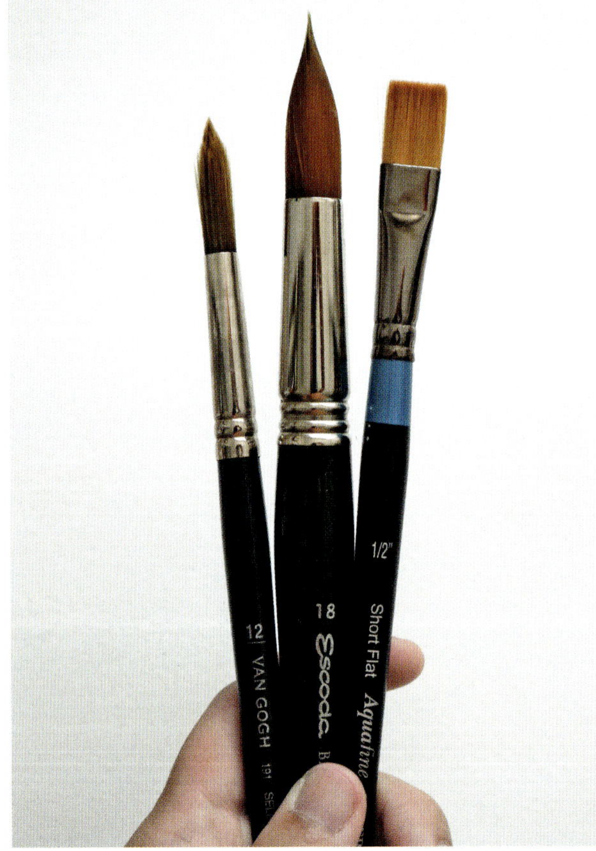

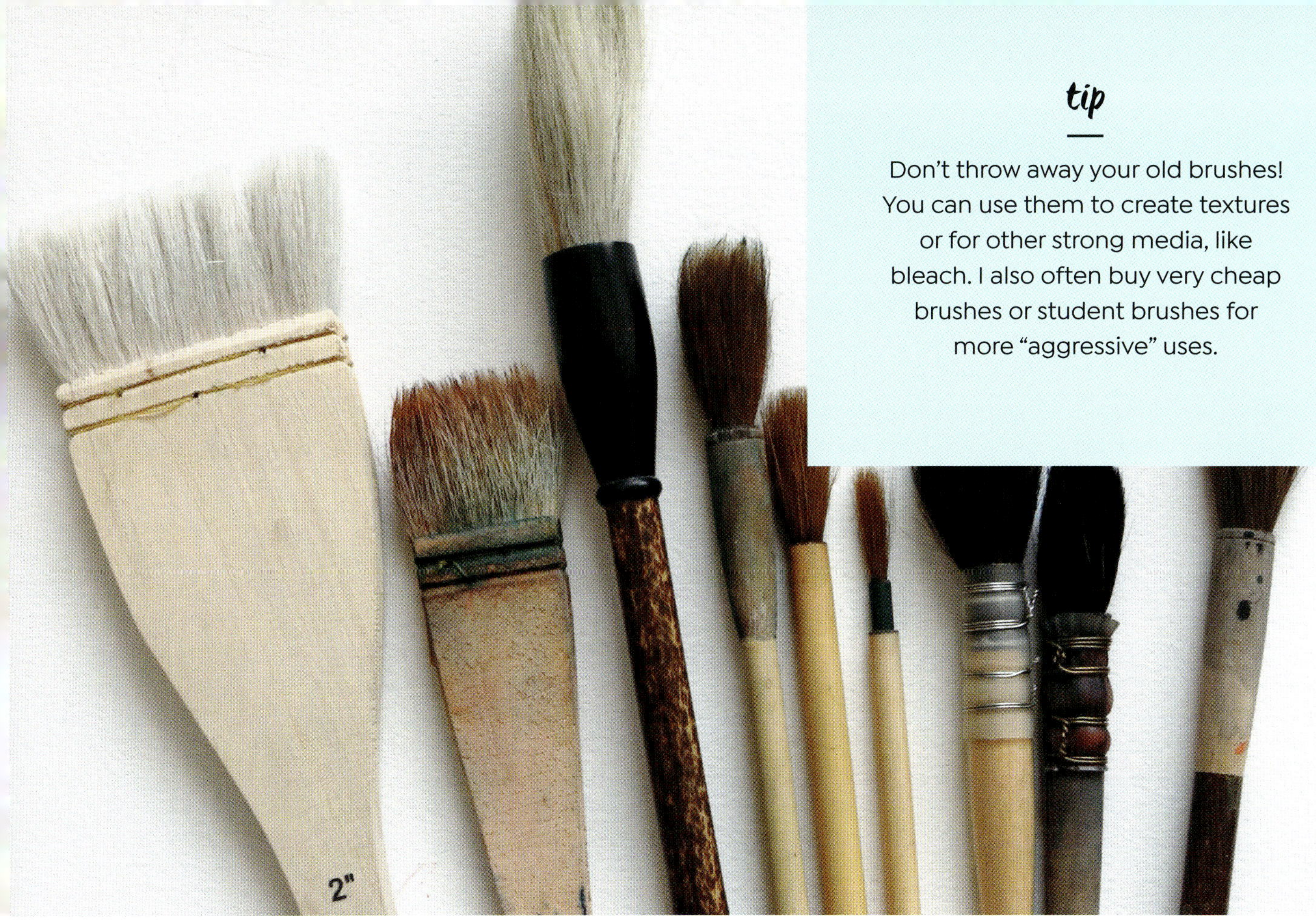

tip

Don't throw away your old brushes! You can use them to create textures or for other strong media, like bleach. I also often buy very cheap brushes or student brushes for more "aggressive" uses.

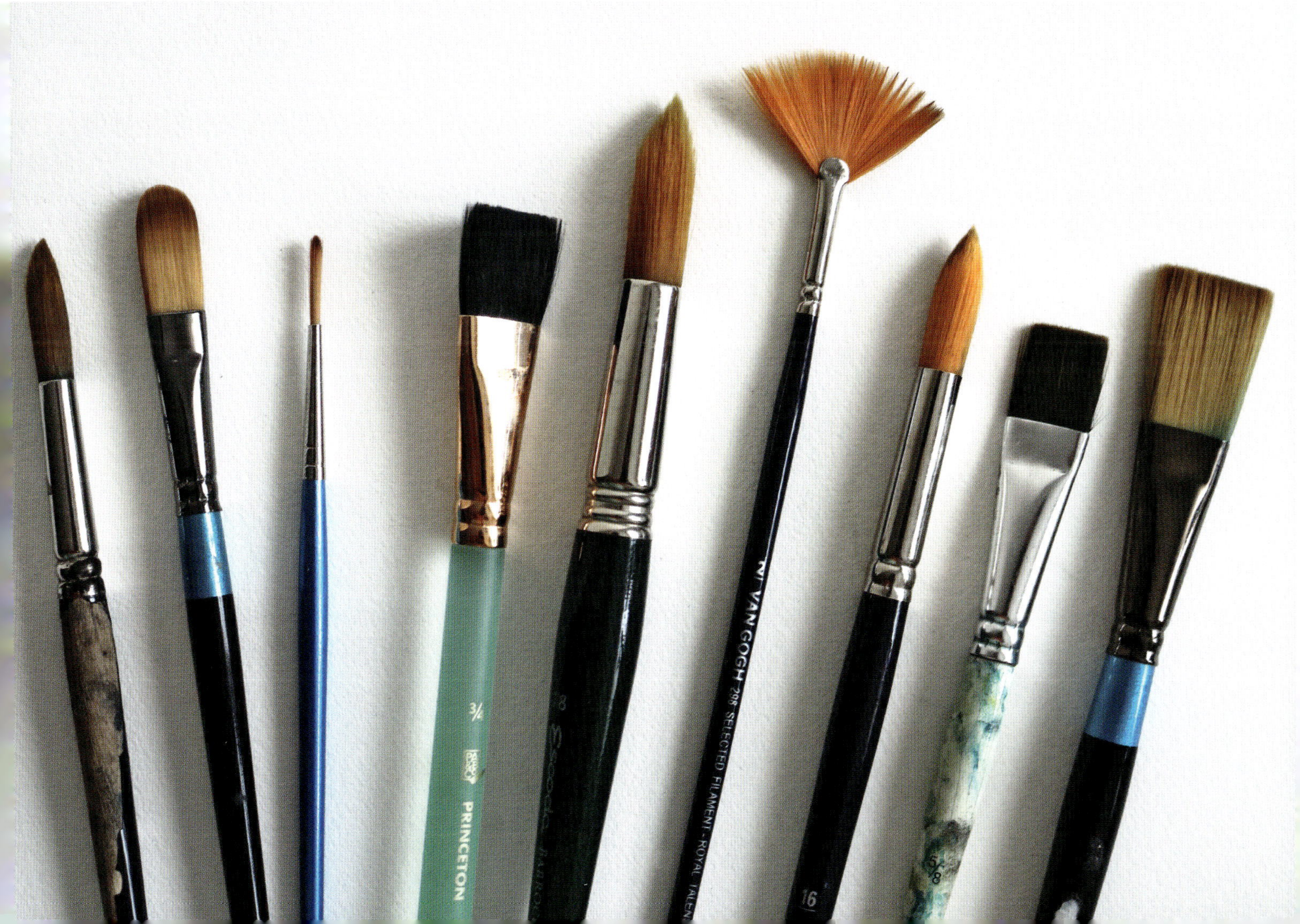

OTHER SUPPLIES

In addition to the basic and essential materials that we need to get started in watercolor, we can gradually include other supplementary materials. Below, I share some of the tools that I use. Feel free to include what you think is necessary and works for you.

tip

If you don't have a palette, you can use a regular plate from your table settings to mix colors.

PALETTE

Pan watercolors usually come with a built-in palette, but it's always a good idea to use a separate one. You can find plastic, metal, or ceramic ones. Personally, I recommend that you get a ceramic one. They're easy to clean, and the paints mix better. They also come in different sizes. But if you like to paint while traveling, a metal palette is lighter and more comfortable.

PAPER TOWELS

There are several uses for paper towels. You can use them to clean and remove excess water from brushes while you work.

You can use a paper towel as a paintbrush to drag paint or absorb it. You can also create interesting textures with paper towels.

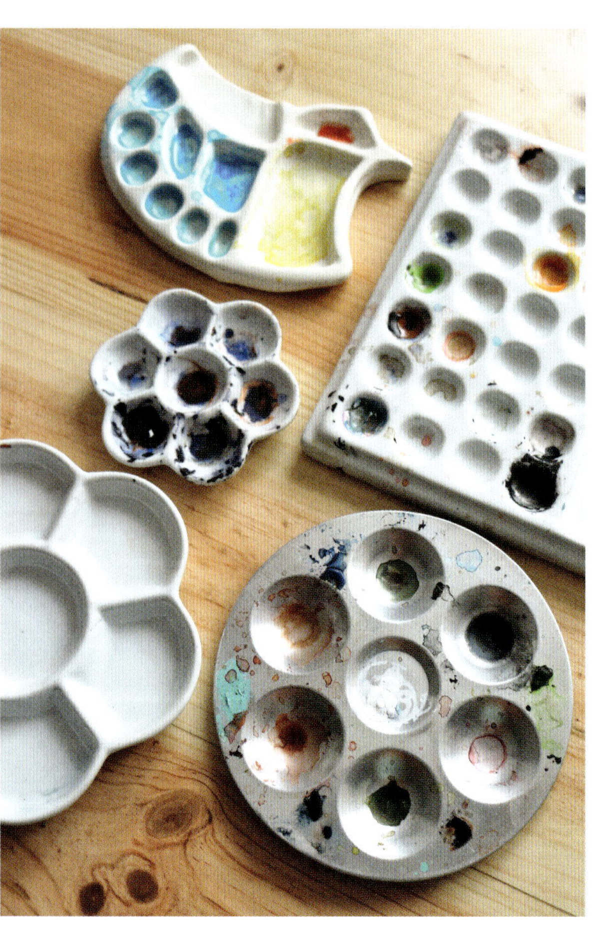

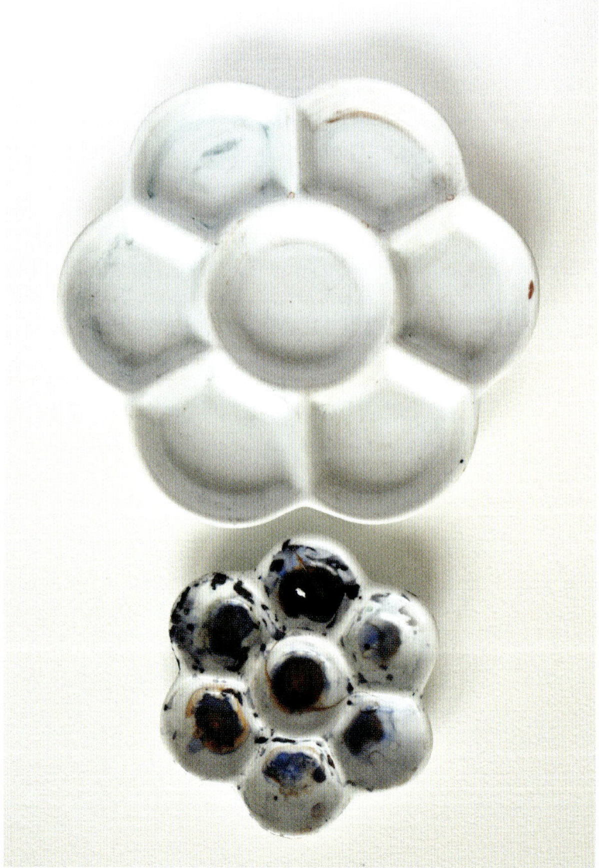

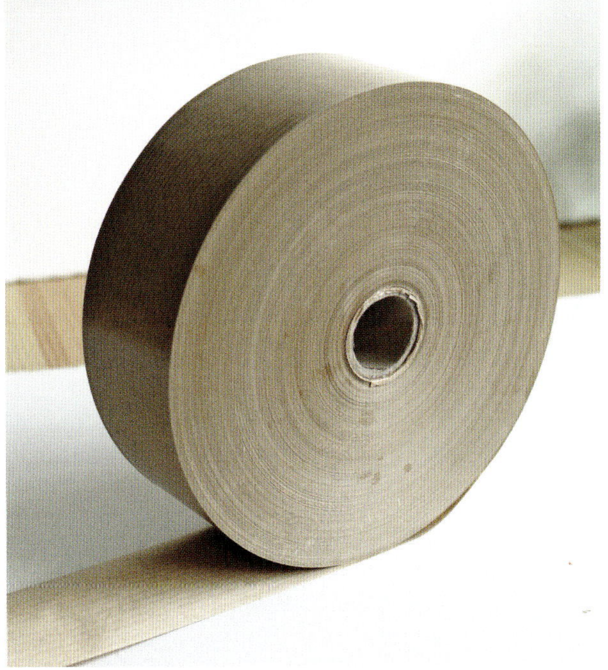

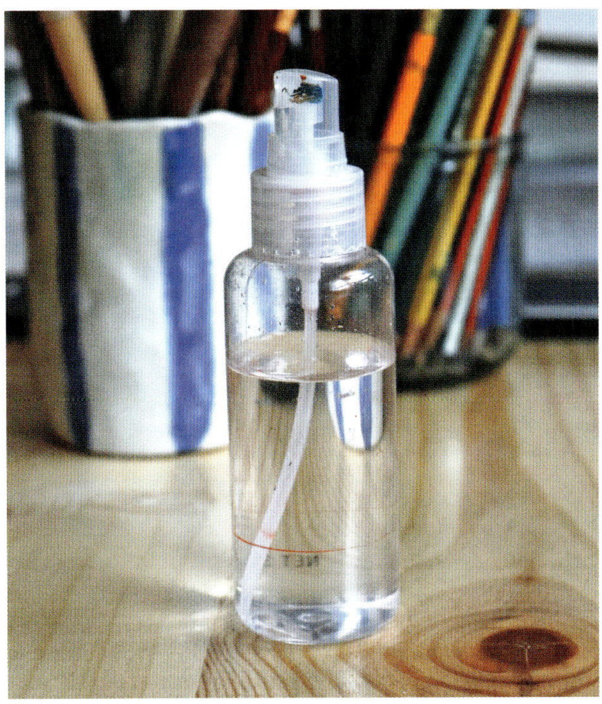

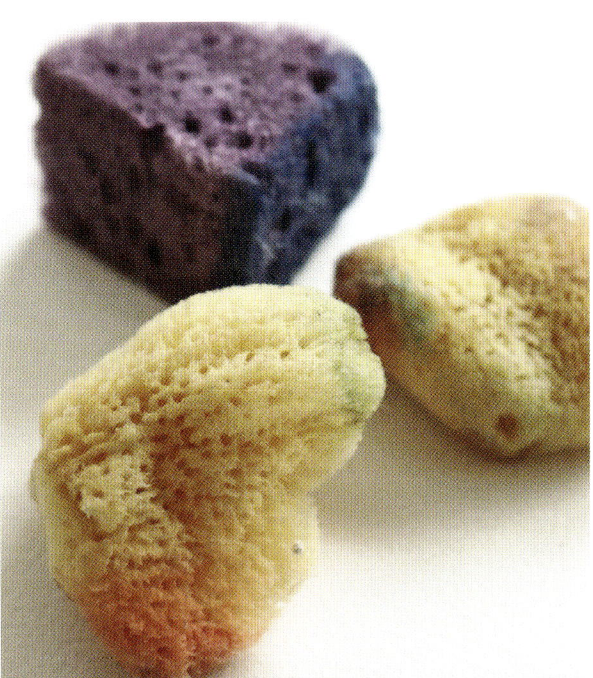

MASKING TAPE

If you paint on looseleaf paper, masking tape helps you attach and stretch the paper to the support of your choice, whether a table, a board, or a piece of cardboard.

You can also use it to reserve light color values or create straight lines.

KRAFT PAPER TAPE

Kraft paper tape allows you to stretch the paper to a board. This way, you can paint without fear of the paper buckling. The tape must be moistened with water to activate the adhesive so it sticks to the paper's edges, and it has to be completely dry before you start working. Once the paper is dry, cut around the edges with a box cutter.

SPRAY BOTTLE

Having a small spray bottle filled with clean water on the table can help you do the following:

» Keep your work wet longer (spray from a safe distance).

» Activate watercolor paint pans.

» Create special effects by spraying on your work.

You can also fill a spray bottle with liquid watercolors and spray directly onto paper.

SPONGE

There are special watercolor sponges, but you can also use regular bath sponges, which are available in varying quality.

Sponges absorb and create light values, they can be used like a large brush to create washes with water or paint, and they can be used to create textures.

HAIR DRYER

When you're in a hurry on a project, you can always opt to use a hair dryer. It's a fantastic way to speed up the drying of your watercolor.

The materials you have and the way you use them are limitless. Dive in and explore your imagination. Don't restrict yourself!

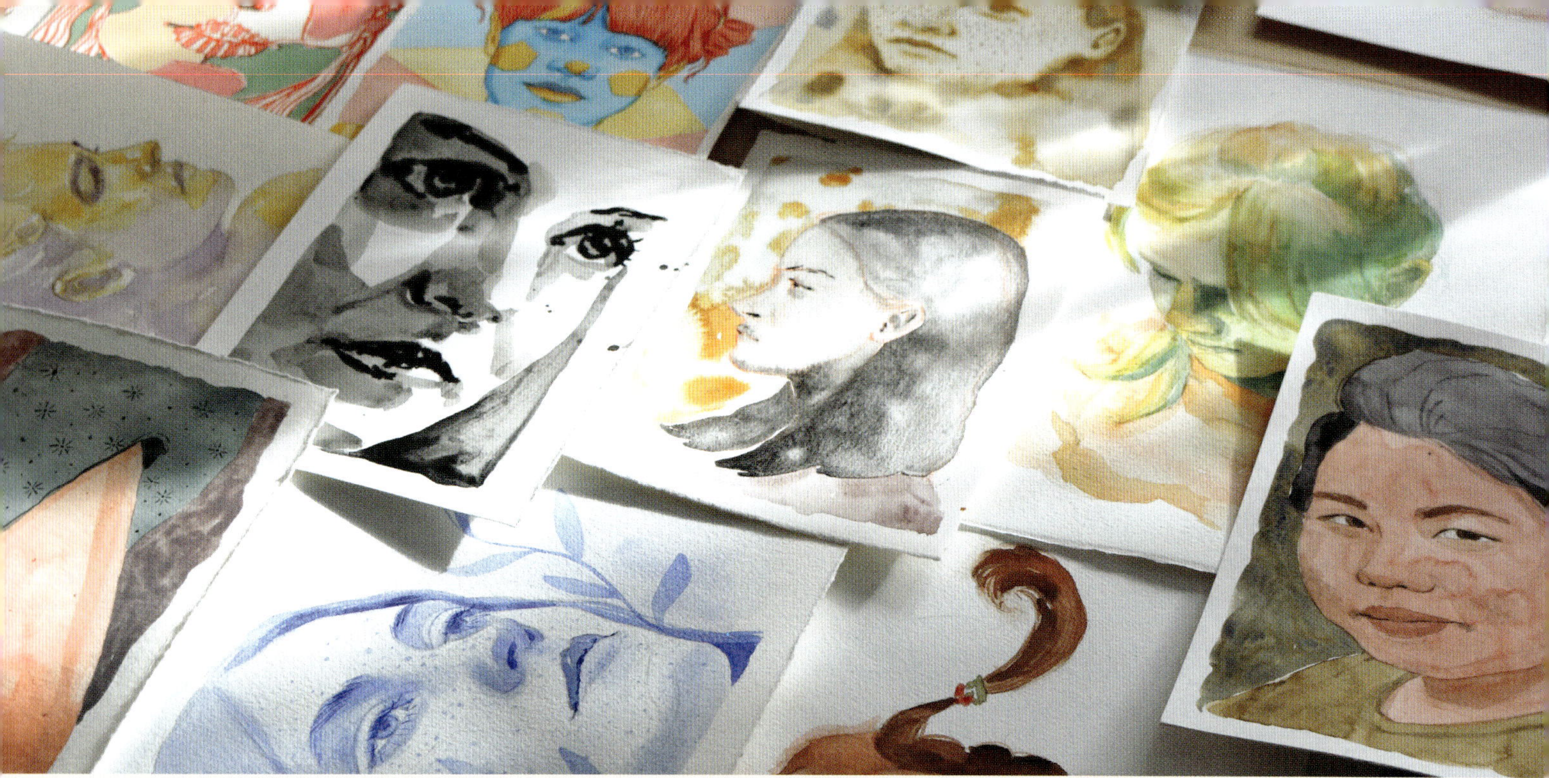

BEFORE YOU BEGIN

In the following lessons, we'll learn several watercolor techniques. But before we continue, there are certain "rituals" that I always do before beginning to paint. Although they might seem obvious, they are still important to share:

- ***Organize your workspace.*** It's important to have a workspace that inspires you to create. We all understand our own order and our own chaos, but maintaining a certain harmony lets you be more fluid in your work.
- If you can, choose a well-ventilated place with clean air and work with ***natural light***. Artificial light changes how we perceive color, and you might err in choosing the right tones.
- You must wash your hands before painting. This keeps you from soiling the paper you're working on, since your hands accumulate oils and dirt.
- Use several water containers. You need one for clean water to create washes, to blur tones, and more. And you need another for dirty water to clean brushes.
- With ceramic palettes, if I want to create new mixtures, I clean the palettes. Others I leave as is, with old paint mixtures, since sometimes I need one of those "dirty" colors, and I take advantage of the colors that were already in the palette.
- When choosing papers, to save time, choose and prepare the papers for your work and have them at hand. This helps avoid distractions.
- Arrange your materials so it's easy to find what you're looking for.

You'll find out over time what gives you peace in your workplace and helps you create.
LET'S GET STARTED!

COLOR

Colors make us feel, they are exciting, they collide, they attract—color is a language unto itself. Because of that, if you learn to speak the language of color, you can express yourself and communicate with viewers of your work, and you'll know how to use colors intentionally and not just casually. Sometimes, we choose colors randomly or decide on too many without giving it much thought, but this can cause a piece to be immediately rejected at first glance or can ruin an otherwise good work.

Although you sometimes use intuition, understanding how to apply color is very important when it's time to start a project. Learning about the color wheel, contrasts, harmonies, color schemes, and so on, and knowing how colors engage in dialogue with each other will provide your work with a big boost in quality and attractiveness.

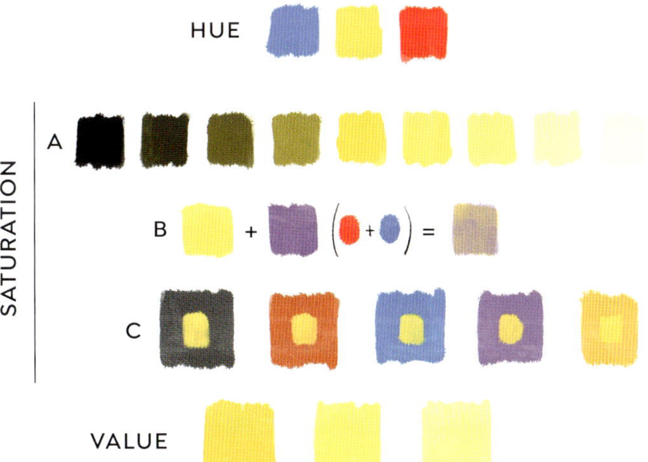

CHARACTERISTICS OF COLOR

Colors have three main attributes: hue, saturation, and value.

1. **Hue.** This refers to the actual color itself. It is how we identify colors. For example, all the shades of yellow are a yellow hue.

2. **Saturation.** This is the degree of a color's purity. The more saturation, the purer the color is. There are several ways to desaturate, or lower, the intensity of a color:

   » **Apply light or dark,** such as with black and white or gray.

   » **Apply the color's complementary color.** For example, to desaturate green (blue + yellow), add the color red. The result will be a more temperate or earthy red.

   » Use **simultaneous contrast.** A color appears more or less intense depending on the color next to it. For example, white appears whiter if it's next to black, and vice versa. Red appears redder when next to its contrasting color: green.

3. **Value.** This is the degree of a color's lightness or darkness. It's what makes us perceive a color as light or dark. The perceived value of colors will vary, depending on the color next to them.

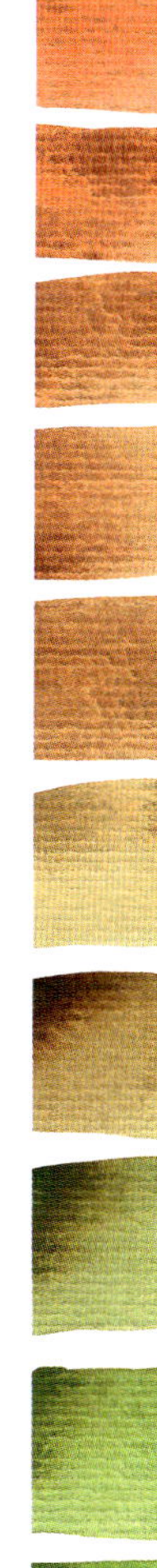

Each color can have a varied hue, according to its degree of saturation and the degree of lightness or darkness.

THE COLOR WHEEL

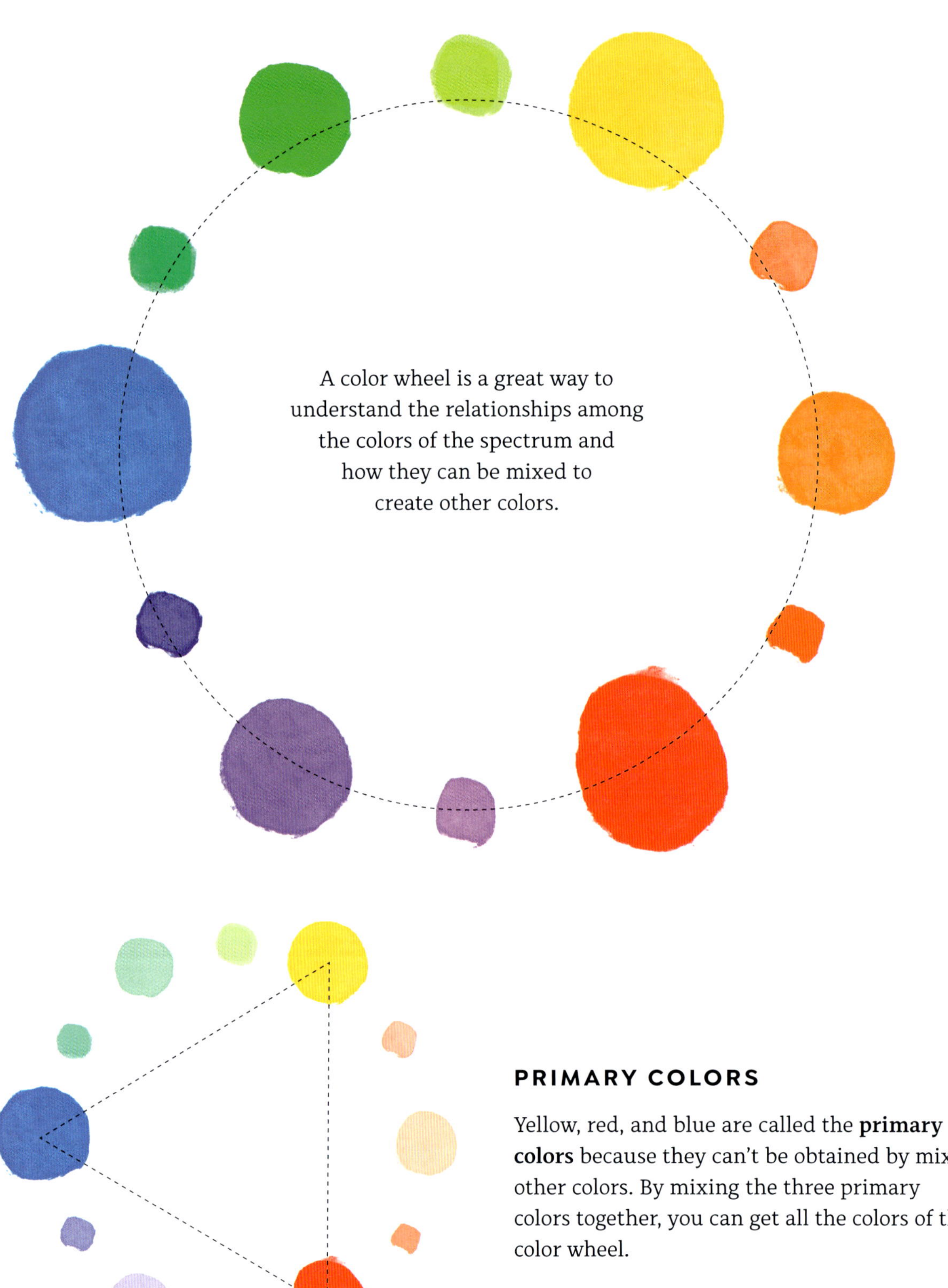

A color wheel is a great way to understand the relationships among the colors of the spectrum and how they can be mixed to create other colors.

PRIMARY COLORS

Yellow, red, and blue are called the **primary colors** because they can't be obtained by mixing other colors. By mixing the three primary colors together, you can get all the colors of the color wheel.

SECONDARY COLORS

The three secondary colors—orange, purple, and green—are created by mixing two primary colors.

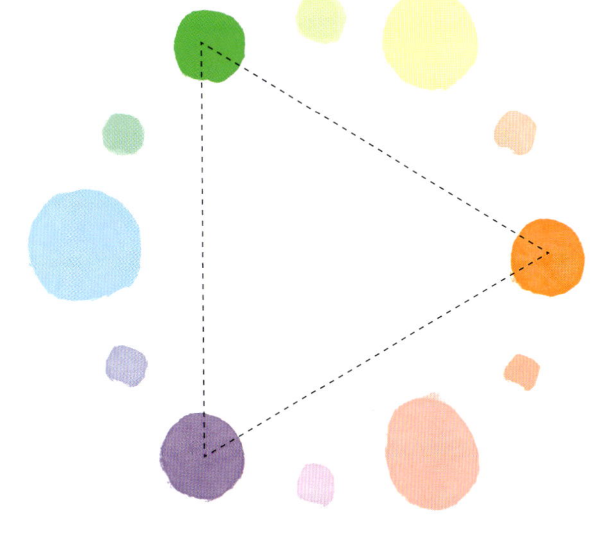

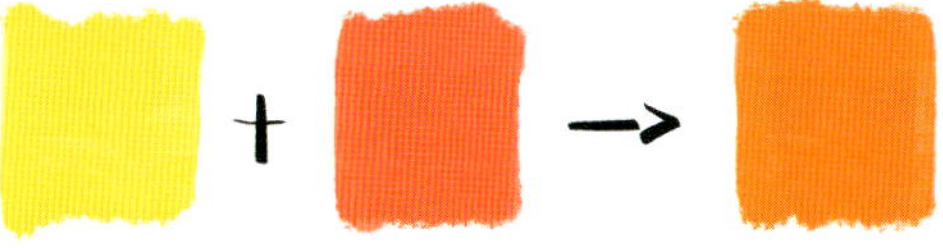

YELLOW + RED = ORANGE

RED + BLUE = PURPLE

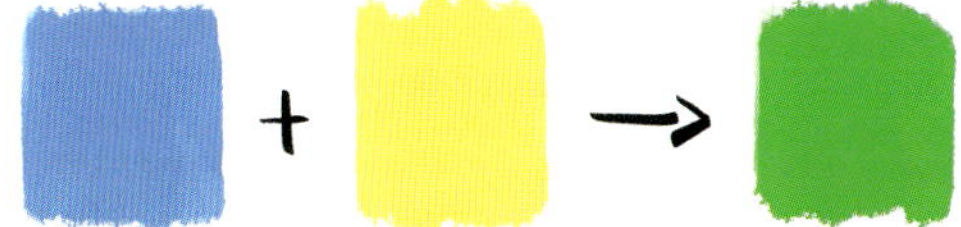

BLUE + YELLOW = GREEN

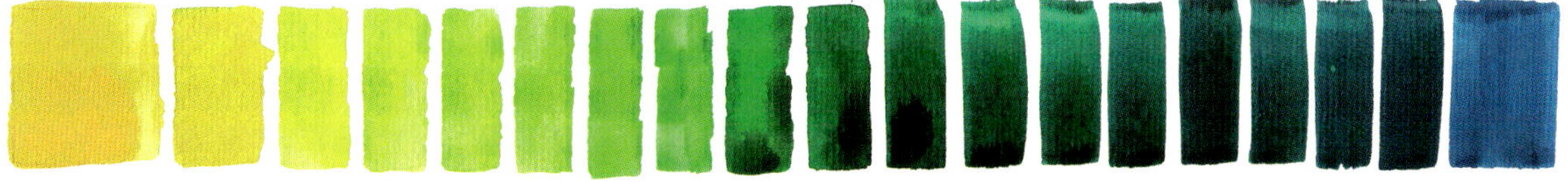

Just by varying the proportion of blue or yellow, you can get an immense range of greens.

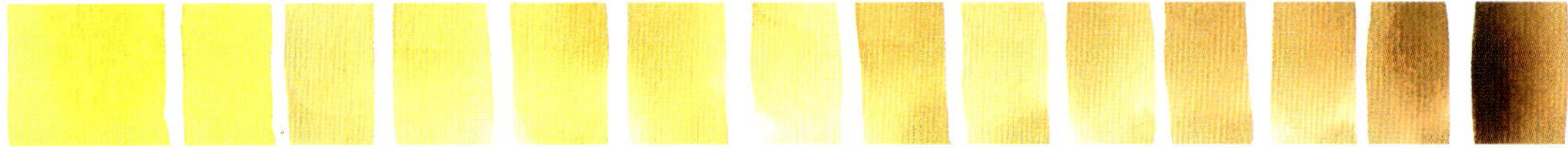

To get warm, neutral, or muddy yellow tones and desaturate them, you can add purple (blue + red), the color opposite on the color wheel.

TERTIARY COLORS

Tertiary colors can be mixed by combining a primary color with an adjacent secondary color on the color wheel. For example: blue + green = blue green.

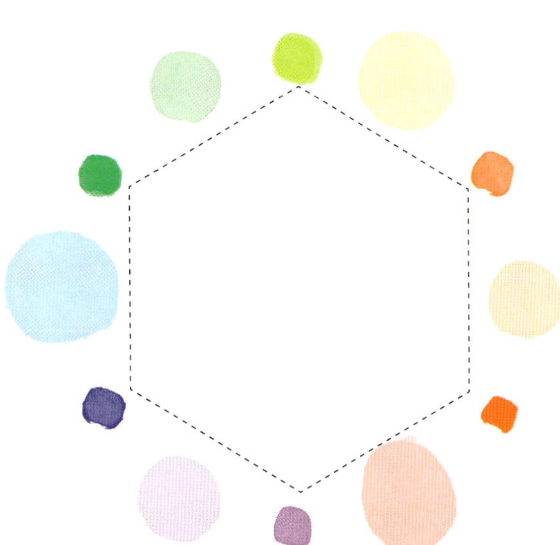

HARMONIES

We perceive certain color combinations as orderly, beautiful, and pleasing to the eye. This makes us feel attracted to certain artworks. At the same time, when we're unable to perceive this coherence, we tend to reject a piece and think that something is off or not working.

Knowing about the visual tensions, the balance or imbalance, in color helps us to create different harmonious sensations in a viewer, as well as avoiding negative ones or ones that might lead them to dislike the piece.

Let's take a look at some of the main color harmonies or schemes.

MONOCHROMATIC

This is the use of a single color, varying its value. With watercolor, you can modify the value by mixing the paint with more or less water.

ANALOGOUS

These are the colors that are close to one another on the color wheel. Together, they create very harmonious color schemes without any contrast or visual tension.

» The analogues of blue are green or purple tones.

» The analogues of yellow are green and orange tones.

» The analogues of red are orange and purple tones.

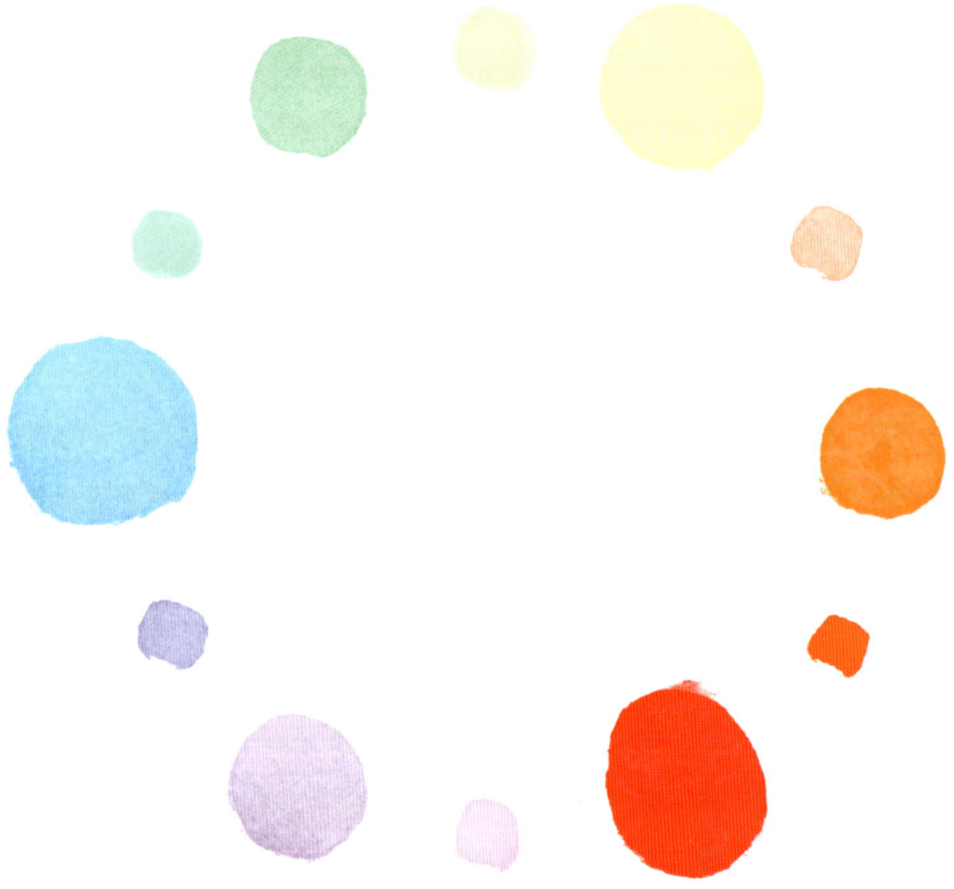

TRIAD

This is a composition of three colors located equidistant from one another on the color wheel at a vertex of an equilateral triangle.

Here are some examples of these compositions.

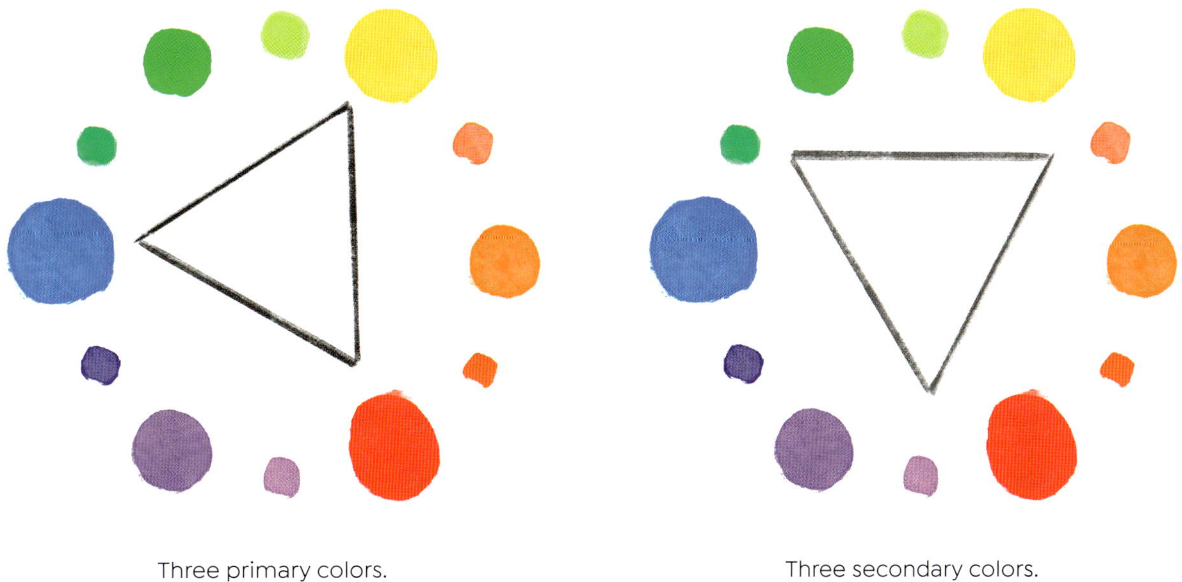

Three primary colors.

Three secondary colors.

ADJACENT/SPLIT COMPLEMENTARY

This is the set of colors that are made up of the analogues of a color's complementary colors. For example, blue with an orangish yellow and an orangish red.

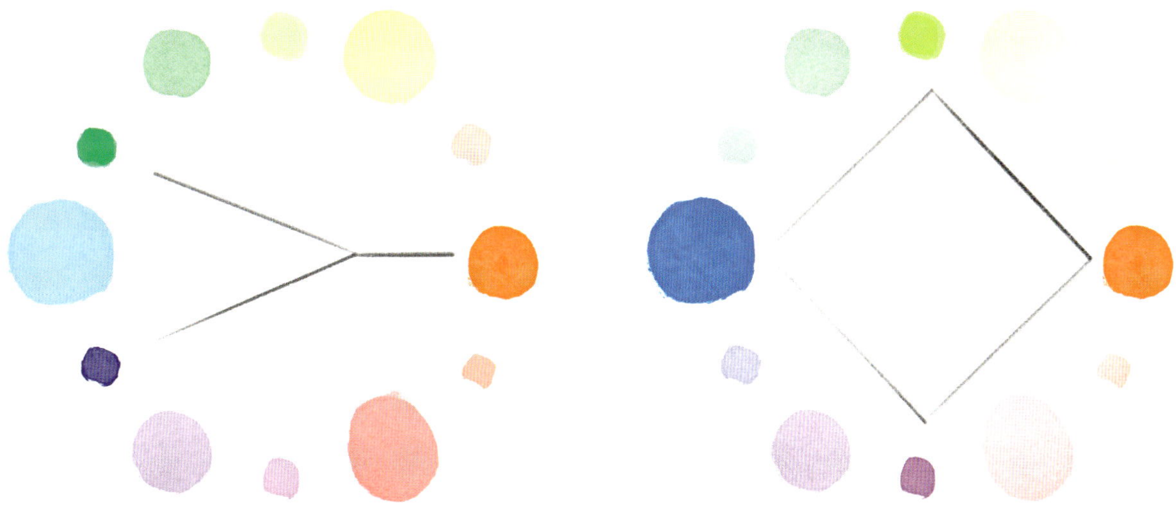

Here are examples of other types of combinations.

CONTRASTS

Thanks to the research and analysis of Swiss painter Johannes Itten, we know there are seven main color contrasts:

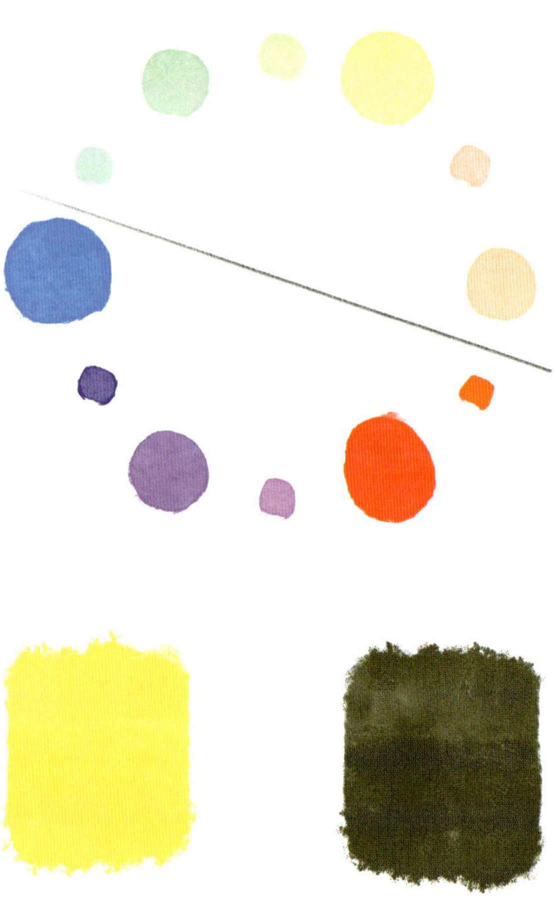

- Contrast of hue
- Light-dark contrast
- Cool-warm contrast
- Complementary contrast
- Simultaneous contrast
- Contrast of quality
- Contrast of quantity

Note: If this topic interests you, I highly recommend the book *The Art of Color*, by Johannes Itten, in which he gives a more extensive and scholarly explanation of color theory.

CONTRAST OF HUE

This is the contrast between pure and bright hues. The three primary colors produce the strongest contrast: yellow, red, and blue. As they lose their purity, the contrast becomes diluted.

LIGHT-DARK CONTRAST

This is the contrast between dark and light colors. The closer a color is to black, the darker it will be. The closer it is to white, the lighter it will be.

On one side of the color wheel are light or bright colors, which are all those that contain yellow—from green to orange—with yellow being the brightest color. On the other side of the color wheel are dark colors—from blue to violet to red—with purple being the darkest color.

COOL-WARM CONTRAST

Colors also have temperature. There are two sides on the color wheel: cool colors are on one side and warm colors are on the other. This contrast results from the clashing of these colors.

We can also create harmonious color schemes using only cool colors or only warm colors.

Keep in mind that the temperature of a color changes depending on the color that's next to it. For example, a yellow can be cooler next to a blue and warmer next to a red.

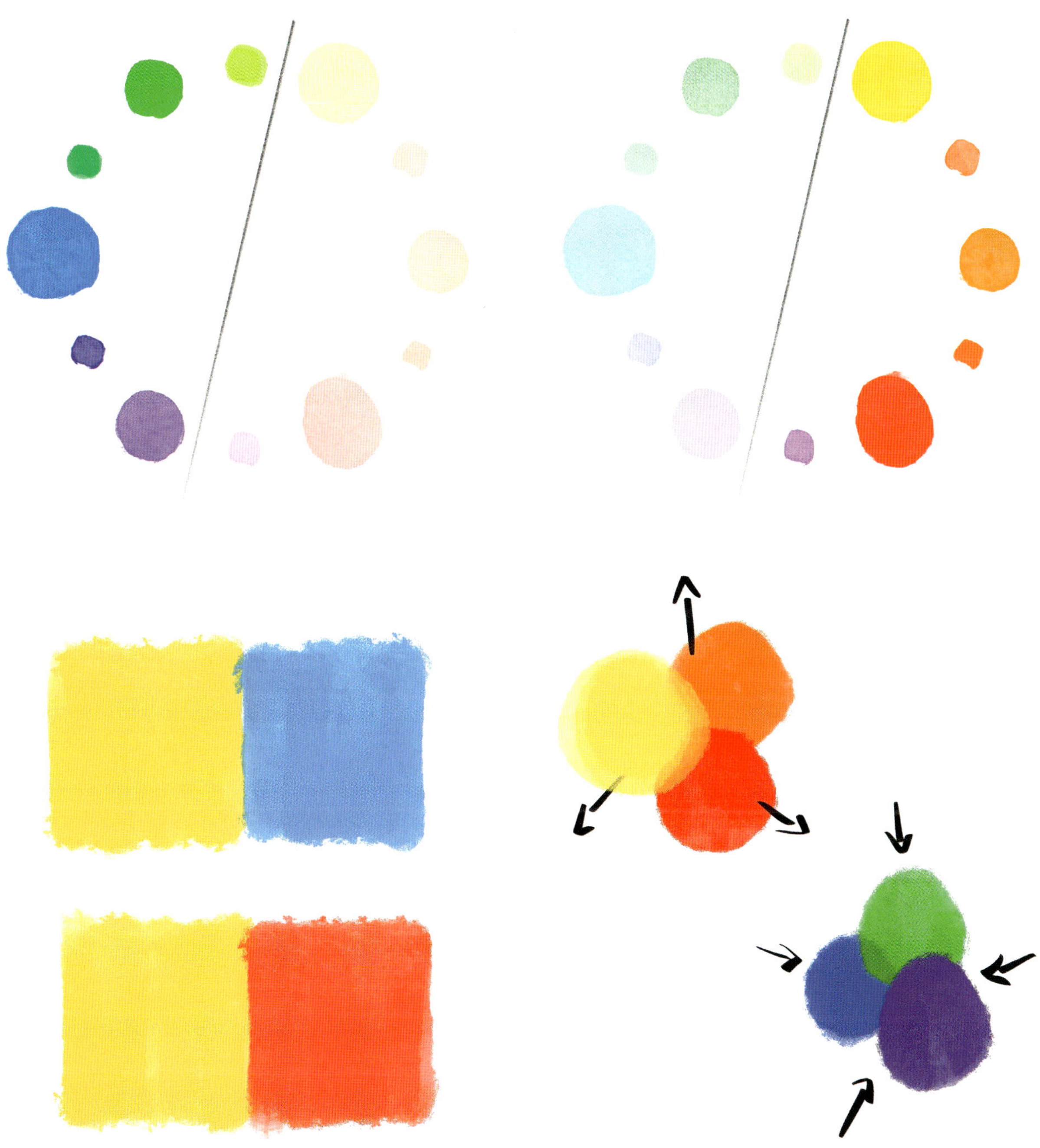

Bright and warm colors approach and move toward the viewer. As their name suggests, they also transmit warmth.

Dark and cool colors, however, move away from the viewer and transmit distance and feeling of cold and darkness. Because of this, they are usually used for shadows.

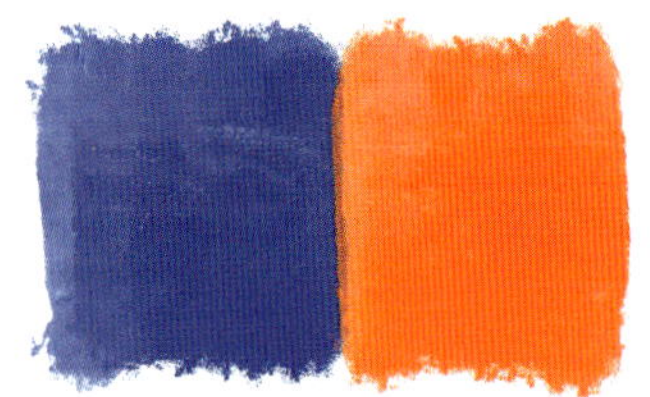

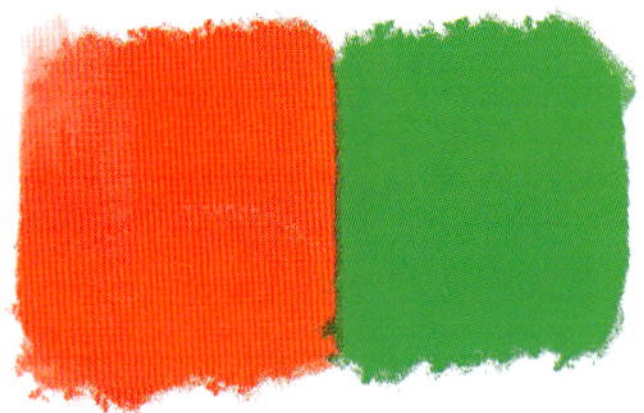

COMPLEMENTARY CONTRAST

Complementary colors are those that are opposite each other on the color wheel. Pairs of colors are thus created that have a strong color contrast. Each one makes the other stand out since they don't have any color in common. These combinations are very striking and visually attractive.

For example, in a portrait, if you paint everything in red hues and apply green to the eyes, it will make our eye move powerfully to the green detail of the eyes. This is a very simple way to highlight a particular detail.

By mixing a color with its opposite color you obtain neutral colors because the colors lose their essence. If you add a little green (blue and yellow) to red, you'll get a terra cotta or earthy red. Personally, I love to make these kinds of mixtures and desaturate colors for a feeling of visual calm.

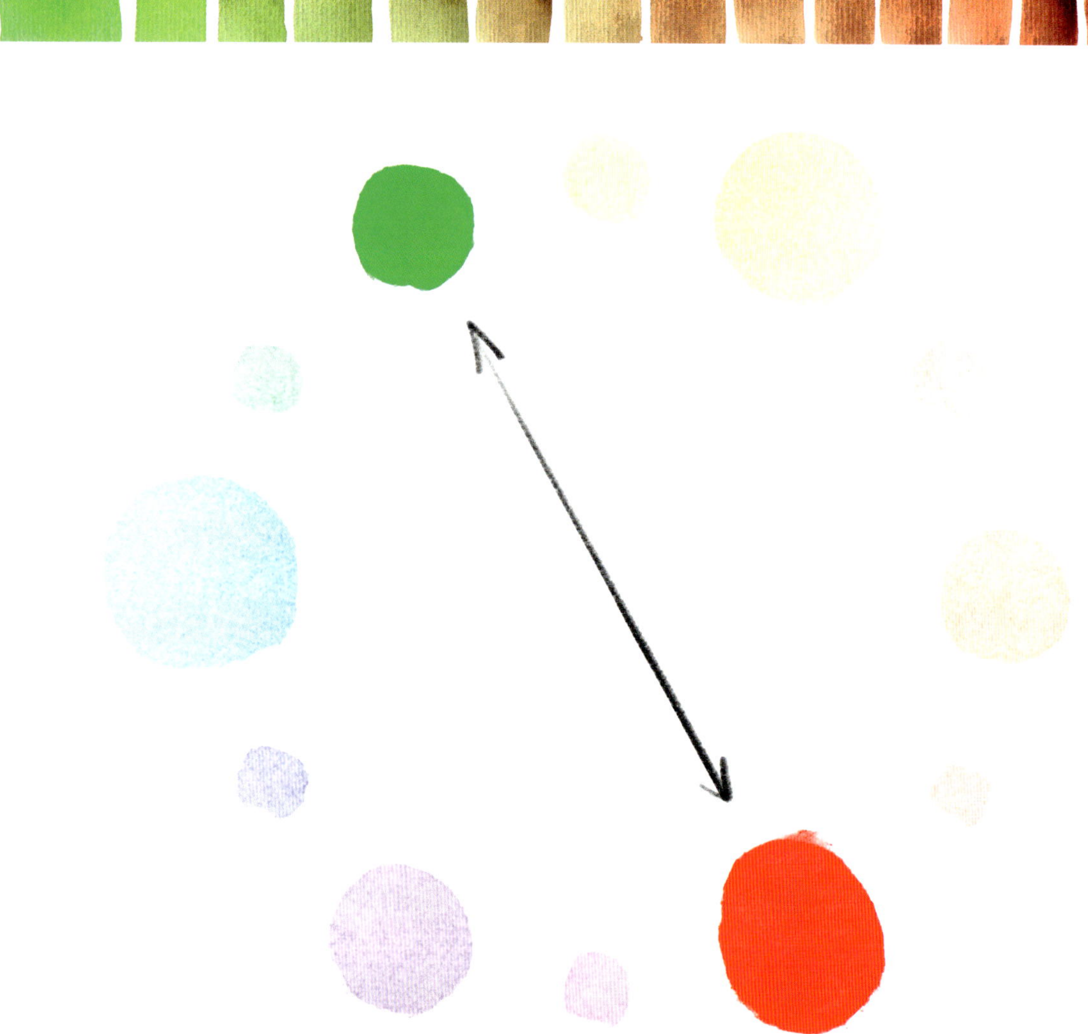

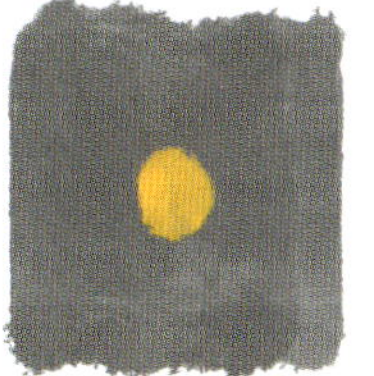

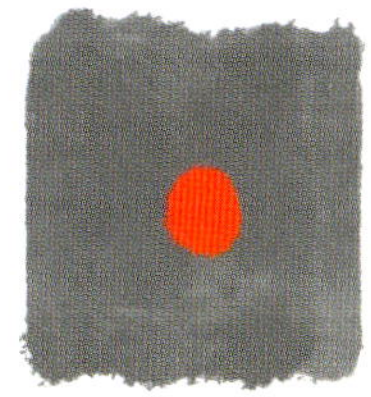

SIMULTANEOUS CONTRAST

This contrast is one of the most complicated since our own physiology comes into play.

When the eye observes a color, it needs to find the complementary color. If the eye can't locate the complementary color, it affects how it sees the initial color. Because of this, we perceive a gray next to a red as a grayish green. If that same gray is placed next to blue, we perceive it as an orangish gray. Therefore, colors vary in their intensity or hue depending on the color placed next to them.

CONTRAST OF QUALITY

This occurs when saturated colors and muted or "dirty" colors contrast with each other. The amount of contrast depends on the degree of the difference of the purity between the colors.

CONTRAST OF QUANTITY

This refers to the quantitative relationship between two or more colors. This is the contrast of a lot with a little, of big and small. There are colors that we perceive as heavier than others because of their brightness or hue. So, to achieve a balance of yellow and purple, purple should occupy more surface area than yellow, since the latter is considered "stronger" and has more visual weight because of its brilliance.

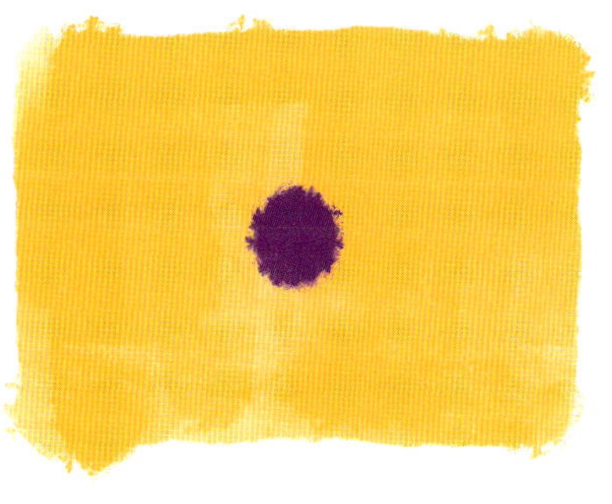
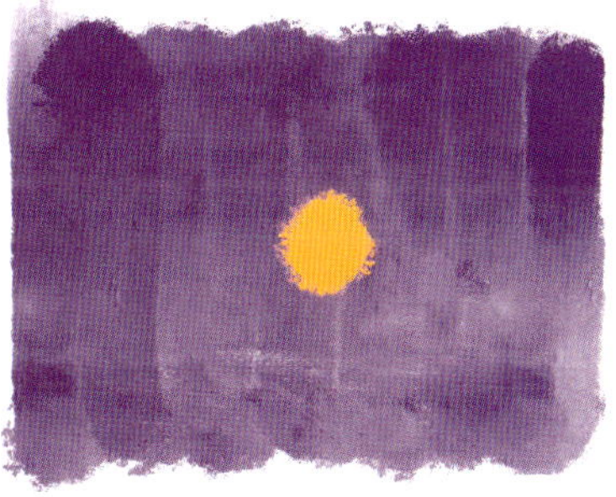

CREATING COLOR PALETTES

Choosing a color palette is very personal. Over time, you'll become more comfortable using certain colors, or you'll use them intuitively. These colors might express a sensation or an emotion or enhance a specific idea or detail. Remember that color also has different meanings in different cultures. If you're curious about this, I encourage you to research the history and psychology of color.

Some people use a certain palette for all of their work, which becomes part of their identity. Others hardly use any color and prefer dark or earth tones for their work. Some use color freely and their work is identified by other visual characteristics like shape. Regardless, feel free to experiment. To me, color is an emotion, a way to express yourself, and whether you use it or not, any choice is valid. I particularly don't like to set limits in terms of using color. I choose to play, experiment, surprise myself, and above all, have fun!

In addition to knowing the color wheel and all the possible combinations of colors, harmonious color palettes, and palettes that work and are attractive, we're going to still try to surprise ourselves with new color schemes.

EXAMPLES OF INSPIRATION FOR CREATING COLOR PALETTES

Here are some ideas for choosing your color schemes.

1. **Use a color swatch book** to make different color combinations. You can choose by intuition or by what appeals to you personally, or you can choose several colors at random like a card game.
2. You can make **your own color swatch book** using paper. On each piece, paint a color that you're using and from the colors you've already mixed. Write down the color names so it's easy to find them or buy them if you run out. This way, you can better identify the colors you frequently use and their possible combinations.

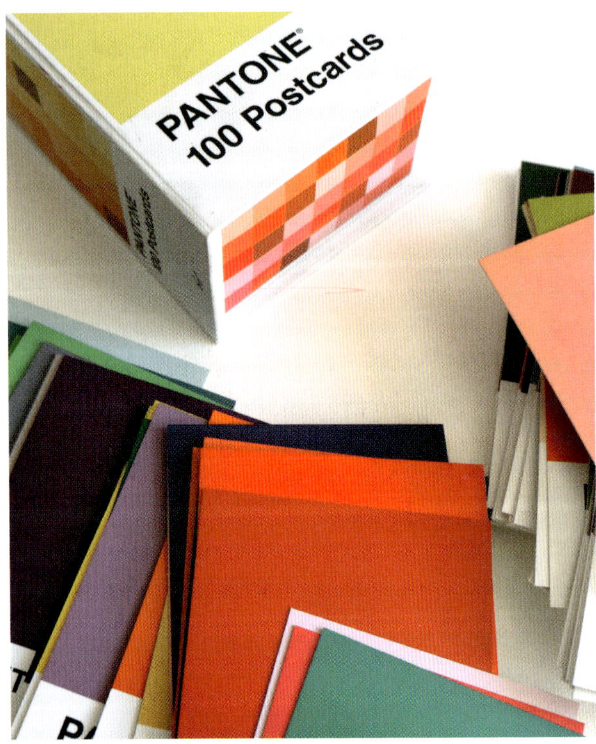

What if the result is a surprise because it never would have occurred to you to choose those colors?

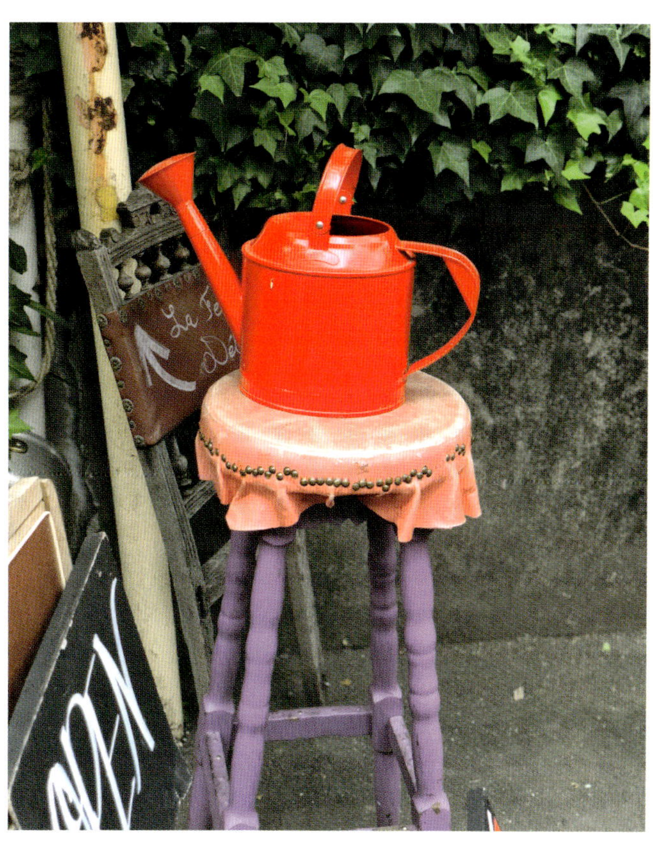

For example, I took this photo in Japan and was very attracted by its colors.

3. **Be inspired by your own photographs.** When you return from a trip, look over the photos you took. Surely, the colors in at least one photo will powerfully draw your attention. Try re-creating those colors and apply them to one of your projects.

4. **Be inspired by nature.** I think there's nothing more inspiring than nature itself—its shapes, its colors, its patterns. Animals like fish have endless unique color combinations, as do insects, butterflies, and beetles. The landscape, the sky, flowers, plants, trees . . . Nature is an inexhaustible source of inspiration. You can even combine colors from different flowers: *daisy + dahlia + yellow lily*.

5. **Be inspired by film.** Film offers an incredible array of inspiration in its frames. If you're short on ideas, take a look at your favorite movies and analyze the colors they use.

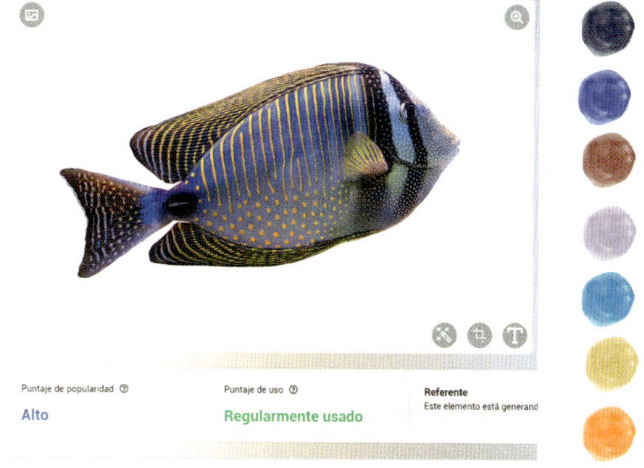

6. **Be inspired by the work of other artists.** Being inspired or making reference to the work of other artists (which is not the same as copying) can help you get rid of a block or give you ideas for new color palettes. Look to the past, too—maybe you'll be fascinated by the Impressionists' use of color.

Can you think of any other ways to create color palettes?

HOW TO WORK WITH WATERCOLOR

When starting out in any technique, it's helpful to know how that medium behaves on different surfaces. The uniqueness of watercolor is that, when mixed with water, it becomes a very spontaneous, random, and surprising technique. That's what makes it so special!

It's true that, at first, watercolors can appear very rebellious, and it can be difficult to achieve what you have in mind. But like everything, with a lot of practice and knowledge about the medium, you can succeed. *Practice, practice, practice . . . That's the true secret.*

It's a lot like learning to play an instrument. On the first day you play the piano, you are not going to be an expert—that would be impossible. Everything requires time, and you should enjoy the process of learning. You don't have to hurry to see your results. It's better to enjoy the actual act of painting and the mistakes that pop up along the way. *Besides, you have to make mistakes in order to learn, so don't demonize the mistake! Instead, consider it an opportunity to create something new or to find an unexpected and surprising result.*

The primary characteristic of watercolor is its translucence. Mixing the paint with water causes translucent layers where the white of the paper creates brightness.

Chance in watercolor is due to the water we mix with the paint. The way we mix the paints is very important and determines how the watercolor settles onto paper. The watercolor is "alive," and it freely arranges itself onto your work surface.

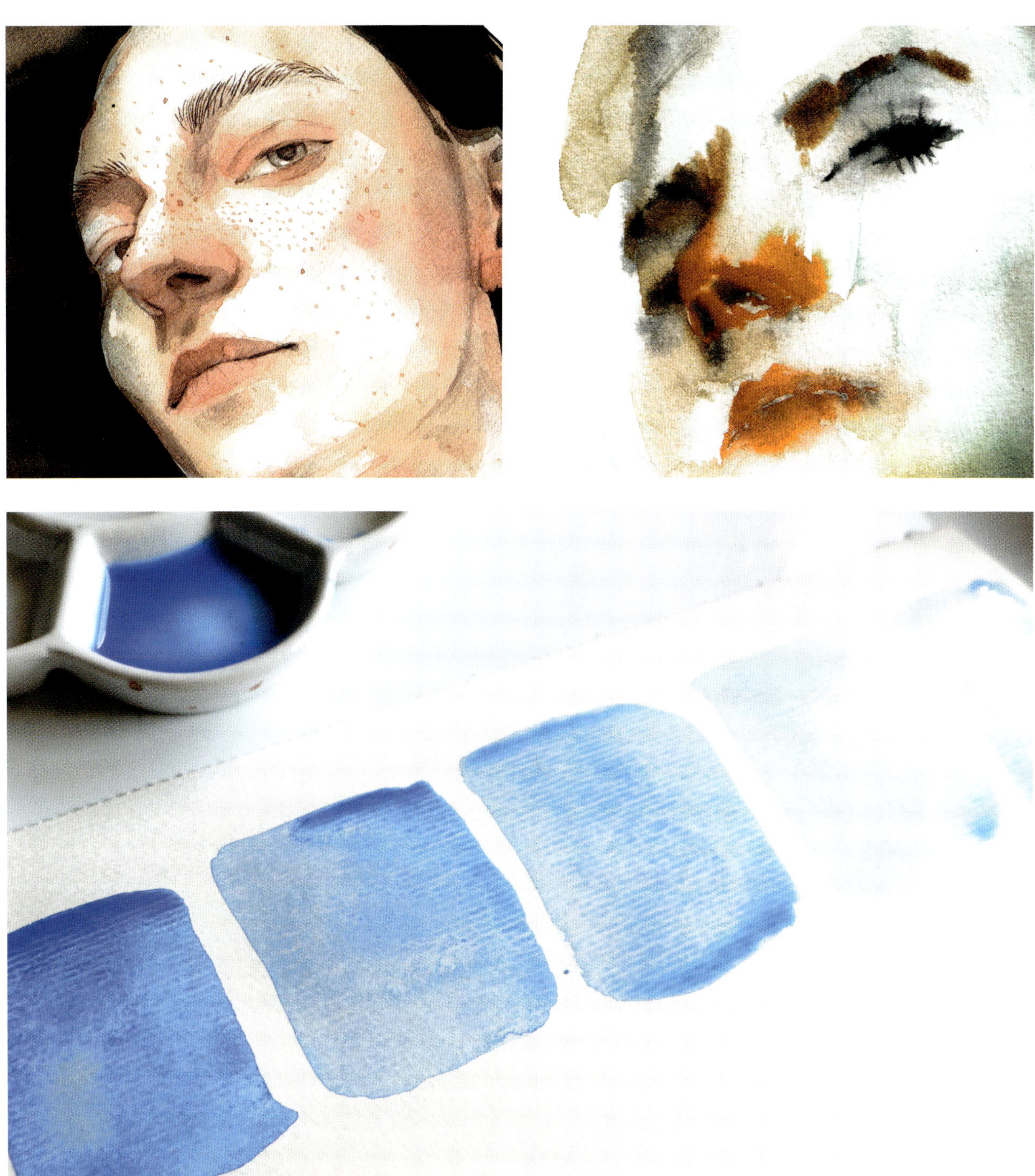

You can work in watercolor technique with a thorough, detailed approach, controlling your brushstrokes and water, or you can surprise yourself and leave it up to chance, letting the watercolors decide.

The amount of water you use provides the transparency that's so characteristic of watercolors.

Before you keep reading, try to let yourself be carried away by the medium. Find your most personal and intuitive side. This is usually an interesting exercise to engage in before learning any other methods.

Watercolor painting has multiple techniques and brushstroke combinations. It's incredible how such a seemingly simple medium can cover so many different styles depending on who is holding the brush. So remember to seek out and add your most intimate, instinctive, and creative sides to your creations.

ESSENTIAL METHODS

In this lesson, I demonstrate some basic techniques to give you a better understanding of how watercolor works.

BRUSHSTROKES

There are two main types of brushstrokes in watercolor: **dry brush** and **wet brush**.

These two strokes can be combined to change their character depending on the texture and wetness of the paper.

Dry Brush

The **dry brush technique** usually uses less water, so the stroke is rougher (especially if you paint on rough paper) and more defined.

Simply dampen your brush and take paint directly from the palette. This stroke is usually easier to control since it uses less water.

You'll get different results with this stroke, depending on the wetness of the paper. On dry paper, you'll get a controlled stroke. On wet paper, the stroke becomes more random with soft or blurred edges.

At right (top two) are some examples of the dry brush technique.

Wet Brush

The **wet brush technique** loads the brush with much more water, so the resulting brushstroke is more transparent.

As with the dry brush technique, for more definition and control, use a wet brushstroke on dry paper.

The result of a wet brushstroke on wet paper will be random and freer. Let the results surprise you and try not to control the brushstroke. Chance is one of the most interesting and unique qualities of this technique.

At right (bottom two) are examples of the wet brush technique.

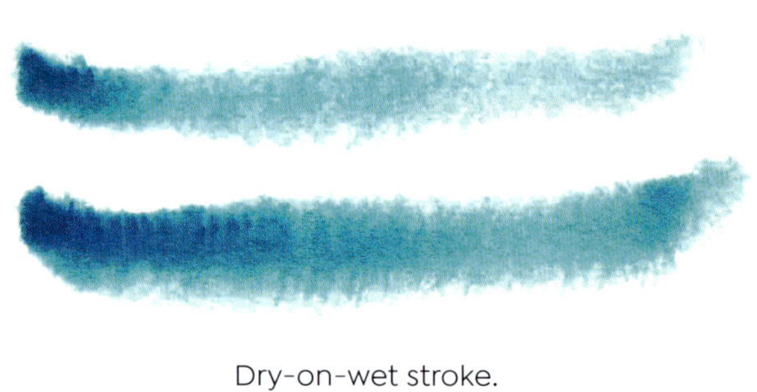

Dry-on-wet stroke.

Wet-on-dry stroke.

Wet-on-wet stroke.

Dry-on-dry stroke.

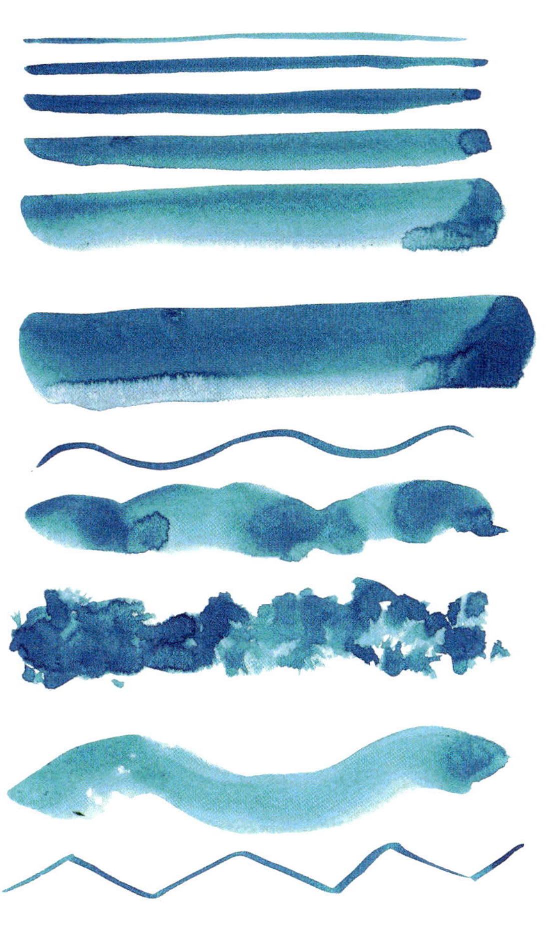

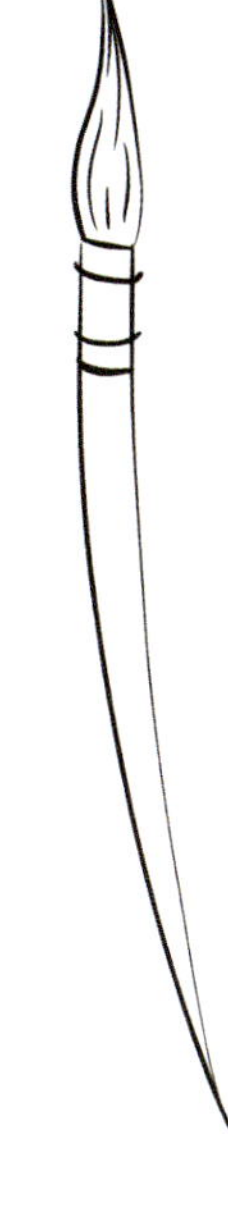

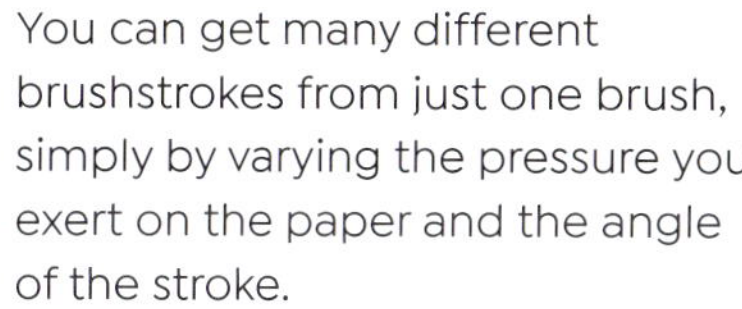

You can get many different brushstrokes from just one brush, simply by varying the pressure you exert on the paper and the angle of the stroke.

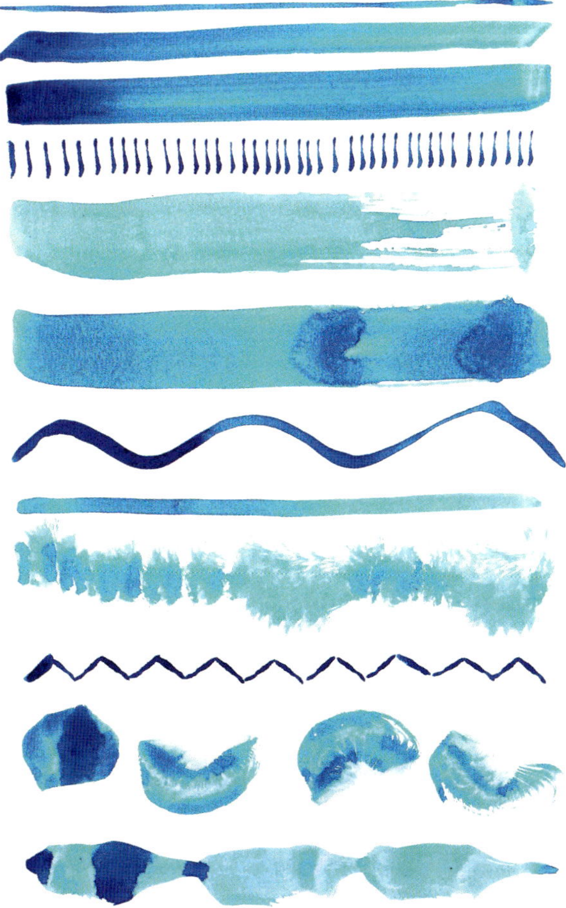

HARD EDGE/SOFT EDGE

When you use a wet brush on dry paper, the edge is defined. It is called a **"hard" edge**.

When you use a wet brush on wet paper, the edges blur and are lost in the wet paper. It is called a **"soft" edge**.

You can see how the stroke is transformed by how it looks on the paper.

(below) Examples of hard and soft edges.

BASIC TWO-COLOR TECHNIQUES

The same brushstroke techniques shown on the previous pages can be applied using two colors, which will show how the colors flow together and interact.

In these examples, we'll use two primary colors: blue and yellow. This way, we can best appreciate the result. Depending on how transparent the colors are, we can see that adding yellow and blue together results in green.

From this, we can conclude that watercolors can be mixed in three different ways:

1. Mixing on the palette itself (yellow + blue = green).
2. Through transparencies.
3. Mixing two wet colors on the paper's surface and letting them move freely.

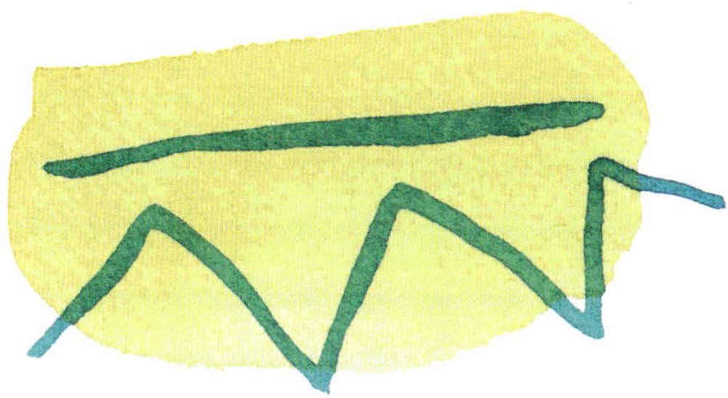

Dry-on-dry stroke.

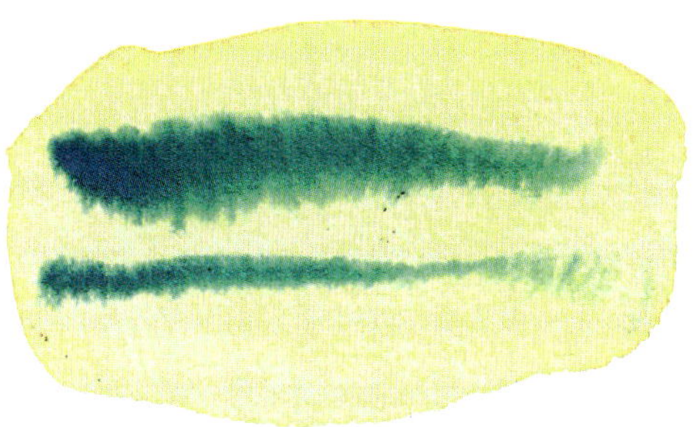

Dry-on-wet stroke.

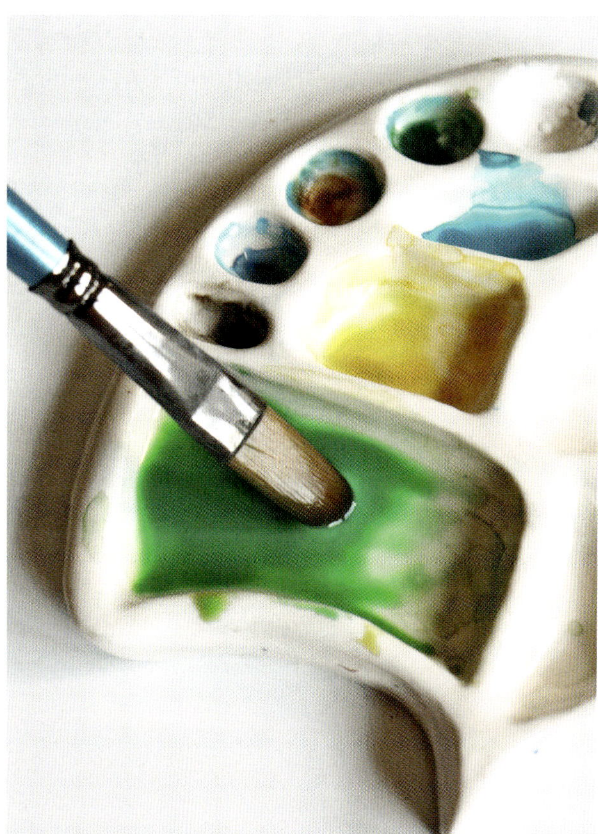

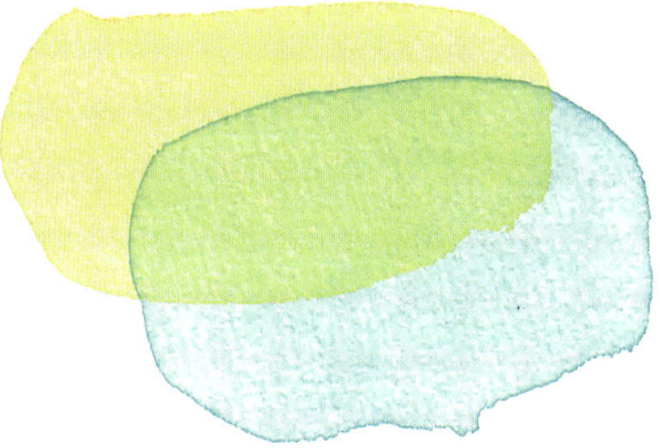

Wet-on-dry stroke.

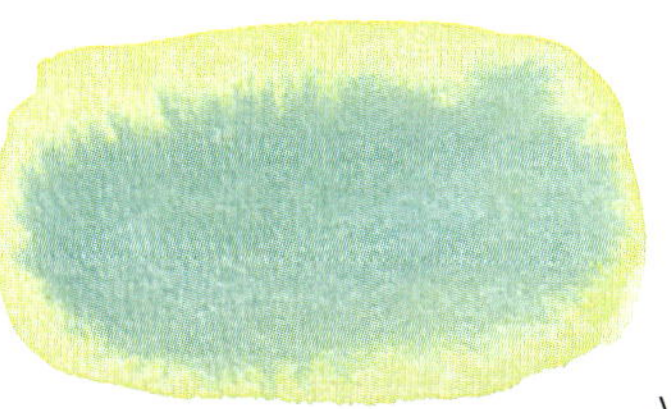

Wet on-wet stroke.

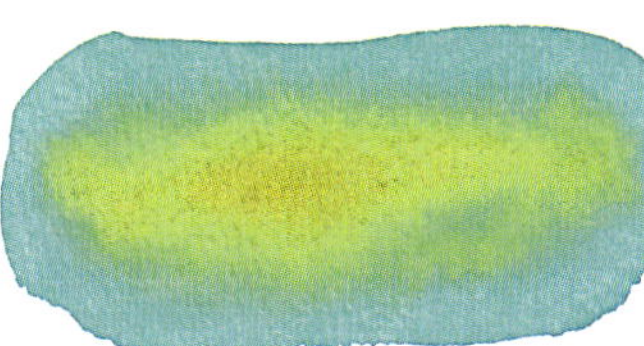

TRANSPARENCIES

As we've already discussed, the transparency of watercolors depends on the amount of water added to the paint. This is one of the most important lessons in watercolor technique because if anything at all identifies this technique, it's translucence.

White paper is what gives **light** to our work.

The **more water** we add to the paint, the **more transparent** the color will become.

With **less water**, the color will be **more opaque**. For example, if you paint directly from a wetted pan watercolor, the color will be more opaque than if you mix paint and water on a palette.

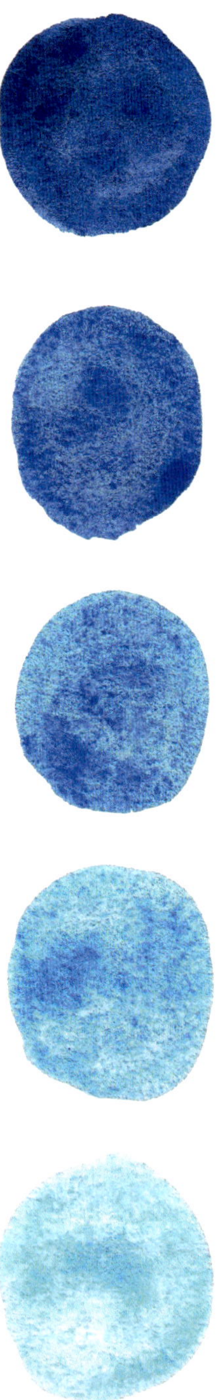

GRADIENTS

The transparency of watercolor makes it perfect for **glazing**, which is nothing more than placing one translucent layer on top of another. The transparency allows you to see the lower layers of paint.

Transparency also offers the opportunity to mix two or more colors. The sum of the two tones results in a third tone, which will be slightly different depending on whether a bright color or a dark color is applied first. In very elaborate works with many layers, the final tones are the sum of the many layers of translucent color.

Many artists start a work by first placing shadows with cool or dark colors (for example, blue, green, violet, red, and brown). Others start by first placing the lightest and brightest colors and then add the shadows. The results of the two methods are very different, and I encourage you to try both ways!

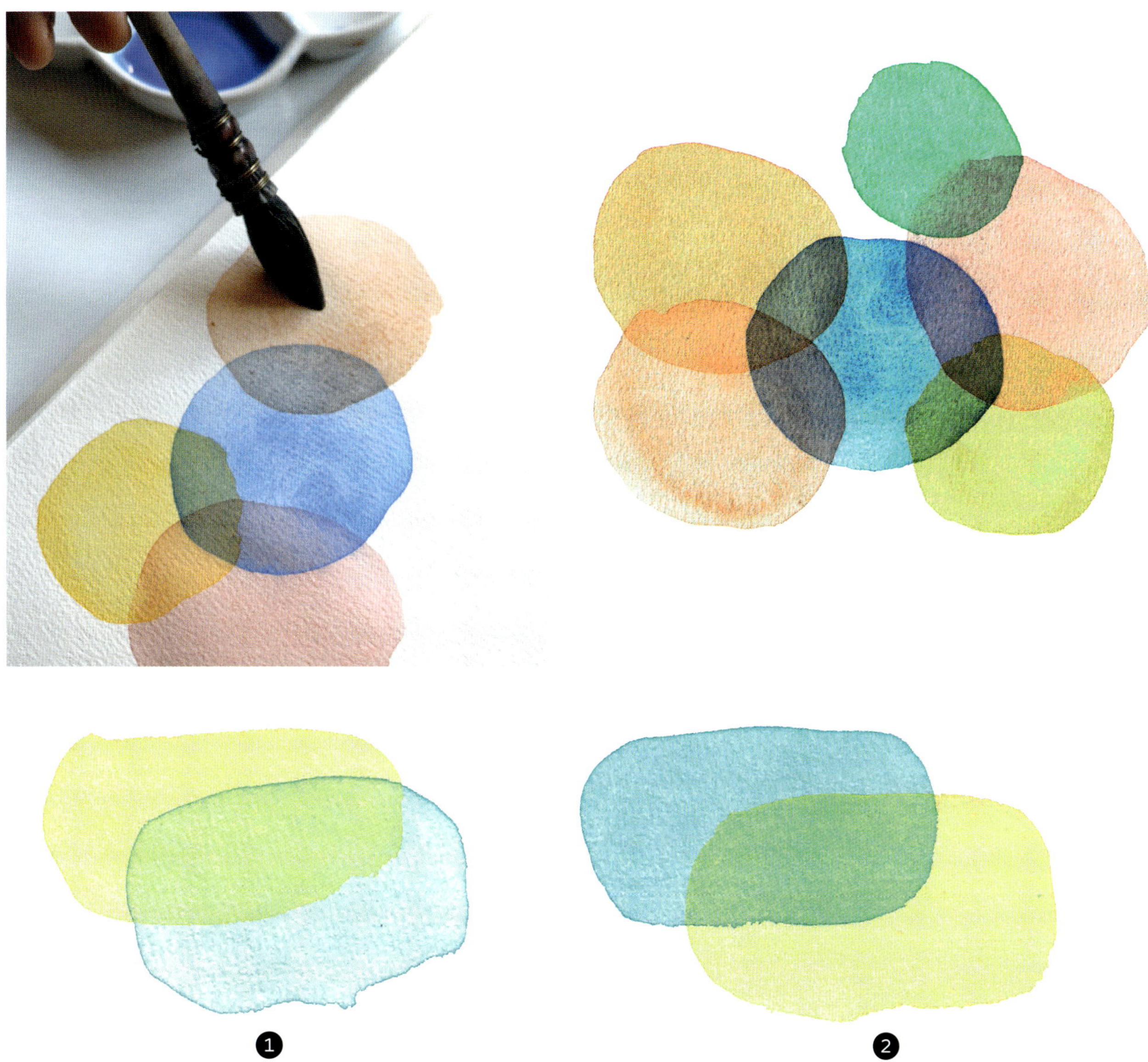

Example 1: First a bright color (yellow) was placed, and then a darker one (blue). Example 2: First a dark color (blue) was placed, and then a bright one (yellow).

SINGLE-COLOR GRADIENTS

A **gradient** is a transition in a color's value—from opaque to transparent, and vice versa. To do this, apply a brushstroke and gradually add water until it becomes as transparent as possible.

This is similar to making a grayscale with a pen, from darker to lighter.

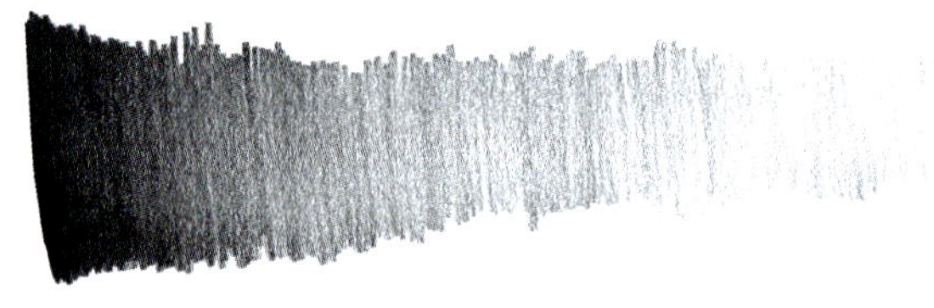

MULTIPLE-COLOR GRADIENTS

A color gradient mixes two or more colors. They usually work best with colors that are close to each other on the color wheel.

For example, from yellow to blue, we'll get green.

However, if we use a gradient with two complementary colors, for example, red and yellow, the gradient will be brown.

You can create gradients to make different color palettes.

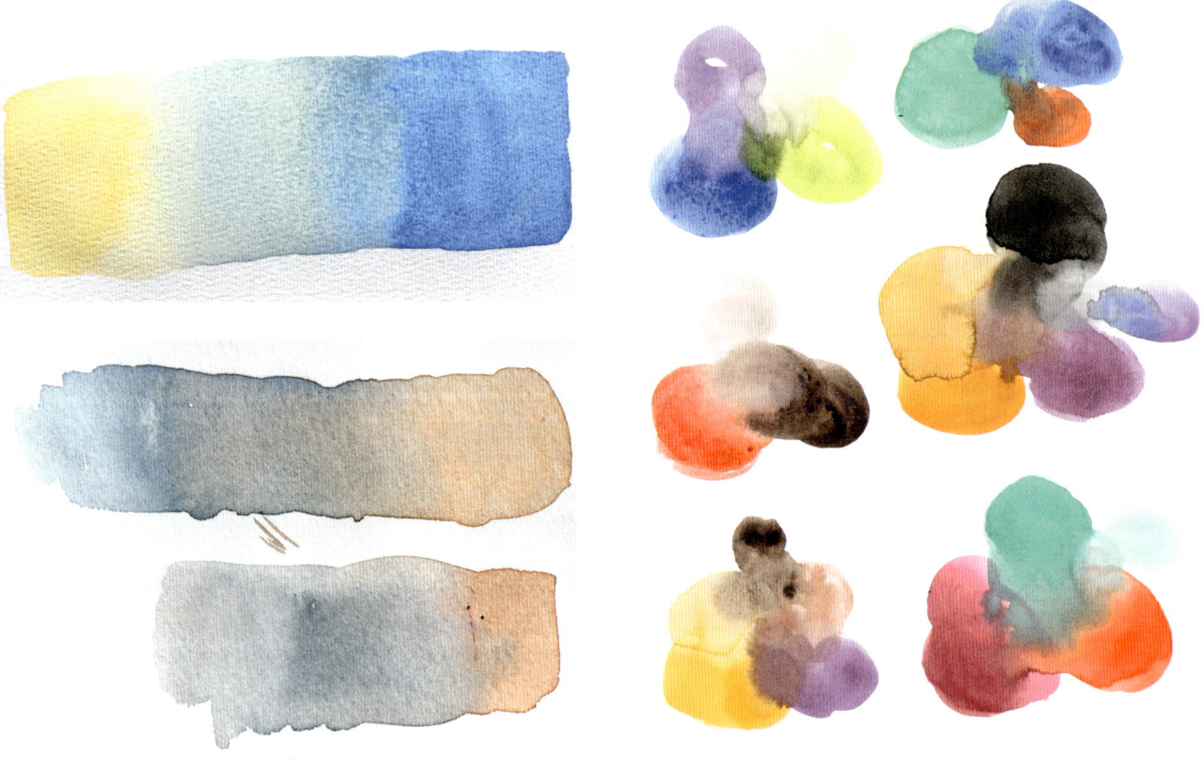

PAINTING WITH LARGE STROKES

It's easier to control small strokes than large ones, but if you want to paint a large surface in a soft, uniform color, without any shifts, the trick is to prepare enough of the color first on a palette so that you don't run out.

With a high-numbered brush that can hold a lot of water, paint as if you were "scrubbing" the paper. It's important not to touch up the area you've already painted too much. Don't rush to dry your brush. While painting on a surface, it's is better to keep the brush wet with the mix of paint and water you've made.

If, in contrast, you want a more spontaneous result or to paint more freely, you can use more water in some areas and more paint in others. Play with the directions of the brushstroke.

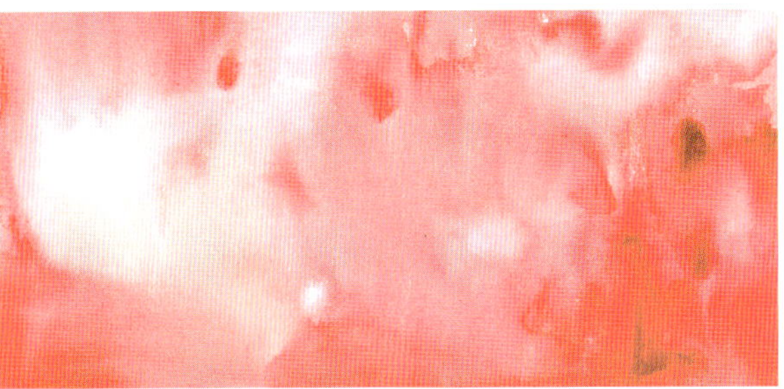

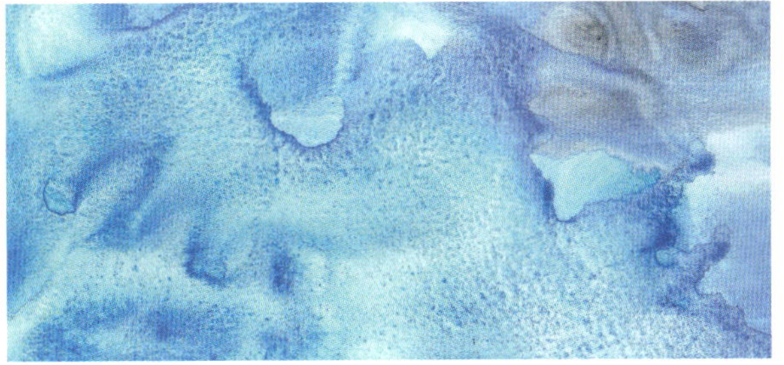

CORRECTING UNWANTED SPLASHES OR STAINS ON PAPER

It's true that watercolor has little margin to make corrections since it dries very quickly. This can have advantages and disadvantages for creating effects.

But if you have an unwanted stain at the edge of your paper, before it dries completely, moisten that area with clean water and then quickly use a paper towel to absorb the stain and lift it away (don't drag the wet paper towel since you could also make the stain bigger).

TECHNIQUES FOR CREATING LIGHT AREAS

We've already talked about the importance of light in watercolor. The light comes from the white of the paper itself. A color will look bright or opaque depending on the amount of water we add to the paint.

The traditional way to create light and white is to simply leave paper unpainted—this is what's called **preserving white**.

In addition to this classic way of creating white in our work, here are some other ways to provide brightness and to create points of light.

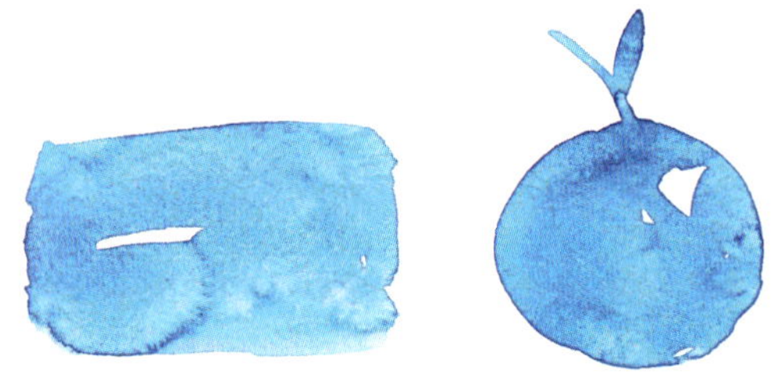

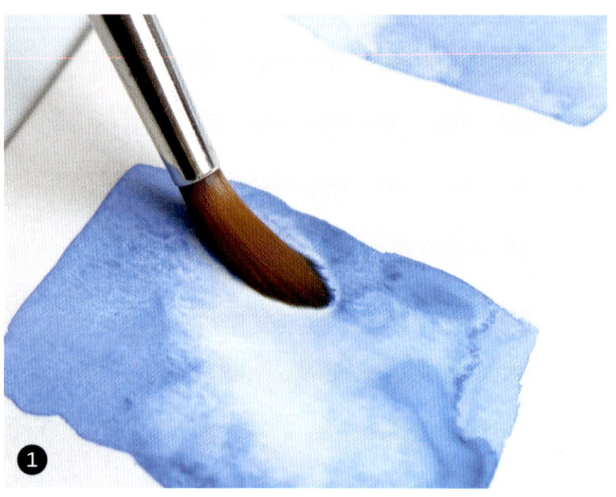

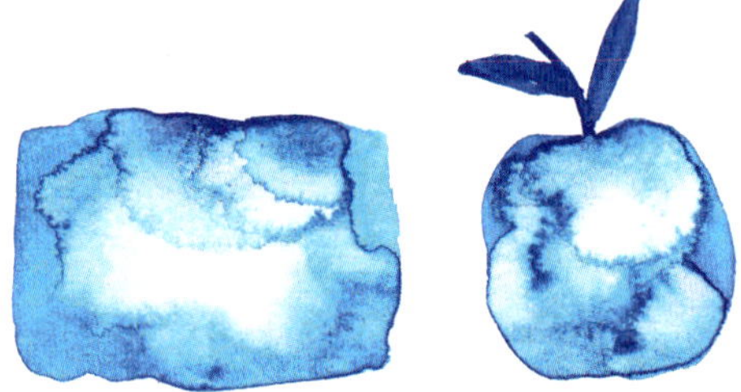

1. Over a layer of watercolor that's still wet, **apply clean water** and let it move and create lightness as it goes. Once dry, you'll have your own surprising watercolor shapes and textures.

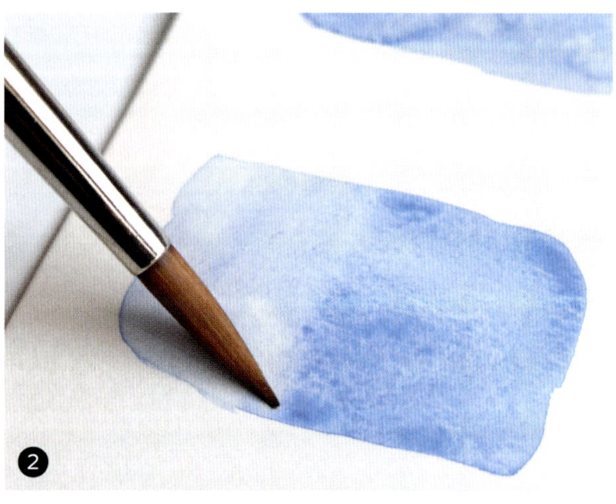

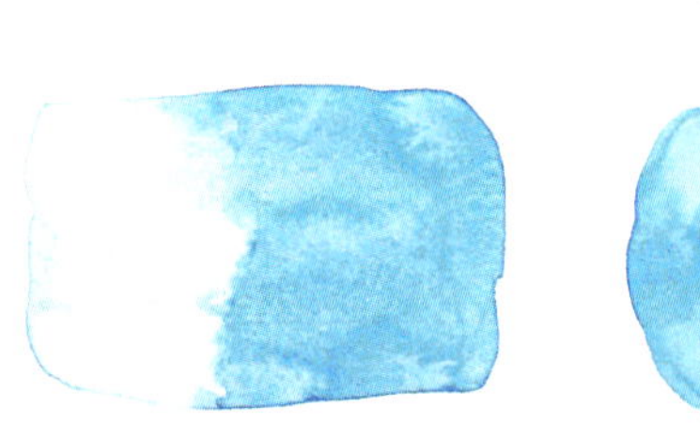

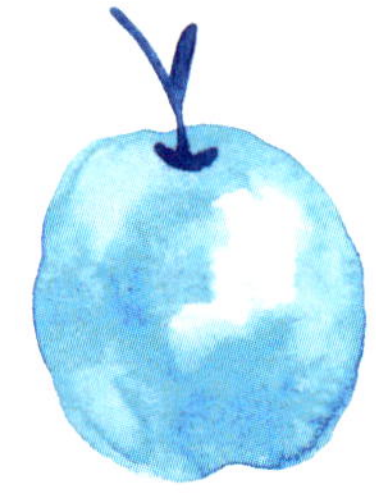

2. With a **clean and somewhat dry brush, absorb** wherever you want to recover light (before the watercolor dries).

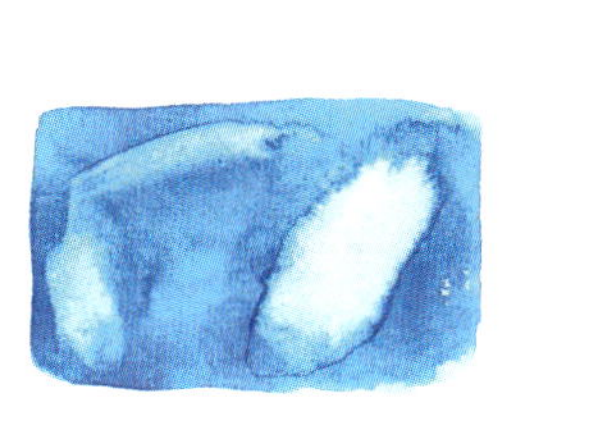

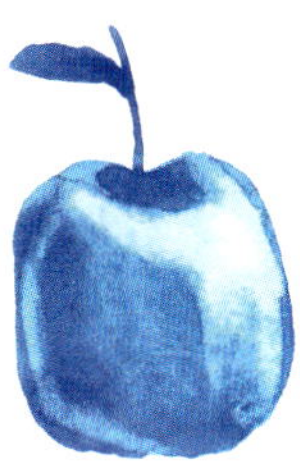

3. Use a **hard and wet brush** to “scratch” a previously dried layer of color.

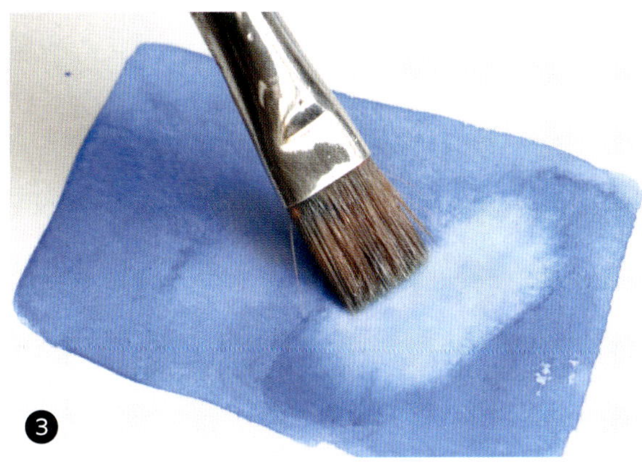

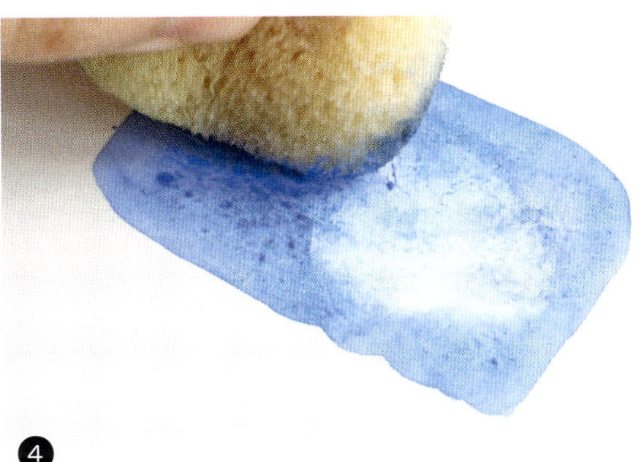

4. Use a **sponge** to absorb or drag.

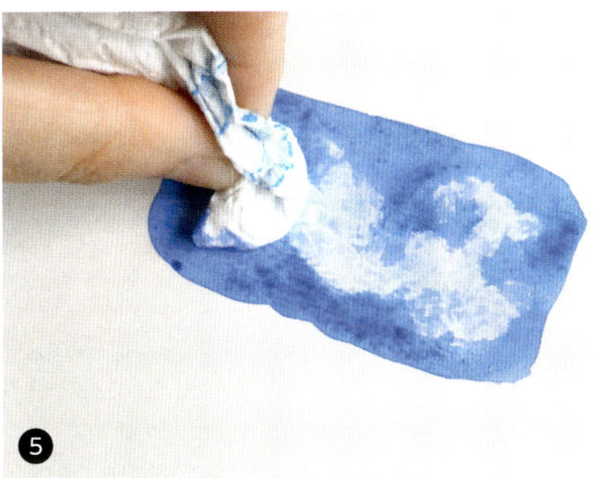

5. Use a **paper towel** to absorb.

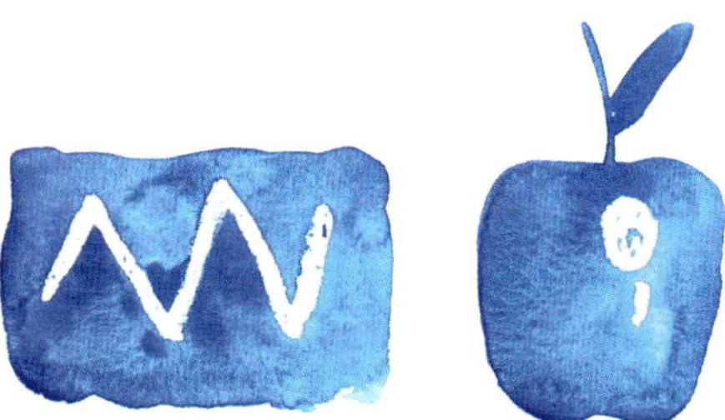

6. Use **wax crayons**, such as Manley wax crayons, where you want points of light. The wax is oily, which repels water, so the paint will not stay in that area.

Once you’ve traced your drawing in pencil, use a white wax crayon in those places where you want to leave light or white. Then, you can brush over the wax without fear!

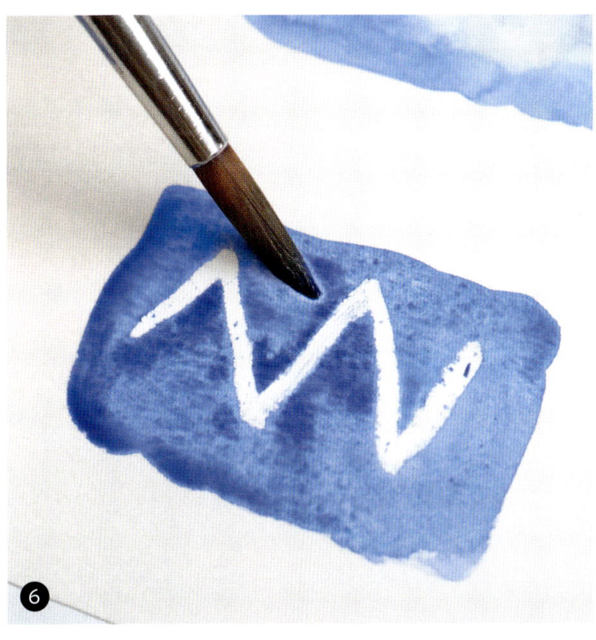

7. There are many brands of **masking fluid** available for sale. They have different applications, either with a brush or a marker to make small, precise reserves. Paint or apply the fluid where you want the paper to show through.

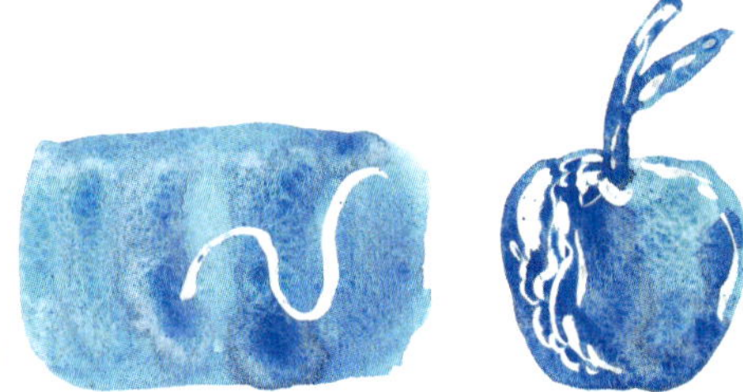

This material creates a thin rubbery colored film. Once it's dry, you can paint on top of it. Once your watercolor is dry, you can remove the masking fluid with your fingertip (make sure your hands are clean so you don't get oils or dirt on the paper). As it dries, you'll see how the white paper and the light reserves you previously "protected" appear.

8. You can create light colors in your work with white paints. If you want powerful and very clean whites and light points, it's best to make sure that you use very opaque white paints such as **gouache**.

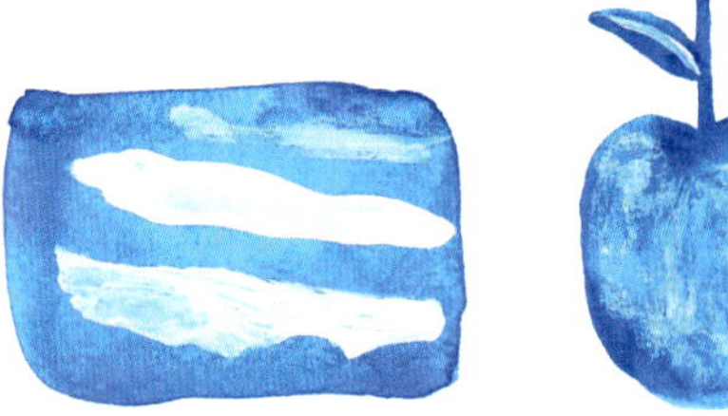

WET-ON-DRY

You can also add gouache to watercolors when they are still moist.

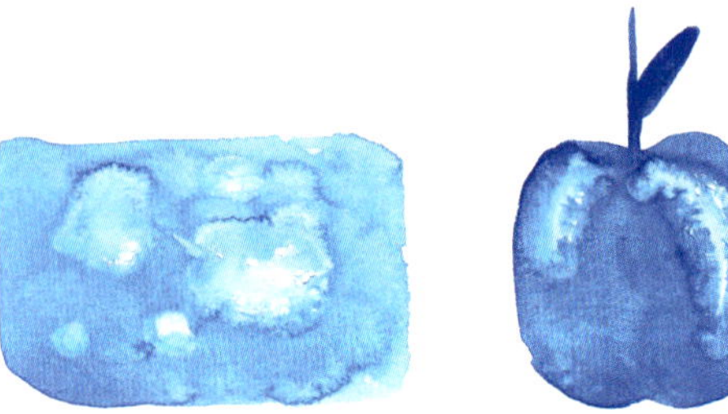

WET-ON-WET

If you add water to gouache, it will lose its opacity, and you can create beautiful white glazes to add brightness and light.

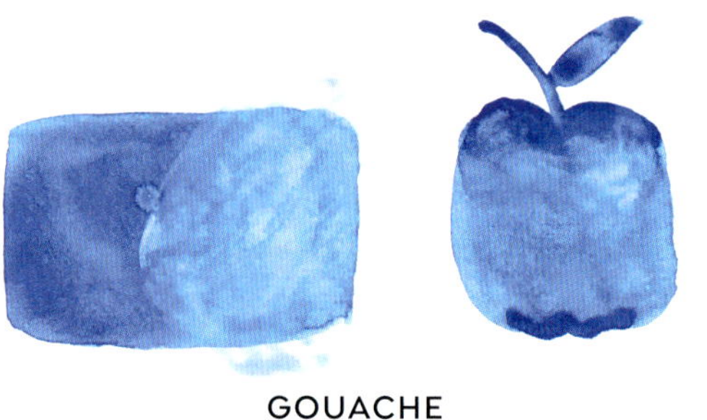

GOUACHE

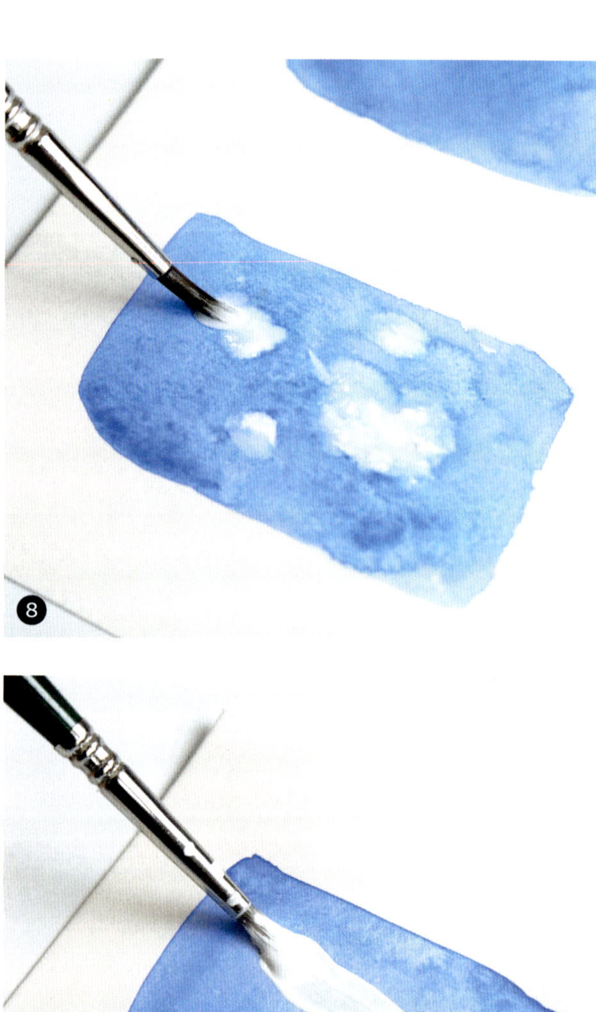

WHEN MIXING PASTEL WATERCOLORS

You can mix either gouache or white ink with watercolors to create pastels. But beware! White makes the colors more opaque and eliminates the transparency of watercolors.

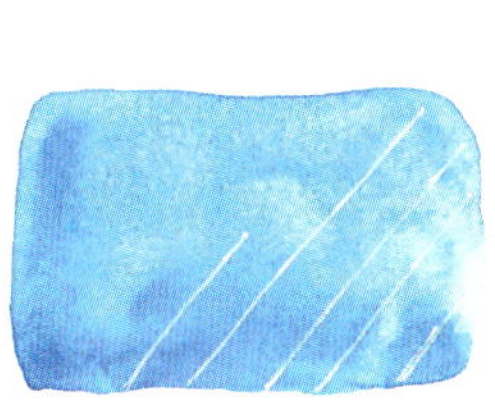

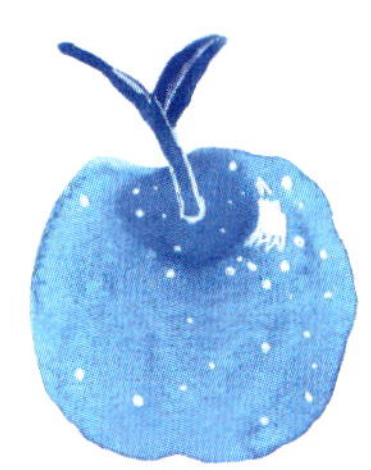

9. A **white pen** (such as Pilot brand) is a good choice for very small and precise light details. Make sure the watercolor layer is dry.

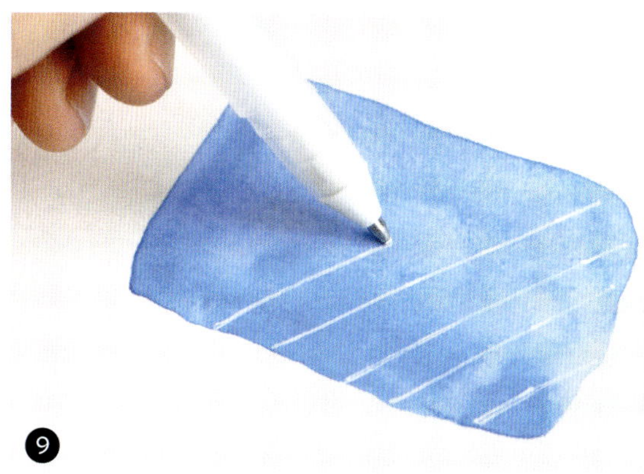

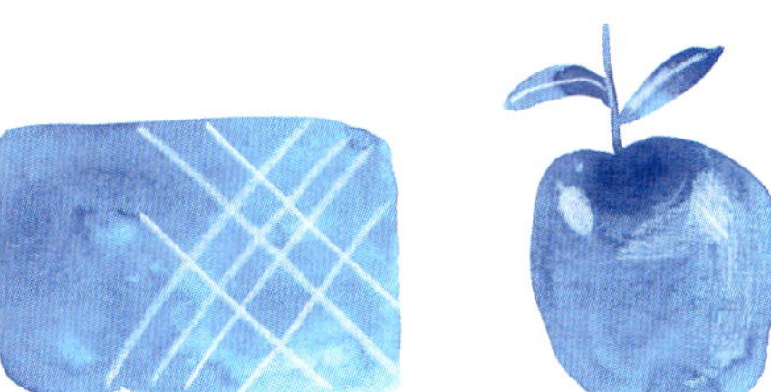

10. A **white pencil** works the same way as the white pen. You can use it when the watercolor is completely dry.

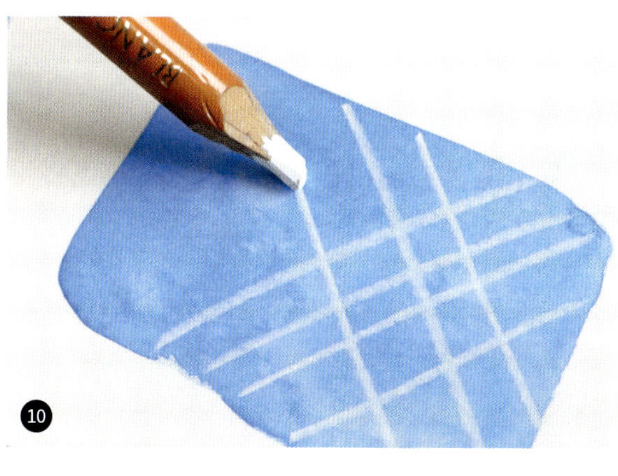

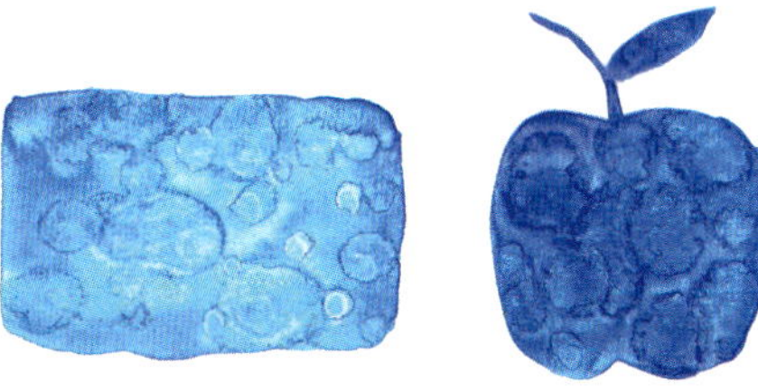

11. **Acetone** creates light in watercolor when it's applied wet on paper, as well as different effects and textures. You have to make sure to use it carefully because it "burns" the paper.

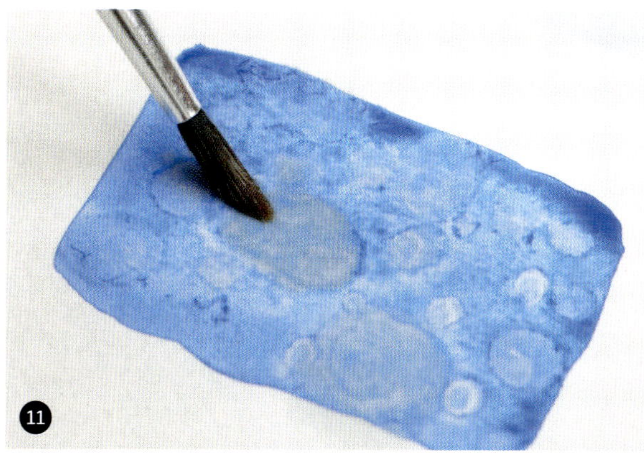

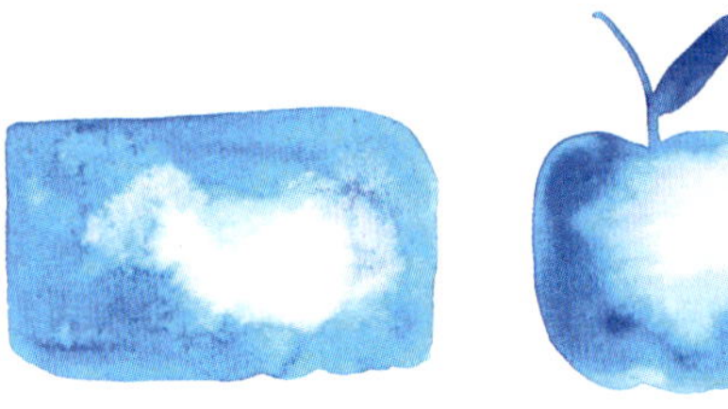

12. You must use **bleach** very cautiously and in a well-ventilated room. The bleach fades the color and creates some surprising light areas on the paper. It should be used while the watercolors are still wet.

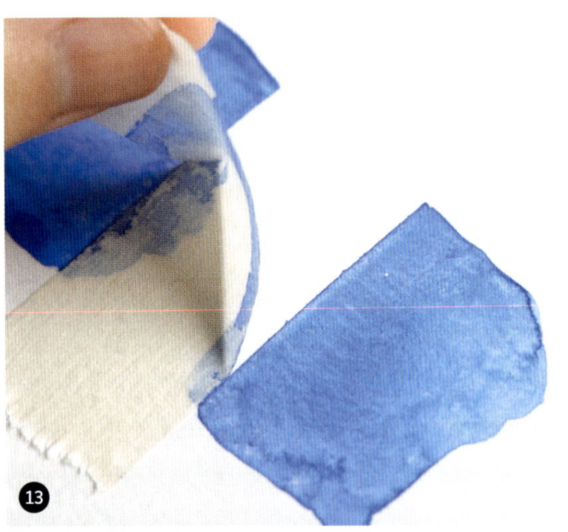

13. Place **masking tape** on the paper where you want to leave a line or area unpainted. Once the watercolor has dried, you can remove it. Low-quality masking tape can tear or lift the paper, so be sure to test yours first!

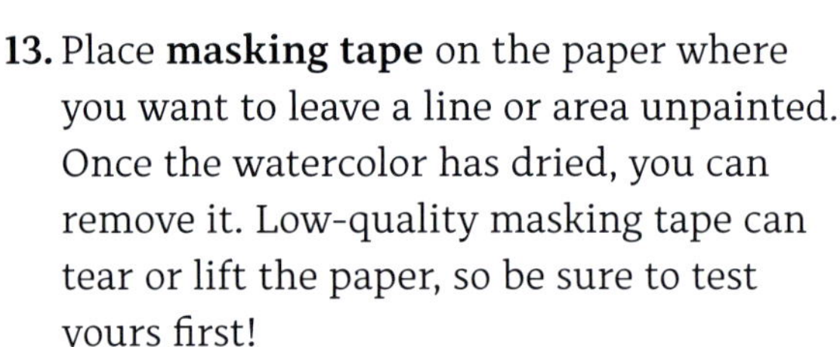

14. Although the method requires a lot of visual practice, you can give volume to the face using light and shadow. In a reference with "real" colors, it can be difficult at first for us to translate those tones into a **color language**. An easy way to identify tonal volume is to modify the reference photo to black and white. When we see the photograph in gray tones, it's easier to identify the light and dark areas.

To make the location of the most contrasting points of light and shadow even more clear, you can further adjust the contrast of the black and white photo. Once you've identified the areas of light and shadow, choose a color palette and assign corresponding gray tones to those colors.

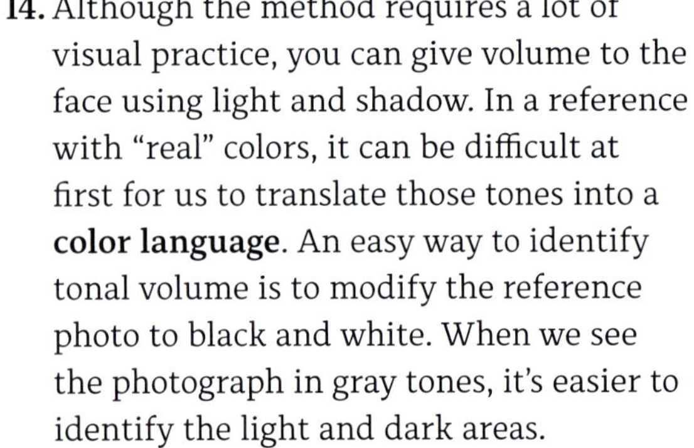

For example, if you use a bright color palette (yellow-orange-green), you'd make the following selections:

» Yellow for the lighter whites and grays

» Orange for the intermediate grays

» Green for the darker grays and blacks

On the next page is an example of choosing a photo and converting it to black and white where we can very easily identify lights and shadows or tonal values.

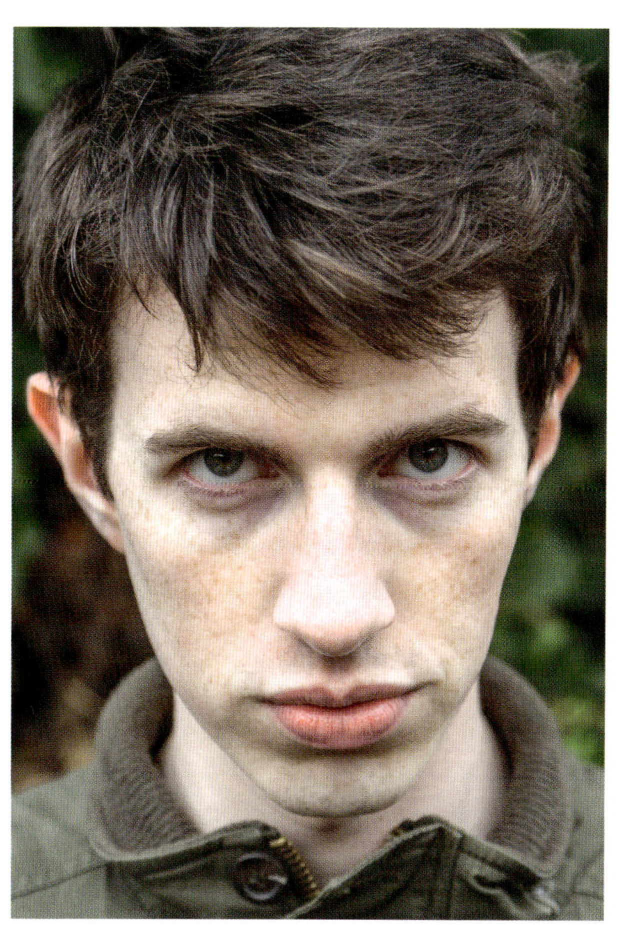
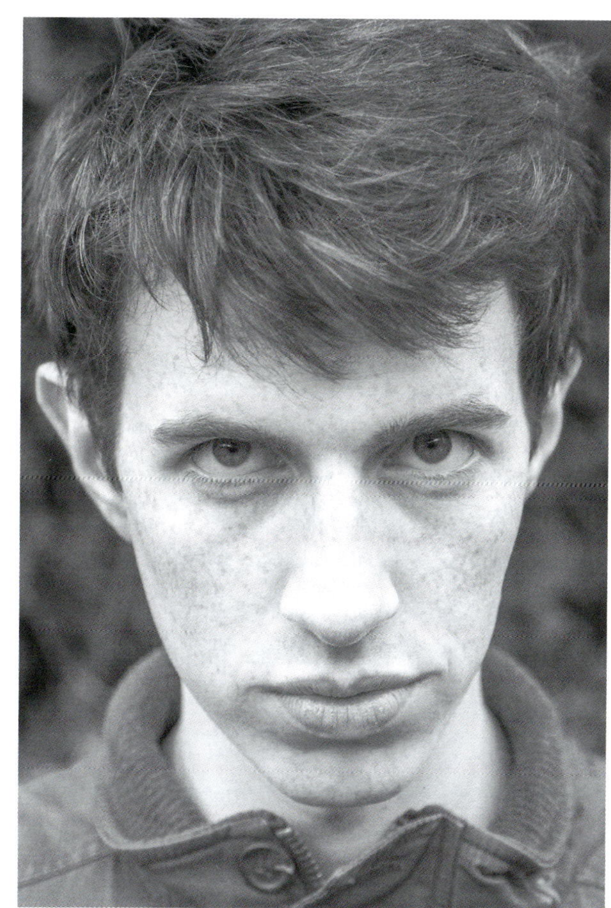
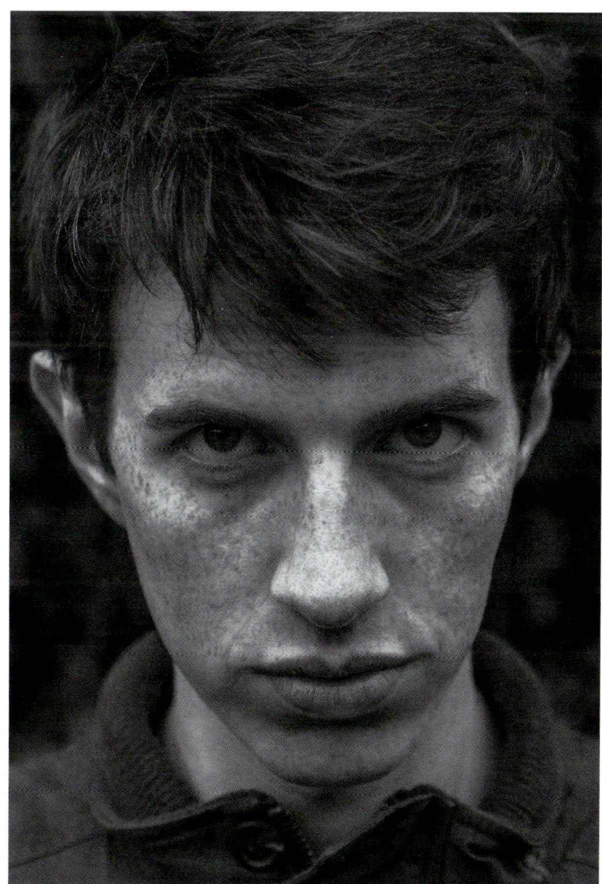
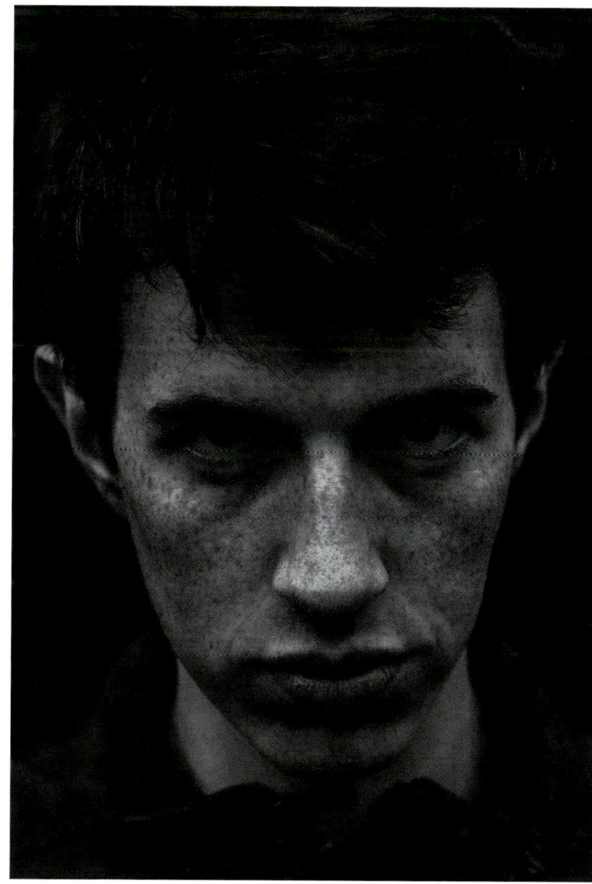

PROPORTIONS OF THE FACE

In this part of the book, I give a brief introduction and simple explanation of the proportions of a face. *There are endlessly different ways to build a face. Each method has its own particular approach, but most of them have similar processes. I explain some of the basics, and you can find a method that best fits for you. Then, I share what works best for me.*

Keep in mind that, with rare exceptions, most people's faces aren't totally symmetrical. So don't worry too much about achieving perfect symmetry.

The portrait is considered one of the most complex themes or subjects to represent. Becoming a good portraitist requires hours of practice. Achieving a realistic portrait requires a lot of observation and knowledge about the muscles and bones that are part of the head. Representing the "soul" of a person also requires practice and is almost always the most interesting step.

In this book, I want you to have fun and learn about a simpler approach to portraiture. Personally, I love portraits made by children for their spontaneity and innocence when it comes to drawing. Children draw very original and out-of-proportion portraits that have their own character, which makes them very special.

Drawing is a very freeing activity, and you don't have to be an expert to be able to express yourself by drawing. "Awkward" drawings, or ones that are not based on basic rules or theories of drawing, also have a lot of charm. Not everything has to be faithful to reality or to specialized standards of beauty and harmony. Above all, feel free and have fun when you draw. Pour out your personality into what you create—we all have our own language, and that's what makes us unique.

The best advice is to know all the rules to be able to break them.

Making an awkward or disproportionate drawing also requires skill, and most artists who draw this way are aware of the standard proportions of a head.

That said, it's usually possible to determine who draws in an awkward style intentionally and who does so due to a lack of knowledge. My advice is that you learn about proportions to be able to be free to draw as you wish.

It's true that in following the rules, you can lose a certain "freshness" or spontaneity. Many artists choose to paint in a more childish way and set their knowledge aside. We can always ignore rules and draw more freely and outside what we learn in school. How you express yourself in drawing has no limits or boundaries. Having knowledge about the rules doesn't have to restrict your imagination. It can actually help you expand your horizons just a little bit more.

Before you continue reading the next lesson, take a sheet of paper and a pencil and draw a face with all features. Then, compare those results with the ones in the next lesson.

FRONT VIEW

We begin our lesson on proportions by drawing a full-face portrait in front view.

1. Draw an egg shape and divide it in half horizontally. That dividing line is the height of the eyes, as incredible as that might seem.
2. Divide it in half with a vertical line. This divides the head into two sides and is the axis of the nose. (A)
3. Place a second horizontal line above the eyes. This is where the eyebrows go. Now, we have the upper part of the head, eyebrows, eyes, and chin.
4. From the line for the eyebrows to the chin, divide it in half again. This is where the base of the nose goes.
5. From the base of the nose to the chin, divide the area into three equal parts. The first third is for the center line of the lips.
6. The width of the nose is calculated as the halfway point of the line from the base of the nose to the eyebrows. The result is the proportional width of the nose based on the height measurement of the head. (B)

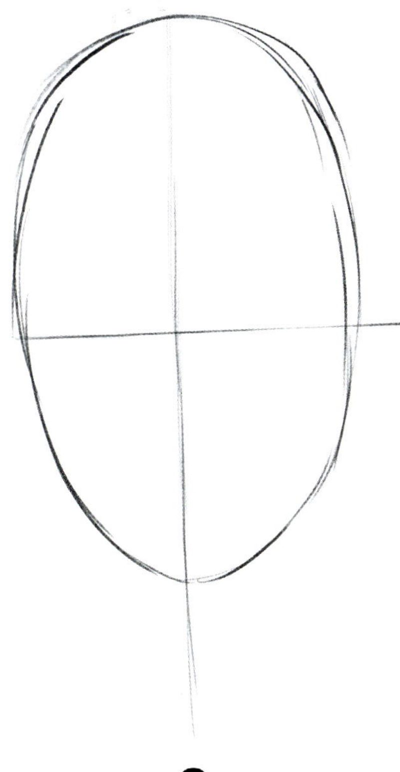

A

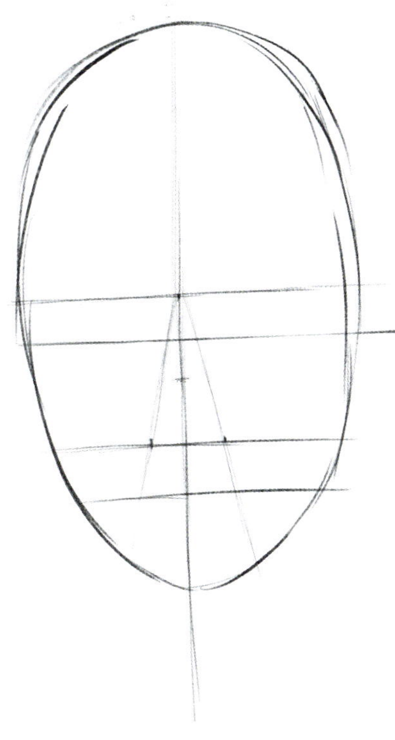

B

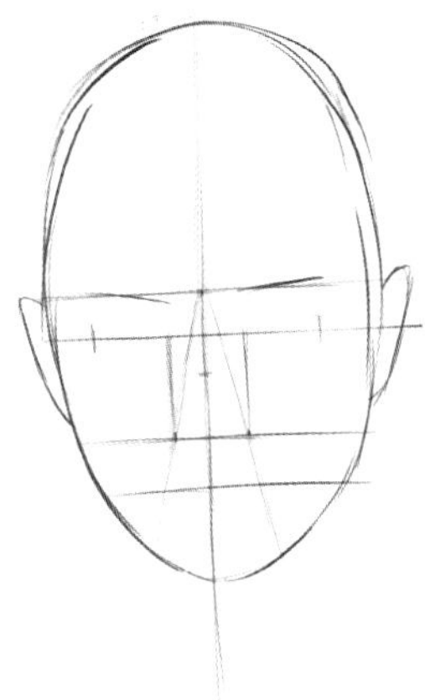

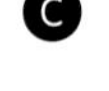

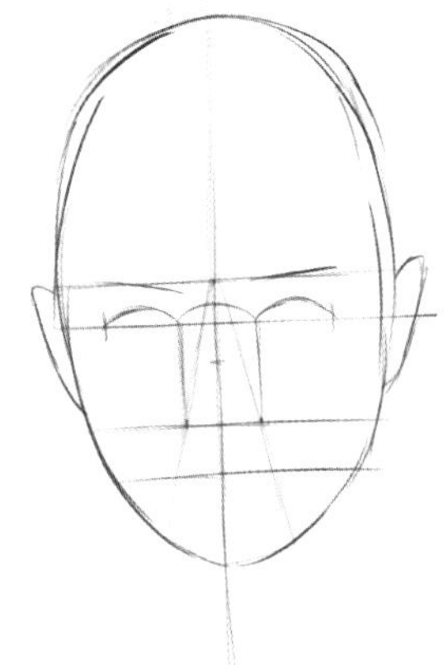

D

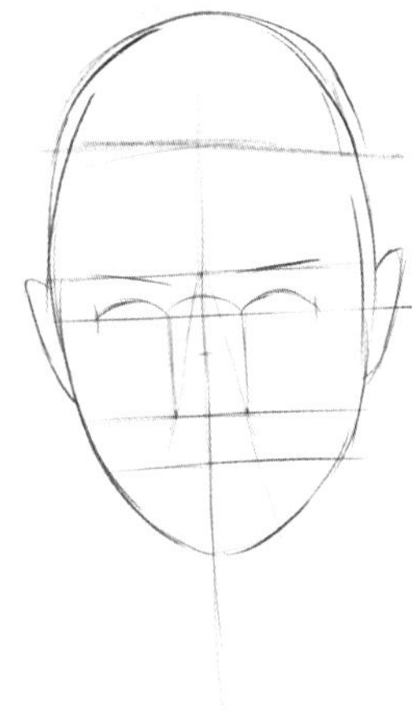

E

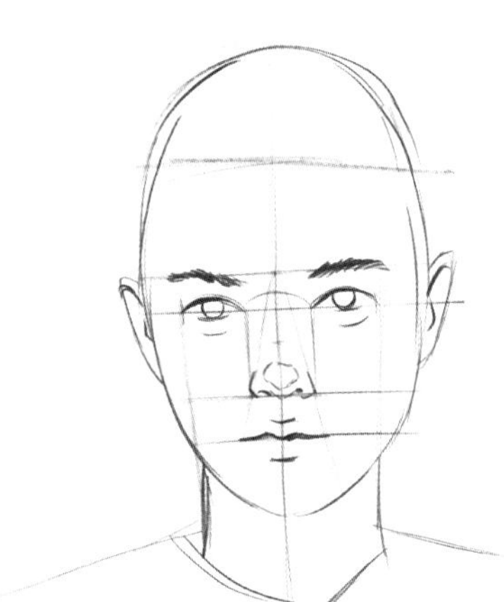

F

7. Once the width of the nose is determined, draw two vertical lines toward the horizontal line for the eyes. That's where one edge of the eye goes. The size of the eyes usually corresponds to the width of the nose. (C)
8. For the septum, draw two vertical lines, one on either side of the nose to the line for the eyebrows. (D)
9. The edges of the mouth usually line up with the center of the pupils.
10. A harmonious face corresponds to the face being divided into three equal parts, which is a very basic guide to help you easily draw a proportionate portrait (E):
    - From the chin to the base of the nose.
    - From the base of the nose to the eyebrows.
    - From the eyebrows to the forehead.
11. The ears usually go from the base of the nose to the eyes or eyebrows. (F)
12. The width and height of the neck depend on the person, but you can roughly approximate by drawing a line from the outer edge of the eyes.

See next page for the remaining steps in this process (G–K).

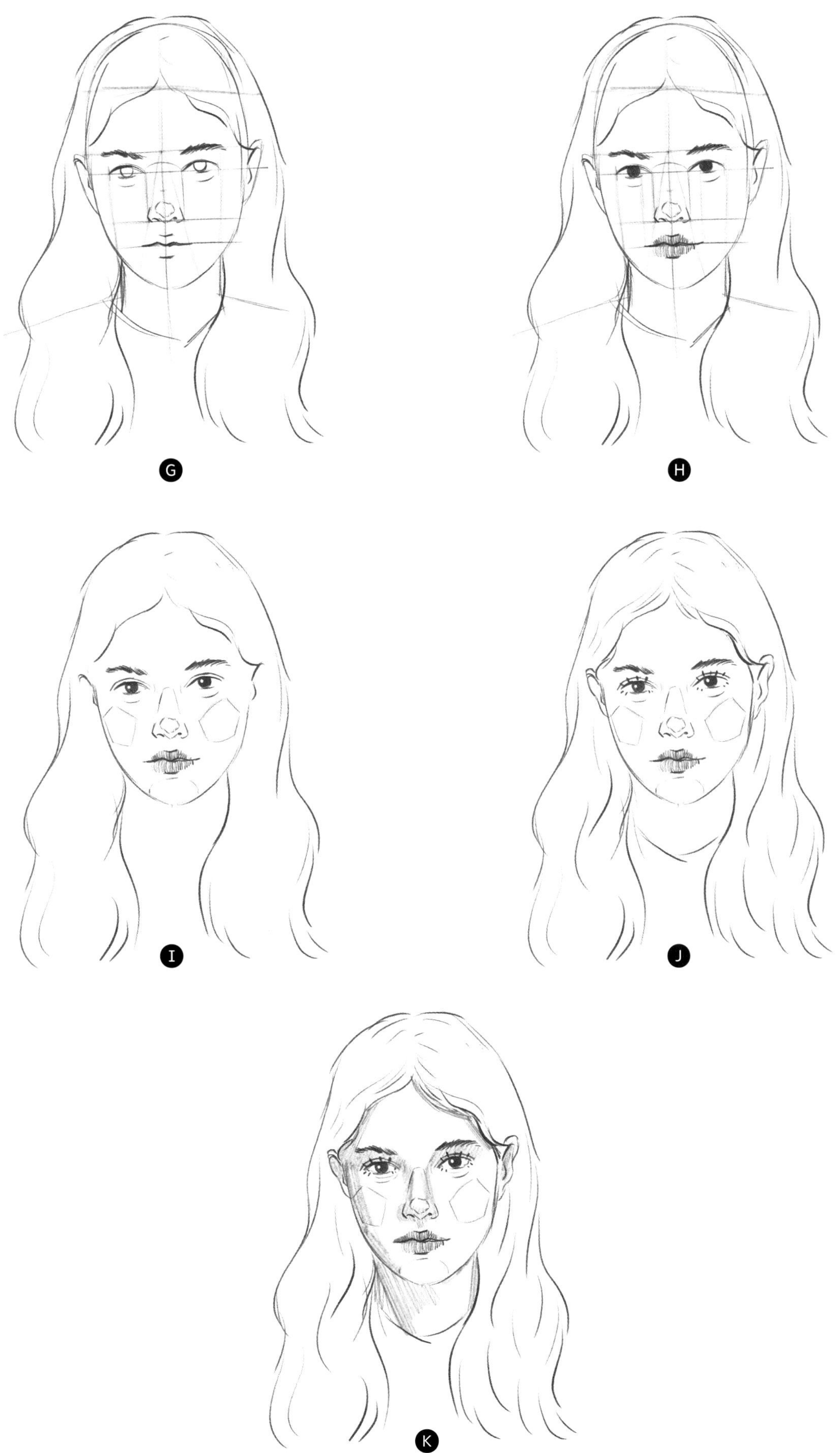
G
H
I
J
K

PROFILE VIEW

The process of drawing a face in profile follows the same proportions, measurements, and steps as drawing a face from the front. You can start with an oval or a circle.

Looking at a face in profile, you'll notice that the ear is located at about the middle of the head, and that an equilateral triangle is formed by the chin, the ear, and the eyes.

Here's a simple sketch as an example.

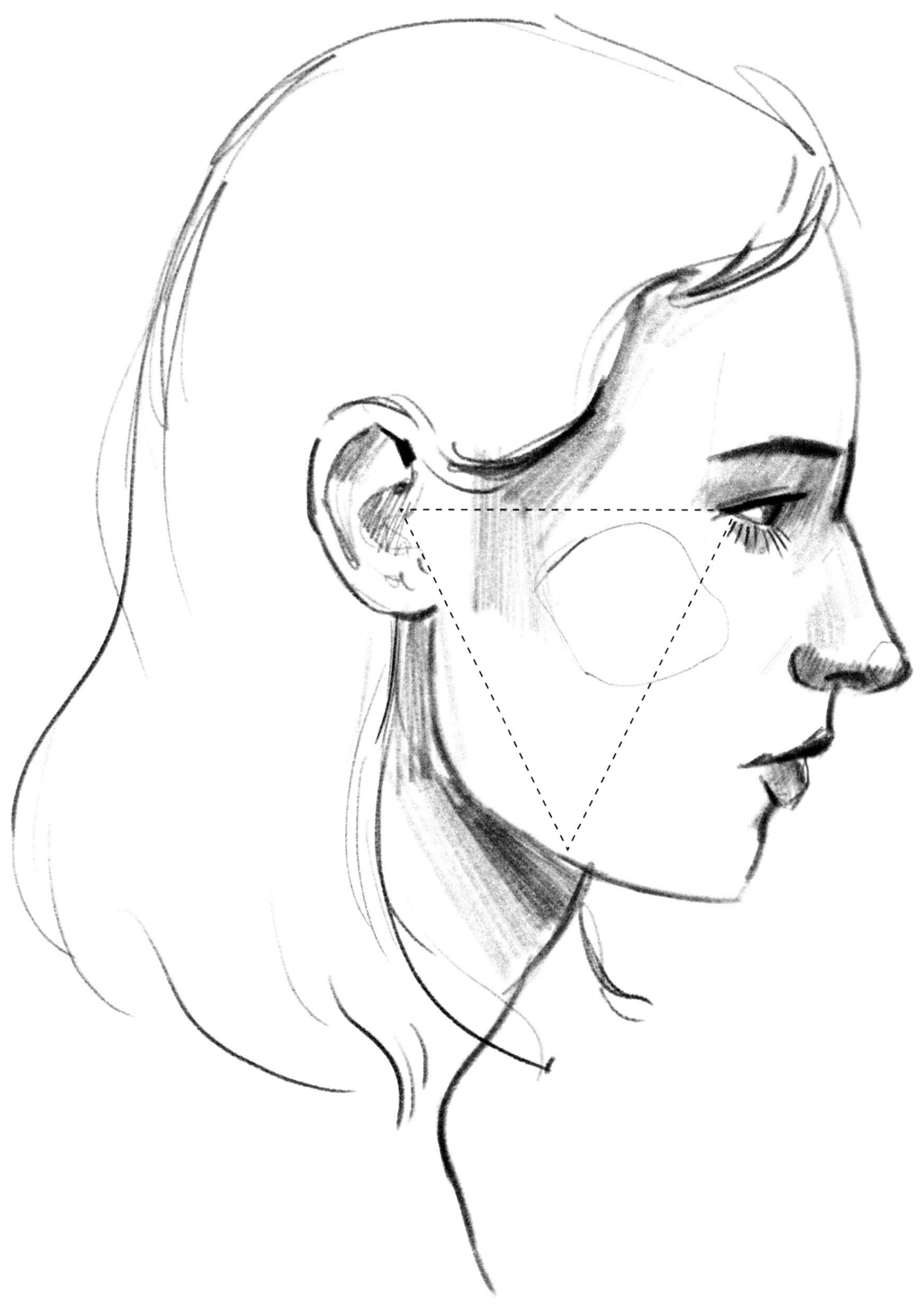

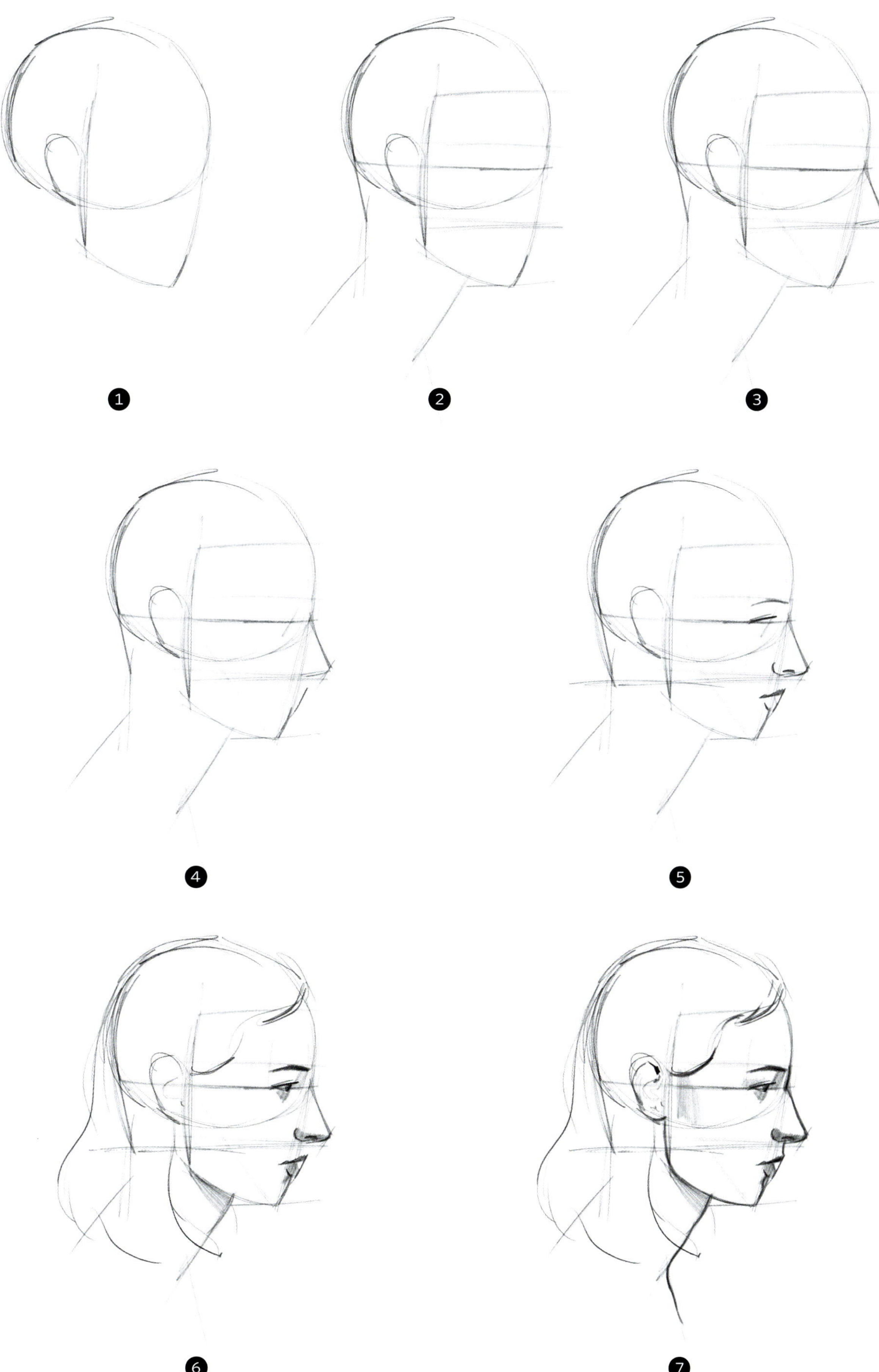
1
2
3
4
5
6
7

THREE-QUARTER VIEW

To draw the head in a three-quarter portrait, imagine an egg shape as a three-dimensional sphere. Set the main axes on a slight diagonal to help you place the eyes, nose, mouth, and ear.

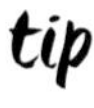

To help block in your portrait, look at a reference photograph and draw the main directional lines.

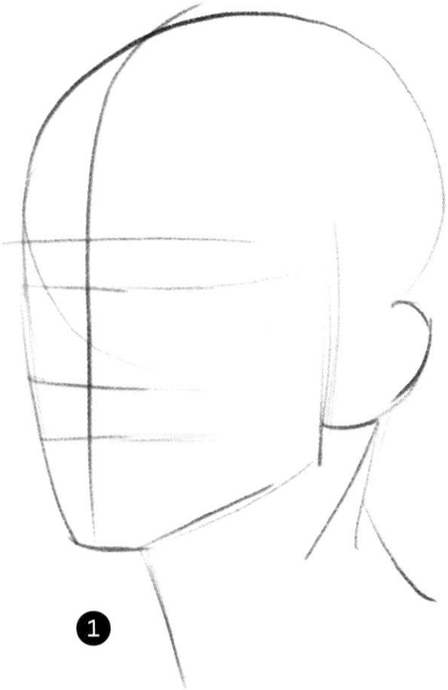

1

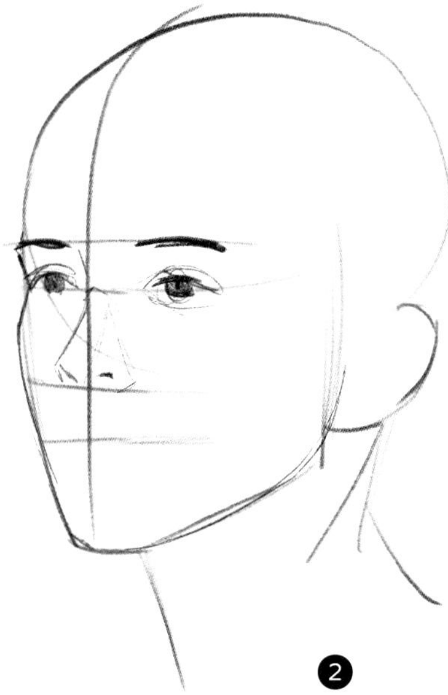

2

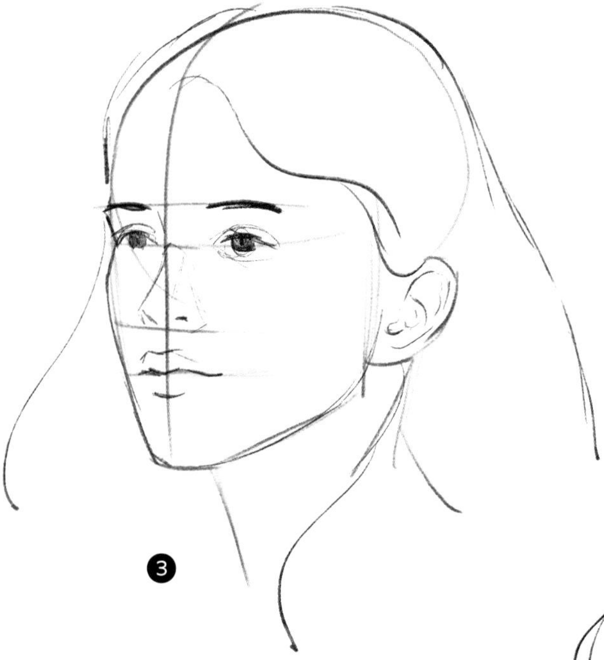

3

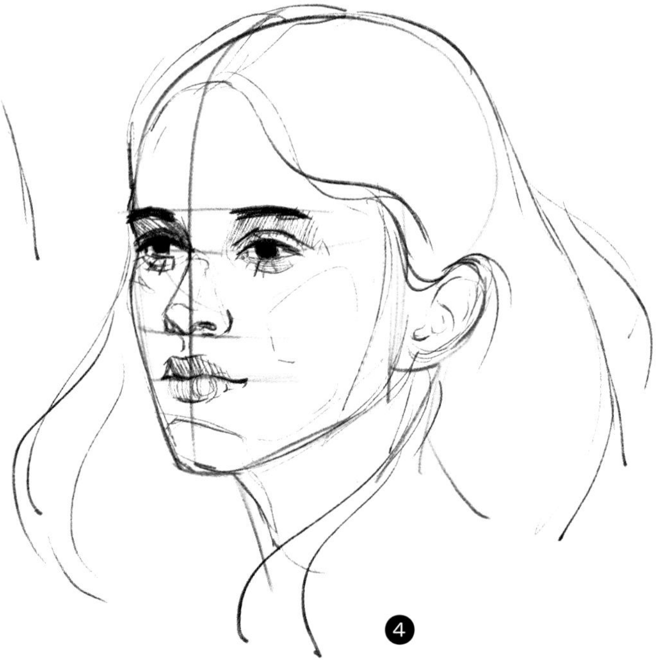

4

BREAK THE RULES!

Once you've learned the rules, it's time to play and have fun. Be daring—modify the height of the lines to obtain disproportionate, original portraits and to create different characters. Try using geometric shapes instead of an oval. Start with a square, a circle, a triangle, a rectangle, and so on. What other variations can you think of?

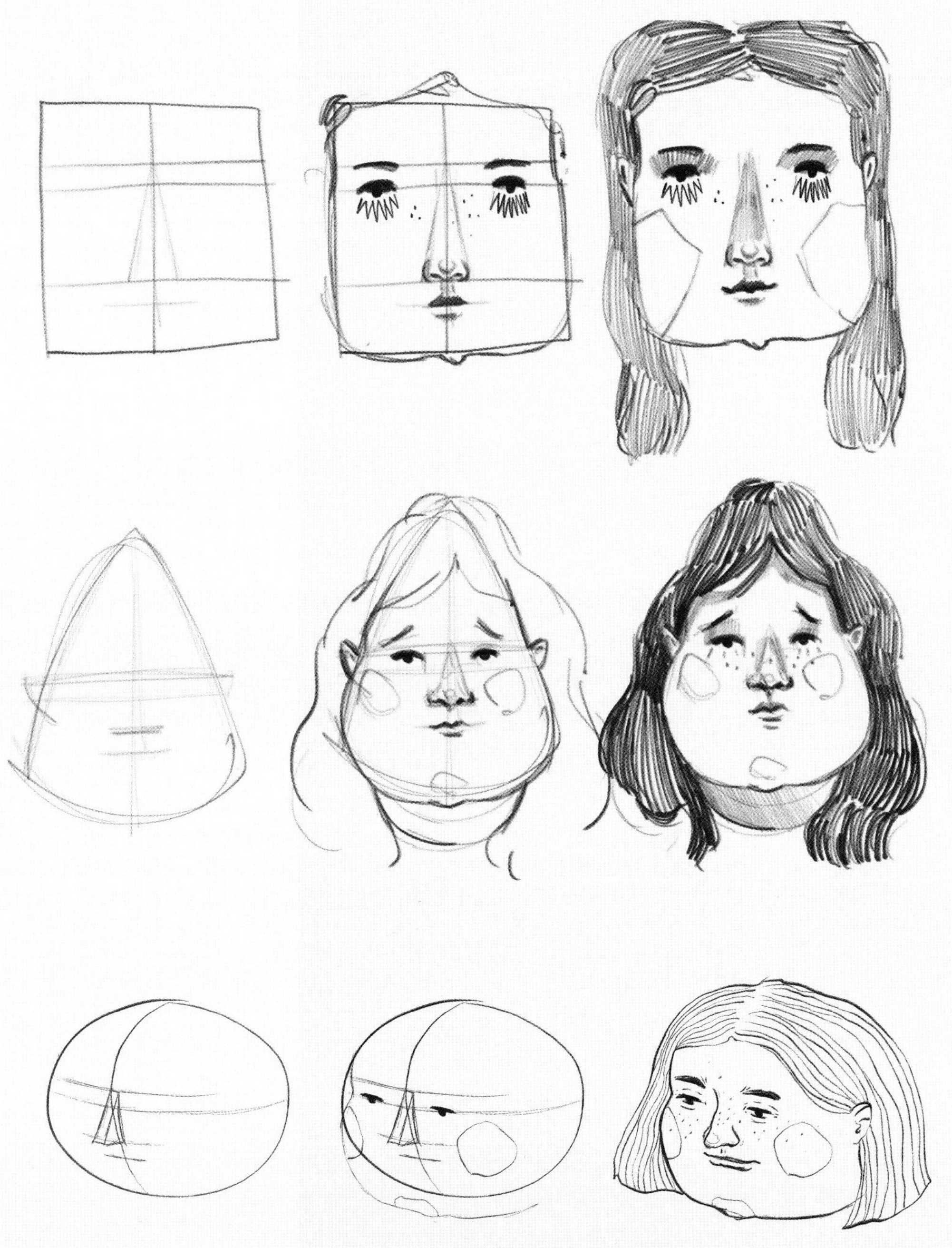

Some examples of disproportionate faces.

TRANSFERRING A REFERENCE IMAGE

Learning to draw takes a lot of time and practice. If you're not there yet and have trouble blocking out a portrait, you can use simpler methods to transfer an image to paper:

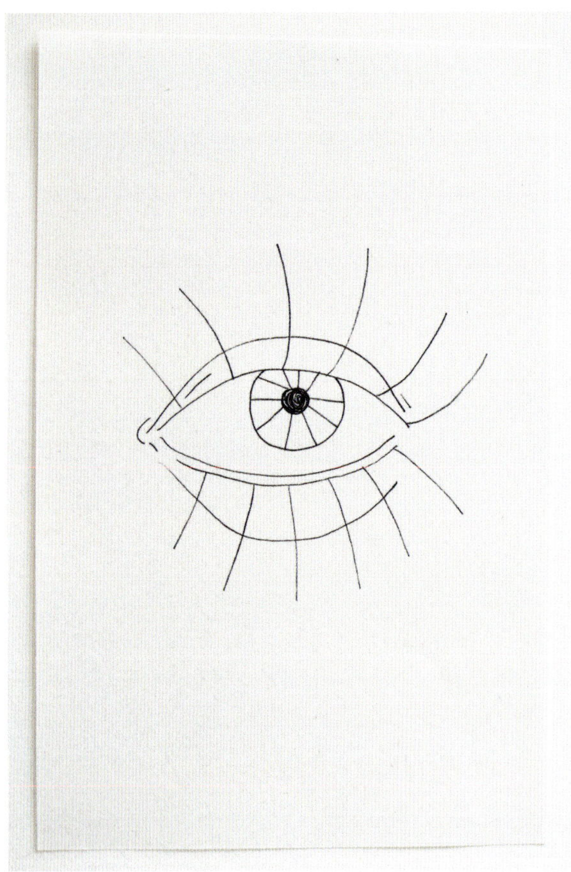

1. Use a window to trace the image:
   - Lay a blank piece of watercolor paper on top of the image you want to copy.
   - Tape both papers to a window that's bright with sunlight.
   - Trace the image.

2. Trace the image with charcoal.
   - Flip over your image and evenly cover the area with charcoal. (A)
   - Take your watercolor paper and place the image on top of it, so that the charcoal is in direct contact with the watercolor paper. Secure the papers to a table with masking tape. (B)
   - Go over the basic shapes with a pencil. (C) If you pick up the paper, you'll see that a drawing has been created. (D, E)
   - With a brush, gently remove the excess charcoal. You can also remove small areas with an eraser. (F)
   - Add more details if desired.

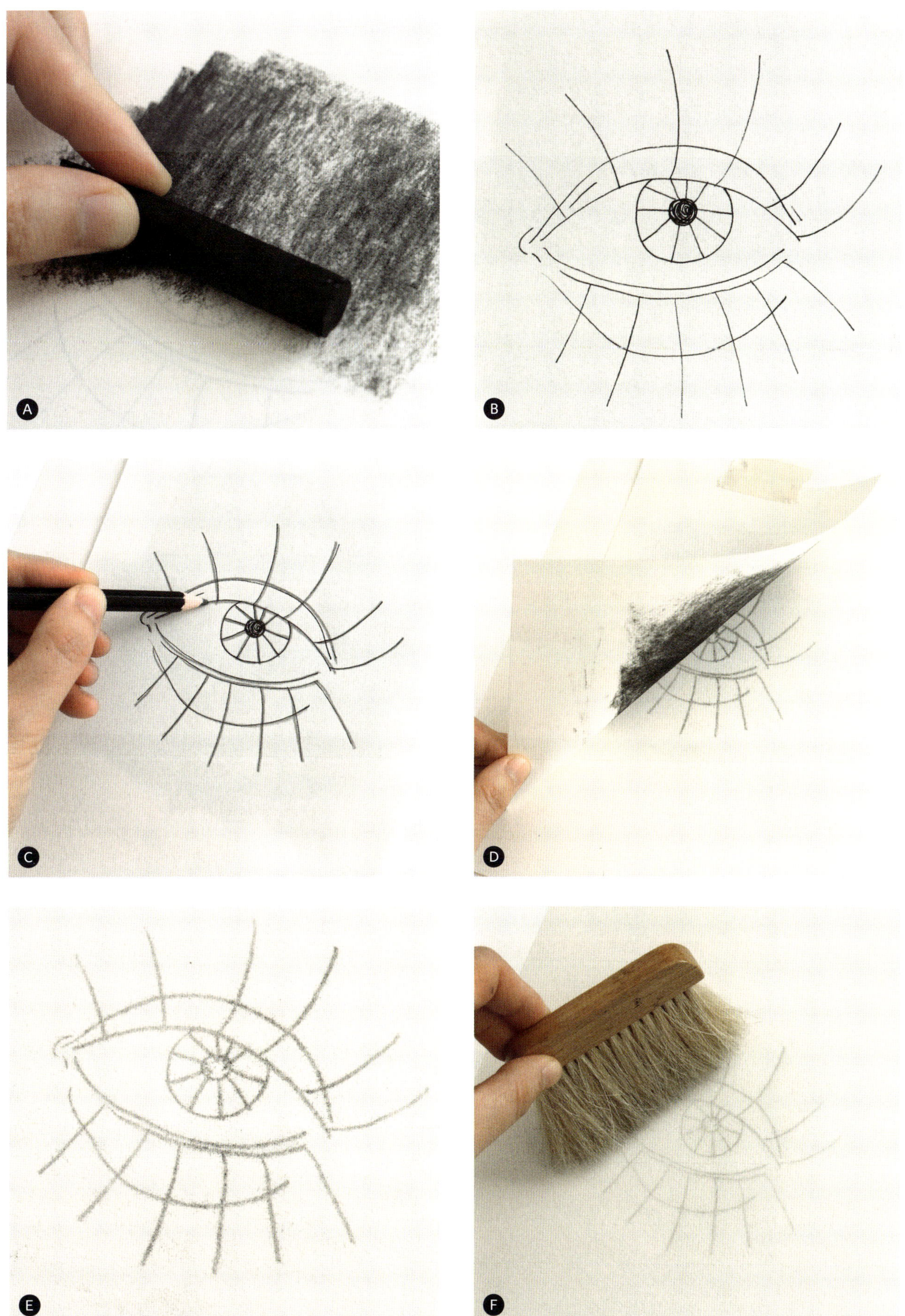
A
B
C
D
E
F

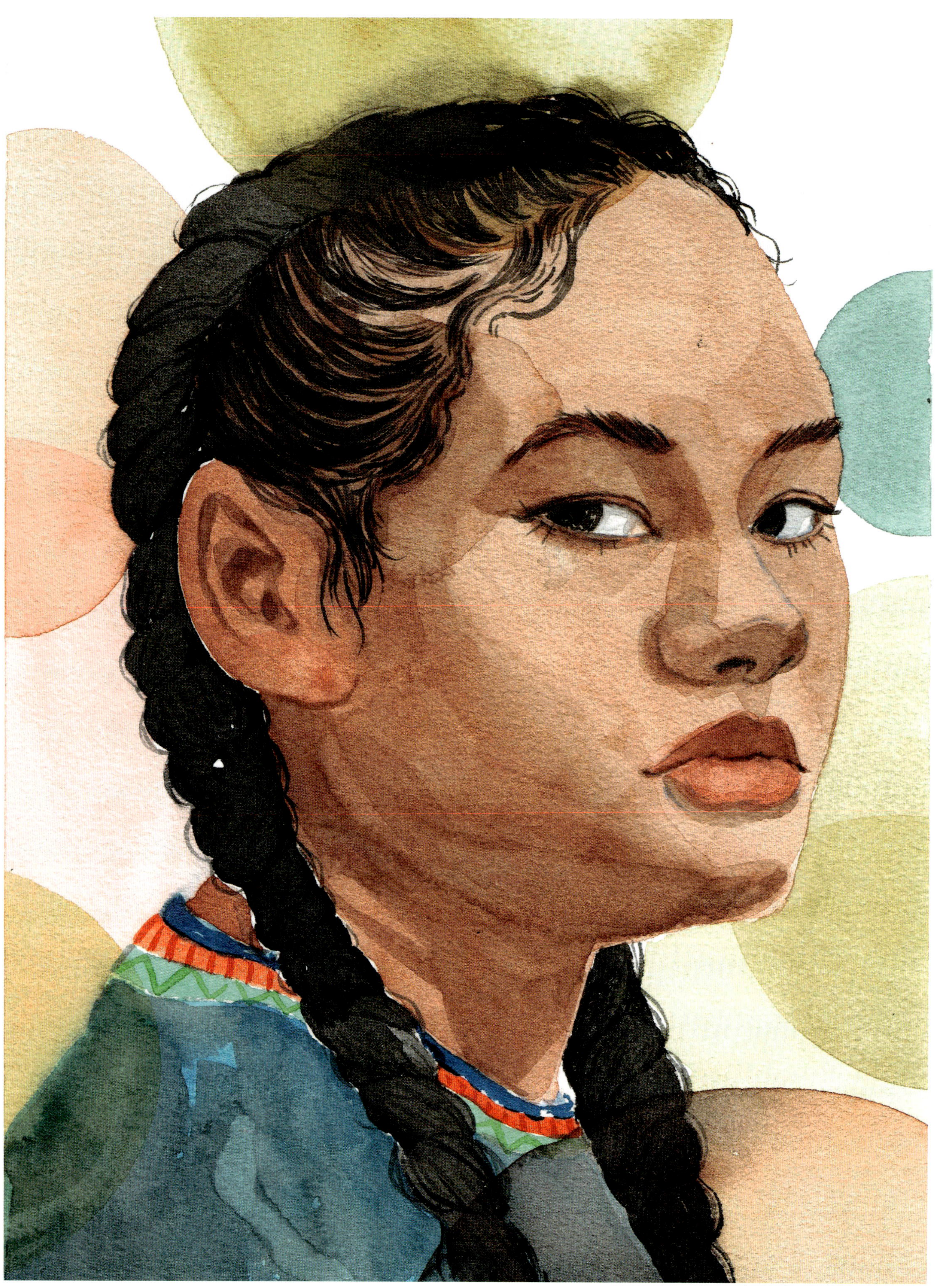

2

CREATIVE PORTRAITS

COLOR + BASIC WATERCOLOR TECHNIQUES

This chapter presents portrait lessons that introduce essential techniques and tips for working with watercolor and that also use various palettes and color combinations based on the color wheel. I've also used different types and weights of paper, from lightly textured to high gloss, to show how that feature might affect the finished results. I recommend stretching the paper to a board or piece of cardboard with masking tape or kraft paper tape so the paper is smooth and doesn't buckle.

Though I've used photo references as a starting point, I used them only as general guides, avoiding focusing on reproducing them exactly so the painting process would flow more easily and I could concentrate on the lesson at hand. Feel free to use your own reference, or you can use your imagination—whatever works best for you!

MONOCHROMATIC

The best way to start experimenting with watercolor is by using a single color. It's an excellent exercise! As we've already mentioned, you can apply more or less water to vary the intensity of the tone. By using a single color and by superimposing layers, you can create portraits with simple contrasts and gradually practice placing the lights and shadows.

> **tip**
>
> Save the photo you're using as black-and-white. That way, you can see the portrait in different shades of gray, which will help you locate areas of light and shadow and areas of greater contrast.

WET-ON-DRY

For this portrait, we'll use a single color, varying its intensity and transparency by adding water. We'll work from fewer details to more details, from the **general to the particular**.

We'll start with more diluted paint and translucent layers. As we develop the portrait, we'll use more opaque paint so the details are increasingly more defined.

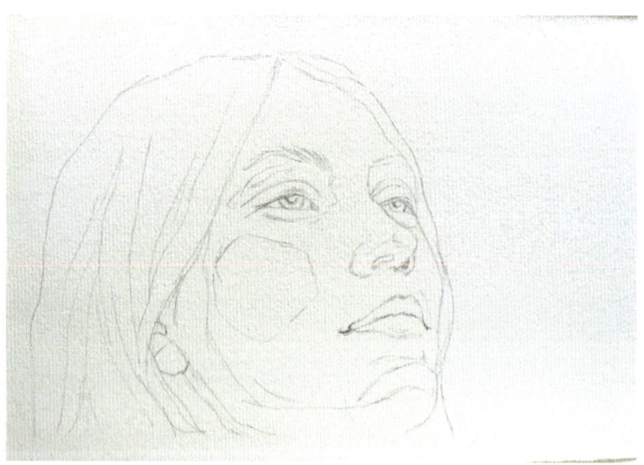

1. First, draw your portrait. The level of detail you draw is up to you. You can make it very detailed to have more certainty when painting. Note that a hard pencil won't smear as much as a soft one.

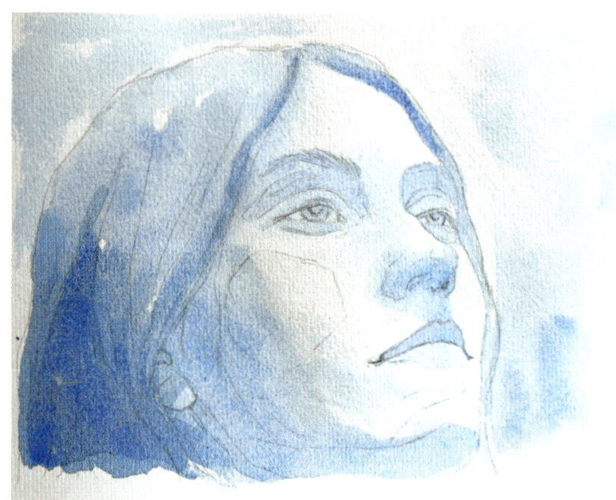

2. Choose a color you like. I've chosen blue. Place the color on the palette and add a lot of water. With this mixture, create a first layer and place the main shadows. Let each layer dry so that you can place the next strokes precisely.

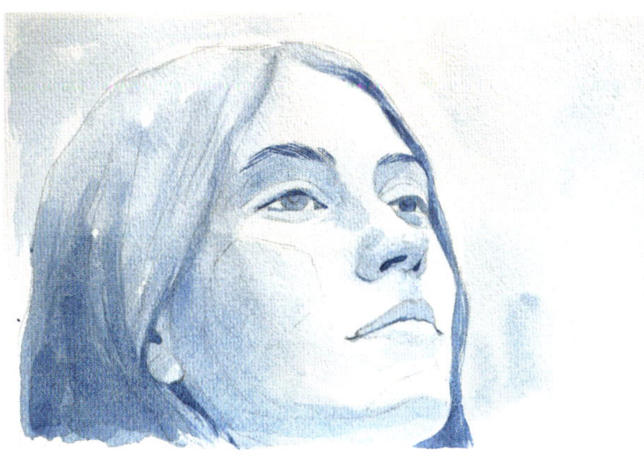

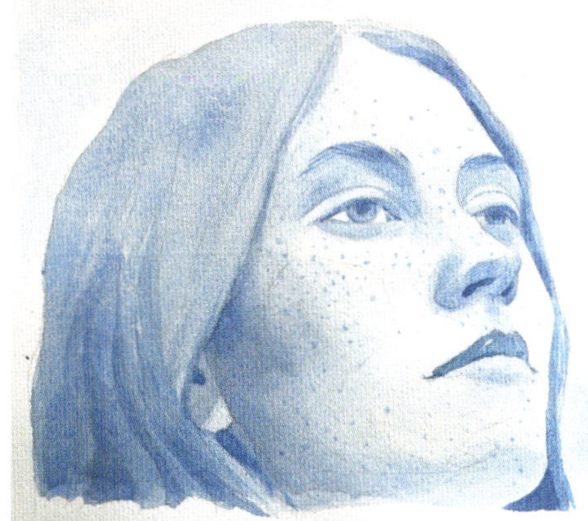

3. Add more paint to the original mixture to make the blue a little more opaque. Use this mixture to paint the slightly darker areas of the portrait.

4. Keep adding the layers as needed to give your portrait volume and contrast. This type of portrait works with two simple layers or with as many as you want. Always make sure that you let each layer dry so you can apply the next coat with precision.

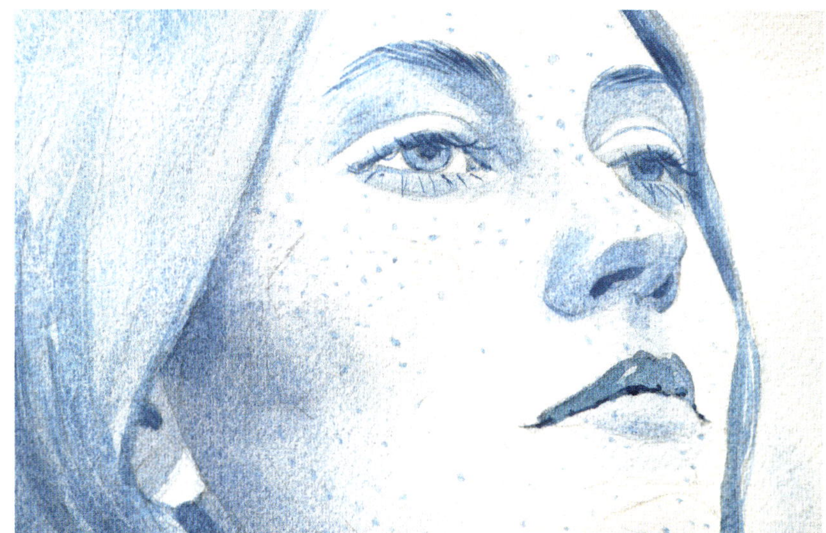

5. Using a round brush for greater precision, add darker details, such as the eyelashes, eyes, lip line, nose, eyebrows, and freckles.

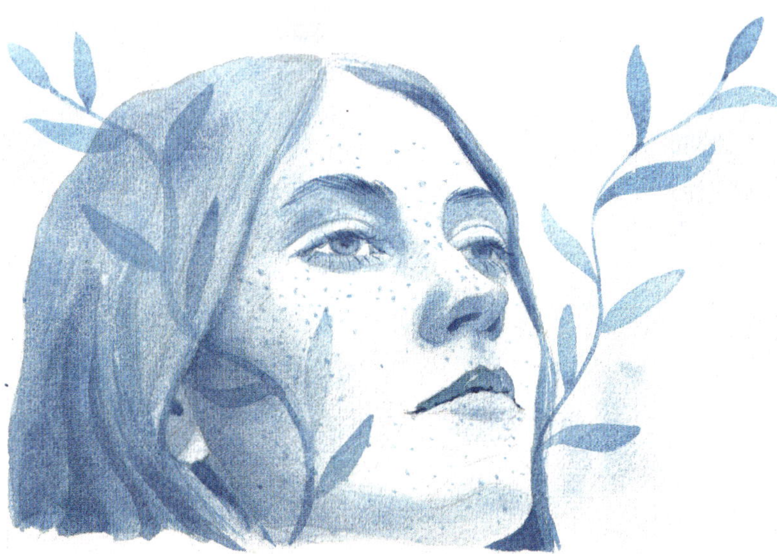

6. Once the portrait is finished and dry, you might choose to add some extra decorative details. In this example, I adorned my portrait with very translucent leaves in the same color.

WET-ON-WET

Here's another portrait in a single tone that varies the transparency and opacity of the paint to create a range of values.

This time, I moistened the entire paper with clean water and then worked the subsequent layers in wet. As you can see, this creates a fluid atmosphere. The brushstrokes merge and the strokes' edges are blurred. I added the most defined details—the upper lip, eyes, and eyebrows—after the first application of watercolor had dried.

This technique is very fun and surprising because you're not in total control. You have to let yourself go!

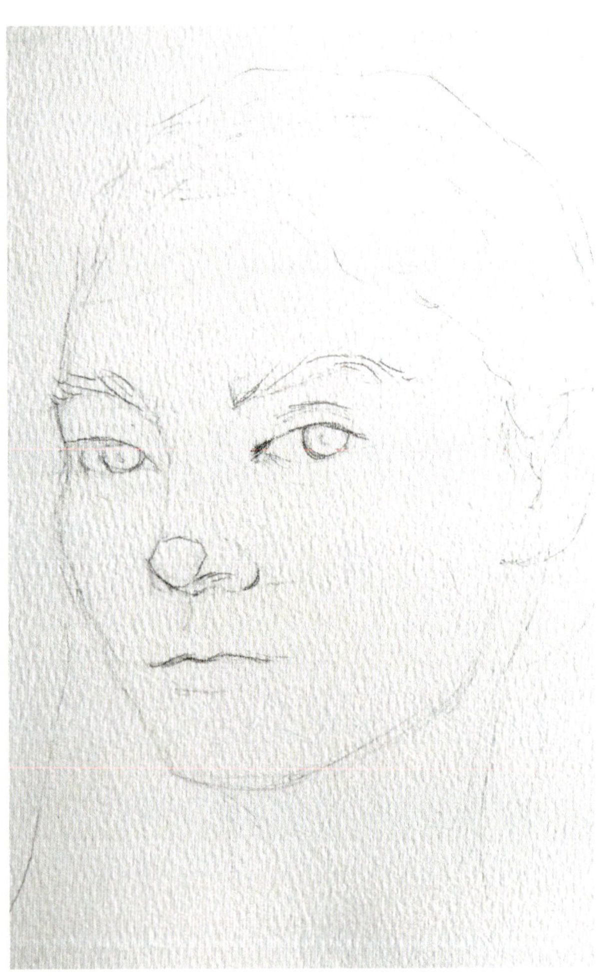

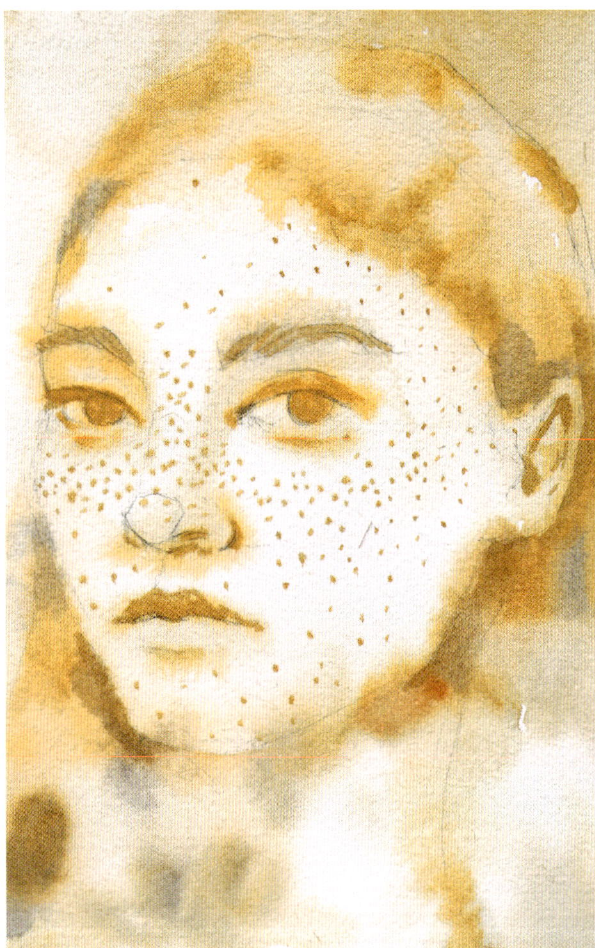

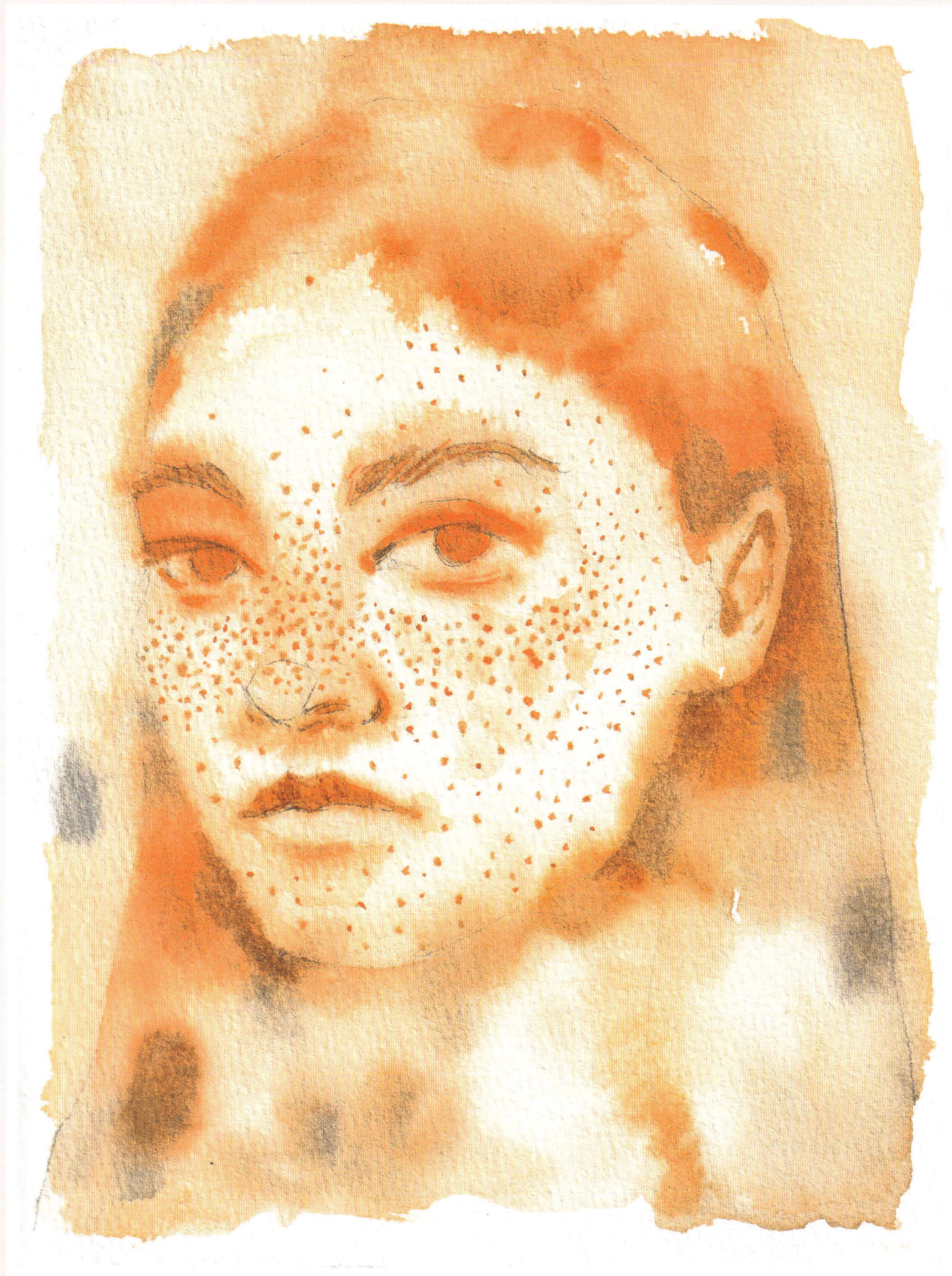

PRIMARY COLORS

For the following portrait, we're going to use the three primary colors: yellow, red, and blue. These three colors combined create a very strong and striking contrast. We're going to use the pure colors without mixing them together. If you mix them, you'll get earthy colors, and they'll lose their purity.

Use your imagination and get creative with how you use them!

FLAT COLORS/WET-ON-DRY

In this simple portrait, I played with blocks of the three primary colors.

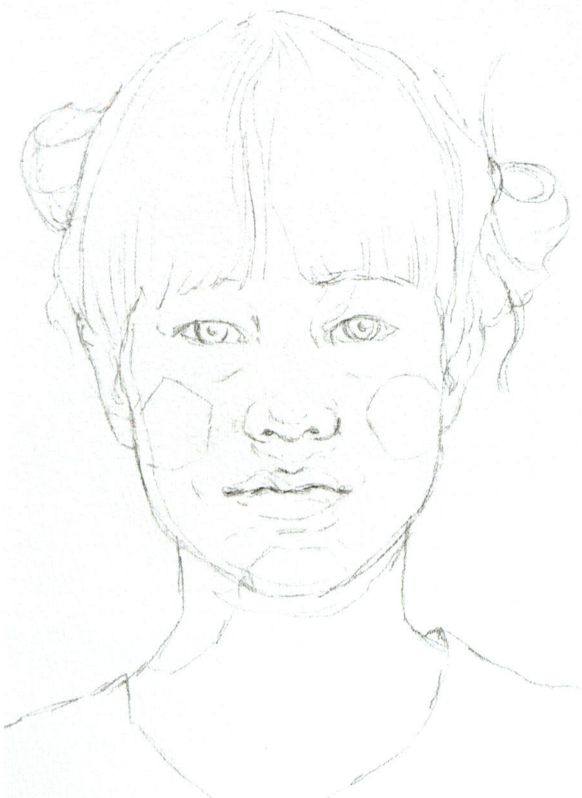

1. I assigned a color to each element: blue for the face; red for the hair; and yellow for the details on the face and shirt.

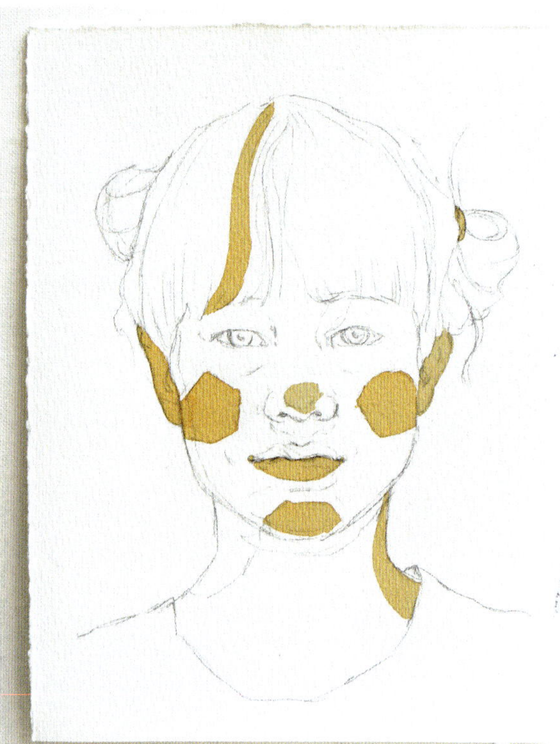

2. I made layered washes in each of the blocks and let them dry so they didn't mix together.

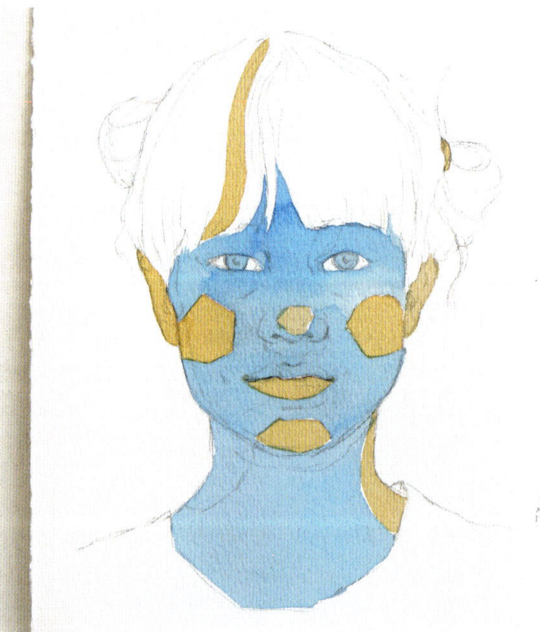

3. In subsequent layers, I defined slight shadows on the face with a wet and defined brushstroke using the same blue that I used for the base.

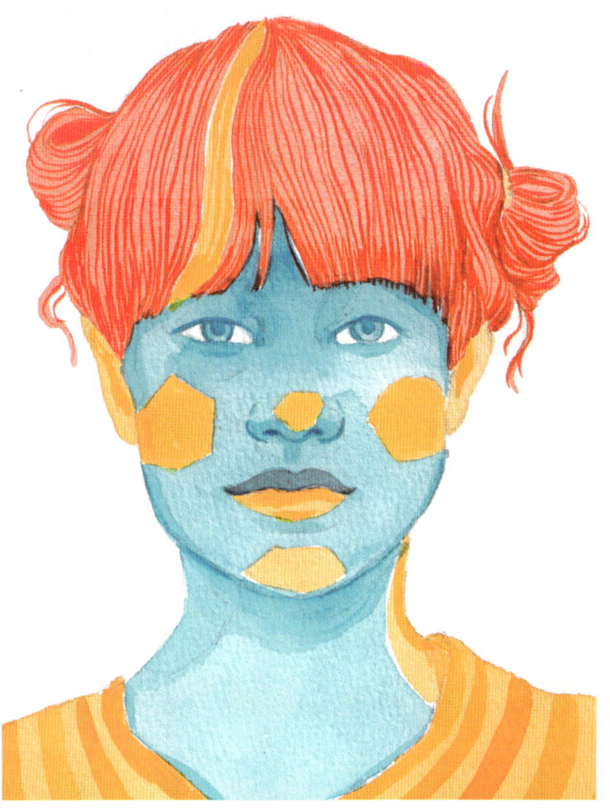

4. Next, I filled in and added texture to the hair (with fine, wavy lines) and added a pattern to the clothes. Then, I added the last details on the face, retracing the small areas of eyelashes, nose, mouth, and so on to add more contrast and force with the color.

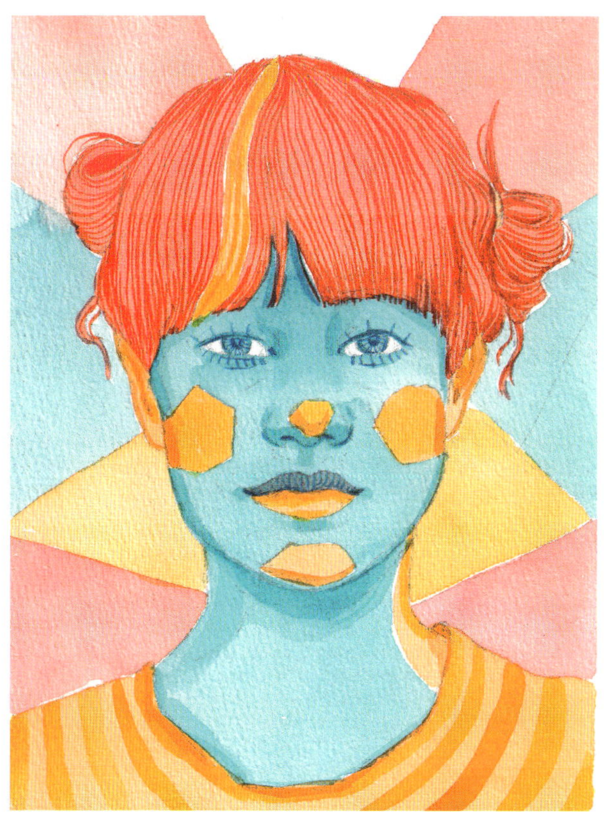

5. Finally, I used the same primary colors for the background, creating a simple geometric pattern. To add a sense of distance, I diluted the colors with a lot of water. I let each color block dry so that the edges are clean and defined.

WET-ON-WET

This is an example where I used the three primary colors, but this time, I worked wet-on-wet, allowing the colors to merge, superimposing several layers. I gradually built up the portrait by adding more color.

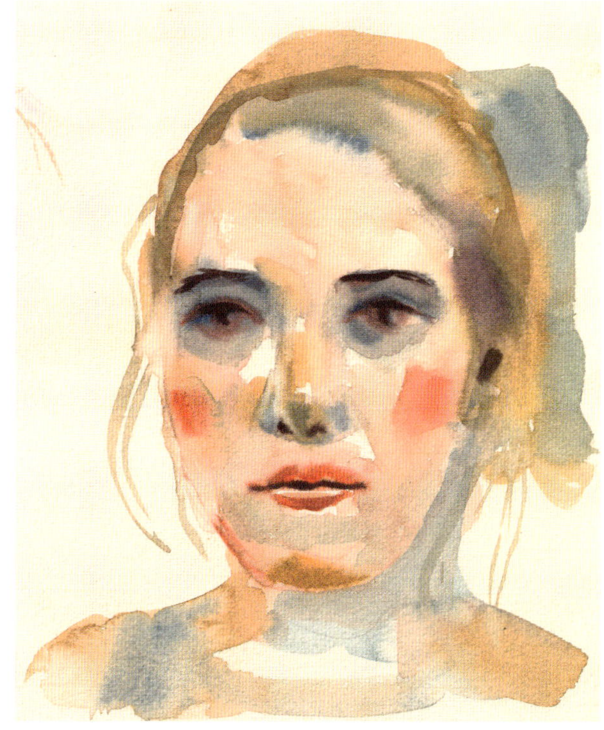

SECONDARY COLORS

Secondary colors are the sum of two primary colors in the same proportion. For example, 50% blue and 50% yellow = green. Combining the three secondary colors creates very harmonious colors that are pleasing to the eye.

In the following portrait, we'll use orange, purple, and green, superimposing very diluted layers of color to create beautiful glazing. I used a very simple geometric shape: the circle.

If you want, you can use short, loose strokes or any other style that comes to mind. The goal is to superimpose translucent layers with the wet-on-dry technique and be patient!

Notice how tonal variations emerge from the sum of the colors as you add layers.

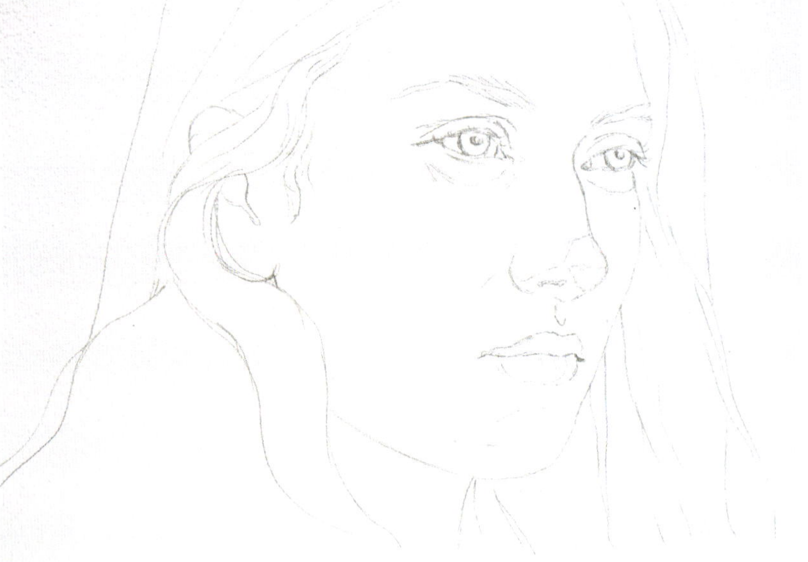

1. I started with a pencil drawing.

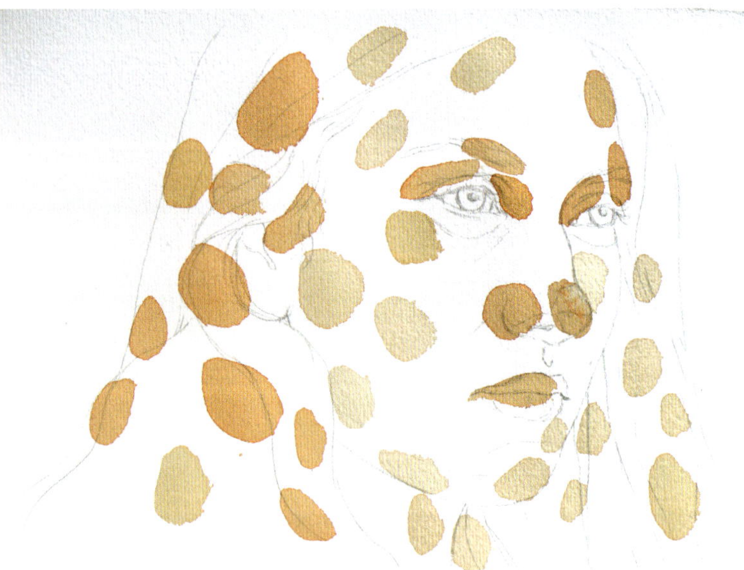

2. I began painting with orange, applying it liberally across the portrait. I was careful using it around the areas of the nose, lips, and eyes to give them depth.

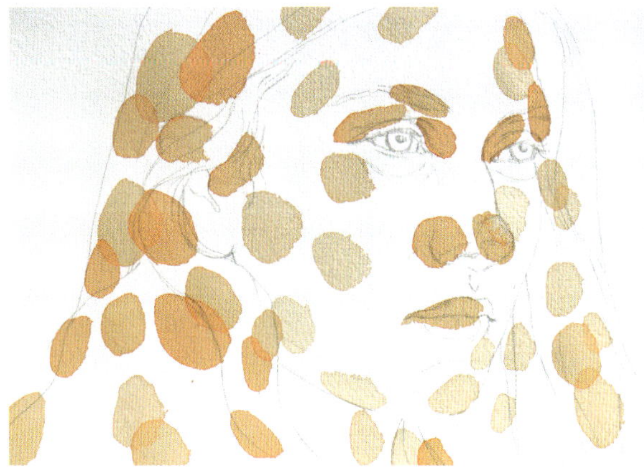

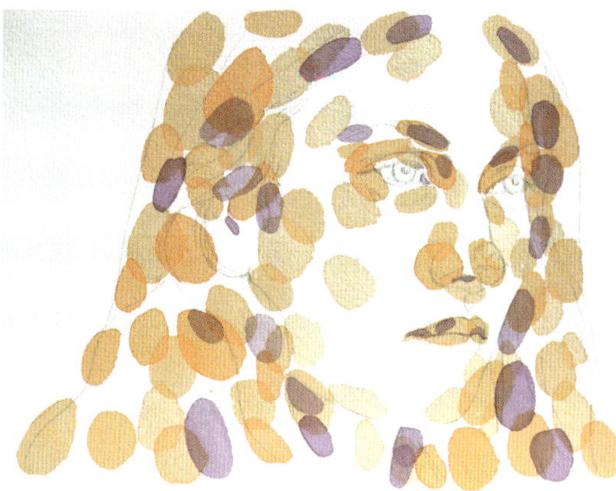

3. I let this layer dry and painted more circles. It's important that the layers are sufficiently translucent so that your first layers are visible. Repeat this process as many times as you see fit.

4. Next, I added purple to the portrait using the same method, placing it in areas to give the portrait volume. Accentuate the shadows by layering on more color, adding contrast. Repeat the process if necessary with a new layer.

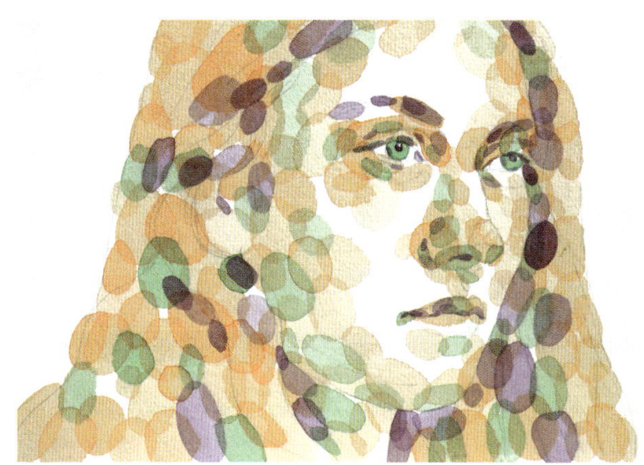

5. Lastly, I added medium tones of green. On a value scale of black to gray to white, green would equal gray. A key like this can help you translate colors to a grayscale and make it easier for you to add color to your portraits (see "Preserving White" on page 42). Place the green where you would use shades of gray for the light and shadows.

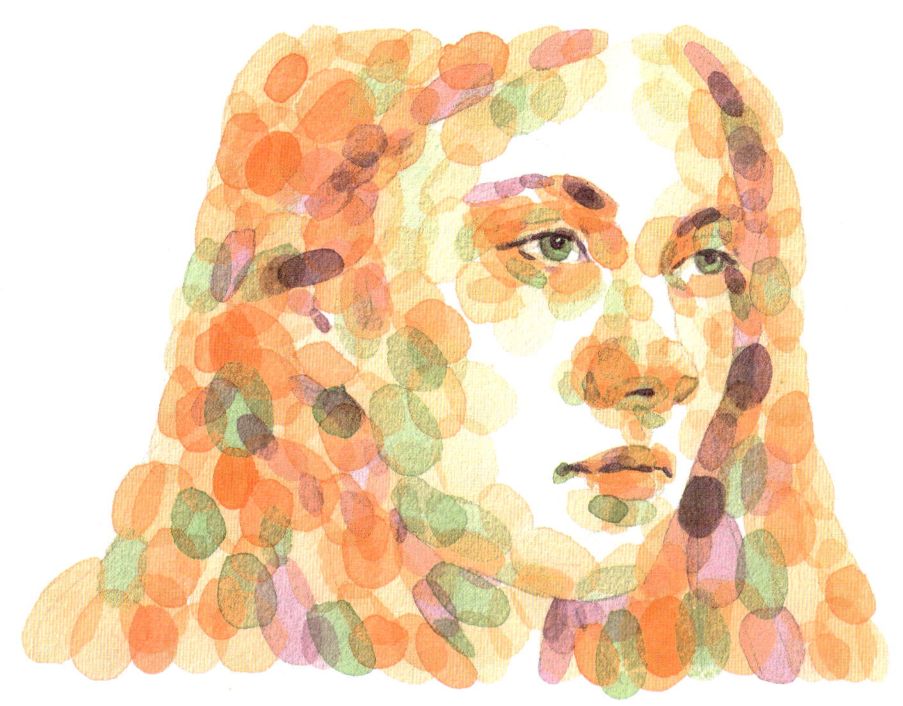

COMPLEMENTARY COLORS

Complementary colors are those colors that are opposite each other in the color wheel. This creates color pairs that have a strong contrast, and each color makes the other stand out.

Let's look at some examples using primary colors and their respective complements.

COMPLEMENTARY: YELLOW-PURPLE

For this portrait, I used a **white Manley wax crayon** to reserve the light areas. I suggest that for these examples, you use portraits that have clear contrasting light and shadow as a reference.

In this color pair, yellow is the color of the light, and purple is the shadow.

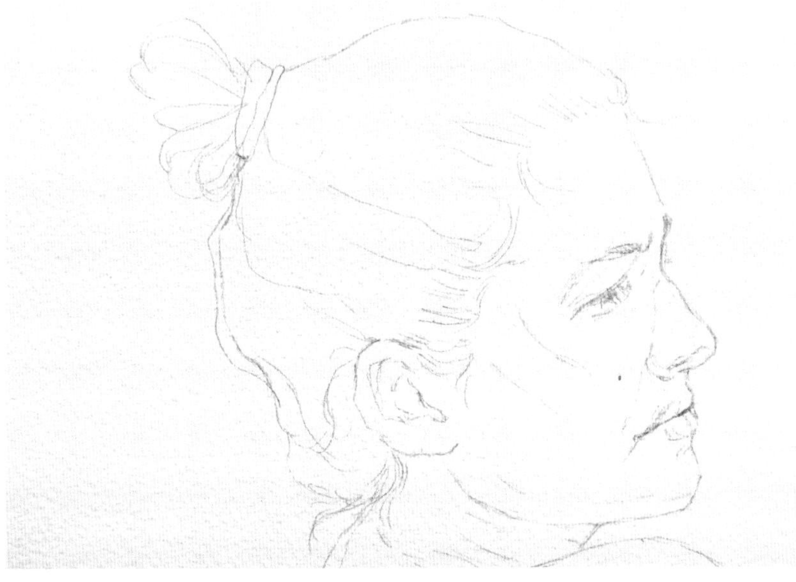

1. Draw the main outline of your portrait.

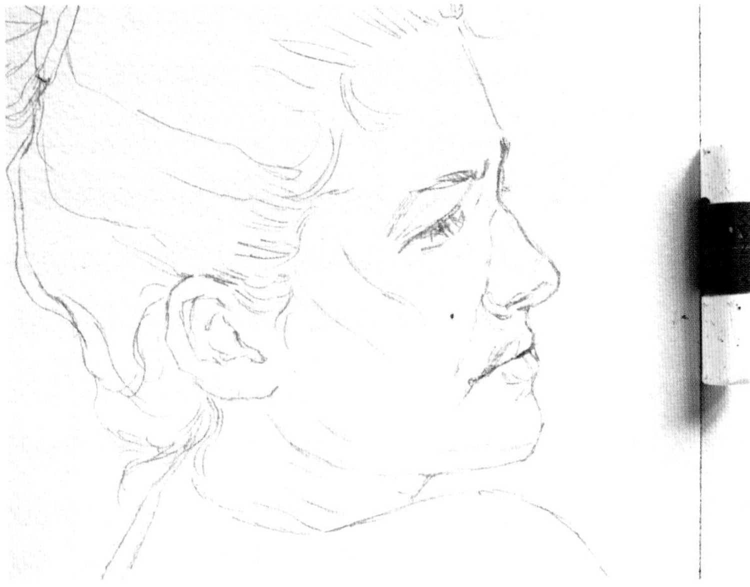

2. With a white wax crayon, add the points or areas of light that you want to remain completely white.

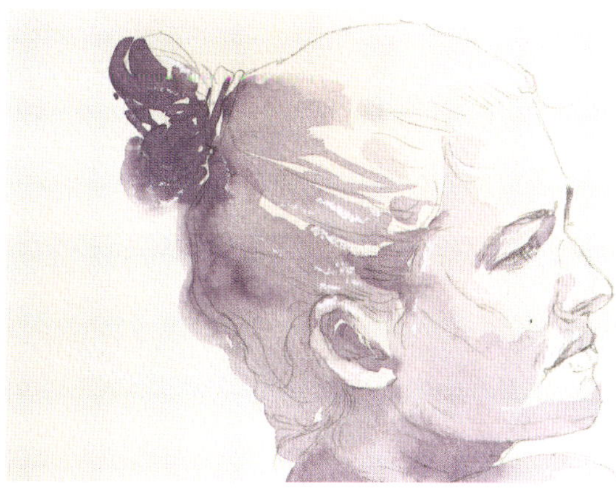

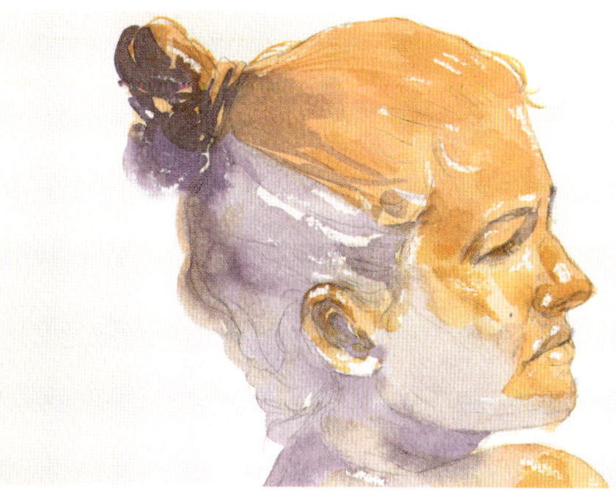

3. Prepare the purple on a palette, using water to dilute the opacity. With a very wet, soft brushstroke, place the shadows using a round brush. Paint without fear! The wax crayon will repel the water. To blur a brushstroke, wet the brush with clean water and dilute the color.

4. While this layer dries, prepare the yellow on your palette in the same way. With a wet brush, paint the area of light evenly and without worry. Once again, the paint will not take to the light areas where you used the wax crayon.

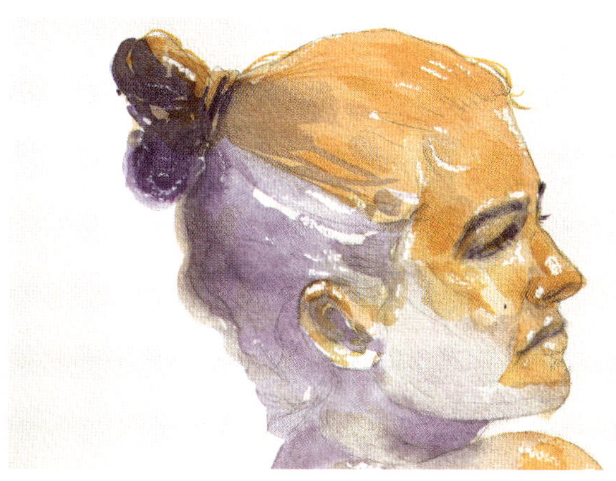

5. Once the yellow layer dries, you can add more intense color to some of the areas. You might opt for a finer brush for small details. In this example, I made some of the yellow areas more vibrant. But I didn't add more layers of purple because if it were any darker, it would become more opaque and one-dimensional. I wanted that part of the shadow to fade into the background to hint at distance.

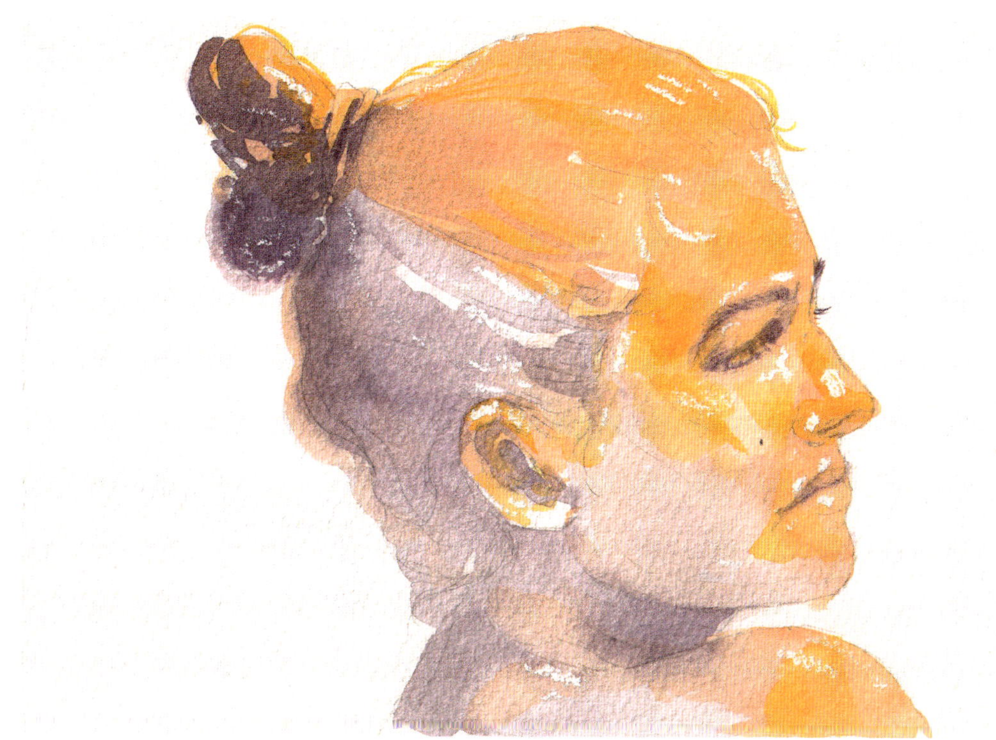

COMPLEMENTARY: BLUE-ORANGE

For this portrait, we'll build a face with decisive wet brushstrokes, without gradient at the edges. We'll add wet layers on top of dry layers. At the same time, we'll try to reserve light areas on the paper.

This color pair contrasts light, the color orange, and shadow, the color blue. There is also a temperature contrast: blue is a cool color, and orange is a warm color.

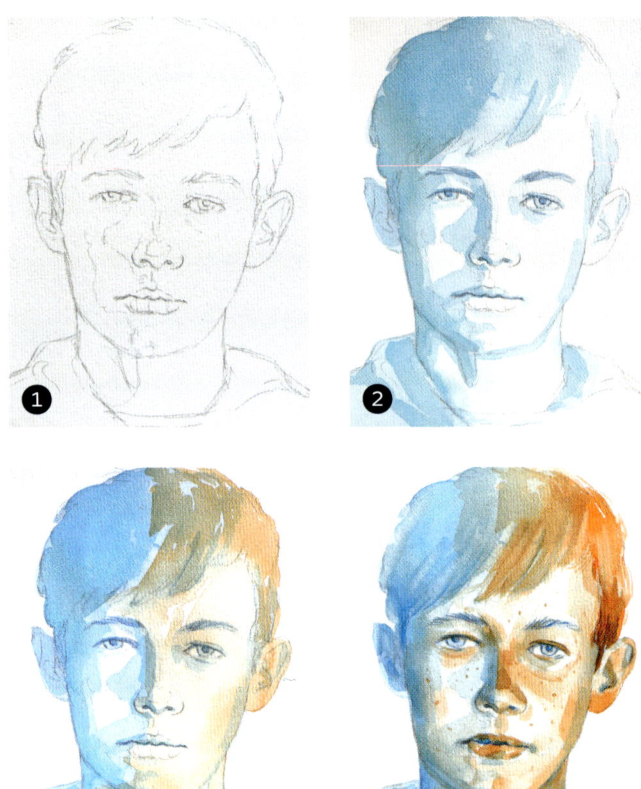

1. Start by tracing the outline and details of the portrait using a hard pencil, being careful not to press too forcefully on the paper.
2. Place the shadows with the blue hue, which you've already diluted with water on your palette. Let dry.
3. With the orange, apply a wet brushstroke across all of the light area. Reserve some light areas from the paper itself. Let dry.
4. Find the middle hues of the shadow and apply more layers. Start with one color, let it dry, and add the other color. Be careful that they don't mix together while wet, which will make the colors look muddy. Work in stages to shape the shadows. Finally, with a sharp-tipped brush, make a highly pigmented paint mixture on your palette and add the last details.
5. Note that with the overlapping of blue and orange, a new color has emerged—green. This orange must have more yellow in it, which is why there are greener or greenish brown hues.

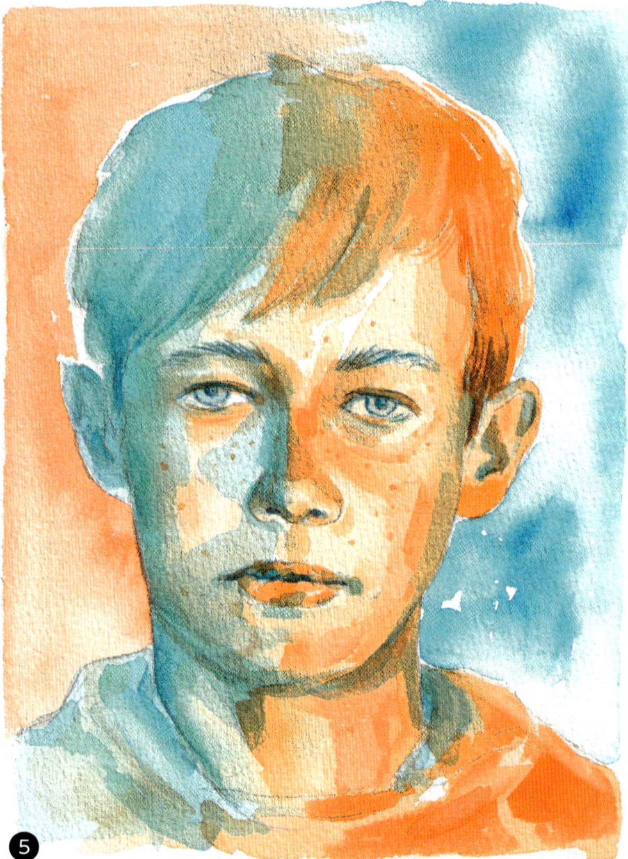

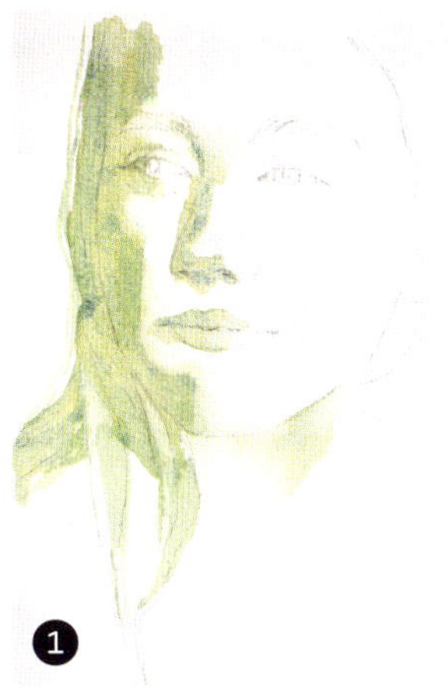

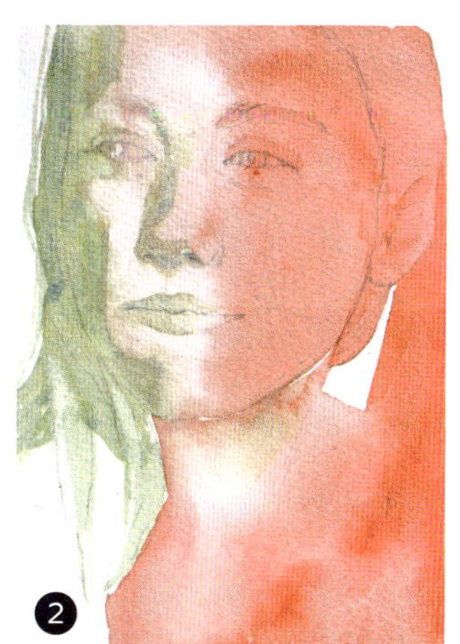

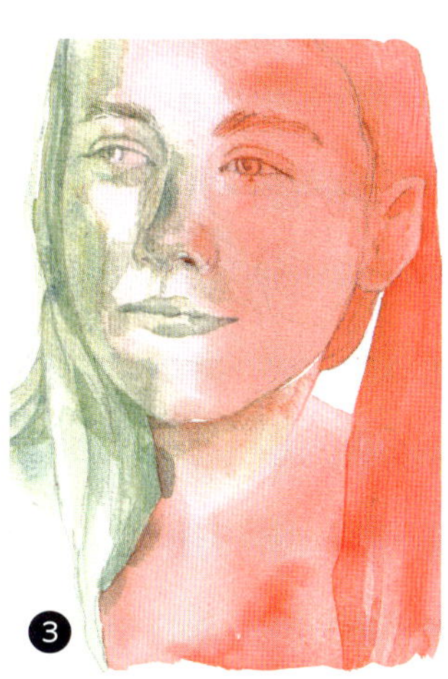

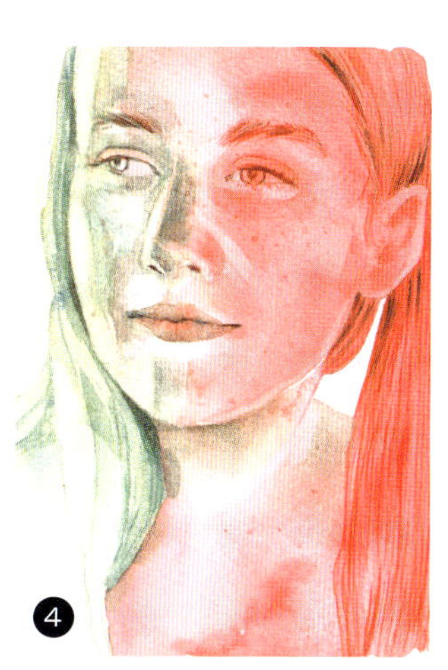

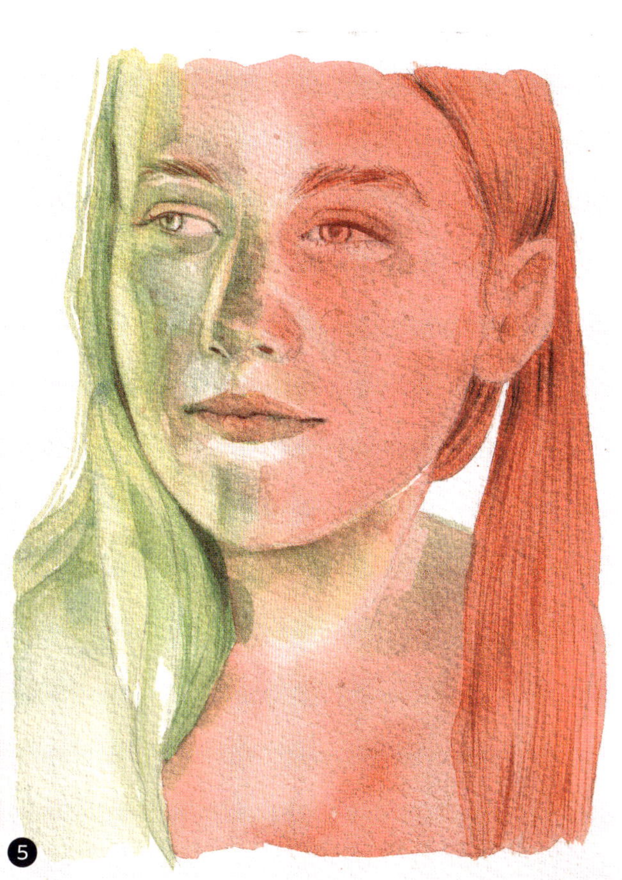

COMPLEMENTARY: RED-GREEN

This last portrait is very similar to the previous ones. The only thing that has changed is that I blurred the edge of each brushstroke with clean water to create soft color transitions and to avoid hard edges.

1. Very wet layers give shape and volume to the face. I used a round brush with a fine tip to define details such as the eyes, nose, mouth, and hair.
2. I used green for the light area (because it contains yellow) and red for the shadows. I still wanted to reserve the paper's white in some light areas with a very wet, transparent layer.
3. Red and green are the complementary pair that's most visually balanced in terms of tonal value and luminosity.
4. In the layers where both colors intermingled subtly, an earthy tone emerged.

ANALOGOUS COLORS

Analogous colors are the colors that are found next to each other on the color wheel.

» The analogues of the color blue are green or purple hues.

» The analogues of the color yellow are green and orange hues.

» The analogues of the color red are orange and purple hues.

If you limit the palette for a project to a range of analogous colors, you'll achieve another kind of color harmony.

For this portrait, we'll use the color blue and a range of one of its analogues, green.

As always, I've gone from less to more. Taking into account the lights and shadows of my reference portrait, I placed the blues in the shadows and the greens in the lights. But you can explore and arrange things as you see fit instead of being guided by lights and shadows.

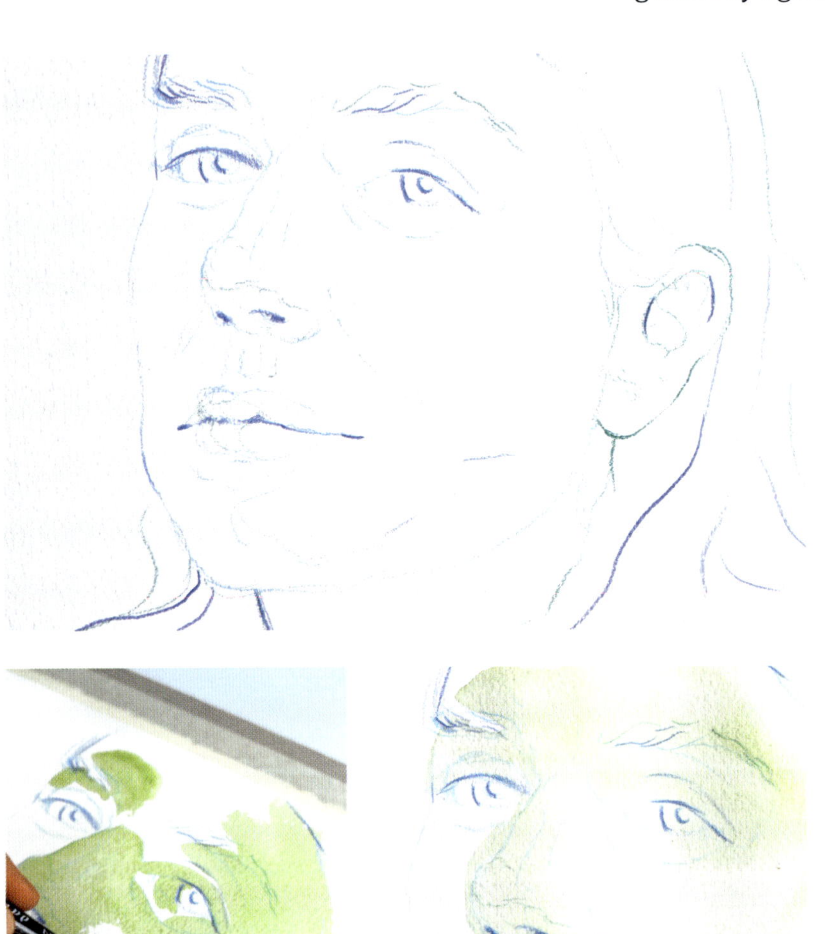

1. I traced the outlines of the portrait in blue and green pencil.

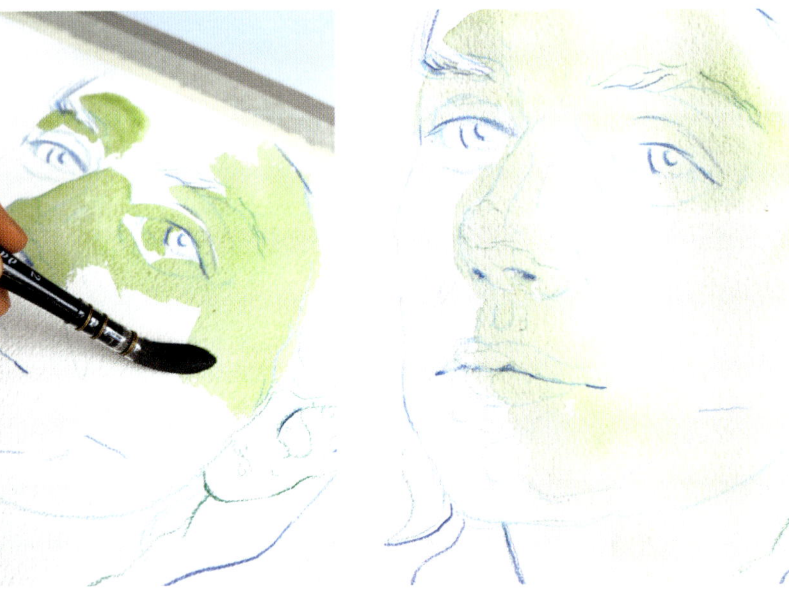

2. I started with an even, wet layer of green in the illuminated area of the face and then let it dry.

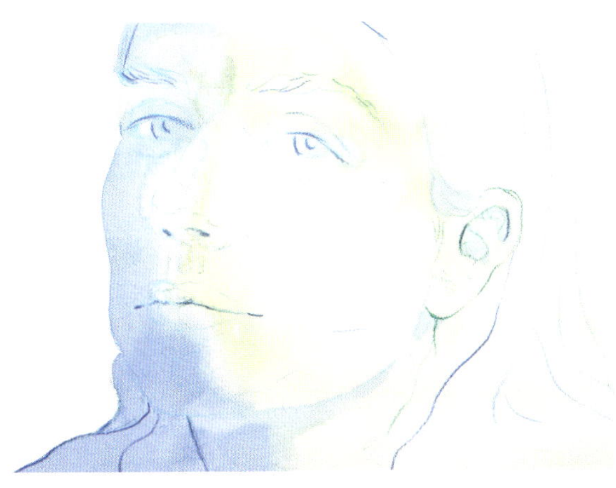

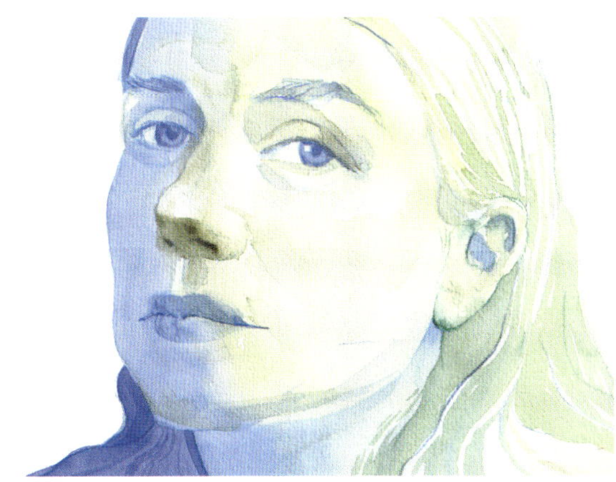

3. Later, I repeated the same technique for the areas with shadow with a diluted blue hue. In the middle, where the colors collide, I made a smooth transition by adding clean water to avoid a hard edge and to integrate it with the green base. Then, I added touches of blue in the shaded areas of the green layer.

4. Once the layers are dry, you can give volume to the face by adding more layers, always in green and blue tones. Use a brighter green (one that has more yellow in it) for areas of more light and a more intense blue for shadows to create a nice contrast.

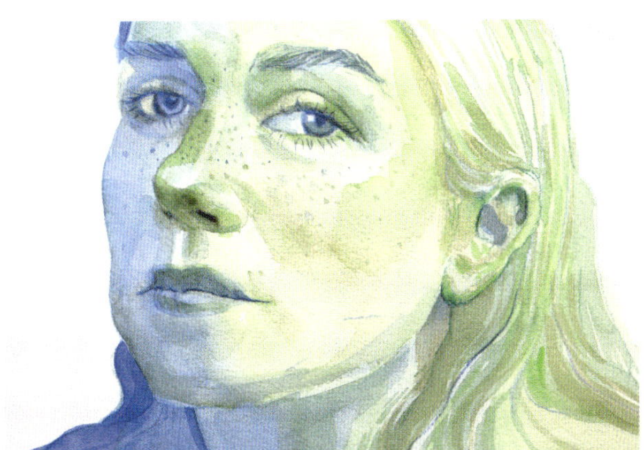

5. Finally, you can add more detail to the portrait with the help of a fine-tipped brush and a highly pigmented paint mixture.

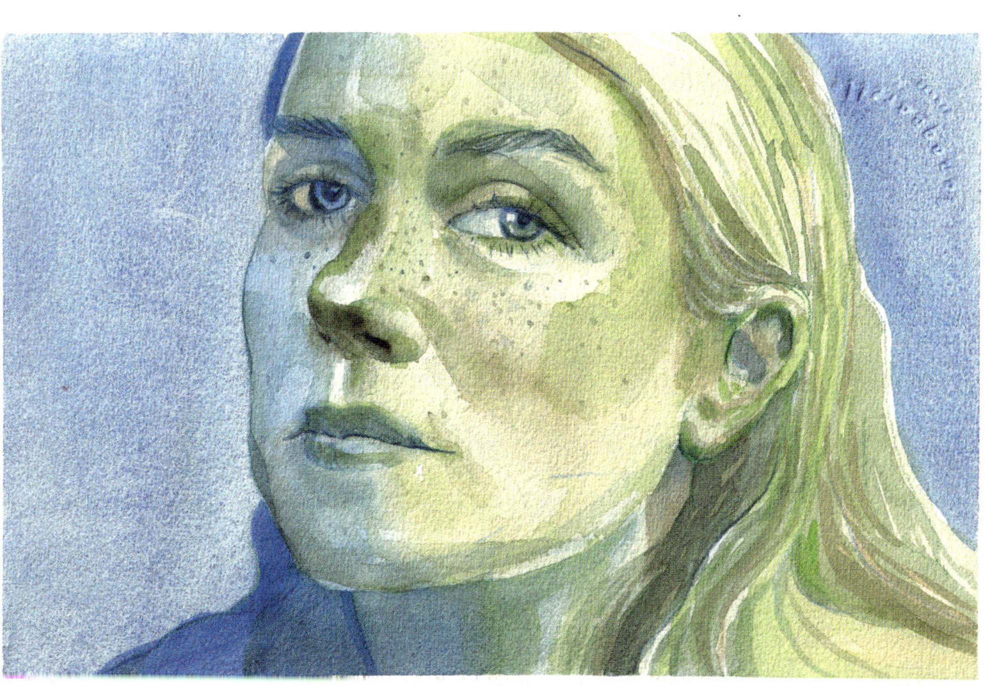

BRIGHT COLORS

Bright or luminous colors contain yellow.

The following portrait is an example using a color palette of bright colors. When you reduce a palette to a certain color scheme, you need to translate the chosen color scheme into shades of gray to help you place light and shadow. (See "Examples of Inspiration for Creating Color Palettes" on page 30.)

Keep in mind that within the green color scheme, very bright greens contain a higher proportion of yellow, and darker greens contain a higher proportion of blue. Play with these variations to paint the light and shadow.

As you can see in the example, I've put very bright greens (with a lot of yellow) in areas of light.

For the middle tones, I chose green and added more blue to darken it.

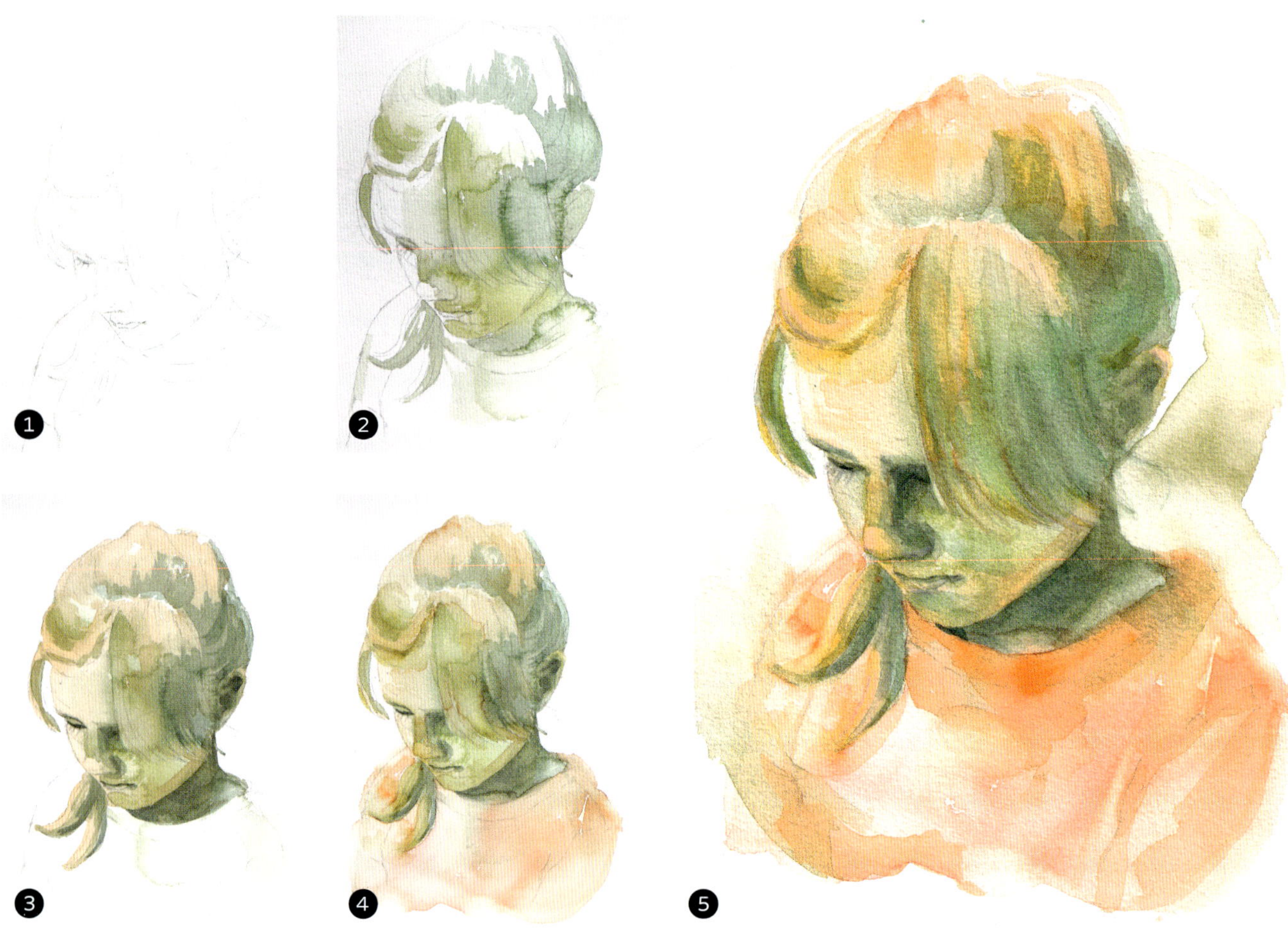

DARK COLORS

In this portrait, I used a dark color scheme to show colors from the other side of the color wheel, from the blues through to the purples and reds. Note that none of these colors contains yellow, which is also a simple way to identify dark colors.

I used this color scheme with very **translucent** layers painted using the wet-on-dry technique. This way, even though I used a range of dark tones, it's still very bright. If I had wanted it to be darker, I would've added more layers or more color. The white of the paper in the background adds a lot of light to the portrait. To reduce the light, you can simply paint the background with a color from the chosen range. Try some tests and experiment to find all these variations of light and color!

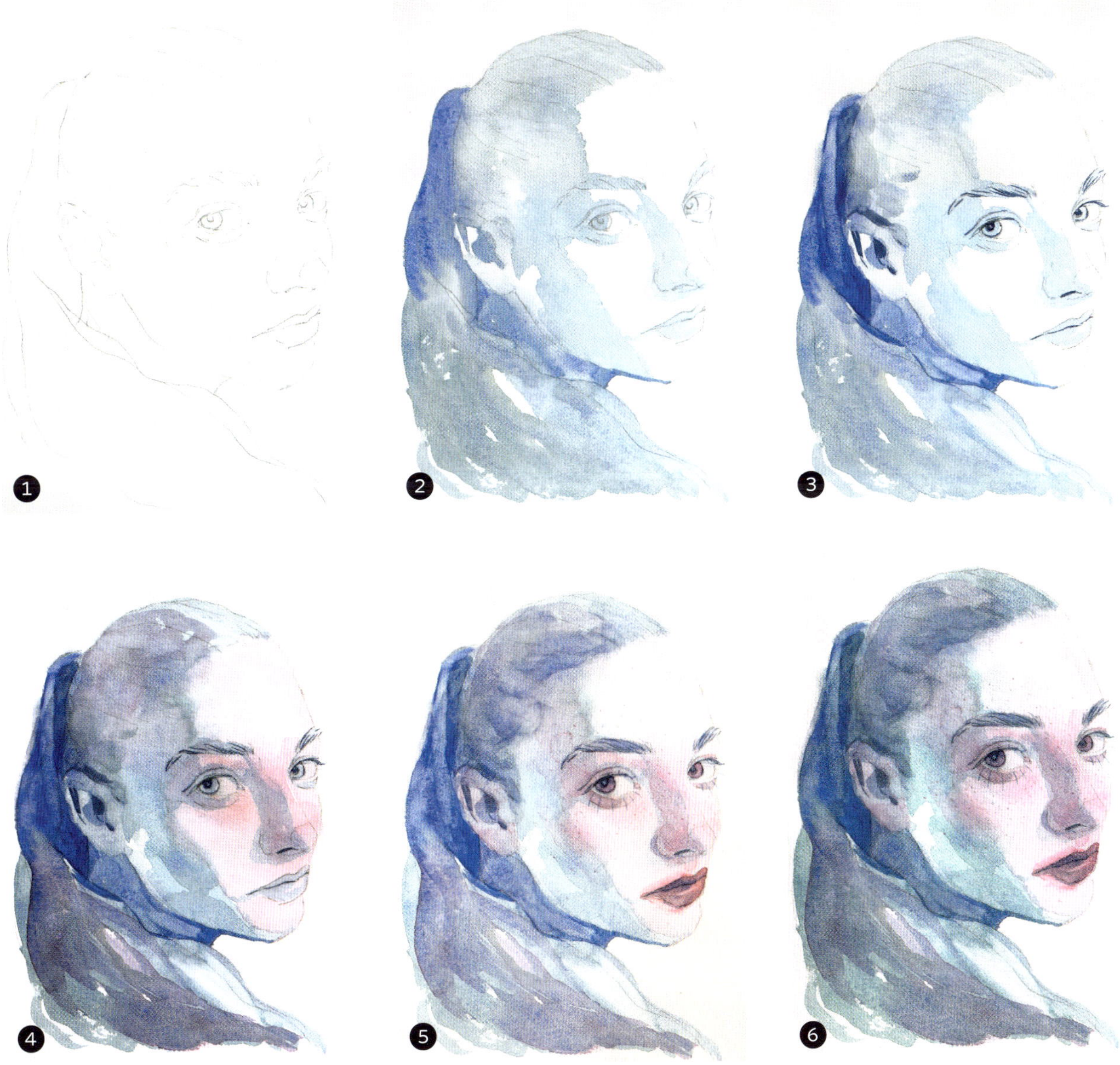

WARM COLORS

Warm colors range from yellow to purple. Colors that contain yellow and red are considered warm colors. Some green hues can be considered warm if they have a high percentage of yellow and some red.

Colors can rise or fall in temperature depending on the color that's next to them. For example, a yellow that's next to a blue seems cooler than when that same yellow is next to a red.

For this portrait, I used layers of very flat colors using the wet-on-dry technique. I didn't blur the edges with clean water because I wanted a sharp, defined stroke.

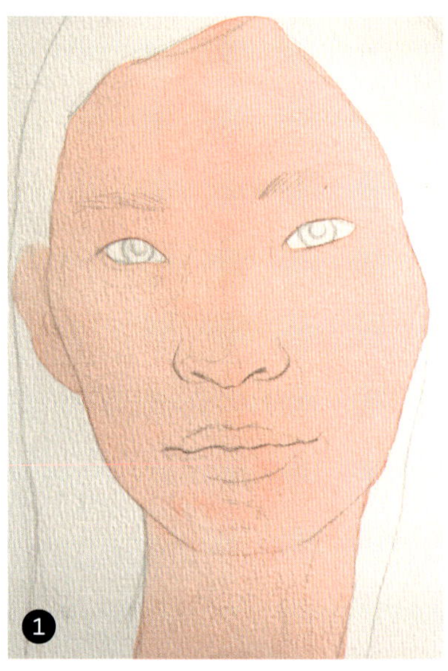

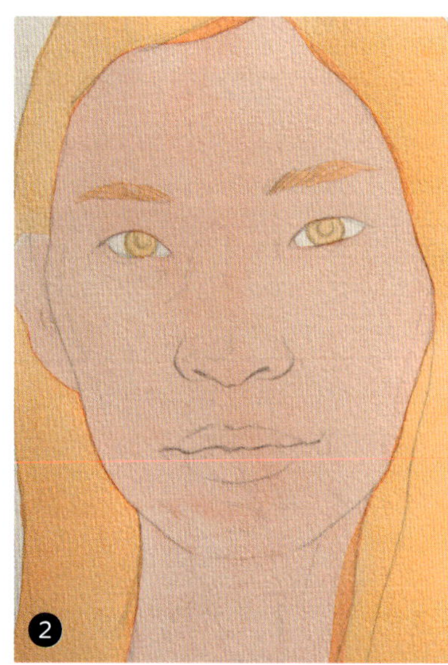

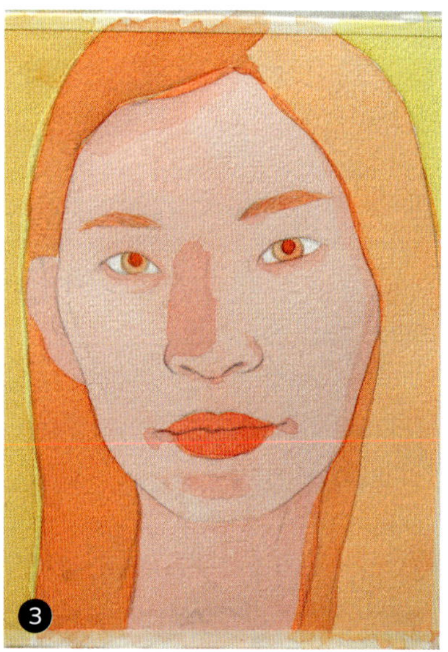

1. Trace the outline of your drawing. With a high-numbered brush, trace a wet, even layer for the face.
2. Once it's dry, add color to the hair and other features until you finish all the main sections.
3. When dry, apply translucent layers on top of the areas with shadows to add volume.

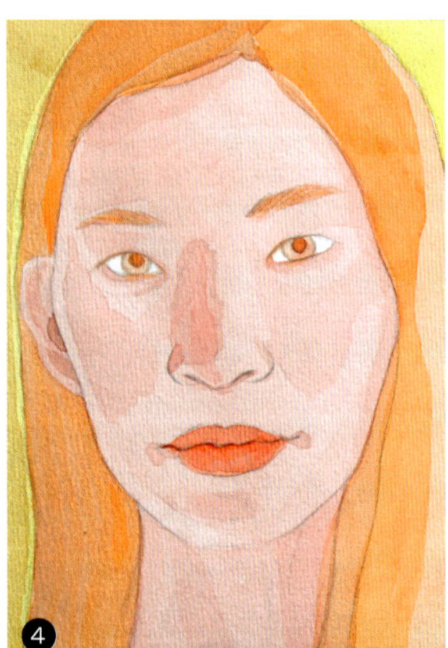

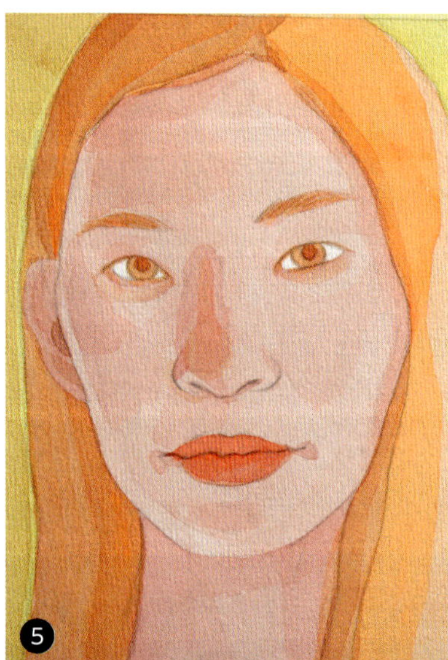

4. Let it dry and repeat this process as many times as necessary.
5. Finally, with a fine brush, add detail to the areas you want to highlight and where you want to create contrast.

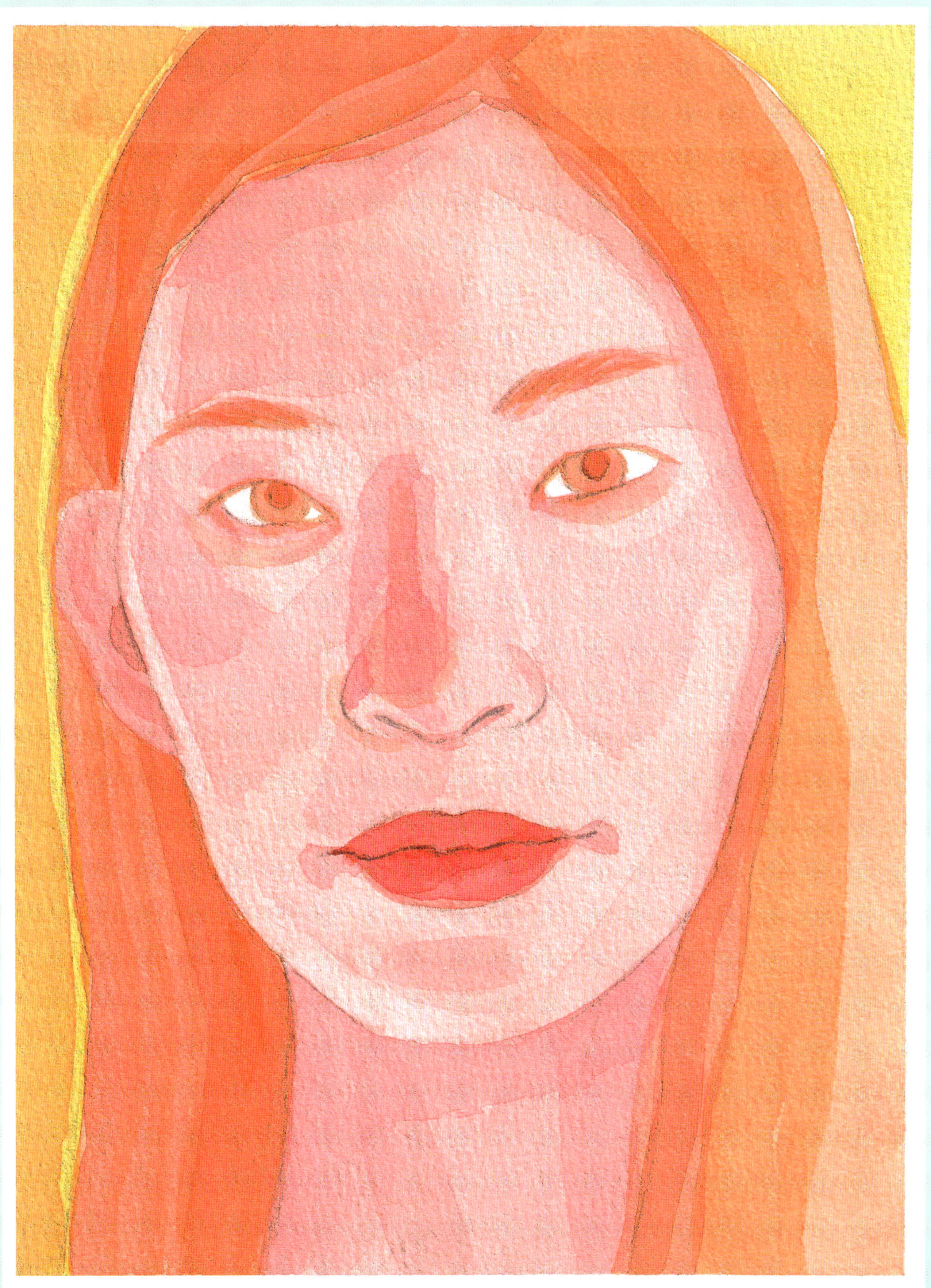

LIGHT-DARK CONTRAST

For this portrait, I chose bright colors (yellow and orange) for the light areas and dark colors (blue and purple) for the shadows. This creates a **light-dark contrast** using colors on the color wheel.

This is a very good exercise for practicing precision, keeping a steady hand, and employing patience. You can use any brush you want, but for this exercise, I recommend a low-numbered brush so that you can get finer strokes for making precise lines and adding detail.

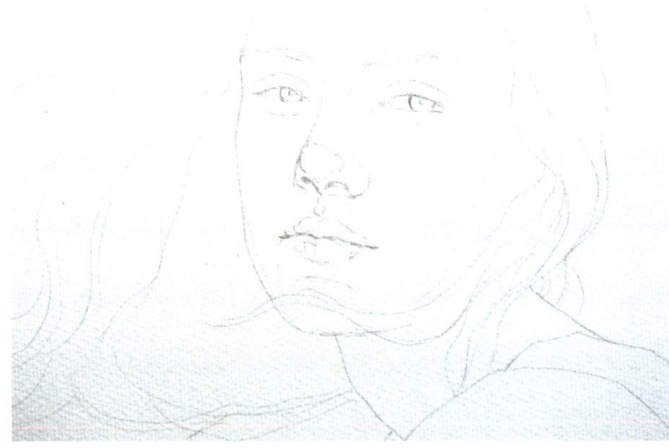

1. Use a sharp pencil to draw your portrait.

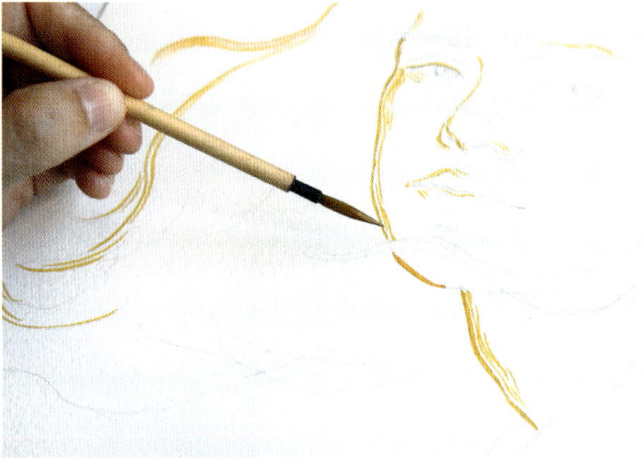

2. Use the brightest color, in this case, yellow, to draw lines for the highlighted areas.

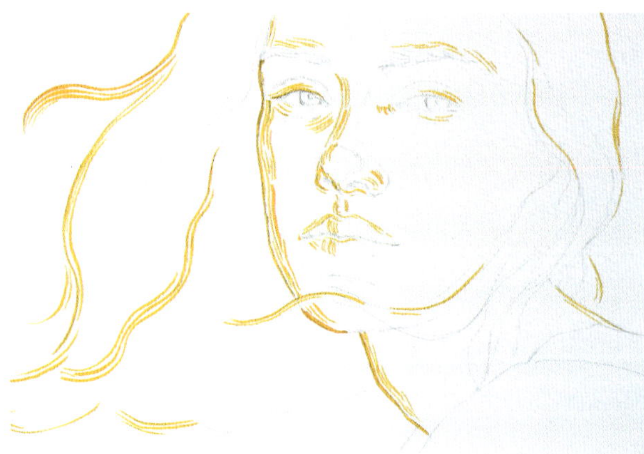

3. Fill in your portrait gradually, letting the direction and volume of the face guide you.

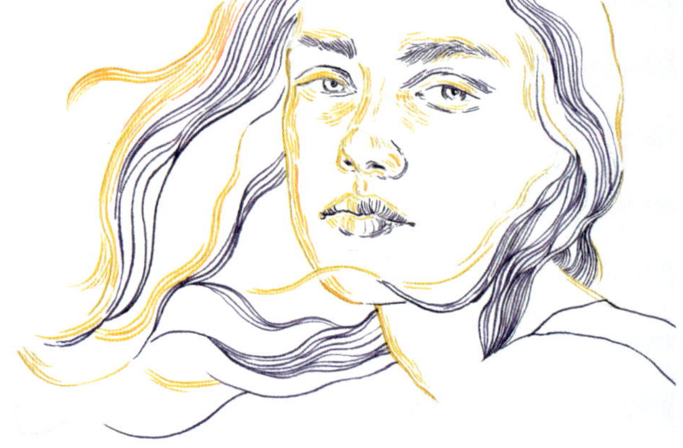

4. Once you determine where the light is, choose the darkest color (dark purple) and draw lines in the areas with more shadows.

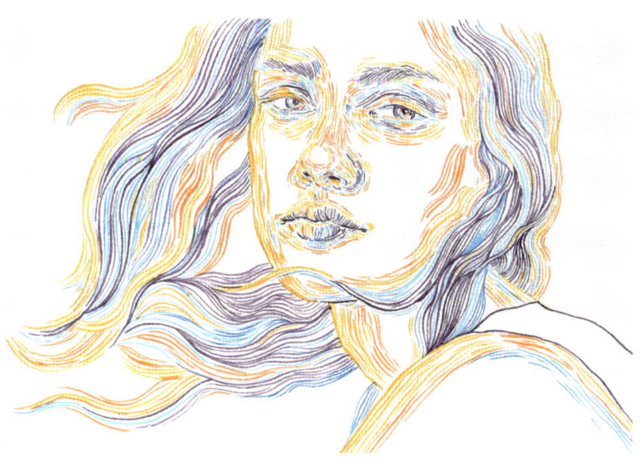

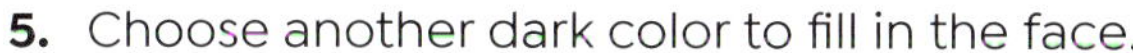

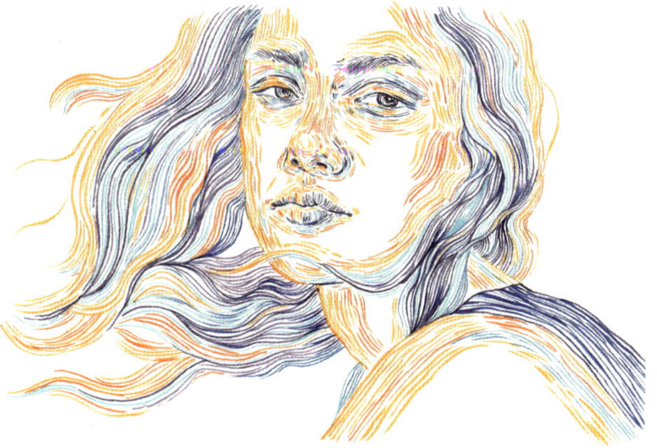

5. Choose another dark color to fill in the face.

6. Continue to fill in the face with your color scheme until you are satisfied.

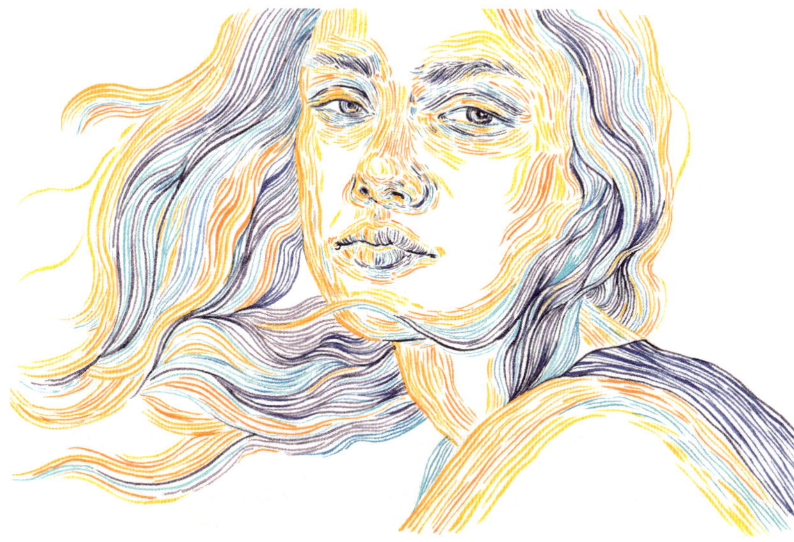

7. Note that in the lighter areas, I added yellow and orange, and in the darker areas, I used blues and purples.

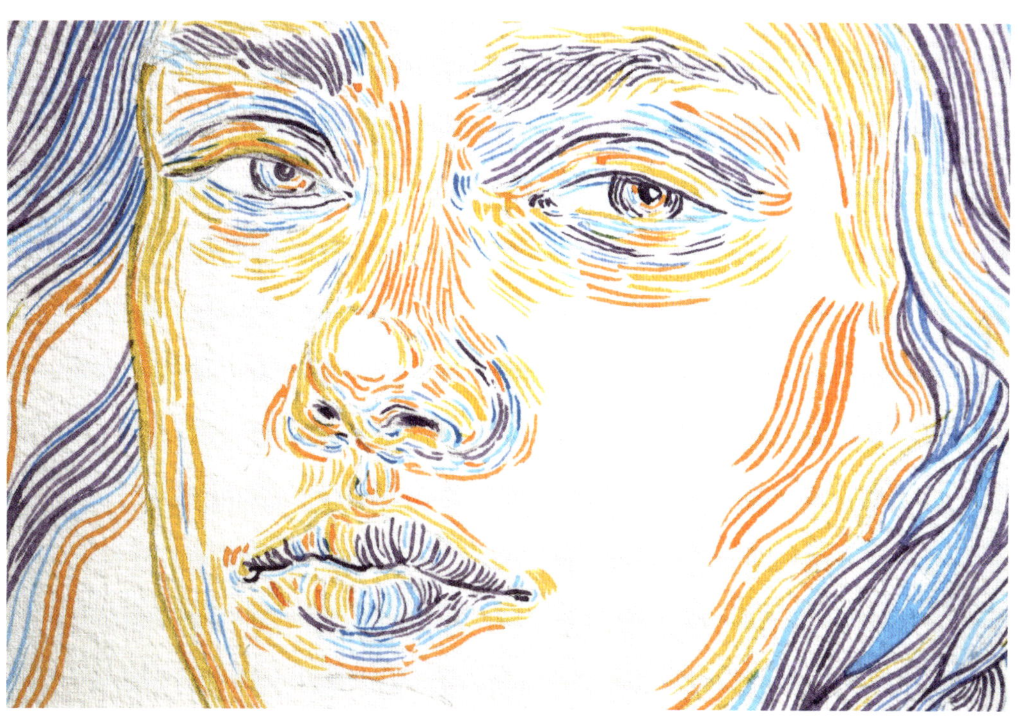

For the fill pattern, I used lines, but you can invent any other kind of pattern. What other patterns come to mind?

NEUTRAL COLORS

A neutral color scheme is identified by colors with reduced purity, meaning that they have been mixed with black or white or a complementary color has been added.

I personally prefer the second option of using complementary colors to get neutral, earthy, temperate colors that are calming to the eye.

SKIN TONES

You can re-create a variety of different skin tones by combining very basic colors.

When you look at the vast assortment of skin colors, you see that they range in tone from reddish, to yellowish, to brownish, and that some are paler or darker, and others are more pink or tan and so on.

Skin tones also change depending on the surrounding light and what *color* that light is. The same portrait can be painted using different shades of color for the skin tone depending on how the light and shadows fall.

Through the mixture of the three primary colors, **yellow**, **red**, and **blue**, you can achieve infinite earthy tones by gradually varying the proportions. Quinacridone Magenta is also widely used to achieve skin tones.

When you mix yellow and Quinacridone Magenta, you create a very saturated pink-orange tone. If you add a little blue, it lowers the intensity of the mixture for a more natural color.

To achieve darker tones, you can use the earth tones on your palette. For example, you can mix the color Toasted Sienna Earth with either yellow, red, or blue, depending on the skin tone you want to achieve.

Adding water or the color white to that same mixture will further modify the shades. If you add more water to the mixture, you will have softer, more delicate and translucent tones. If you add white to the mixture, you will have more pastel skin tones. (Remember that white dulls colors, so use it sparingly or test ahead to see results.)

Don't limit yourself to using only primary colors. Experiment with versions of different colors. For example, adding Lemon Yellow instead of Yellow Ochre or using a red instead of Quinacridone Magenta will create diverse outcomes.

On the next page are examples of color mixes where I have experimented with different shades and quantities. I encourage you to get a piece of paper and start testing out different color combinations to see what different skin tones you can create. Remember to adjust the paint proportions and add water to make even more variations.

Feel free to paint your faces blue, green, or pure unmixed magenta! There is always room for fantasy.

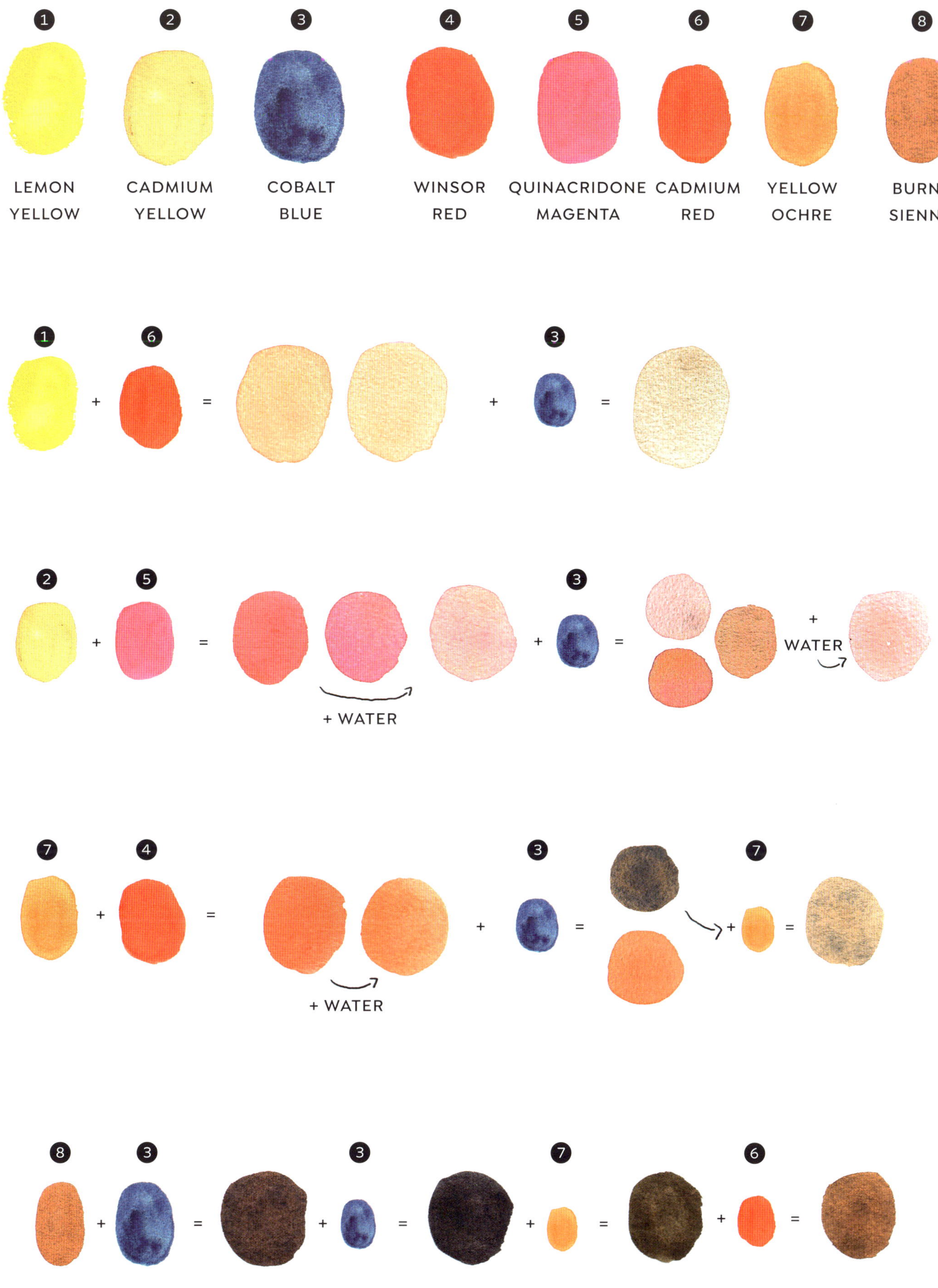
1
2
3
4
5
6
7
8
LEMON YELLOW
CADMIUM YELLOW
COBALT BLUE
WINSOR RED
QUINACRIDONE MAGENTA
CADMIUM RED
YELLOW OCHRE
BURNT SIENNA
1
6
3
2
5
3
+ WATER
+ WATER
7
4
3
7
+ WATER
8
3
3
7
6

EXAMPLE 1: NEUTRAL COLORS

In this portrait, I used a color scheme of colors with reduced purity:

- *I added a little red to the green.*
- *I added a little yellow to the purple shirt.*
- *I mixed red and yellow with a pinch of blue for the warm skin tone.*

1. I worked in blocks: background, T-shirt, hair, and face. All is done with the wet-on-dry technique, letting each section dry so that the edges of the colors don't mix.
2. I wanted a very simple light and bright portrait, so I captured and reserved the brightness of the paper.
3. Once the first layers dried, I added a second layer using the same color but with a little more pigment for the shadows of the face, to darken the area and reduce some of the paper's brightness.
4. Finally, I added some final touches in the areas with greater contrast, around the ears, eyes, nose, and edge of the T-shirt.

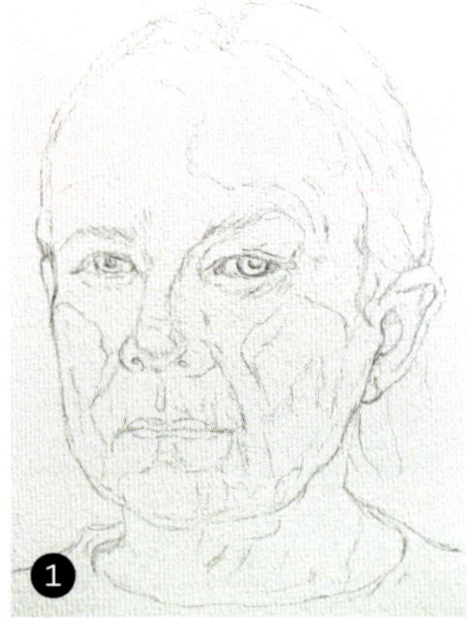

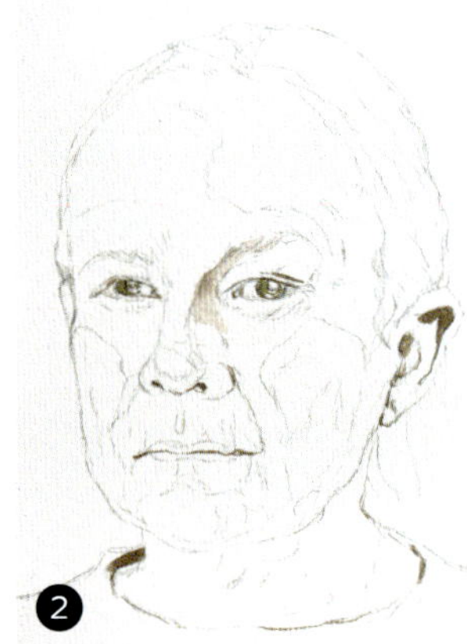

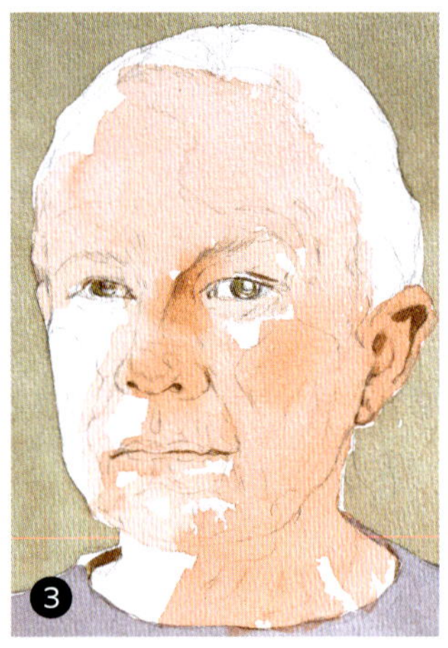

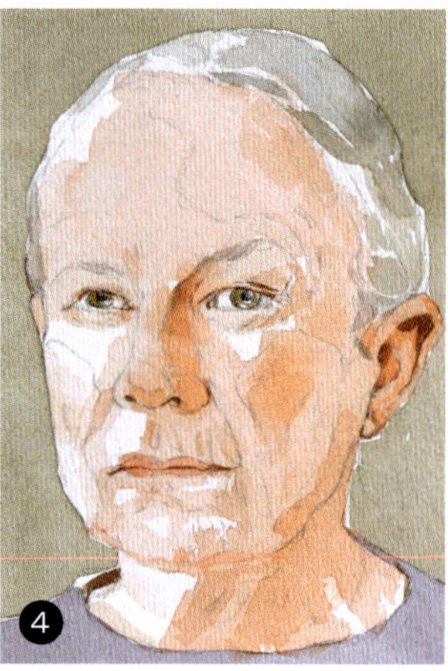

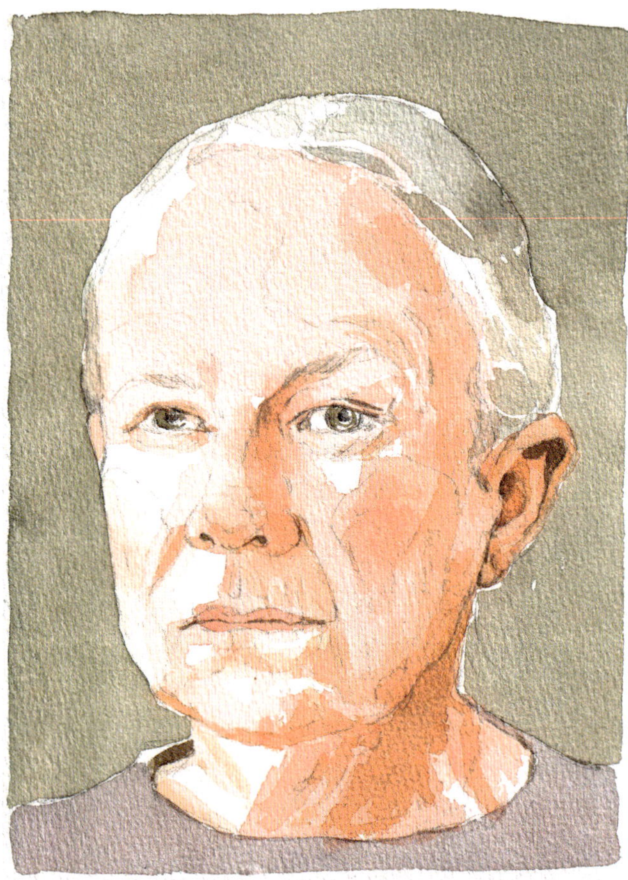

EXAMPLE 2: OPAQUE LAYERS

In this portrait, I wanted more opaque layers, so I added less water to the mixed color than in the previous example.

Coincidentally, in this case, chance created some random, grainy textures. Sometimes, mistakes result in unexpected and surprising things. Notice that the texture of the background, shirt, and face created some marks and stains that make the layers seem not completely smooth. This happened because I didn't clean my palette, and there was a trace of bleach in the mixtures from a previous exercise. The result was those random stains, and I liked them a lot.

I'll most likely have to experiment with the amount of bleach to get the same effect again because when something happens by chance, it's not easy to reproduce. You also have to keep in mind that the paper you use can create different finishes.

When I want muddy hues, I usually use the dirty colors that are left in my palette from other mixtures.

As in the previous exercise, I started painting broad layers and applied successive layers in wet-on-dry. I then used a fine-tipped brush to define the details.

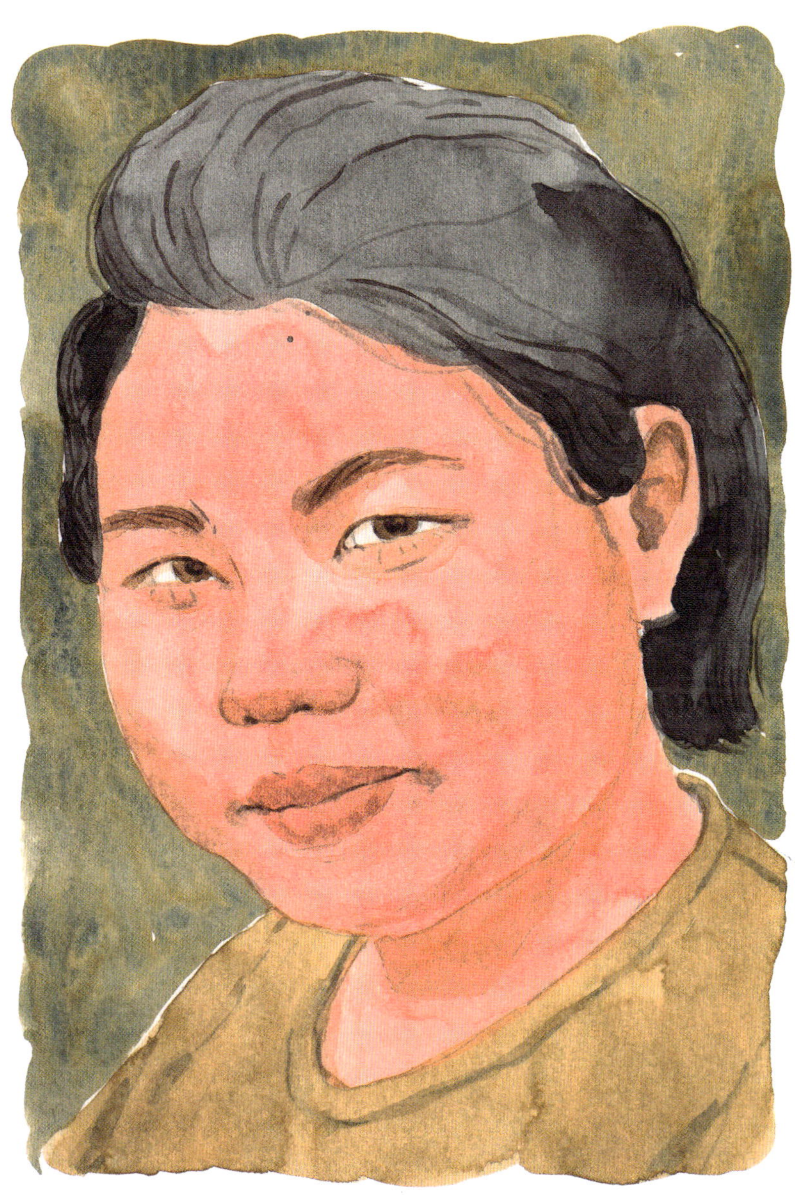

OTHER COLOR EXAMPLES

Here are some examples of alternative color palettes. Once you know the possibilities that the color wheel offers you, you can explore color and create your own color palettes (see "Examples of Inspiration for Creating Color Palettes" on page 30), either by using specialized materials (for example, saturated colored liquid inks) or by creating your own color combinations.

Before you color a project, do some simple blends on a piece of scrap paper to see what combinations you find most interesting. Remember that a restricted palette works great and is easier to apply!

You can also combine different *types* of materials. For example, blend your watercolor with liquid inks plus gouache. A mixture of three different techniques can lead to an amazing result.

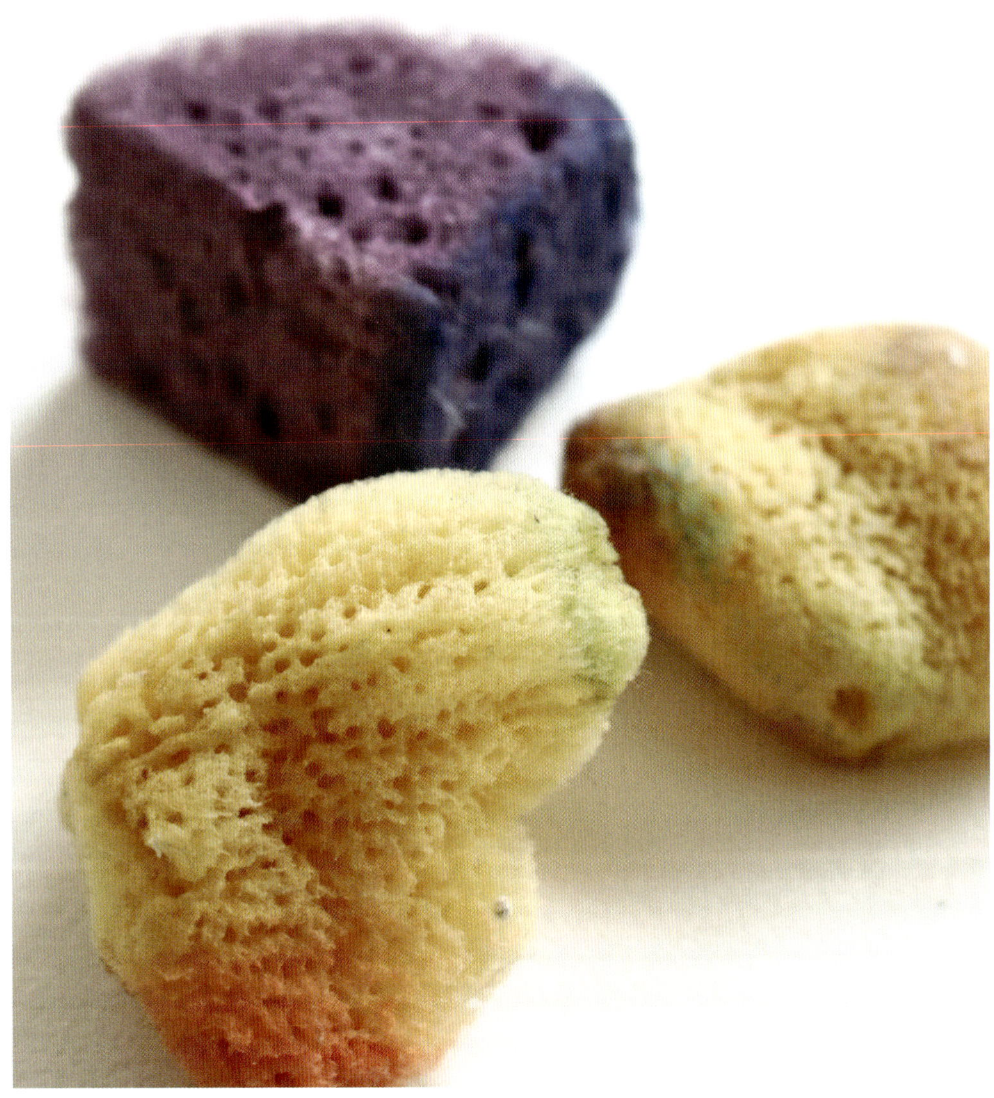

HIGHLY SATURATED AND VIBRANT COLORS

This portrait has a joyful and light feeling thanks to fluorescent colors and liquid inks. I wanted to let myself be carried away by chance, and I allowed the strokes and colors to flow and blend into each other. I wasn't very careful about placing light and shadow. I just wanted to have fun. There are times when things don't make much sense and that's fine too. This type of exercise is good for letting go and not being afraid of the result. Just enjoy the process.

For this type of brushstroke, it's important that you prepare the colors beforehand in your palette because each stroke must be kept wet so it can combine with the next brushstroke.

Apply as many layers as you want. Play with the wet-on-wet and wet-on-dry techniques.

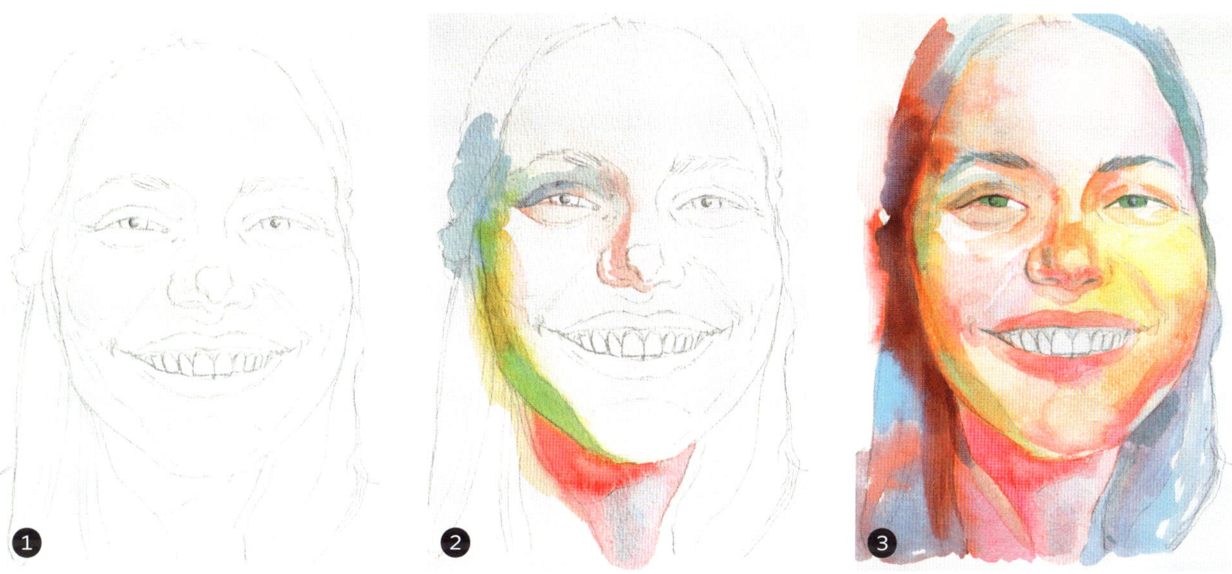

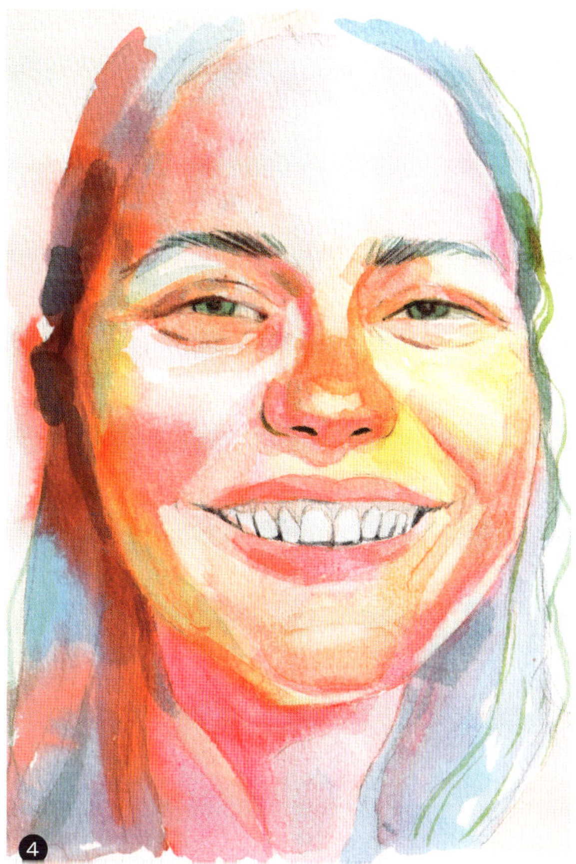

RESTRICTED PALETTE

For this portrait, I reduced the color scheme to greens, browns, and pinks. This color scheme fascinates me, with each color contrasting against each other.

I used various techniques: wet-on-wet, wet-on-dry, and if you look closely, you'll see that the details of the fluorescent pink have a coarse, rough texture. I did this by applying paint directly from a pan watercolor moistened with very little water. As always, I first applied larger brushstrokes and carefully worked in the details.

For the background, I used very translucent layers and the wet-on-wet technique. This makes the trees seem less detailed, and they fade into the background, providing a feeling of distance.

Remember: A very opaque color seems closer and a more translucent than one that seems farther away. Compare the tree on the right with the ones on the left. Which seems closer to you?

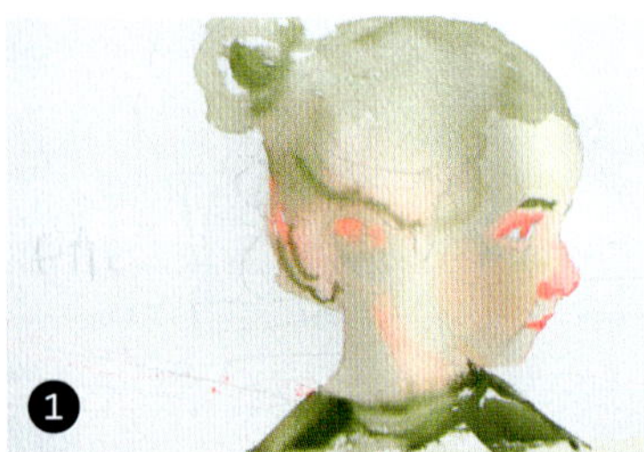

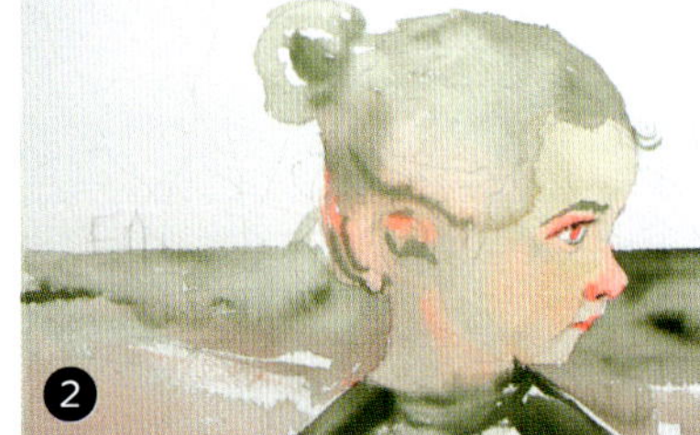

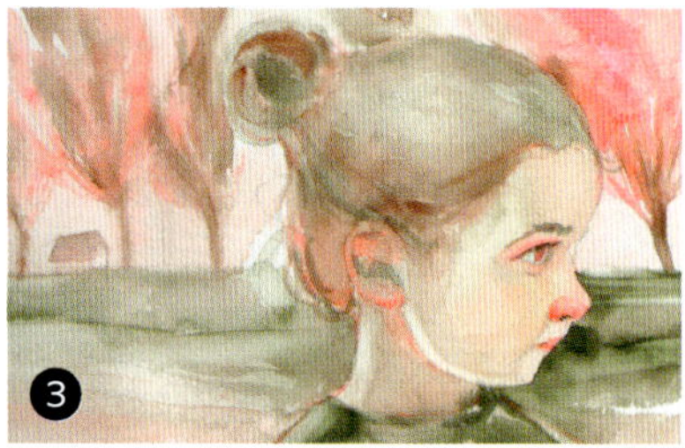

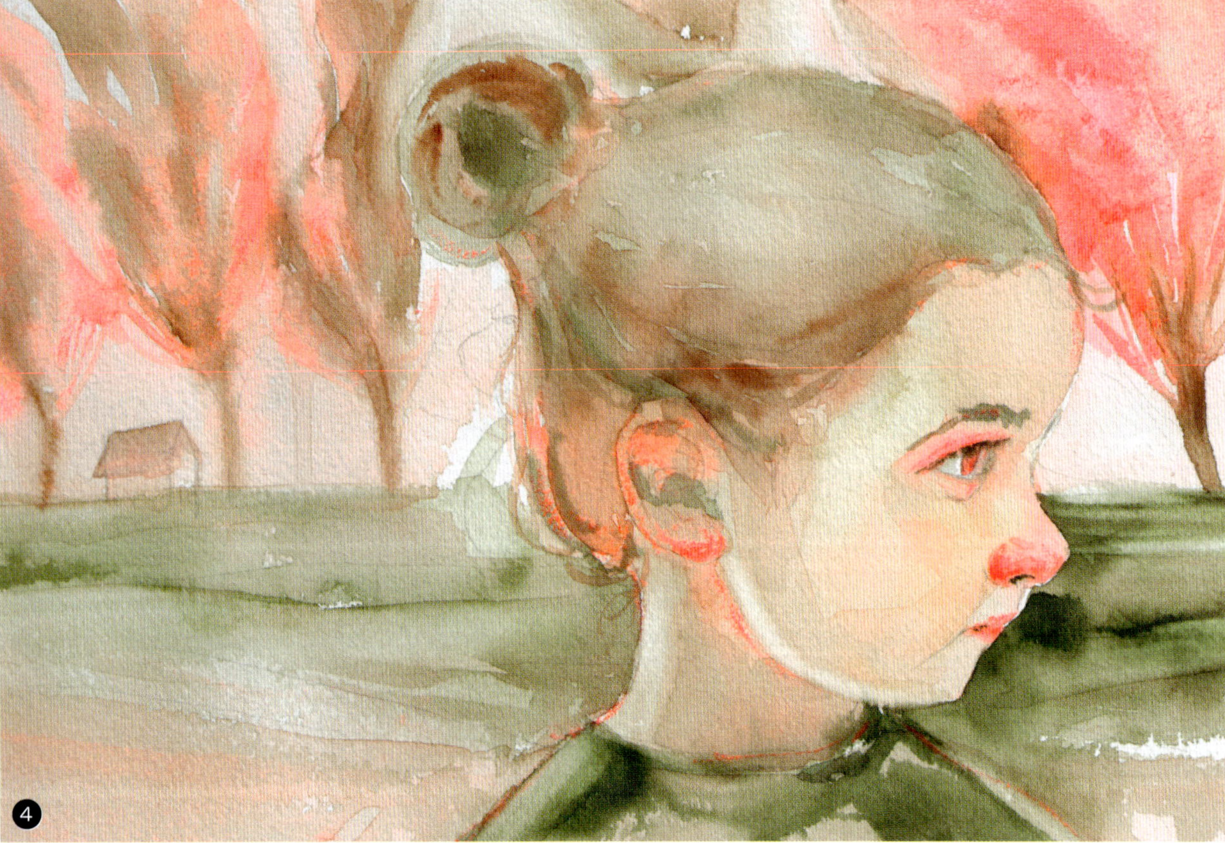

EXTENDED COLOR PALETTE

This portrait is an example where I used several hues, trying to reproduce the colors from the reference photograph.

I steadily applied wet-on-dry layers to give volume to the face. I blended the edge of some of the brushstrokes for a smoother transition to shadow. In others, I left a hard, unblended edge.

Once the layer for the skin was dry, I used a fine-tipped brush to paint the hair with a highly pigmented color to give it a lot of energy.

I added a background with bubbles on several planes, playing with color and size. I painted the two largest bubbles on top of each other, which diluted the underlying layers a bit. This didn't frustrate me at all—in fact, it made me like the final result even more.

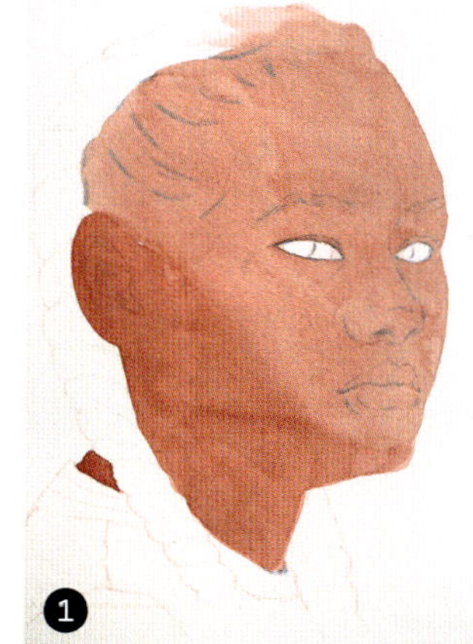
1

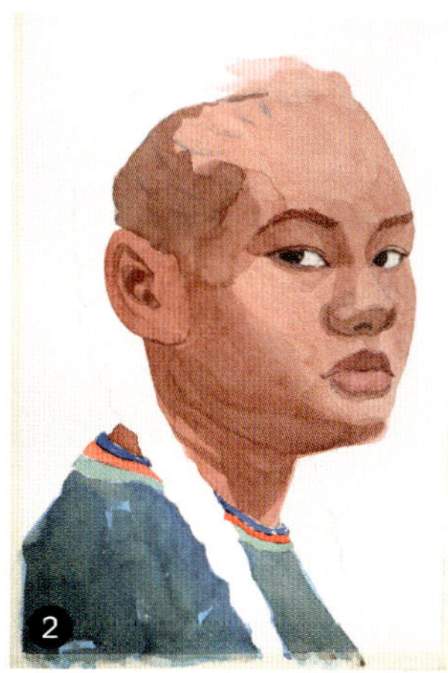
2

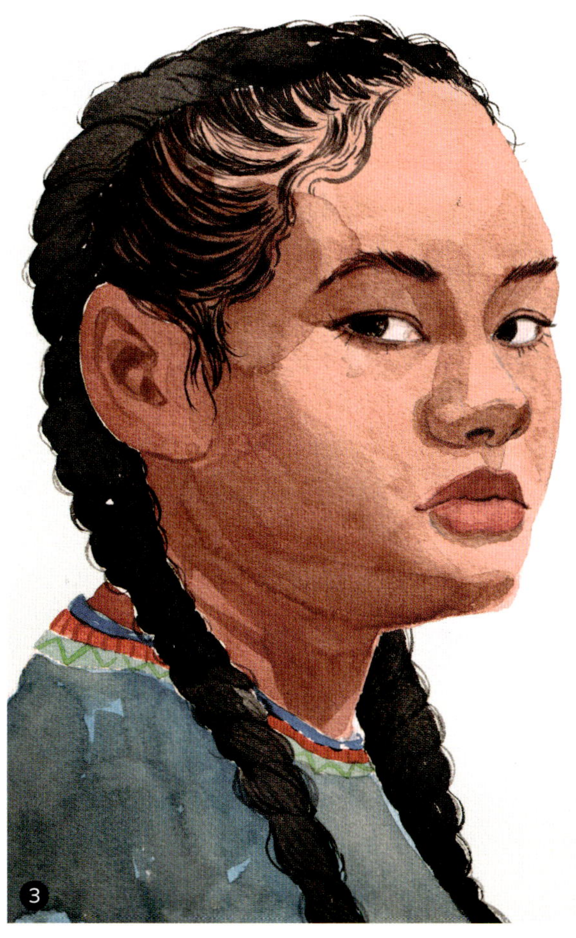
3

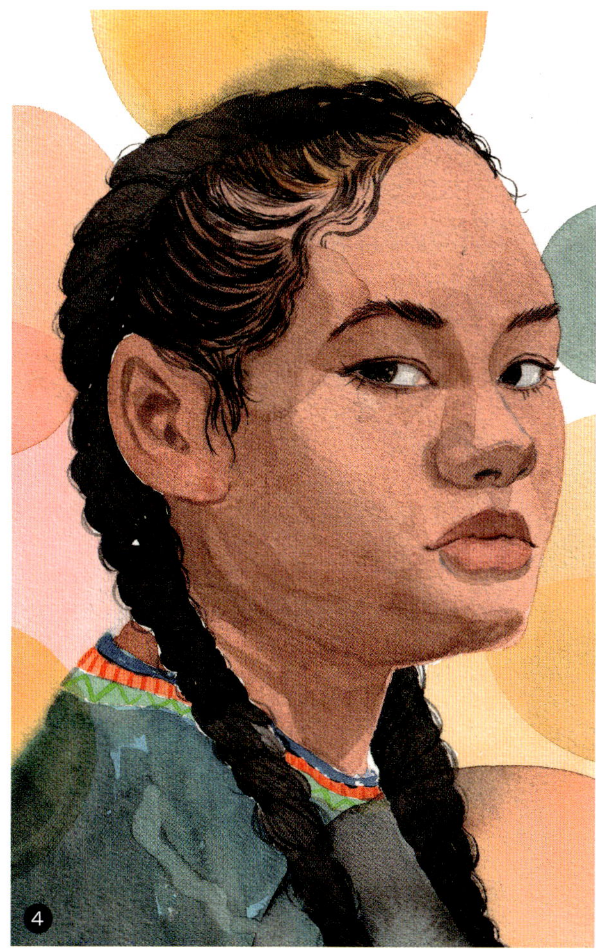
4

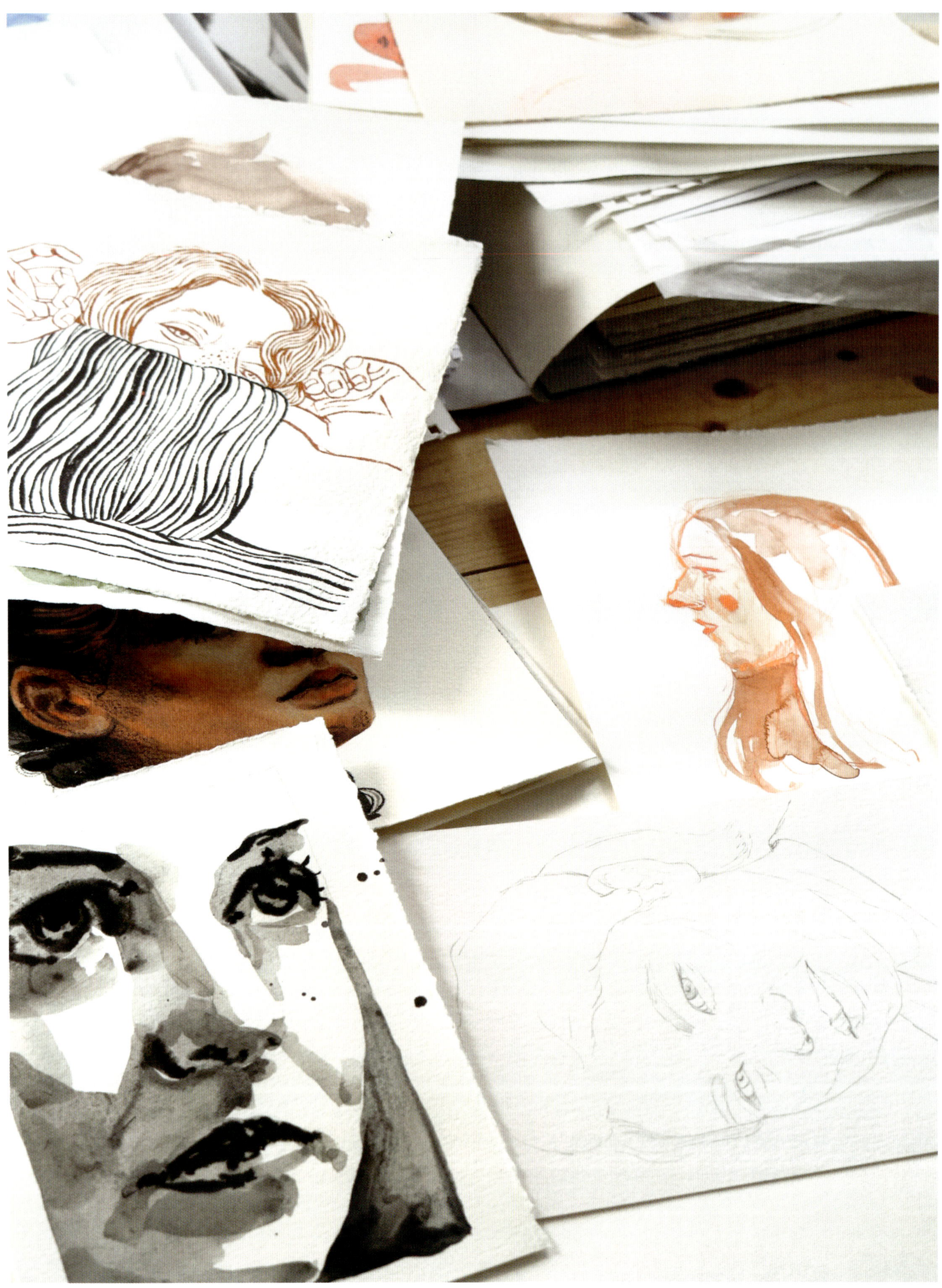

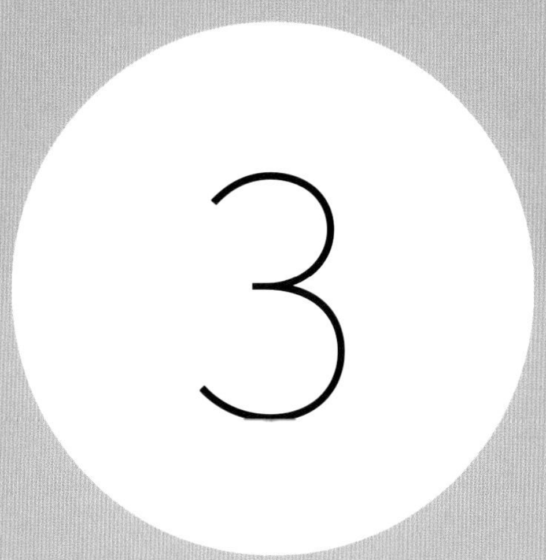

CREATIVE PORTRAITS

WATERCOLOR + MIXED MEDIA

In this chapter, we'll combine watercolor with other materials. I propose several mixed media techniques in the lessons, but feel free to use or mix any materials you want.

I like to watch this process unfold as if my table were a laboratory for creating experiments. Lay out all the materials you have in front of you. Start experimenting with how they mix together. For example, what happens if you use the watercolor paint *before* or *after* a pencil? The results will be quite different. With some trial and error, you'll see how some techniques work better together than others. You'll like some more than others, so give yourself the freedom to play around and make mistakes. You might be surprised! These types of exercises are very creative. They help feed our imagination by not having limitations and allowing us to break the rules. The most important thing is to enjoy the process and don't worry about the result.

WATERCOLOR AND PENCIL

There are two ways to combine watercolor and pencil. Changing the order in which you use them changes the result. Let's look at each one.

LESSON 1: PENCIL FIRST, THEN WATERCOLOR

The technique used in this portrait is drawing the portrait in pencil first and then coloring it in with watercolors.

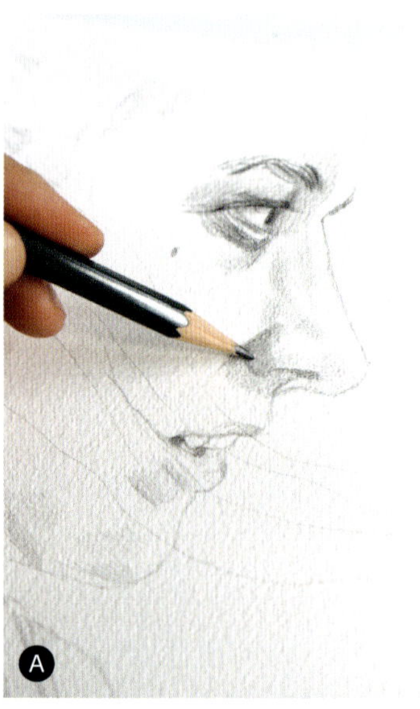

A

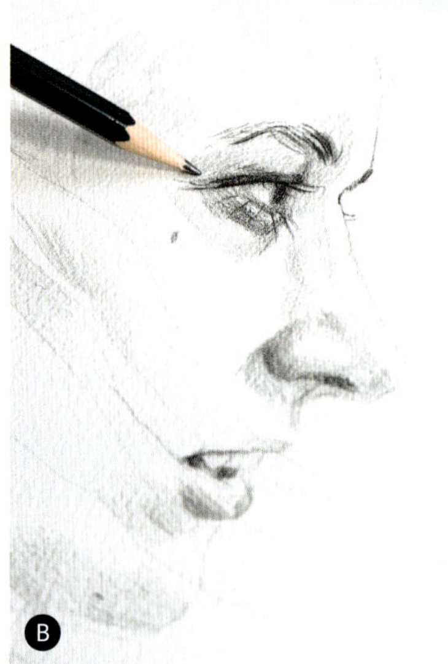

B

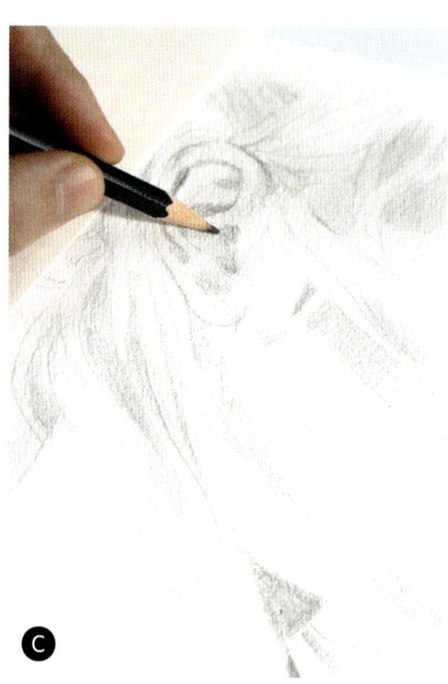

C

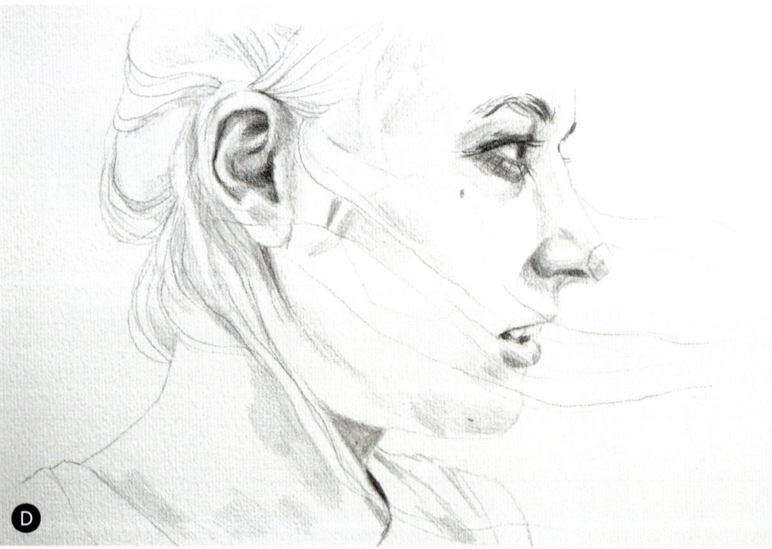

D

1. Use a pencil to draw and shade your portrait. You can use H (hard) or B (soft) pencils. First, I blocked out the figure and then started shading, beginning with the areas of the least contrast and progressing to the areas with the most contrast. I usually start with hard pencils and finish adding contrast with soft pencils or oil-based pencils. (A–D)

2. When you've finished the shading, you can "fix" the pencil with a product especially designed to do this: fixative spray. For a cheaper method, you can also use hairspray, but it can deteriorate the paper in the long run. Or you can choose to use nothing at all. If you use hard pencils instead of soft ones, the work will get less murky when you apply water to it.

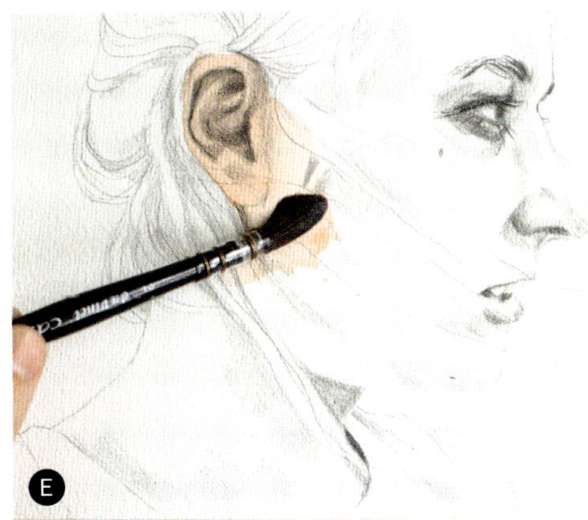

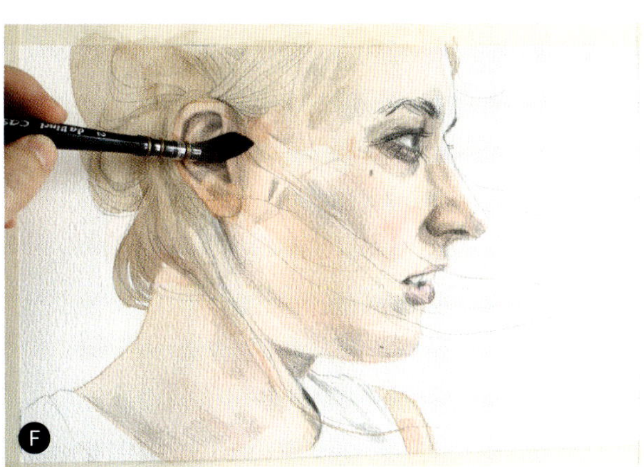

3. Prepare the colors you'll use and start painting washes in each part of the portrait: face, hair, and so on. Stop to let it dry after each color block if you don't want the colors to mix. (E)

4. In the next layers of color, you can define details and add color to the lips, eyes, nose, ear, and hair. (F–H)

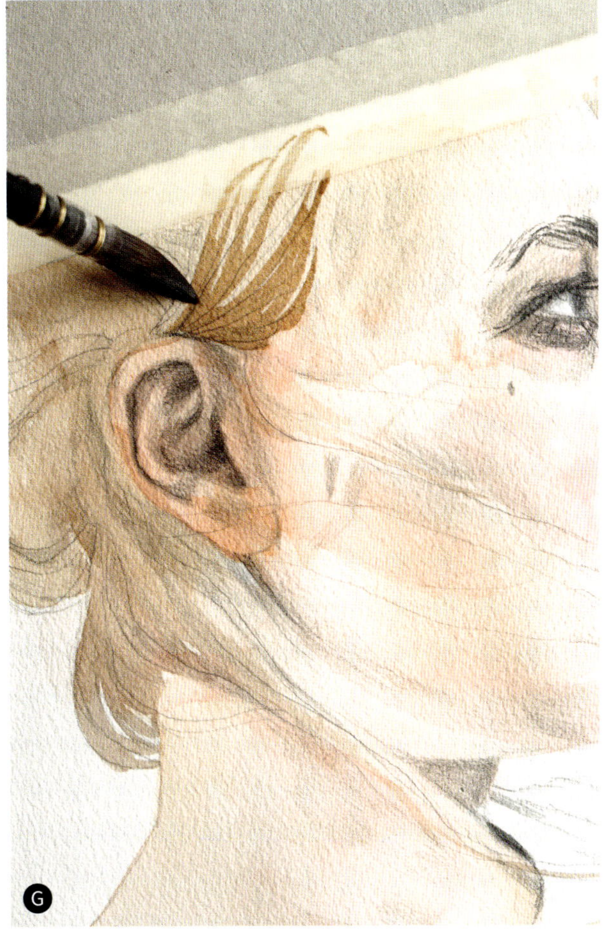

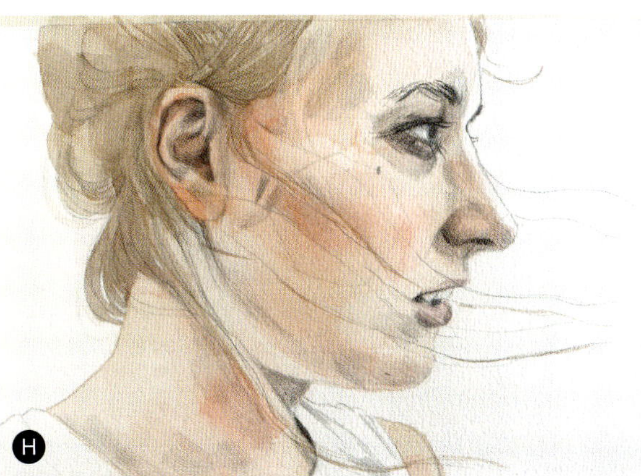

tip

Remember that once the drawing is finished, you can apply watercolor in whatever way you like best: to define the face, to create a color gradient, to add layers, using the wet-on-wet technique, and so on.

(continued)

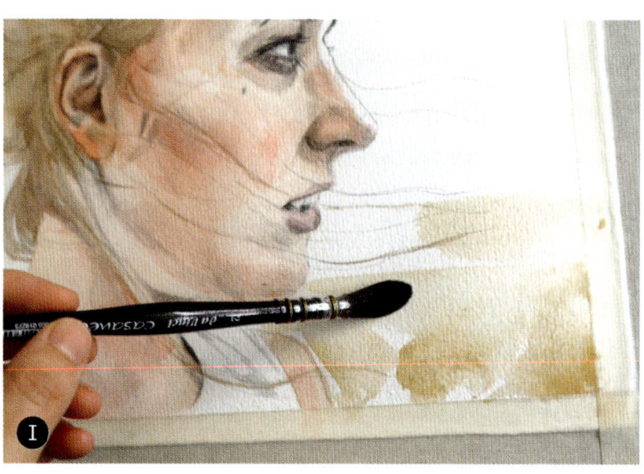

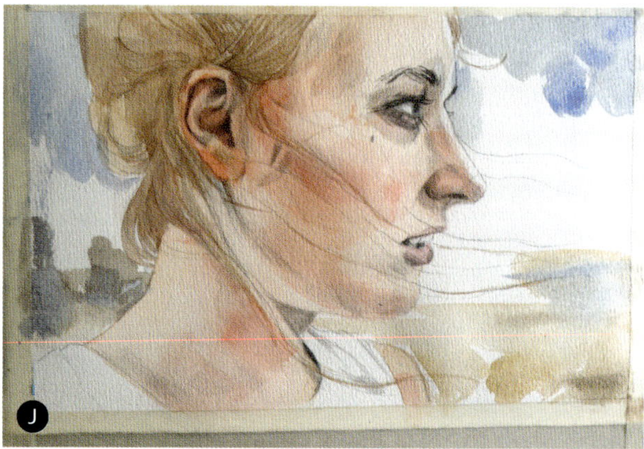

5. I wanted to give depth to the portrait by creating a background. I simulated a landscape with loose brushstrokes and gradients. (I, J)

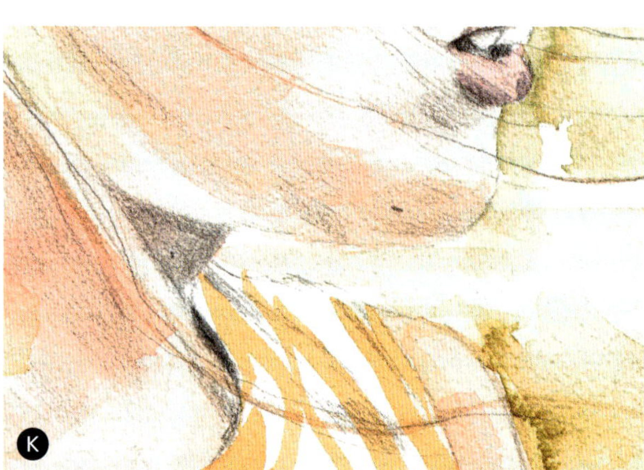

6. Finally, to create a simple striped pattern on the shirt, I added some thick lines, really pressing the brush to the paper.

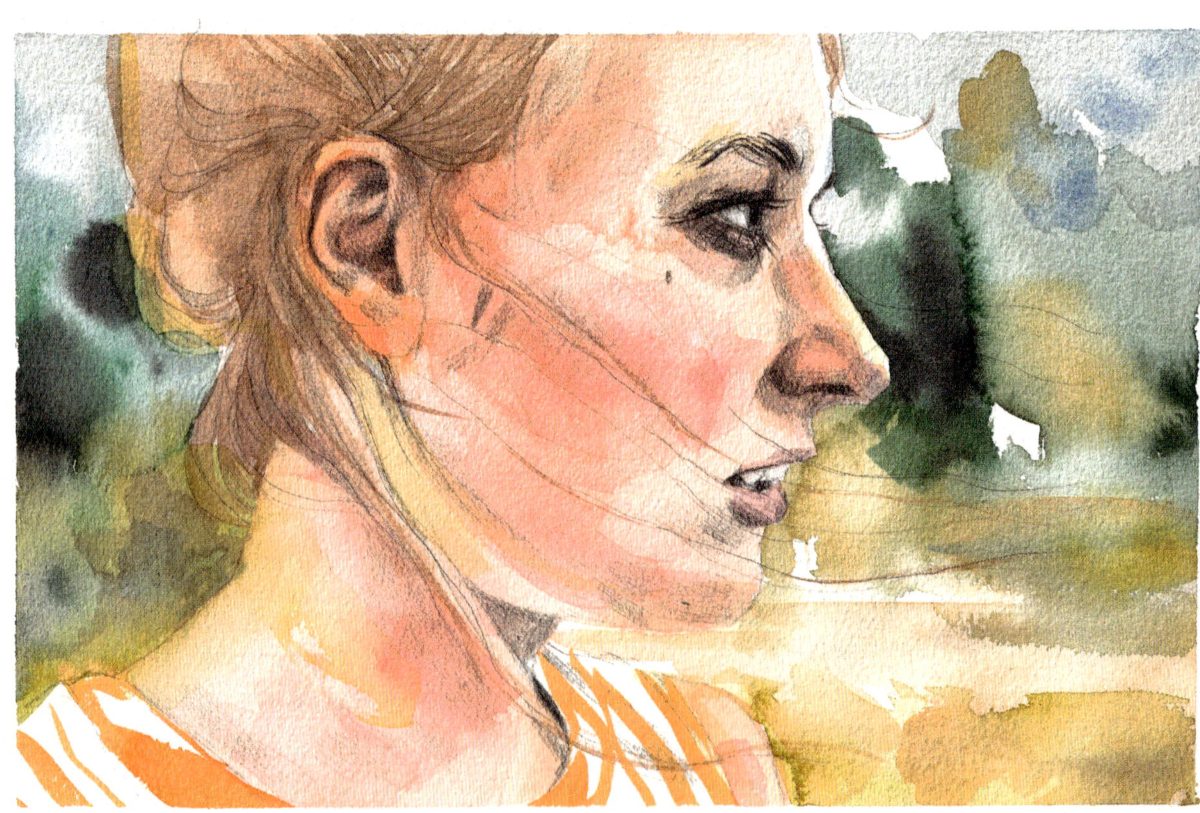

LESSON 2: WATERCOLOR FIRST, THEN PENCIL

The second technique is to paint with watercolor first, and once it's dry, add shadows and details with pencil, yielding a very different result.

1. Use a pencil to draw the outline and details of the face. I used a hard 2H pencil. (A)

2. Evenly paint a layer of color all over the face. I usually leave the eyes unpainted, reserving the white from the paper. Before this layer dried, I applied white ink to the light areas (wet-on-wet). This way, the white ink is integrated into the color layer. (B)

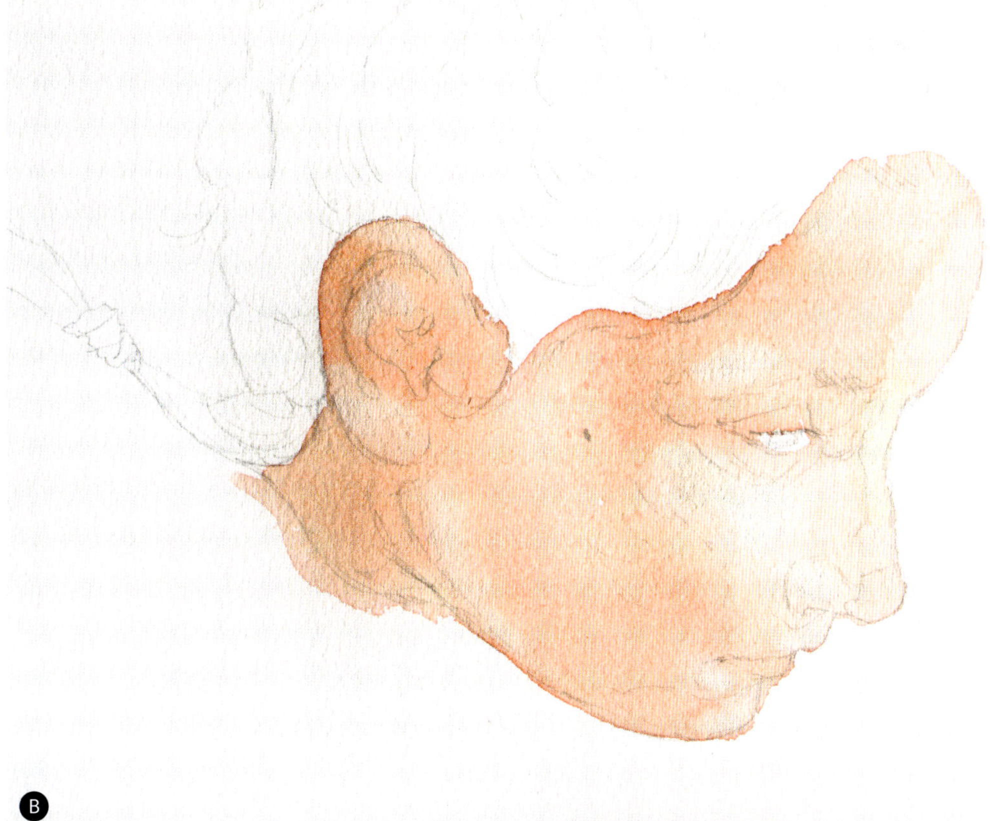

(*continued*)

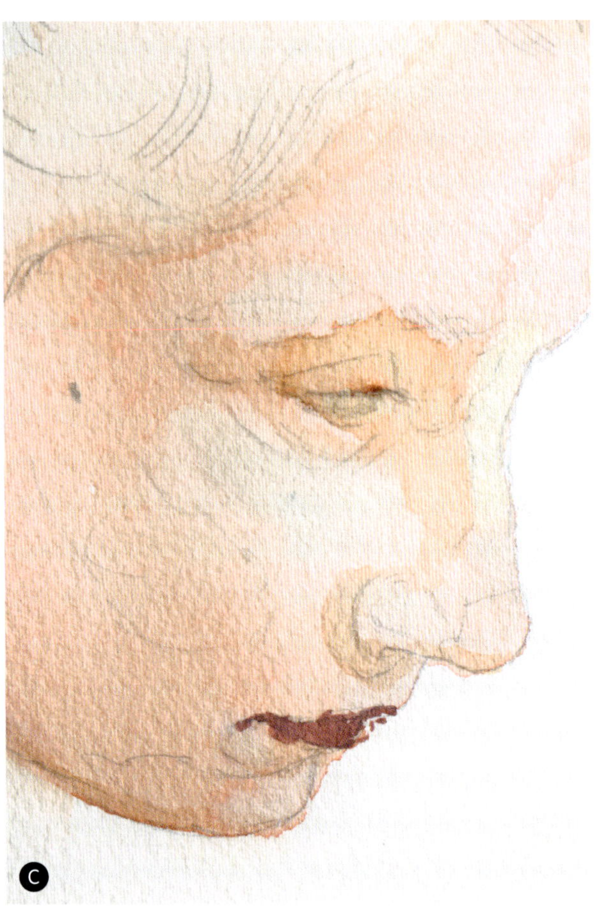

C

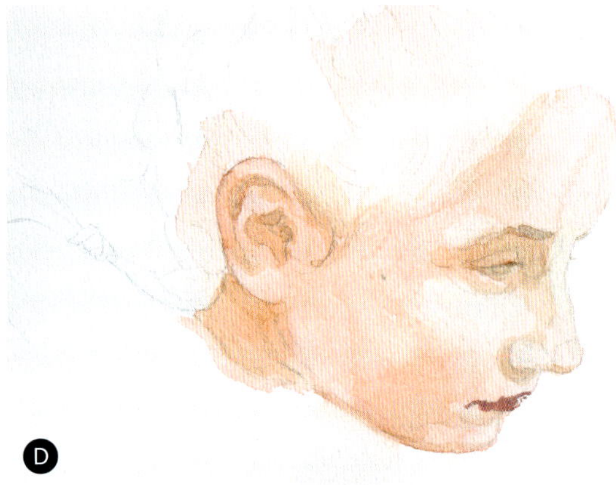

D

3. Once this layer has dried, apply a second color wash in the shaded areas: in the ears, eyelids, nose, and contour of the face and neck. Paint the area around the mouth to give it shape and volume. (C, D)

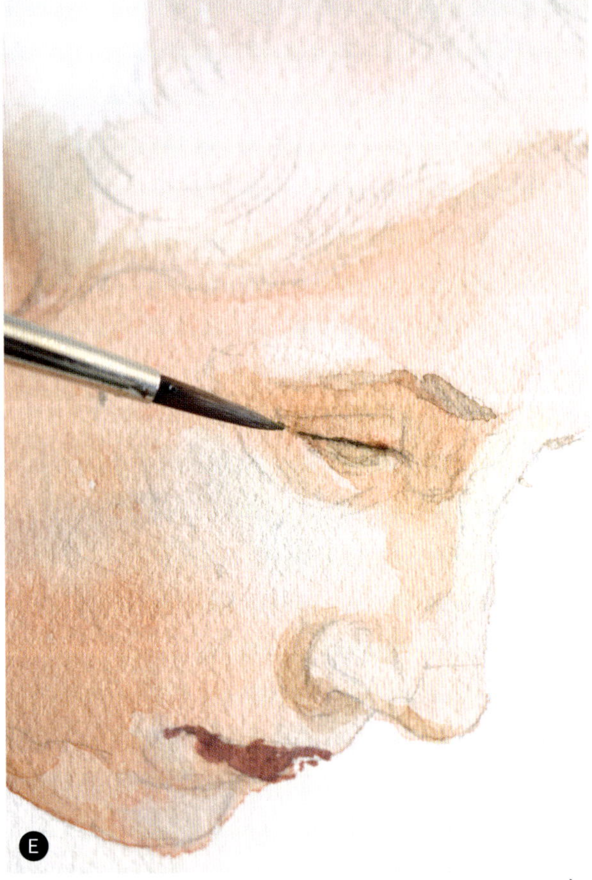

E

4. I reapplied a third layer of color to try to get more shadows and add more volume to the face. With a round-tipped and very fine brush, I detailed the eyebrows and eyes. (E)

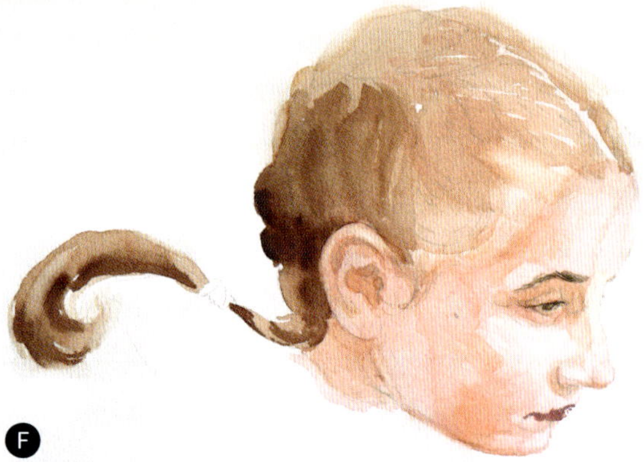

F

5. Following this same process, I added color to the hair, leaving some light areas from the paper in some places. In other places, I applied more color using the wet-on-wet technique. (F)

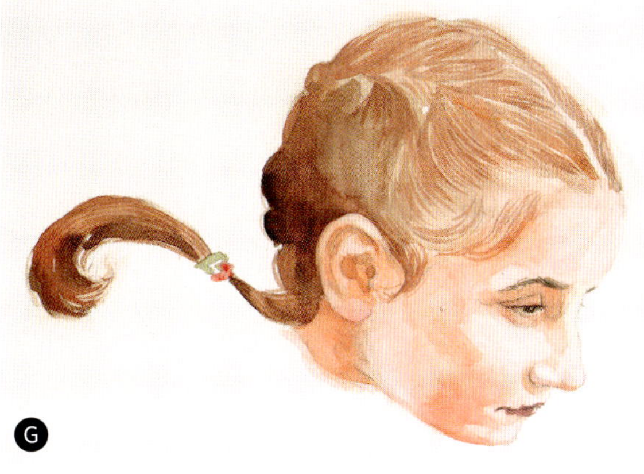

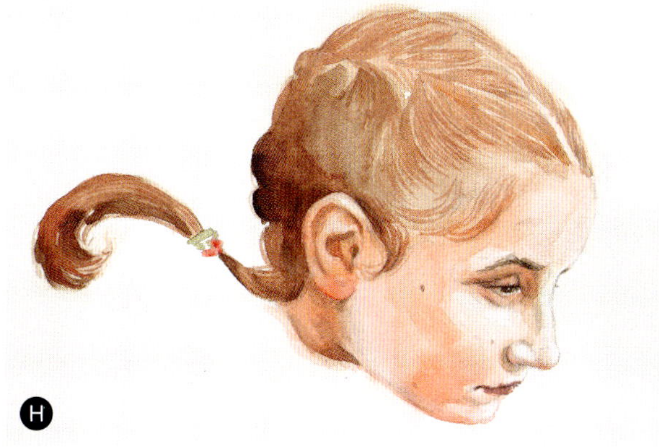

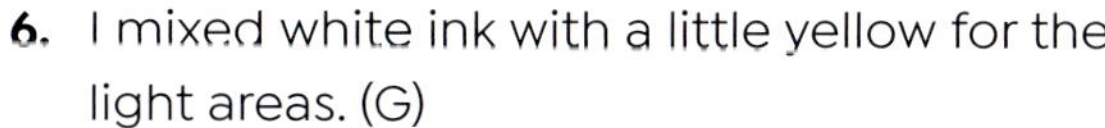

6. I mixed white ink with a little yellow for the light areas. (G)

7. I used a hard pencil to create the shadows and add detail to the eyes, nose, and ear. (H)

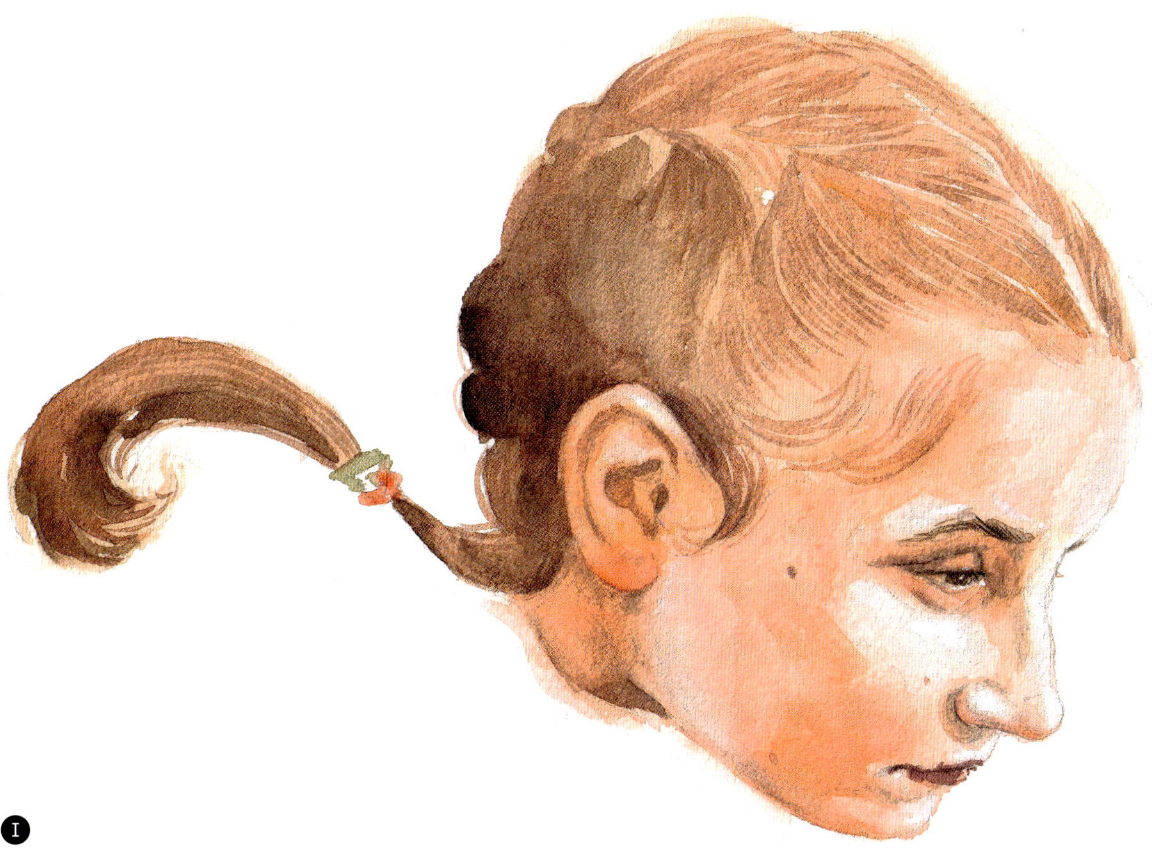

8. Last, I used a mechanical pencil (2B) to add contrast to the areas where I wanted to draw attention. (I)

Our portrait is now finished. The area surrounding the portrait is left empty because the reference model had a prominent white background, and I didn't want any distracting elements.

The color scheme uses warm, autumnal hues. To add a small amount of color contrast, I applied strong, saturated colors to the hair tie. This broke up the monotony of such earthy colors.

WATERCOLOR AND INDIA INK

Watercolor and India ink can be combined in many different ways. I encourage you to experiment and discover all the different results. Here are some examples:

WATERCOLOR BASE AND INK

In this portrait, I used only three colors: Cerulean Blue, Cadmium Yellow, and Quinacridone Magenta. I used hues that have a lot of pure color and are highly saturated and vibrant.

I want pure colors without any mixing, so I'll layer each of these colors, making sure that each layer is dry before continuing. Layering transparent layers on top of each other will create new hues. The technique is wet-on-dry.

Let's look at the process:

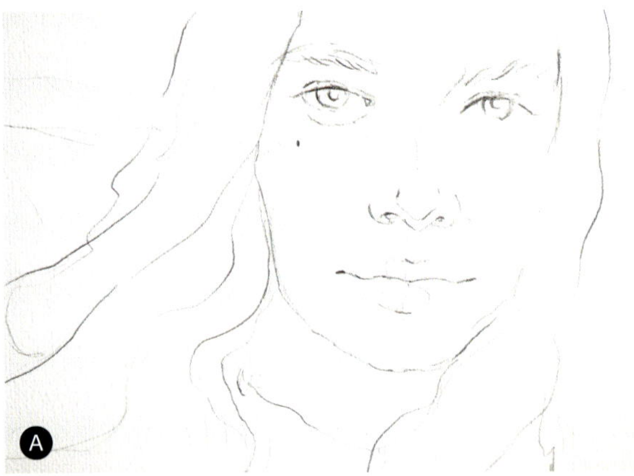

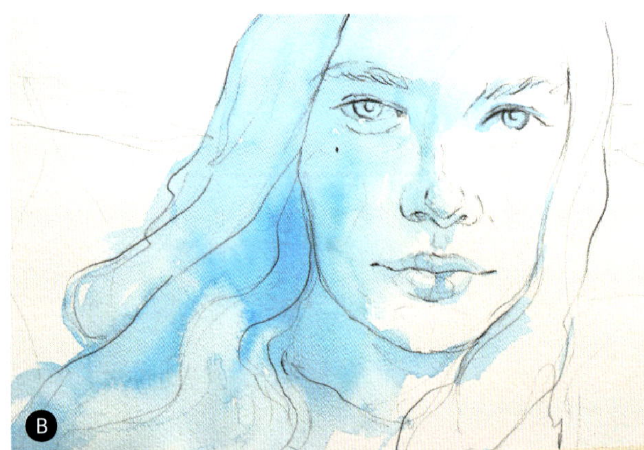

1. Trace the outline of the drawing. Once again, I've used a 2H pencil. (A)
2. With a pipette or dropper, add the colors to the palette. You can reduce saturation with a little water if you don't want them to be so opaque.
3. Start by using the Cerulean Blue to place the shadows. Use a high-numbered round brush so you can load enough paint on it for a wash. (B)

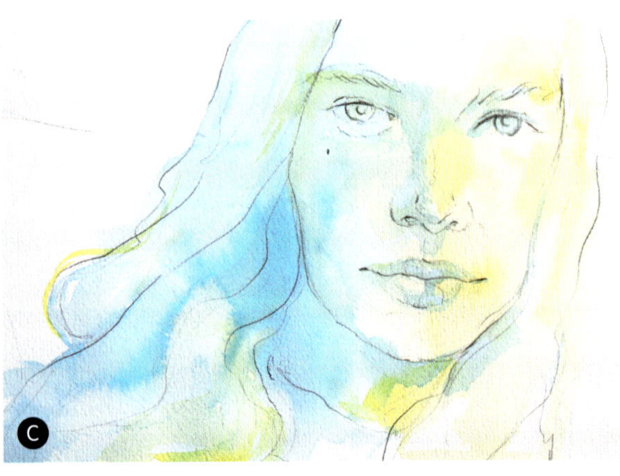

4. Once it's dry, place the light areas with the Cadmium Yellow in the same way. (C)

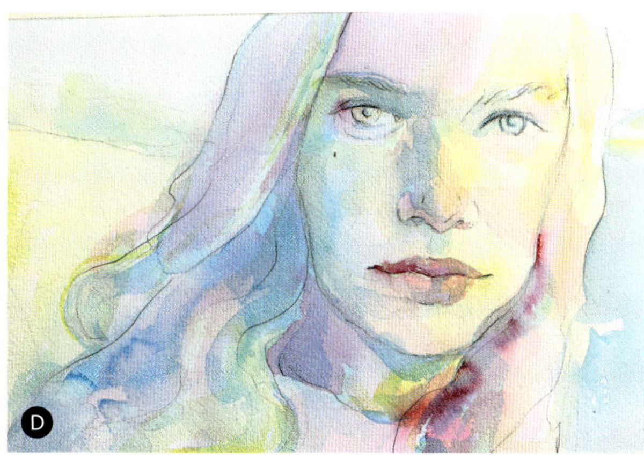

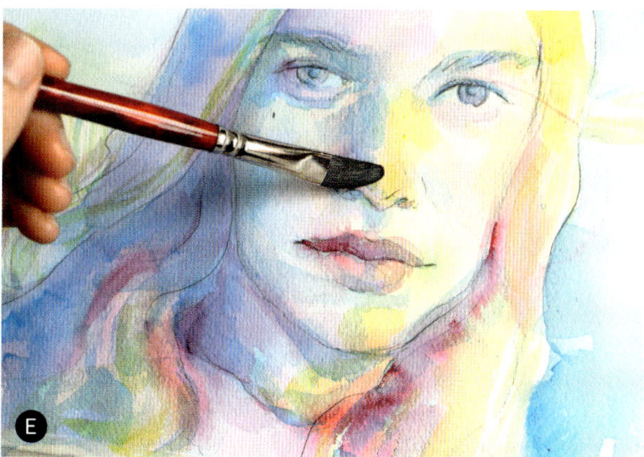

5. Let it dry again before continuing so the colors don't blend. Add a third layer of color with the Quinacridone Magenta in the intermediate shadow areas to pull the portrait together. (D)

6. Note how the sum of the three colors appears on the paper in green, violet, and orange hues.

7. Let it dry and repeat these steps as many times as you'd like, focusing on shadows or lights to create contrast in your portrait. (E)

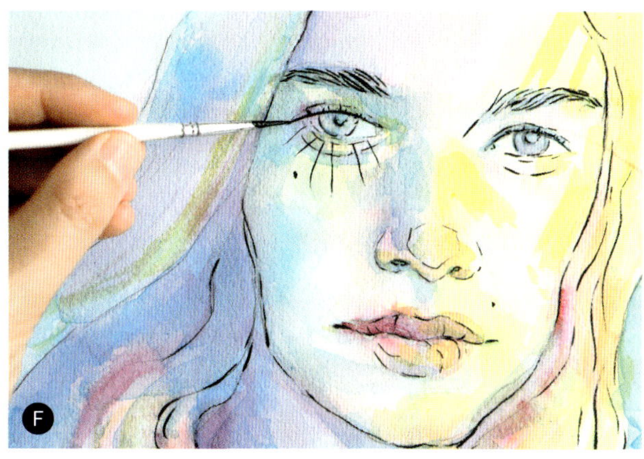

8. I added color to the background using the same shades.

9. When you're satisfied, let it dry. Then, using a very fine brush and India ink, trace over the outline of the drawing. This creates a very striking contrast between the transparency of the watercolor and the opacity of the India ink. Feel free to use any kind of stroke you'd like. Now, we have an amazing watercolor portrait with India ink! (F)

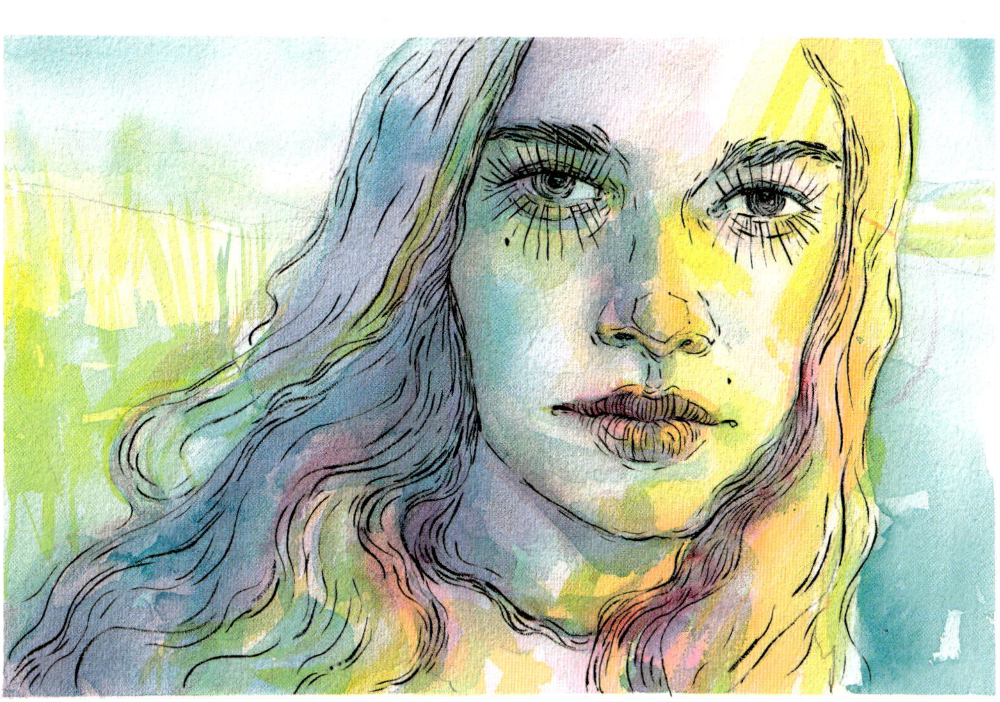

INK AND SECOND WATERCOLOR LAYER

Make sure that the ink you use is indelible and waterproof. Some inks are not permanent, and if you apply a layer of watercolor on top of them, everything can blur together and spoil your work. This portrait has several layers of watercolor, but remember, you can work with only one layer, and the result is just as valid!

1. Use a pencil to trace your portrait. (A)
2. Choose your brush—I used a fine-tipped brush to make very detailed and delicate lines. (B)
3. Once the ink dries, start adding the first washes of color for the general planes of color. (C)

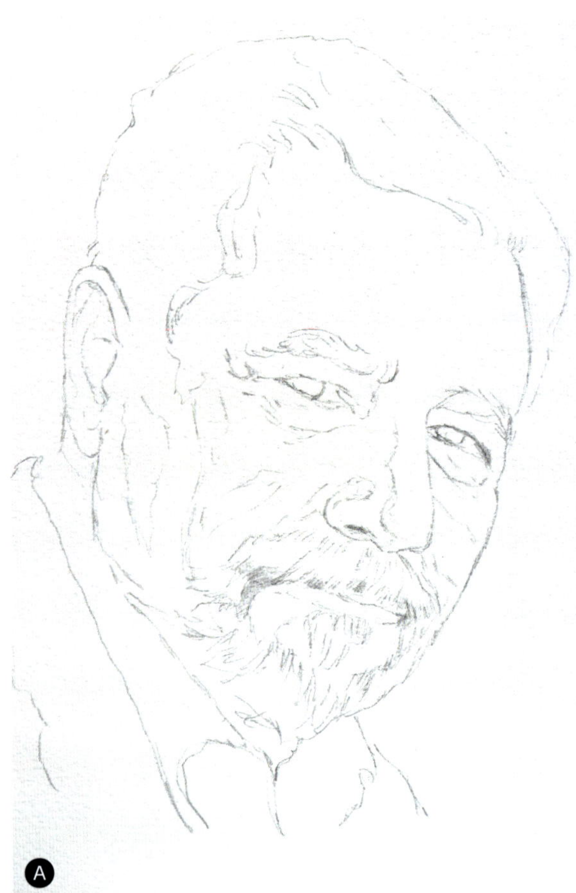

A

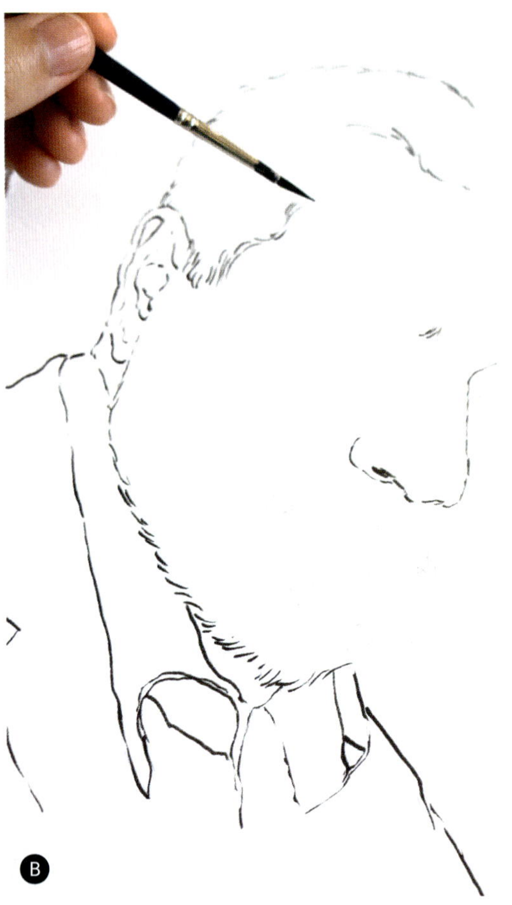

B

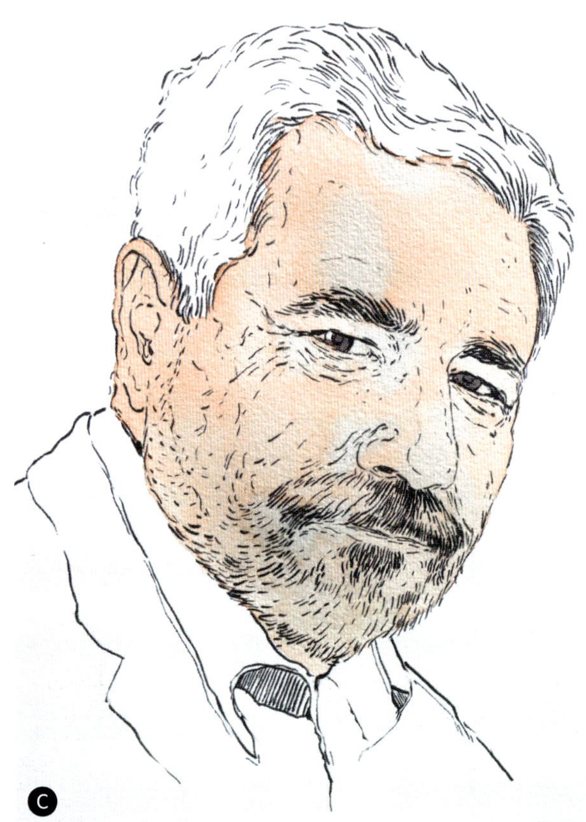

C

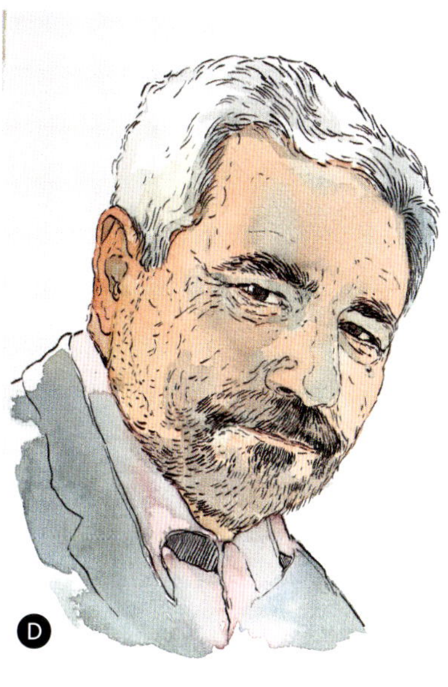

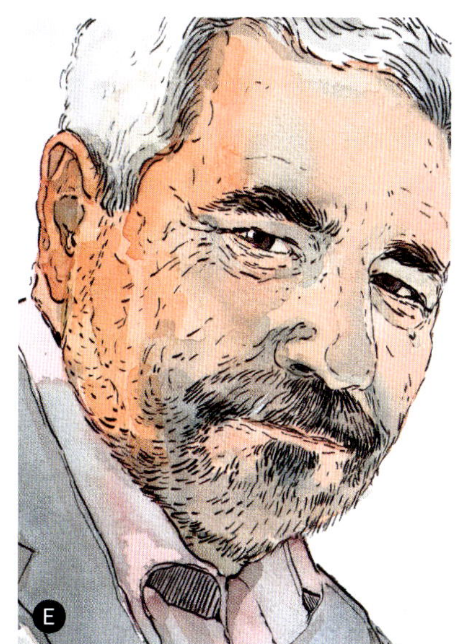

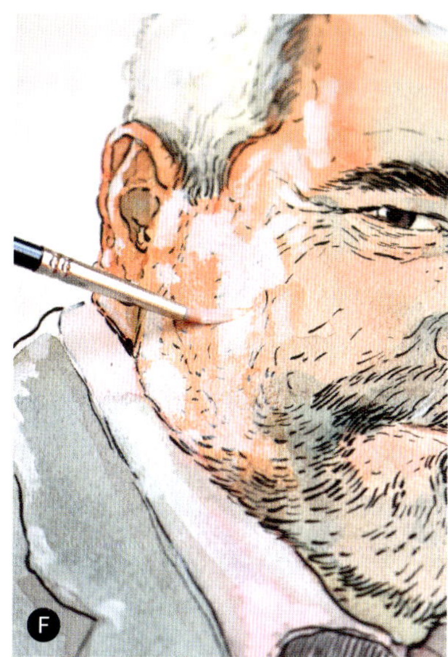

4. Wait for it to dry and then apply shadows to the face. I used a desaturated blue. (D)

5. If the portrait model was illuminated, apply bright color where you see highlights. I used orange. (E)

6. When the work is dry, focus on the details: paint the eyes, mouth, and any shadows for contrast if necessary.

7. After the watercolor is dry, you can apply gouache or white ink to the portrait. I used white ink and focused on adding points of light. With white ink, you can create relatively transparent glazes and then apply opaque white in the areas where you want it very white and to have a lot of light. (F)

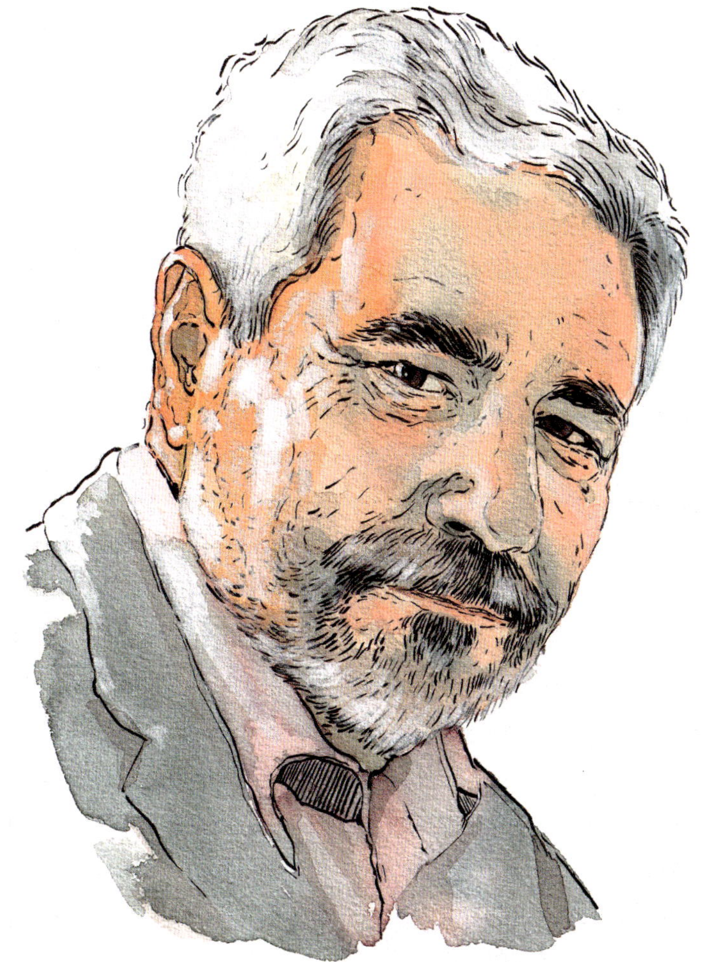

WET WATERCOLOR BASE AND BLENDED LIQUID INK

For this portrait, I chose a very simple example. We're going to work two layers, wet-on-wet. The first layer is painting the face with watercolor and then applying a second layer of ink before it dries. If you apply the ink while the watercolor is still wet, the ink will flow freely to create different shapes and textures. This is a good exercise to let yourself be surprised and not worry about making mistakes.

INDIA INK AND BLEACH

Here are some guidelines for working with bleach:

- Use old or cheap brushes because bleach ruins them. Make sure you designate a brush for bleach only and don't let it touch your watercolor palette or ink containers. If you need to add more color, use a different brush only for your paints and inks.
- Don't mix the bleach *on* your watercolor palette or *inside* an ink container. Use a separate, empty palette to mix colors or ink, making sure to add the colors first and then the bleach. That way, you'll be able to use the mixtures freely, without the fear of spoiling your materials or your paintings.
- Bleach "fades," so when you work it wet, it opens clearings in watercolor and certain calligraphy inks. But this doesn't work with all inks.
- If you use bleach with India ink, it has the effect of creating textures and condensing the ink in wet work. The ink will flow in a more controlled way with bleach than with water.

The following pages show some simple examples of portraits that incorporate bleach.

SAFETY NOTES!

Bleach is a chemical that you must be very careful using.

CAUTION: If you are a minor, only use bleach with adult supervision.

When you work with bleach, make sure you're in a well-ventilated space to avoid fumes.

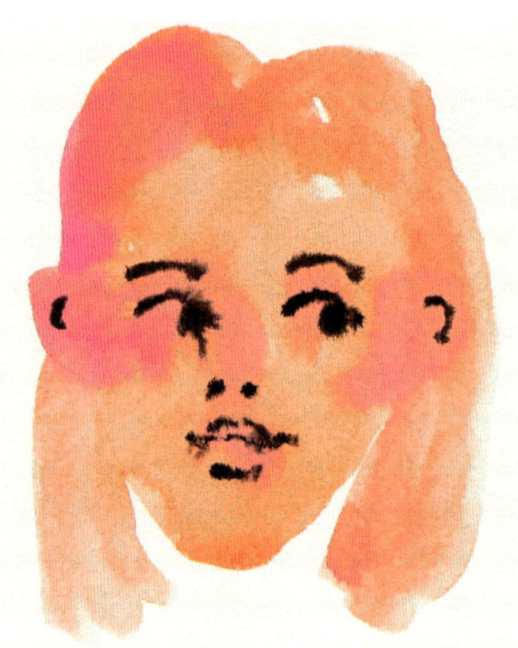

Ink and Bleach: Dry Paper

For this portrait, I used a mixture of ink and bleach.

I drew the main features very subtly with a hard pencil. In my palette, I mixed a transparent gray using ink and bleach (instead of water).

I wanted a very simple result. While I added the first layer of transparent ink in the shadows, I added pure ink with another brush and worked wet-on-wet, taking great care that the first layer didn't dry out.

Note how the ink dissolves in the more transparent first layer and the edges are diluted. If you do this with water, you will not have as much control. The ink flows into the water much more, and it's more difficult to control lines.

Little by little, I repeated this process for the rest of the face. I worked in sections to make sure that the first layer didn't dry out. I reserved the white of the paper in the light area of the face. This creates a strong light-dark contrast between the white of the paper and the black of the ink and makes for a very striking, forceful portrait.

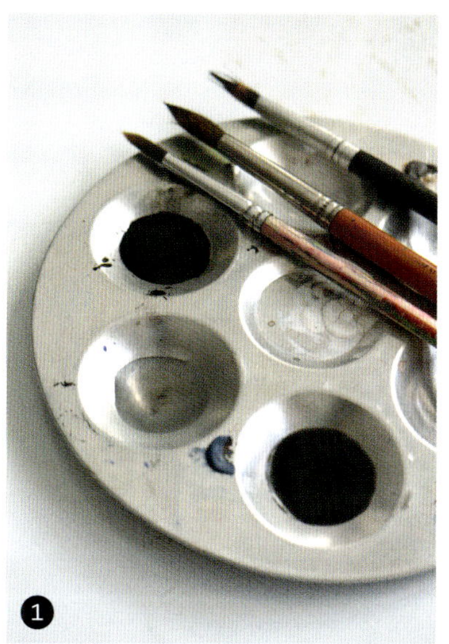
1

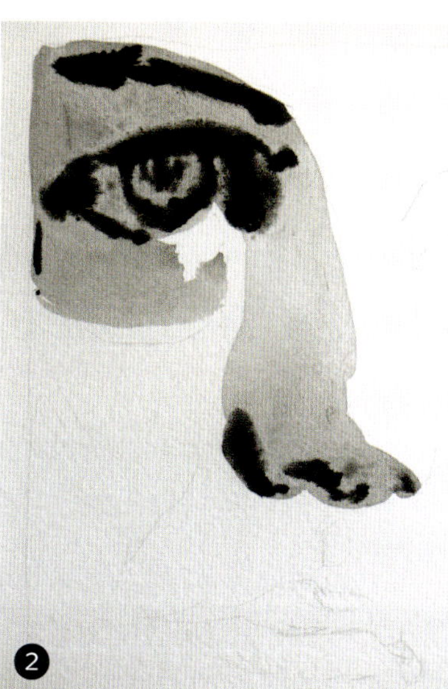
2

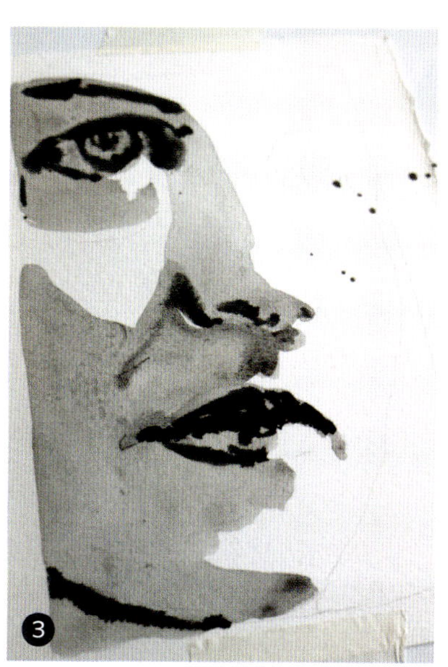
3

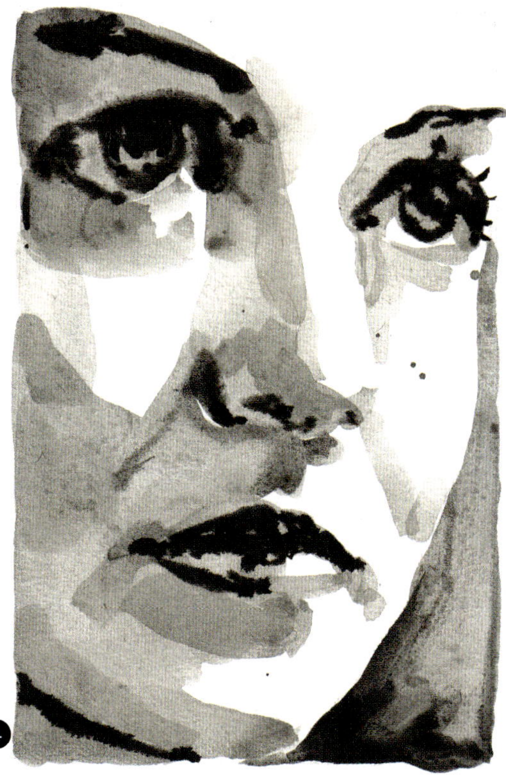
4

Ink, Bleach, and Colored Pencil

For this portrait, I again used a mixture of ink and bleach, but then I used colored pencils to add the details after it was dry.

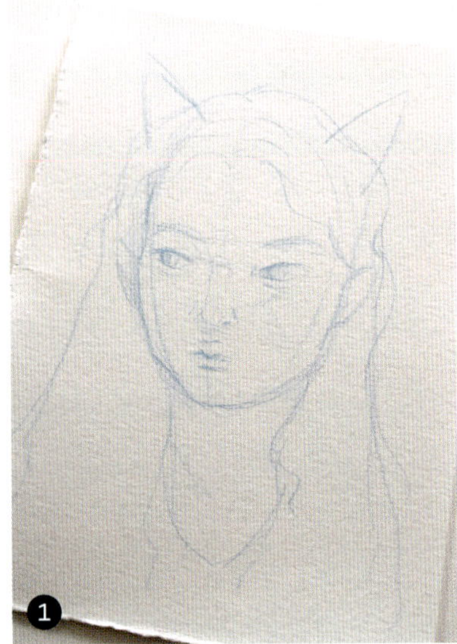

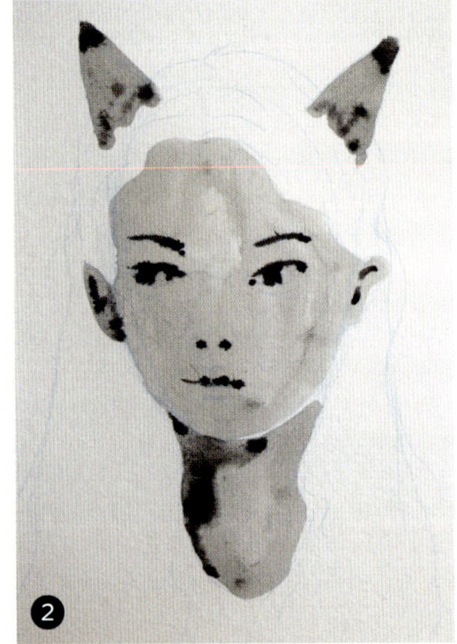

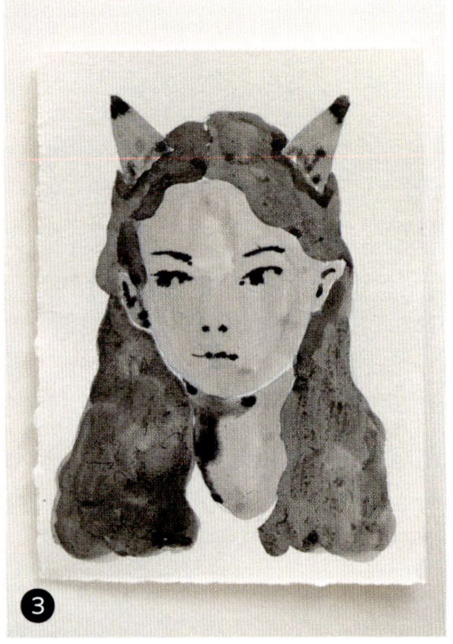

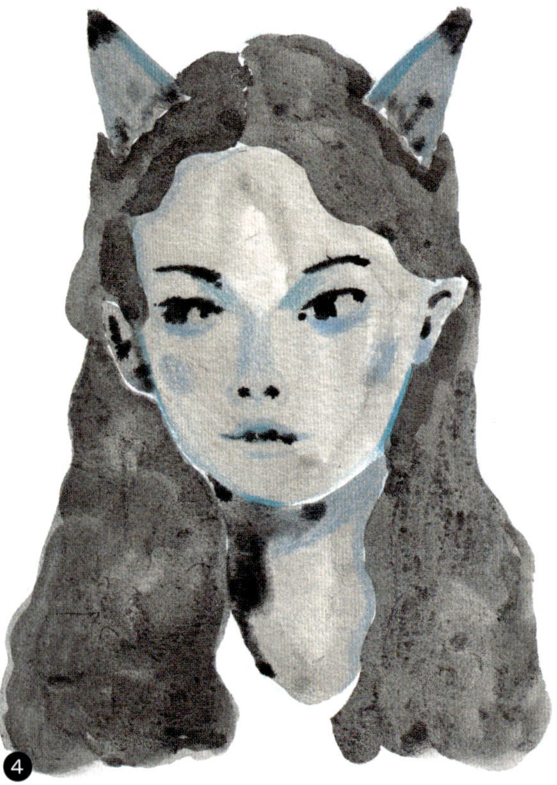

1. In this case, I drew the outline in blue pencil and designed a very simple face.
2. I painted an even, transparent layer in the area of the face and neck using ink diluted with bleach. Remember that the more bleach you use, the more transparent the ink will be. Before it dried, I used pure ink to trace the eyes, nose, mouth, ears, and a light shadow on the neck.
3. Once this layer dried, I mixed another gray hue in my palette with a little more bleach to create contrast for the face without using solid black. I added another layer to the hair. Once it dried, this created a very interesting grainy texture.
4. To add a special touch, I used the same blue pencil I used for the outline to add shading. You can use more colored pencils to finish adding detail to the portrait. Play around and have fun!

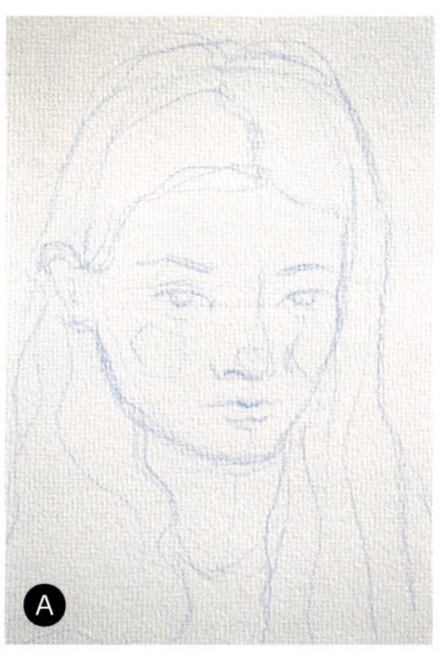

A

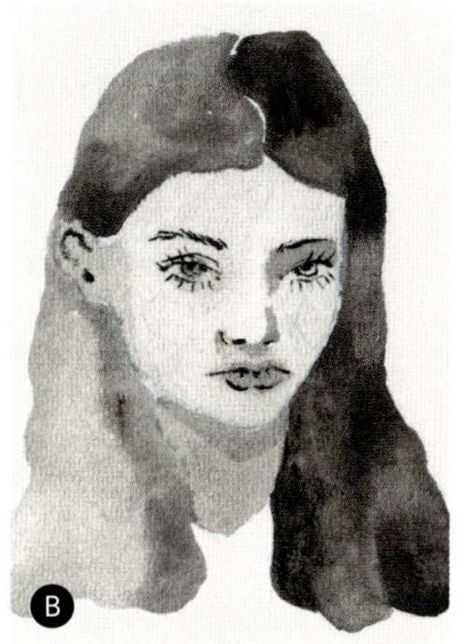

B

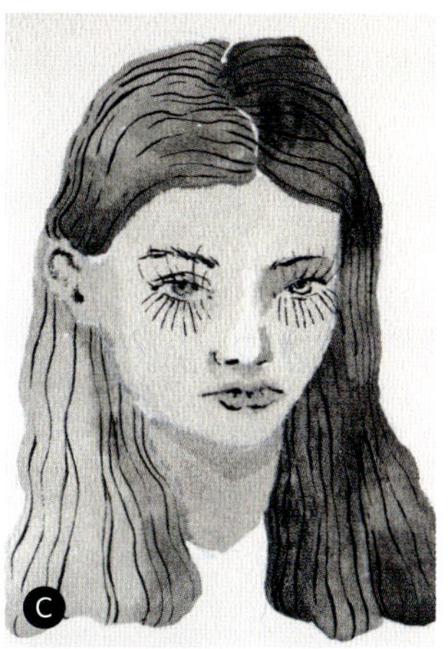

C

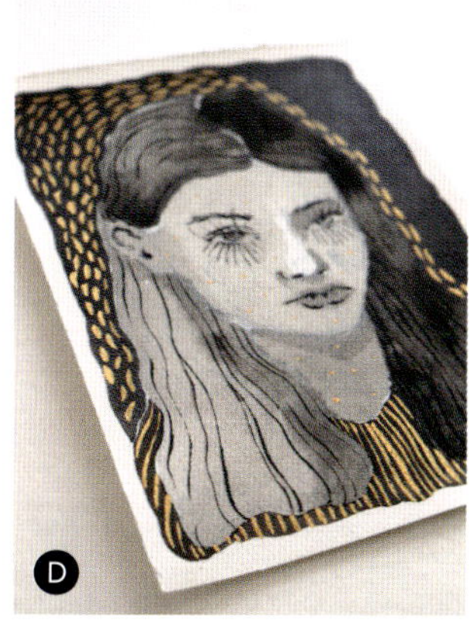

D

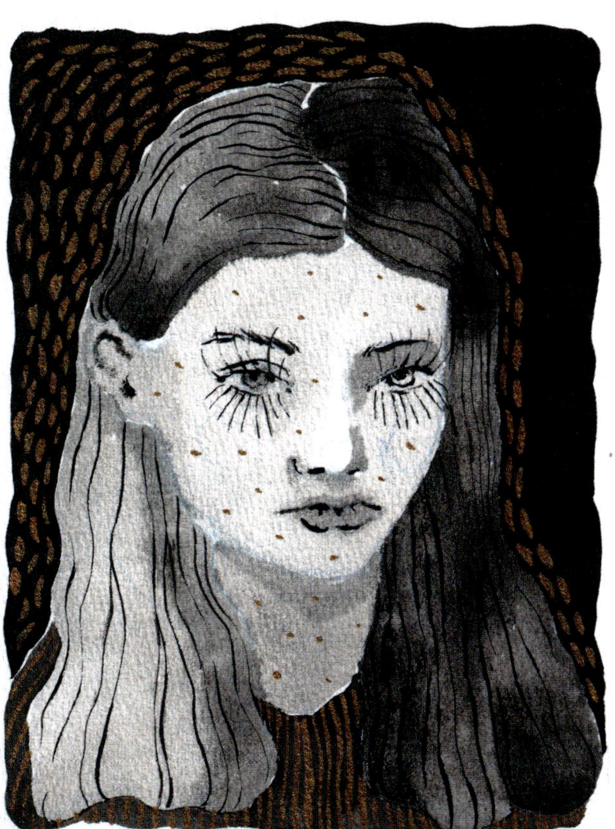

E

Ink, Bleach, and Metallic Watercolors: Wet-on-Dry

This portrait is similar to the previous one, but here, instead of tracing the details in wet-on-dry, the details of the face are dry, with some extra details in metallic watercolor.

1. Draw a simple outline. (A)
2. As in the previous example, paint the face evenly and let it dry before painting the hair. Let it dry again. (B)
3. Once these first layers have dried, you can use pure ink for the features of the face without fear of blending.
4. You can add texture to the hair by adding controlled, fine lines—or however you want! (C)
5. To add more contrast to the face, I used black ink for the background. This way, the light gray of the face projects forward. (D)
6. Finally, I used metallic watercolor for an extra touch and visual richness. I finished the composition using simple patterns of lines and dots. (E) Done! What do you think?

WATERCOLOR AND GOUACHE

For this portrait, we'll combine watercolor with white gouache to make light pastel tones and reduce some of the transparency of the watercolor, since gouache makes the color very opaque. We'll use just two layers of color: base and details.

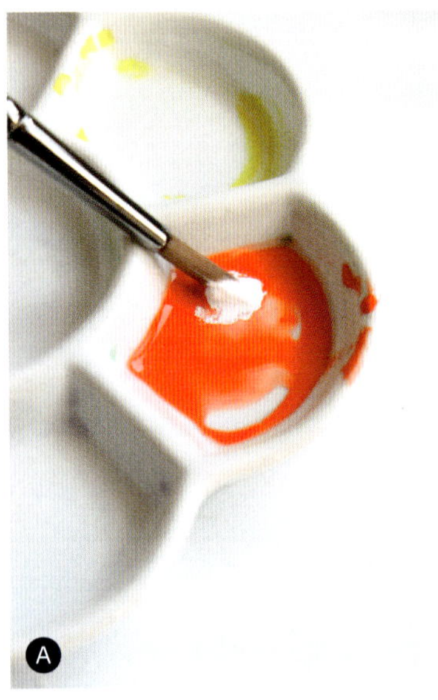
A

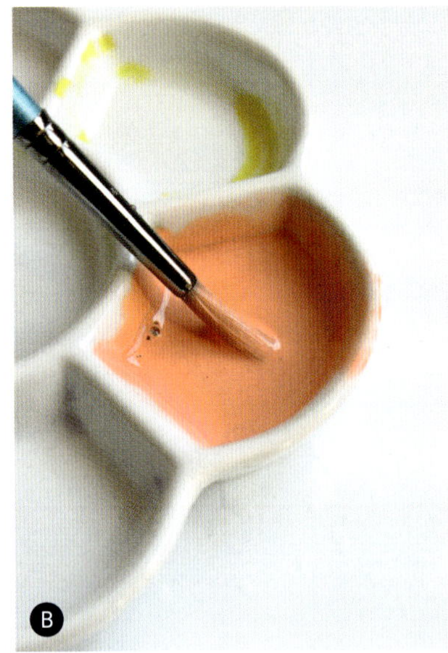
B

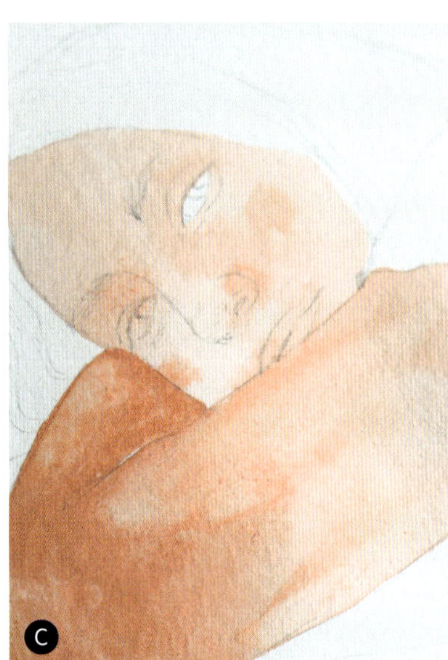
C

1. Draw the outline of your model either from a reference or from your imagination.
2. Prepare the colors in your palette. In this case, for the skin tone, I mixed red watercolor with white gouache. Remember to keep scrap paper on hand for testing colors. (A, B)

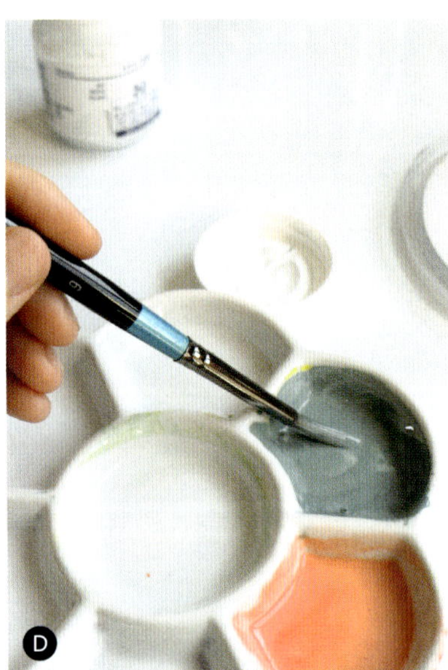
D

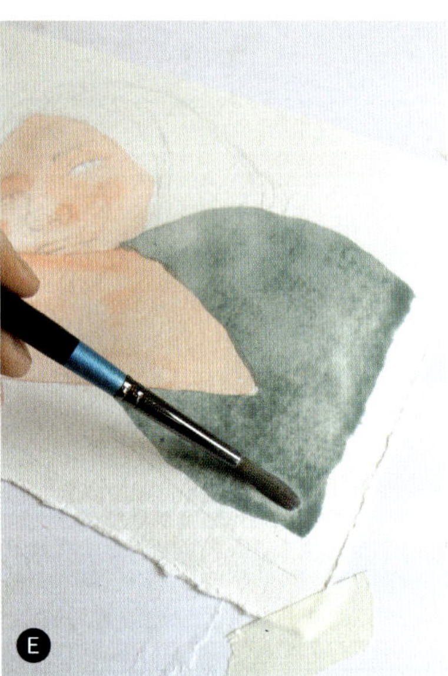
E

3. I painted a base color on the face and arm. I started the brushstroke at the elbow, where it appears darker, and lightened it with water as I went. I added a touch for a shadow so it would blend with the background (wet-on-wet). And I added other shadows once this layer was totally dry. Look closely at the second layer where I added shading and volume: there are both soft and hard strokes. (C)
4. The next color I chose was green, and as before, I added white gouache for a pastel green. I used this mix to paint the shirt evenly and then let it dry. (D, E)

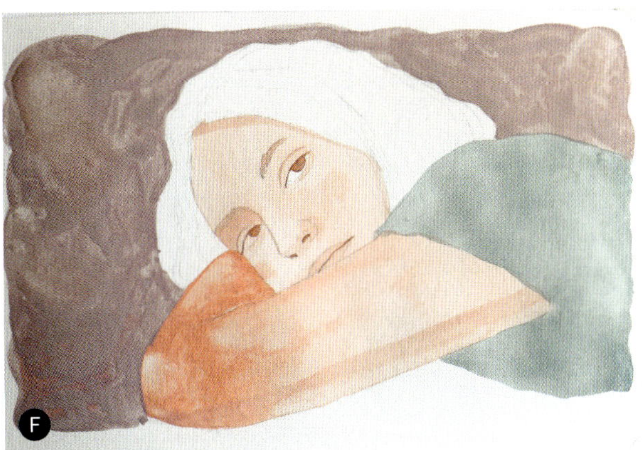

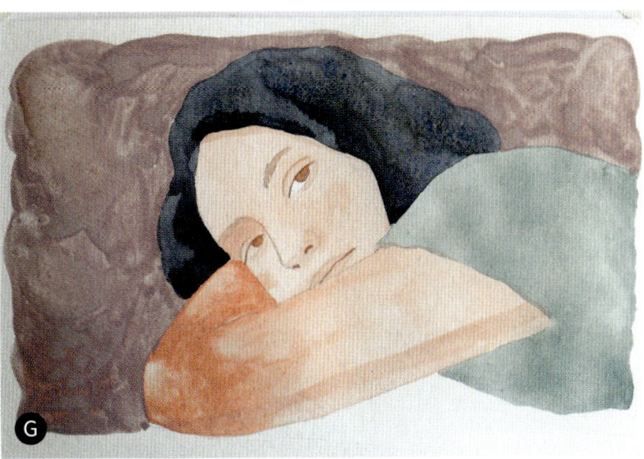

5. For the background, I repeated the same step with another color and painted it in an even layer. I like the textures that were created. (F)

6. Make sure that the face is dry before adding detail or shadows to dark areas: eyes, lips, and nose. While that's drying, you can paint the hair. (G)

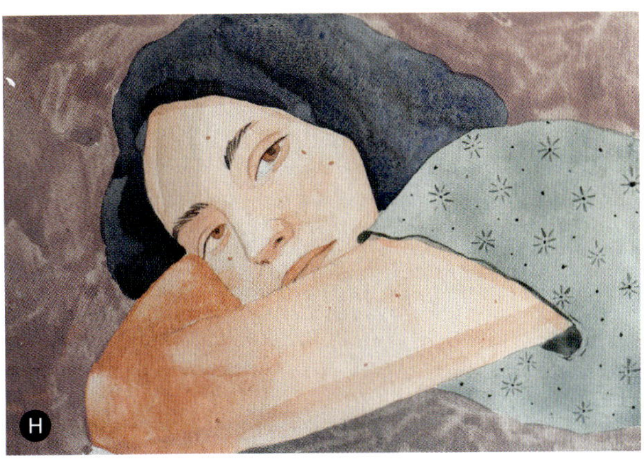

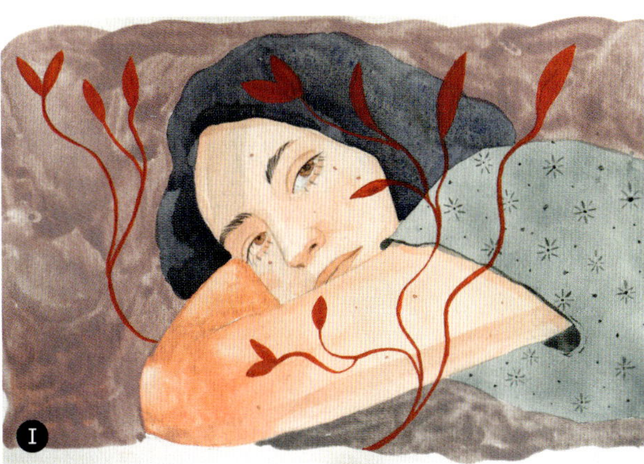

7. Now, we have a portrait that we can consider finished—a simple and clean portrait. But we can also add some extra details! You might want to highlight certain points even more with additional layers of color, add shadows, or create a pattern on the shirt. (H)

8. I wanted to add something else. I used a charcoal pan watercolor with red watercolor (very similar to the gouache result) for an organic element in the foreground. I chose this type of paint because if you use a wet brush directly on the pan, it creates a very powerful, opaque color. These types of exercises are small experiments. Try new things and play around! (I)

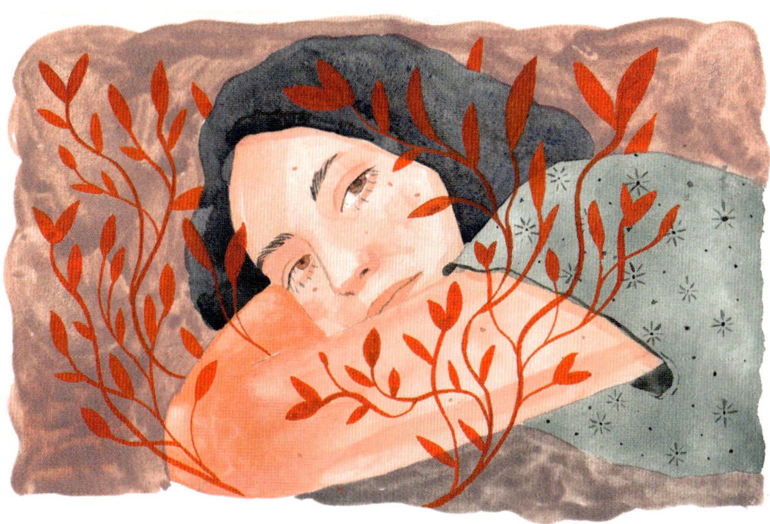

WATERCOLOR AND COLORED PENCILS

This portrait is one of my favorites: painting with watercolor and then highlighting areas with colored pencils.

I use many layers to give shape and volume, but you can use as many as you want. One or two layers is also enough.

This technique creates beautiful, contrasting textures between the softness and transparency of watercolor and the opacity and rough texture of the pencils.

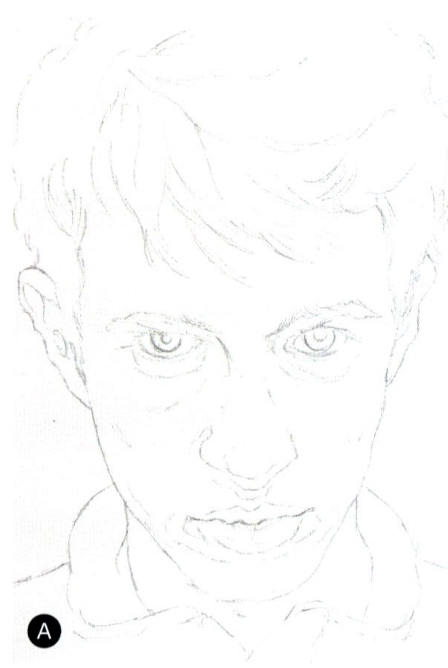

A

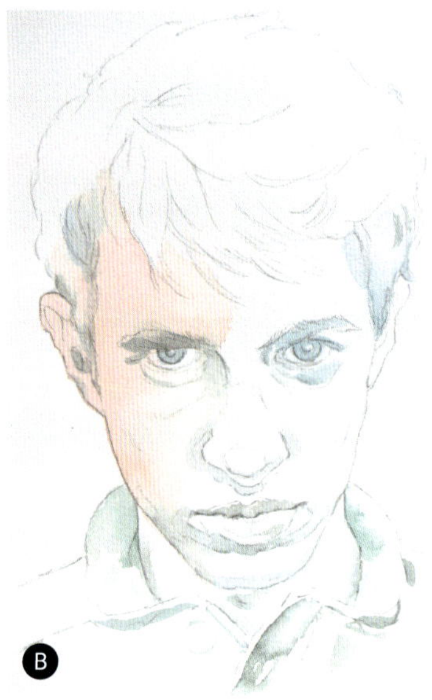

B

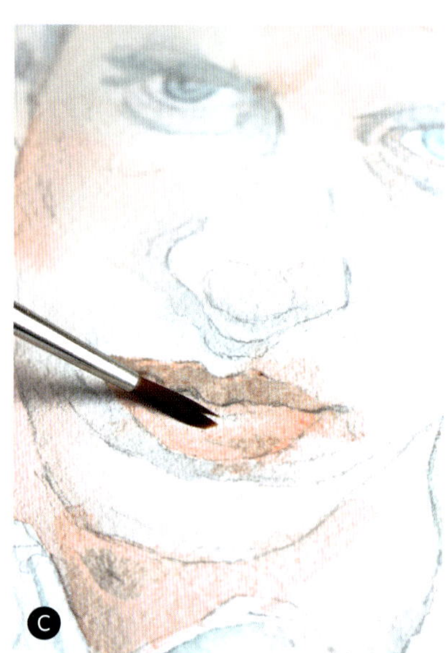

C

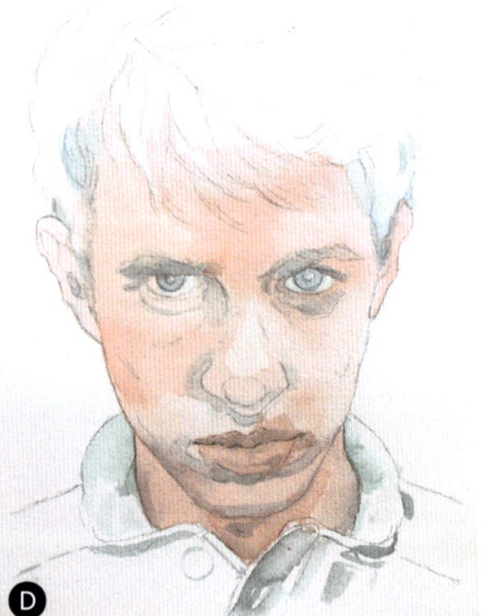

D

1. Use a pencil to gently trace the outline and main lines. (A)
2. Apply a base layer where you will place the shadows. I usually use blue because it's the darkest on the color wheel, but choose another color if you want to try new possibilities.
3. While this layer dries, prepare the skin tones on your palette. Keep scrap paper on hand to mix colors and make sure you're satisfied with them. (B)
4. Apply the second layer of color, taking care to reserve the white of the paper. (C)
5. Apply a third layer of color, varying the skin tone a little to add a greater richness of color to the face. If the previous layer was more pink, make the color brighter by adding a little yellow to it. You can use this color in the brightest areas. (D)

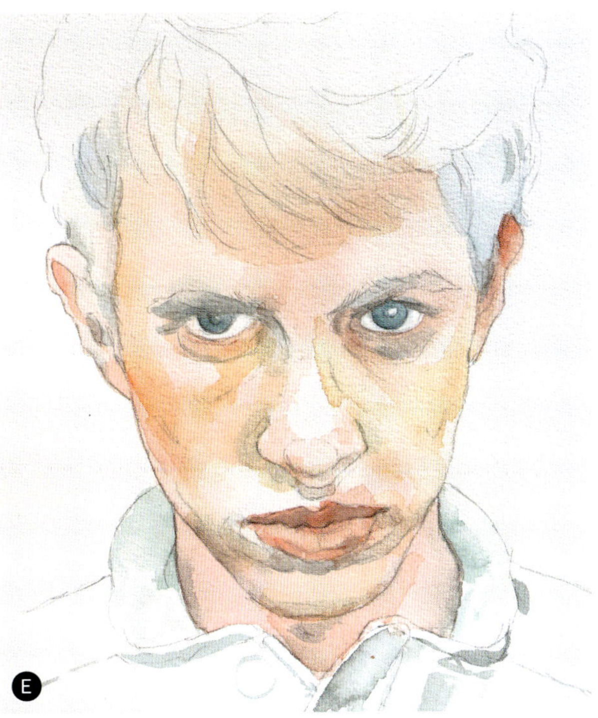

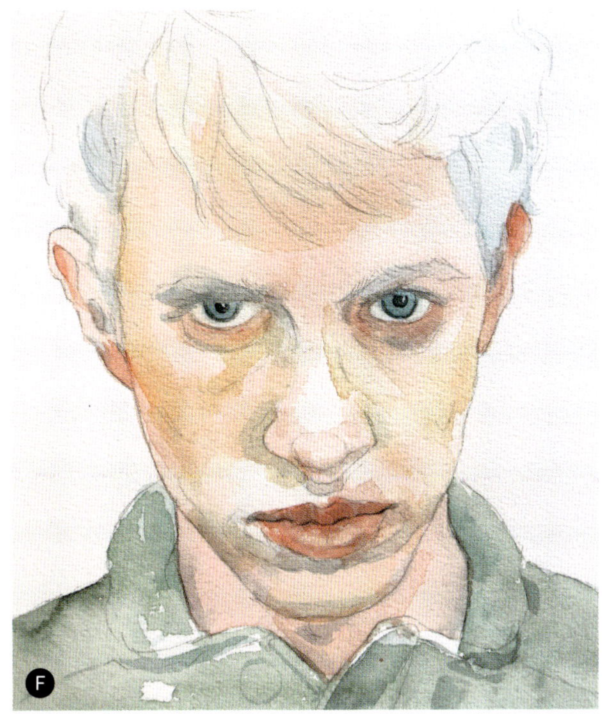

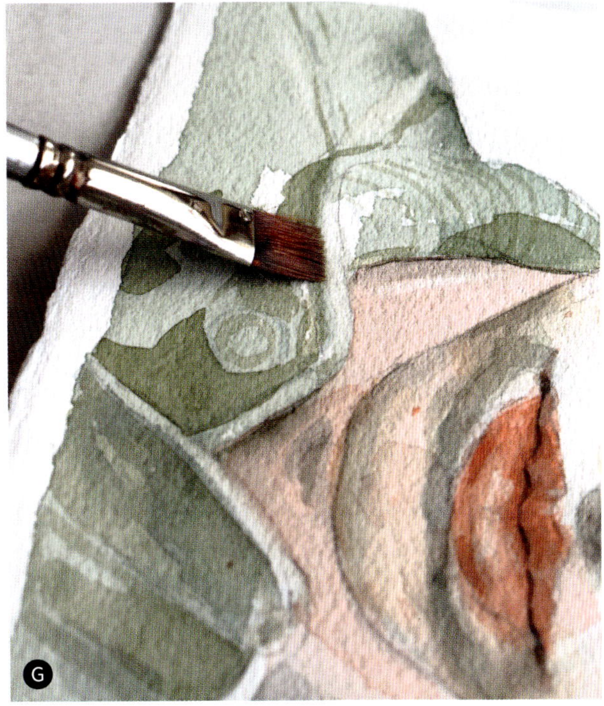

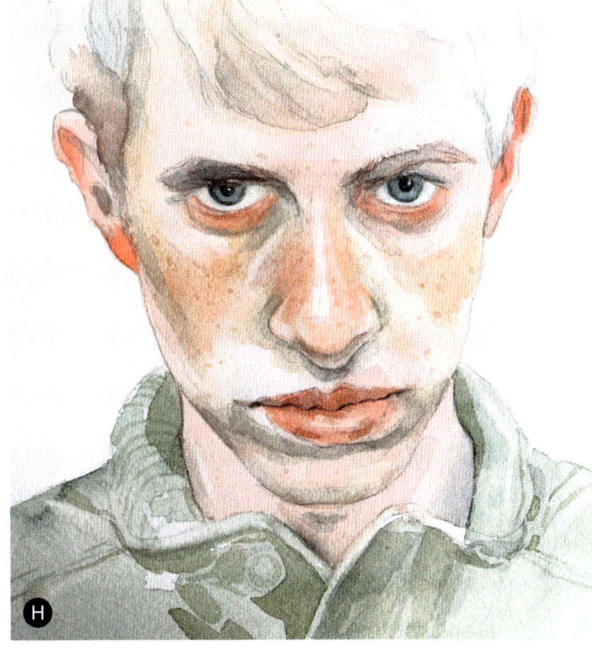

6. For the following layers of color, create the shadows and darker areas to give volume and contrast to the highlights and shadows. Remember that the layering of very transparent layers creates glazes and darkens an area. If you reserve other areas and leave them unpainted, you'll have more light from the paper. (E)

7. For the shirt, use the same technique, from a general and transparent wash of color to a second layer with shadows adding contrast. (F)

8. *When the watercolor is dry, you can recover light areas from the paper. To do this, choose a brush with stiff bristles, wet it with clean water, and scrape it over where you want to recover the white of the paper.* (G, H)

(*continued*)

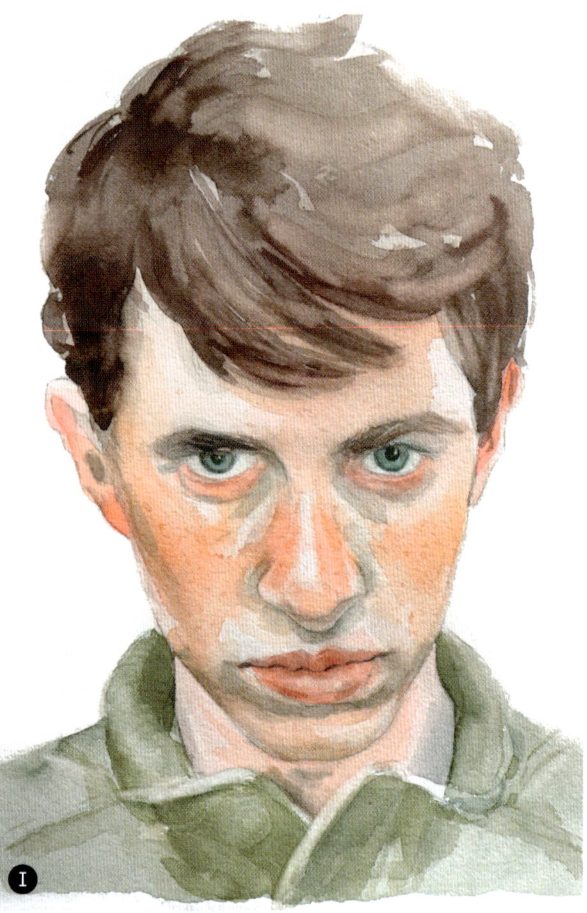

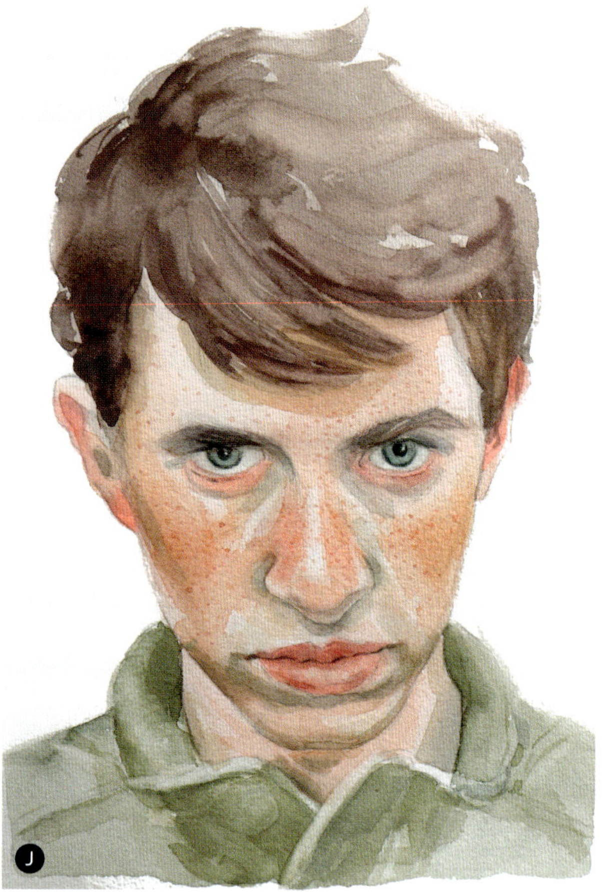

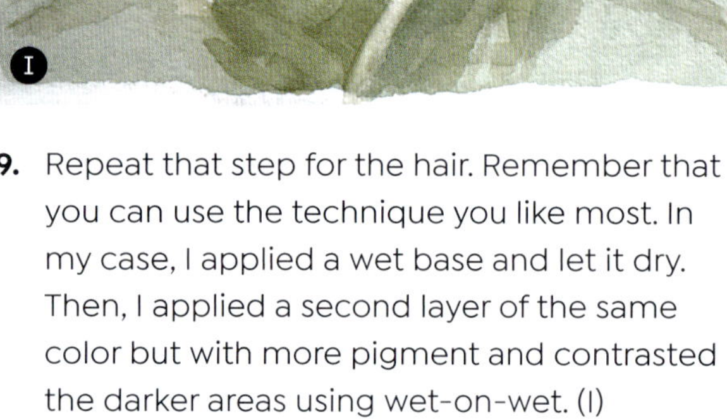

9. Repeat that step for the hair. Remember that you can use the technique you like most. In my case, I applied a wet base and let it dry. Then, I applied a second layer of the same color but with more pigment and contrasted the darker areas using wet-on-wet. (I)

10. Use watercolor to apply the last details you want to highlight and let it dry. (J)

11. Choose your colored pencils. It's best that they work with the hues in the watercolor. Add shading and detail wherever you'd like. In this example, I highlighted some areas more intensely and with more saturation, detailing the eyes and completing the shirt collar with a lined pattern. (K)

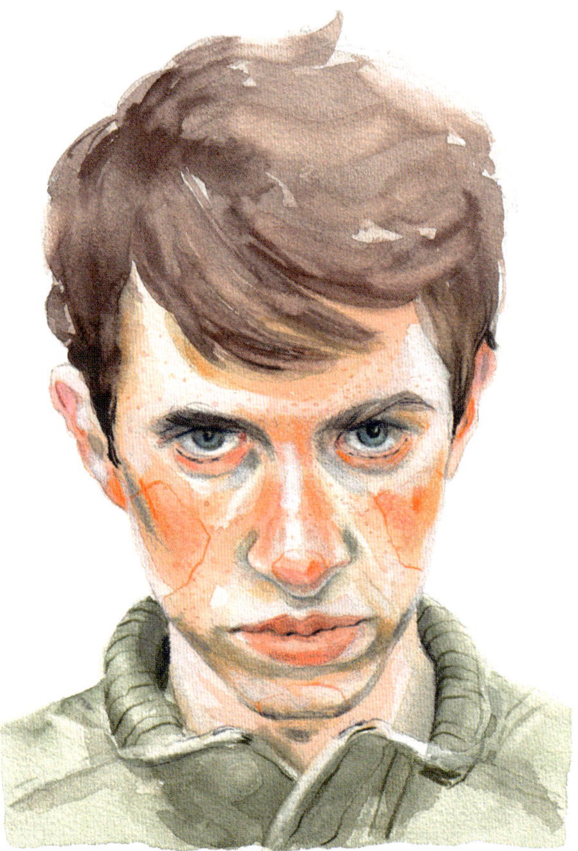

WATERCOLOR AND CHARCOAL

This technique is similar to Watercolor and Pencil (see page 90), so you can review that lesson for a refresher on the concept. Here is a brief, simple portrait.

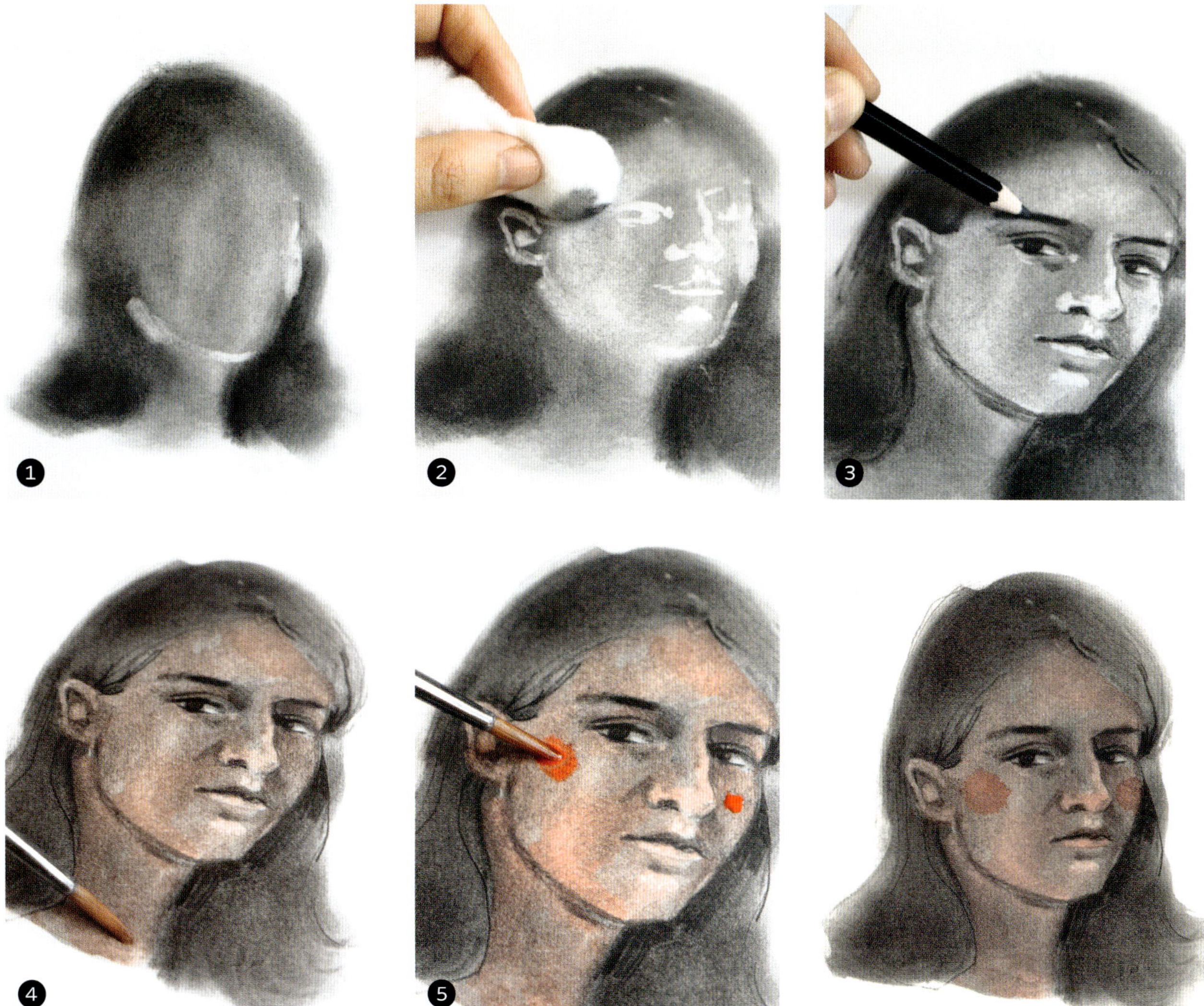

1. I drew a small face freehand from my imagination. I used charcoal powder to shade the whole face. To create this powder, gently scrape a charcoal with a box cutter or scissors and collect the falling dust in a small container.
2. Use a soft cotton ball and a kneaded eraser to pick up the charcoal and create a shape for the head.
3. Create more contrast with shadows around the eyes, nose, mouth, and hair. Use a fixative to set the charcoal and wait for it to dry fully.
4. Gently paint a wet layer of watercolor that's transparent enough for the charcoal to show through.
5. Apply as many layers as you think are necessary.

METALLIC WATERCOLOR

For this portrait, we'll use metallic watercolors and large sections of flat color. Choose where you want to apply the metallic watercolor. In this case, I wanted the hair to be prominent, and I designed a pattern for the clothes.

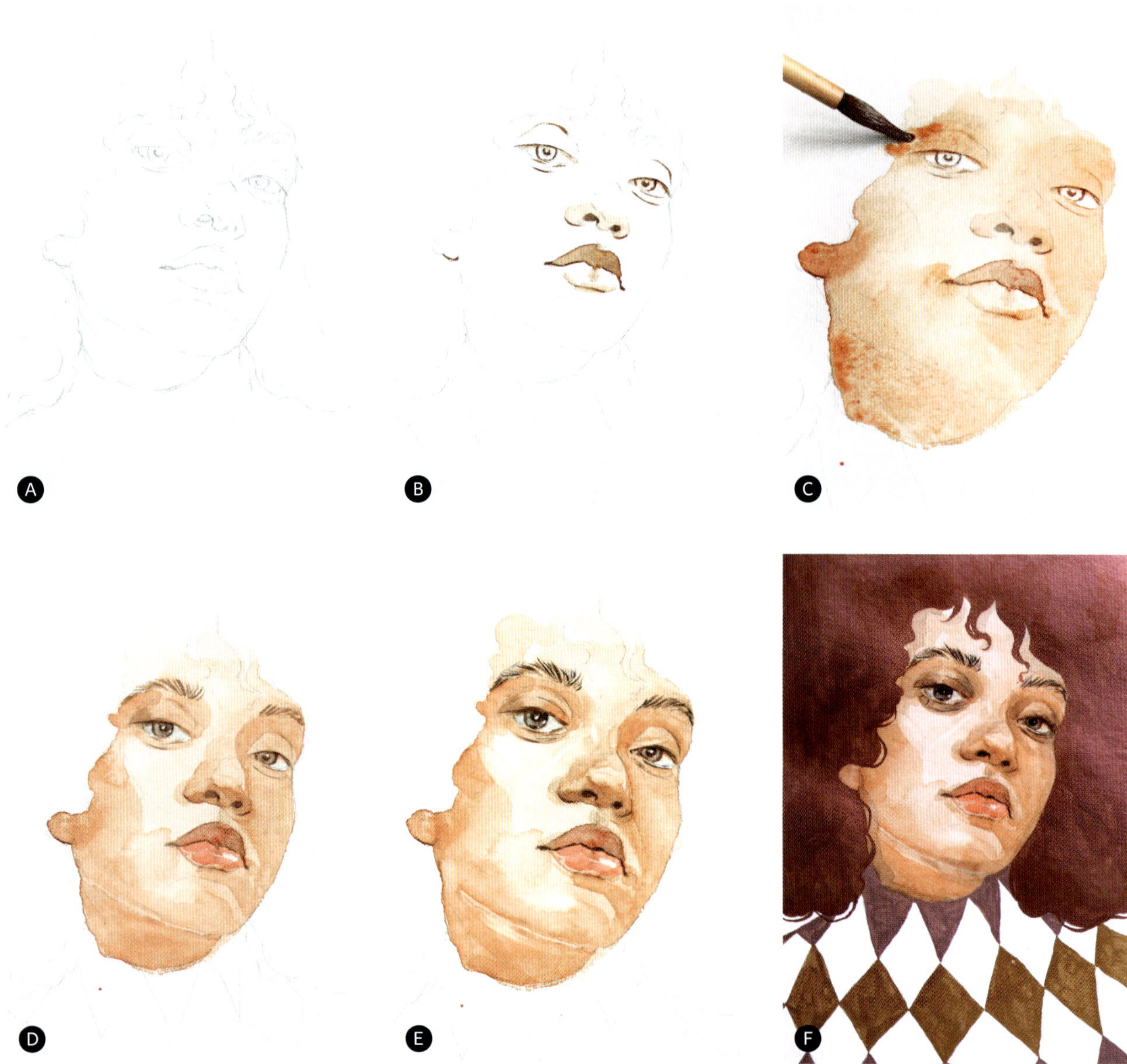

1. Sketch your model with a 2H pencil or similar. (A)
2. Paint the face in layers. The first layer is a general layer with a wet stroke using a round brush that holds a lot of water and paint. (B, C)
3. Once this layer dries, apply another layer of the same color, adding shadows to give volume to the face. Repeat this process as many times as you want. (D)
4. Apply details and contrast in the darker areas around the eyes, nose, and mouth. (E)
5. Last, add the metallic watercolors in the areas you decided on. (F)

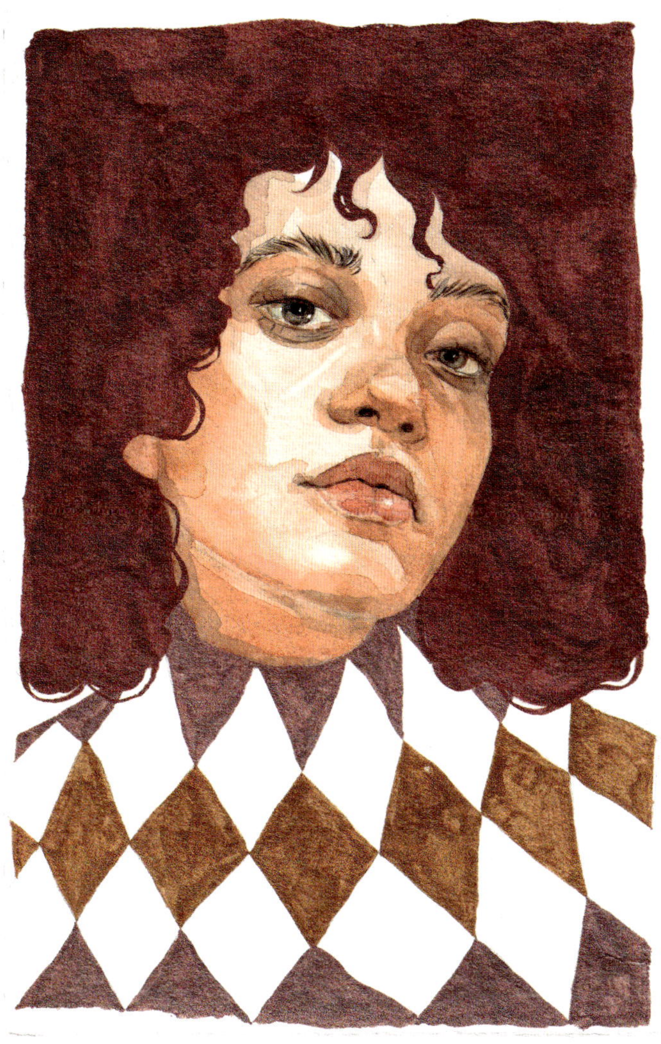

The final result is surprising and very sensational! I love it.

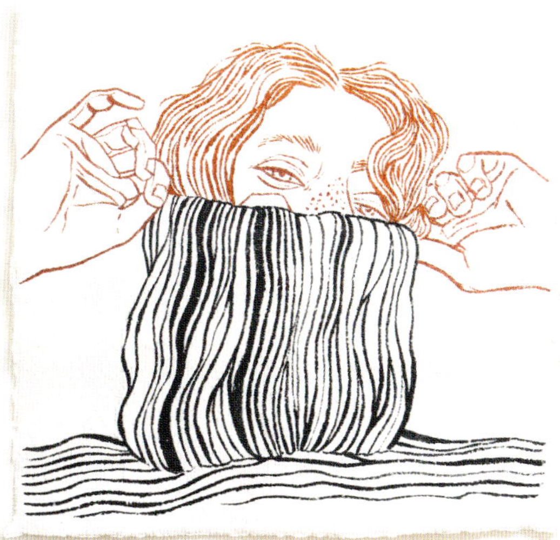

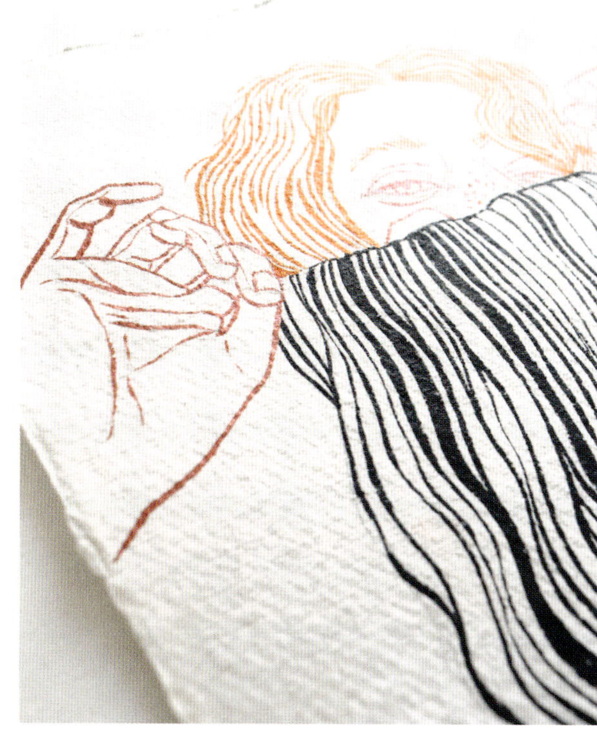

Here is another example using metallic watercolor but with precise and delicate lines. It's a very simple exercise with a beautiful result. Sometimes, less is more. The paper I chose for this project was square with a lot of grain.

WATERCOLOR: RANDOM GRADIENTS

Let's make a portrait with gradient colors. With this technique, it's a good idea to choose your colors and prepare them in your palette. We'll work quickly because we don't want the paper to dry out. This beautiful and surprising technique involves making color gradients and allowing them to blend together, so it's important that the paper stay wet.

If you don't prepare all of your colors beforehand, the paper can dry out while you're preparing your next color, and you won't achieve the desired effect.

This exercise adds spontaneity, daring, and surprise to our work!

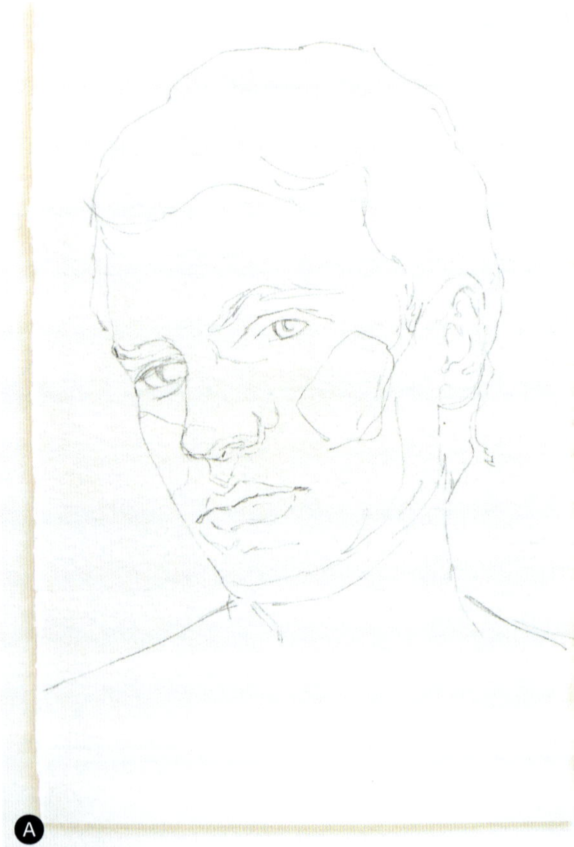

A

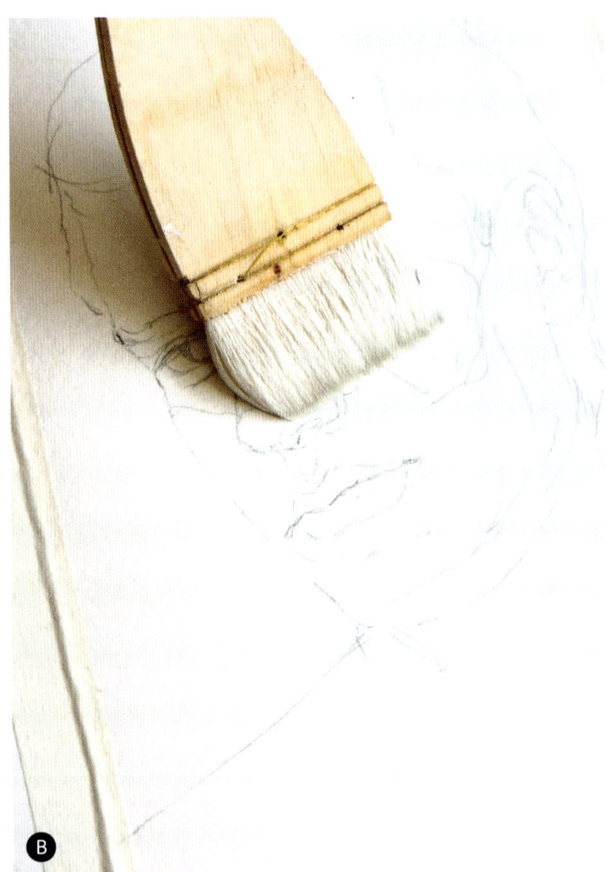

B

1. Choose your reference model and sketch it with pencil. If you want the drawing to be more noticeable in the final product, use a softer pencil (B, 2B, etc.) or draw it in colored pencil. (A)
2. Attach the edges of the paper to a board (cardboard or wood) with masking tape. This will prevent the paper from buckling once it's dry since we're going to use a lot of water.
3. Using a high-numbered brush, wet the entire paper with clean water. This will let the ink and paint mix randomly. (B)
4. It's important to have two water containers: one for clean water and one to clean your brush.

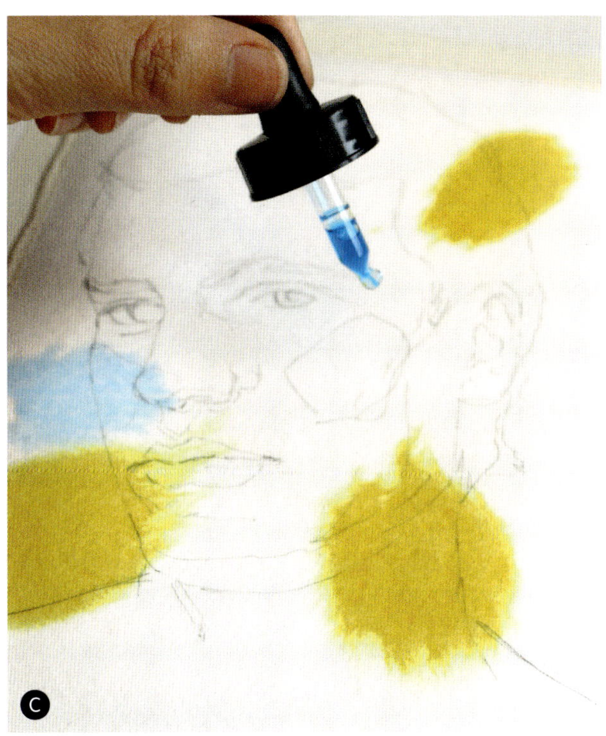

C

5. Go ahead and use your intuition to apply ink and paint using a dropper. You can use bright colors for light areas and darker colors for shadows or surprise yourself and don't think about it too much. (C)

6. Don't get scared when the first layer is still wet and the colors are "scrambled." Once dry, the watercolor settles and creates unexpected gradients and textures. Let the colors flow! (D)

7. Once the layer is dry, apply details to call out the features. Personally, I liked the result without adding many more layers, so I kept it simple, but like everything, keep working as much as you want. (E)

tip

I used Schmincke Tundra Violet for the shadows. Some watercolors have very interesting qualities. The resulting color isn't flat, but instead has texture to it. Although these paints are more expensive, you might want to invest in a few to give a special touch to your paintings.

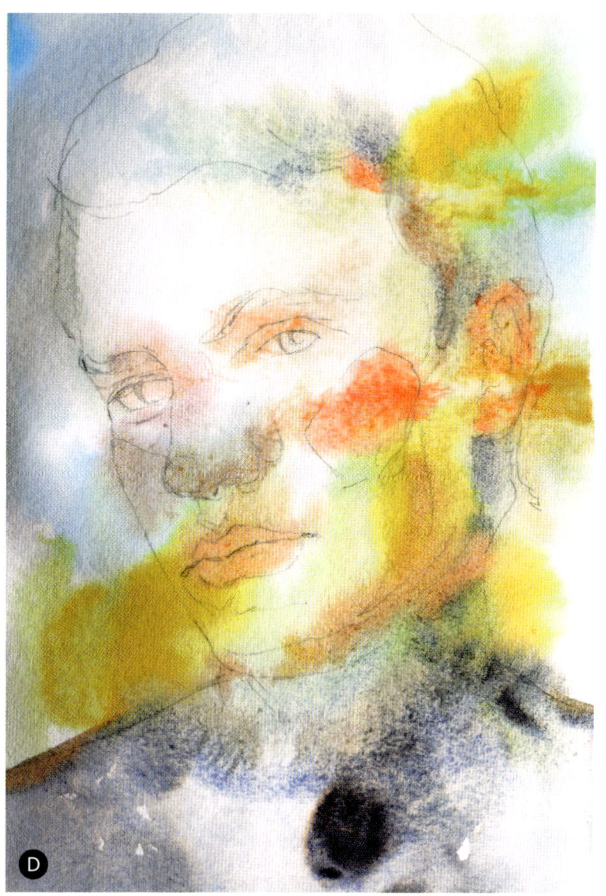

D

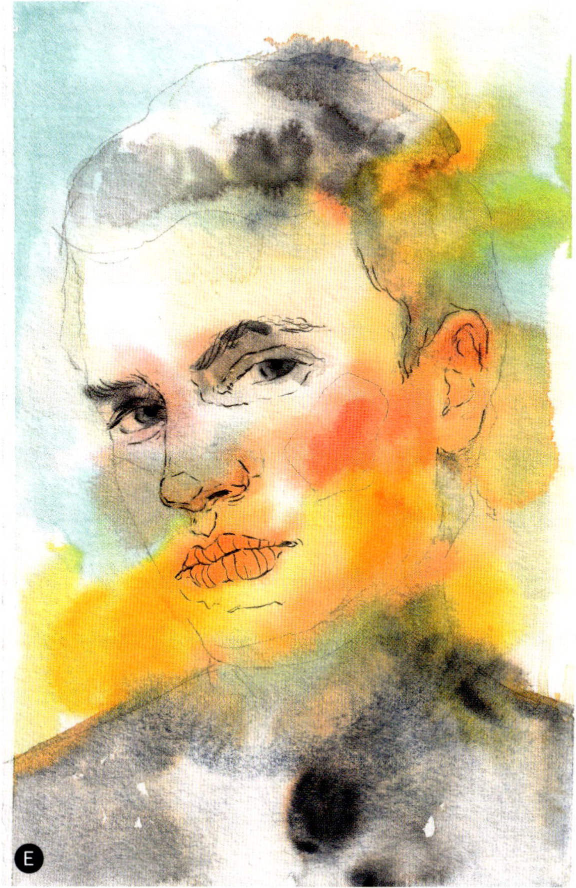

E

WATERCOLOR AND PEN

Who doesn't make doodles with their pen while talking on the phone?

A technique that I like and find very relaxing is drawing in pen—not only because of the characteristic blue ink but for the infinite strokes and different results that can be achieved. You can make loose, messy, or nervous strokes or more delicate and clean strokes. The choice depends on your own taste and ability. Practice making different patterns, shades, and volumes, starting with simpler things.

Because we'll be working with watercolor, it's important to choose a paper that will support the wetness of the watercolor and also allow you to work well with pen. Rough paper will give you a different result from a soft and smooth paper, which will allow the pen to flow better.

WHAT YOU'LL NEED

- For this technique, it's essential that you have a piece of scrap paper to clean the tip of the pen and remove excess ink that accumulates while drawing. If you don't clean the tip of the pen, too much ink can be transferred to your drawing, creating a stained area and breaking up the visual harmony.
- It's also helpful to have another sheet of paper available to cover what you've drawn and to rest your hand on to keep your drawing clean.

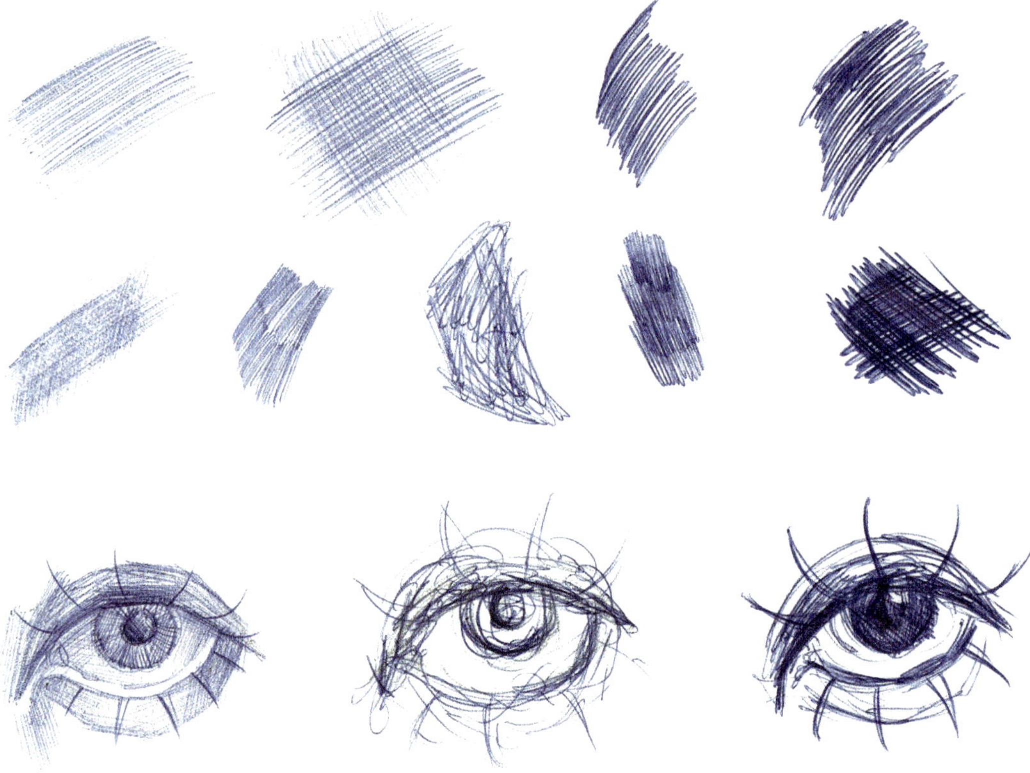

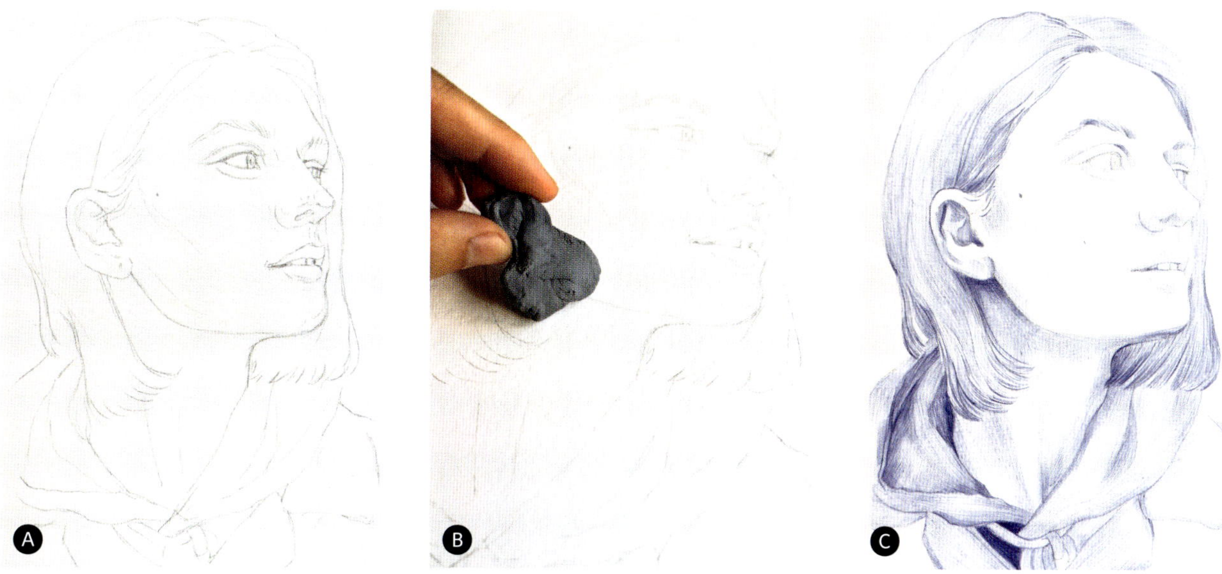

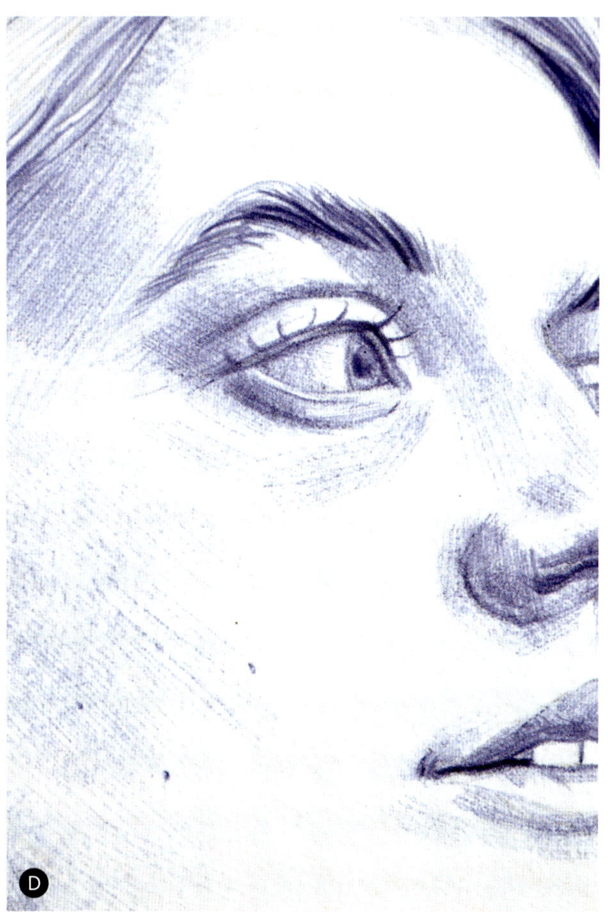

SEQUENCE OF WORK

Personally, I like to go from the general to the particular. Others prefer to shade everything by areas, moving from one area to the next. It's up to you and how you work better. Going from larger to smaller helps me to see the drawing in its entirety, and it's easier for me to work in layers and end by adding contrast and shadows.

1. Start by using a hard pencil to make a sketch. Avoid pressing too hard on the paper. (A)
2. Before you start with the pen, use an eraser to remove any excess pencil, just enough so that you see the drawing but it's not too heavy. (B)
3. Gradually draw the lines and fill in with even patterns. (C)
4. The degree of contrast depends on your taste. The more layers of pen you apply, the darker it will be. (D)
5. Once you've traced your portrait in pen, let it fully dry before applying watercolor.

(*continued*)

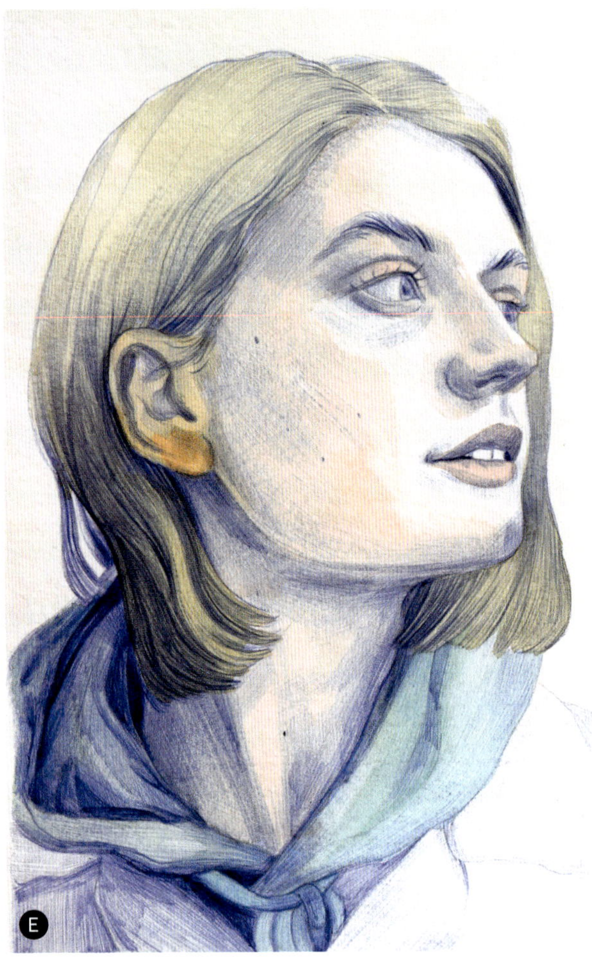

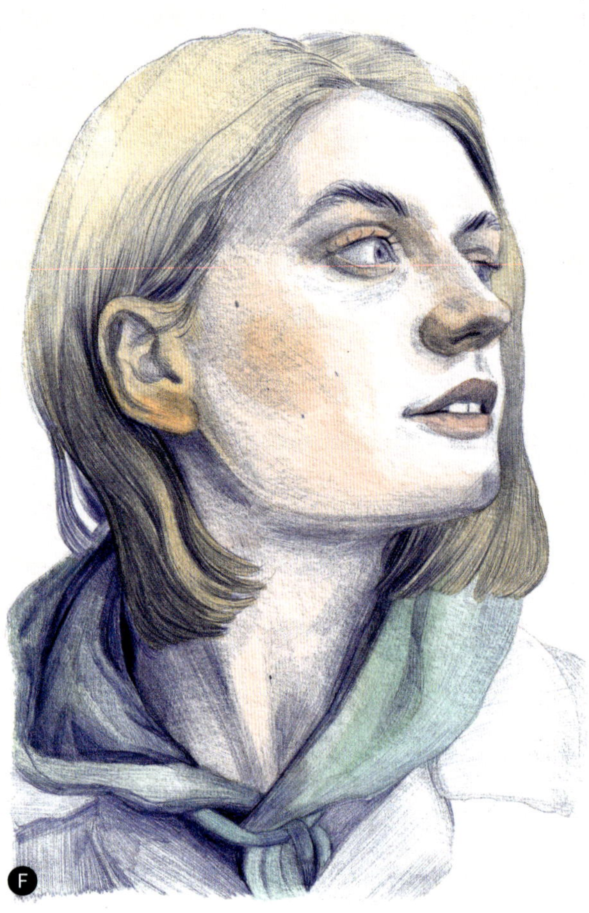

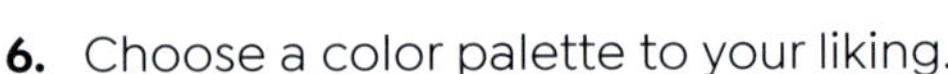

6. Choose a color palette to your liking.
7. Paint each part of the portrait with an even, transparent wash. Let each part dry before working the one next to it so the colors don't mix. In this case, I painted the face first, let it dry, and then painted the hair, and so on. (E)
8. Once the first color layer was dry, I applied a second layer, highlighting the eyes, nose, mouth, cheekbones, and ear. (F)

Because I really like the pen color, I didn't want to use too much watercolor, so I chose to apply only two very transparent layers.

ANOTHER WATERCOLOR + PEN TECHNIQUE

To create a different result, paint first with watercolor and then shade with a pen. The pen will be clearer. This is a matter of personal preference!

CREATING LIGHTS WITH MASKING FLUID

For this portrait, we'll use the masking fluid to reserve small points of light from the paper and be able to use washes of color without fear of making mistakes.

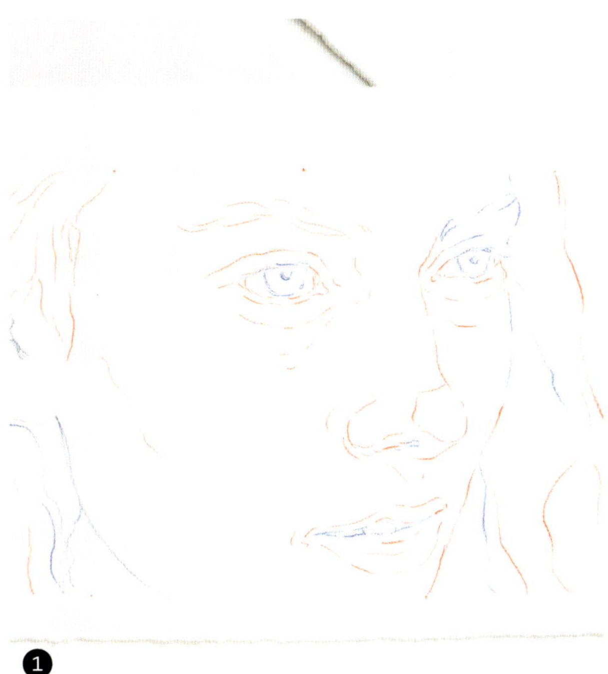

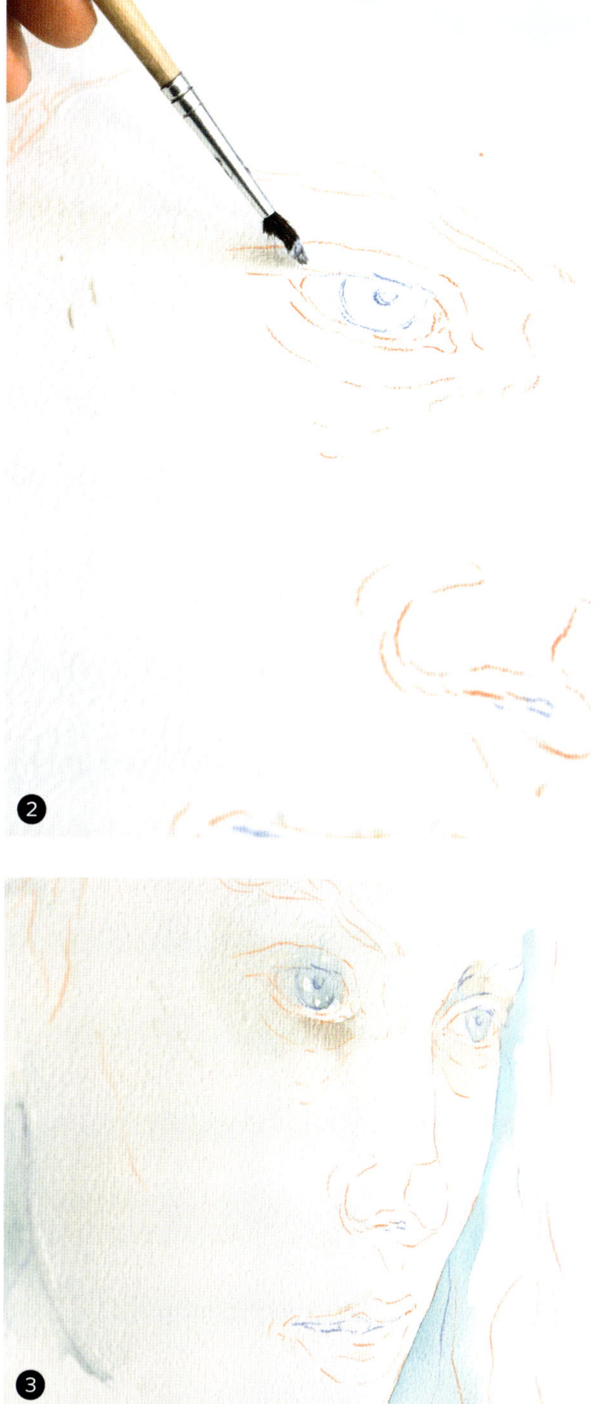

1. I traced the main outline with two colored pencils: blue and orange. These are the main colors I used in the watercolor, so the previous outline is less noticeable.
2. Use an old brush to apply the fluid in the light areas. It can ruin your best brushes if you don't wash them well! Let dry.
3. Once the fluid is completely dry, start painting the first layers. First, I placed the shadows with a very transparent, wet blue and let it dry.

(*continued*)

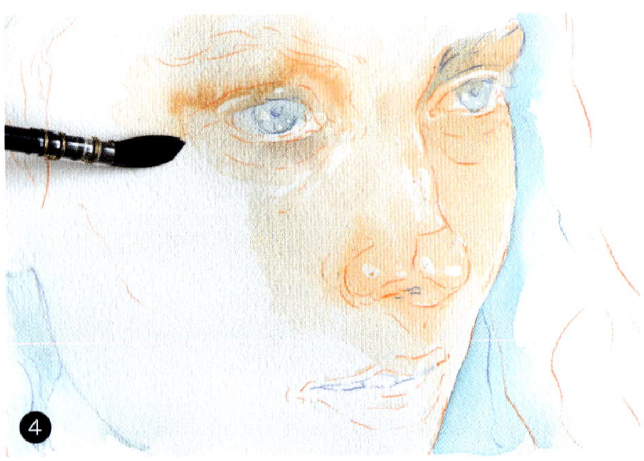

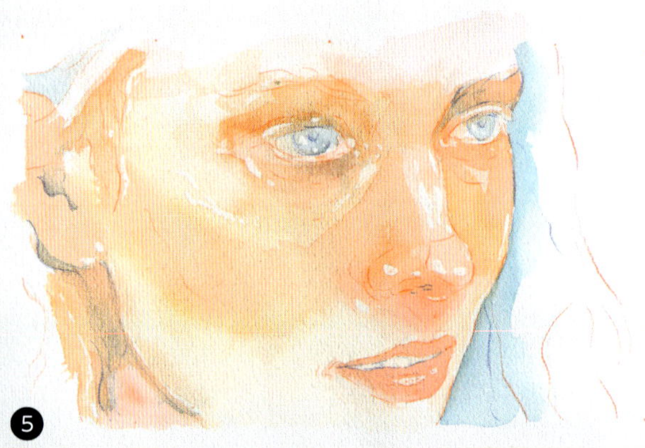

4. I applied a layer of a very transparent orange tone to part of the face. In this case, I wanted to create more impact in the area of the eyes and nose and to leave the rest of the face less finished. The amount of paint and detail on one side creates contrast with the other side that's left more sketchy and without a lot of detail.

5. Continue adding wet layers to add volume and shape to the face, focusing on the shadows. As you add layers of color, the masking fluid becomes more visible. Add as many layers as you think are necessary.

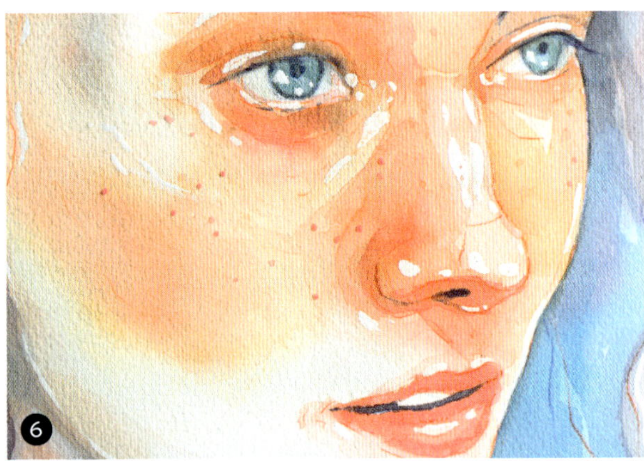

6. Move on to the detail of the eyes, lips, and nose. Note the shadows, the volume, and add small layers of color. Use clean water to blur the edge and blend the color for a smooth transition.

7. With a very fine-tipped brush, choose a darker color to add detail and refinement to the eyebrows, freckles, lips, and so on.

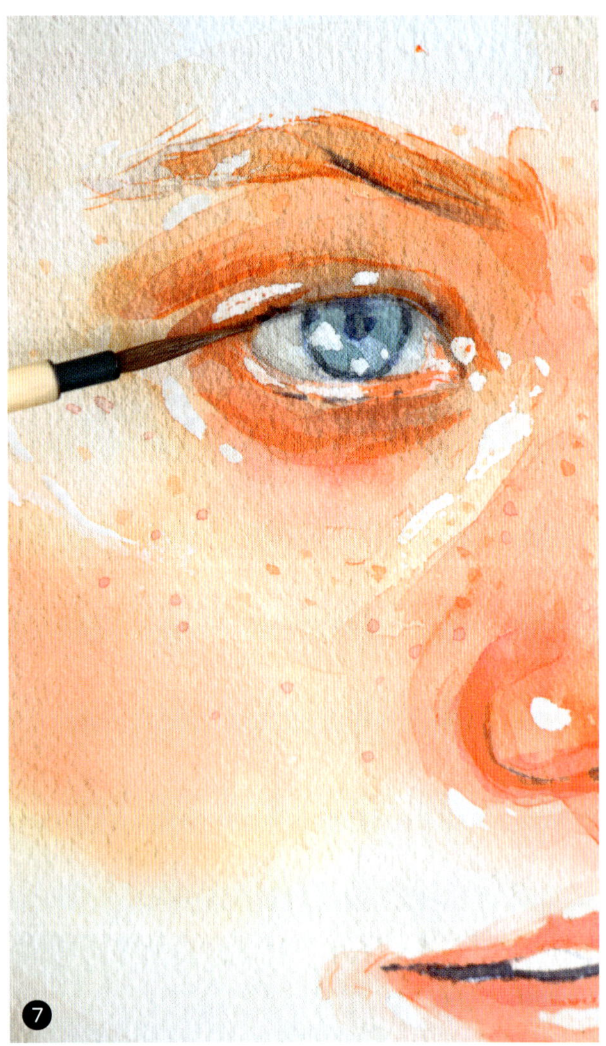

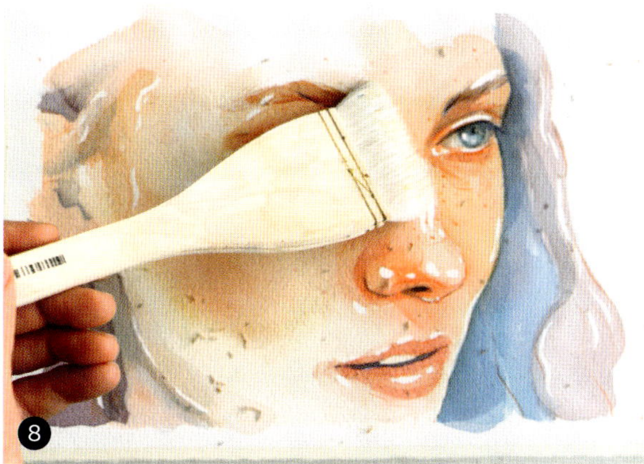

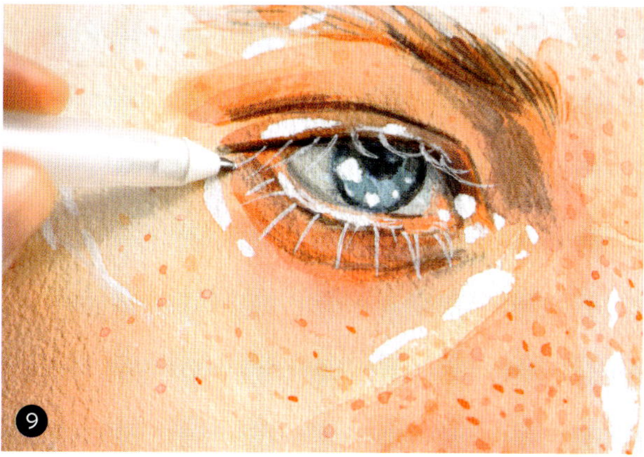

8. When you're satisfied with the result and the watercolor is completely dry, you can safely remove the masking fluid gently with your fingertips (wash your hands first so you don't soil your work). Remove the peeled off masking fluid with a large, soft brush.

9. I chose to add some light shading with a hard pencil.

10. As a general rule, I like to improvise and not have any set plans. I let the portrait take me in different directions than what I had in mind. In this case, it occurred to me to make white eyelashes. I used a white, fine-tipped Pilot pen, which is an excellent option in this case because you can make every stroke precise and very defined.

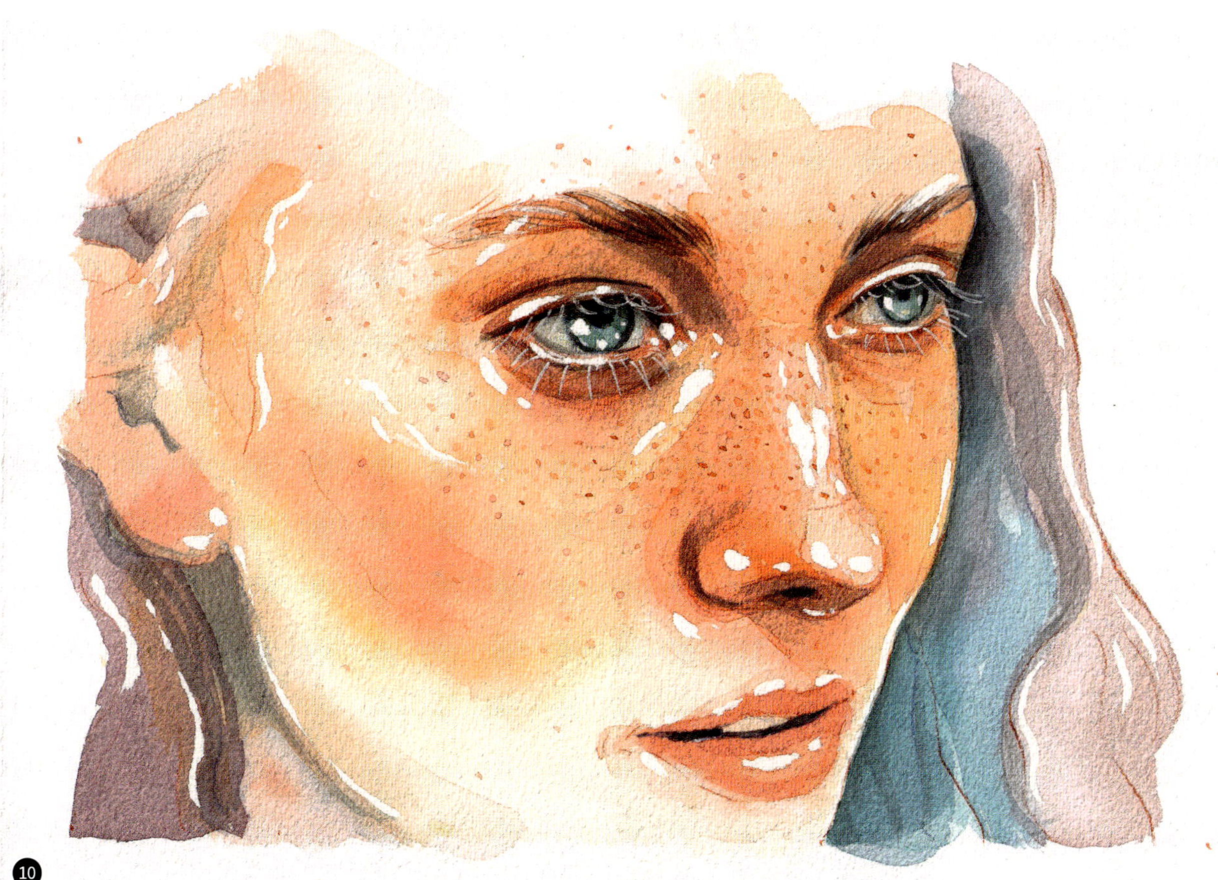

OPENING LIGHT AREAS WITH WATER

For this portrait, we'll play and let the water move us. We'll clear areas very intuitively, using clean water for each stroke or layer and letting it dry. This is a very good way to overcome the desire to control the watercolor. Let yourself go with the flow!

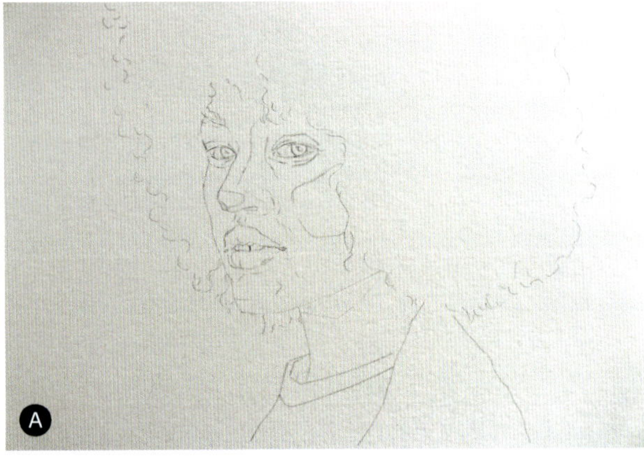

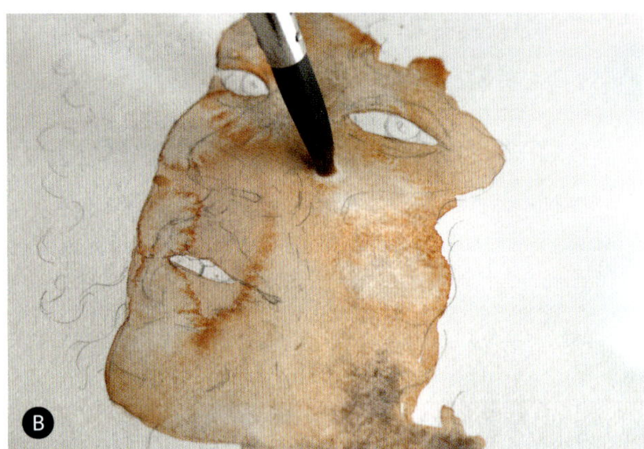

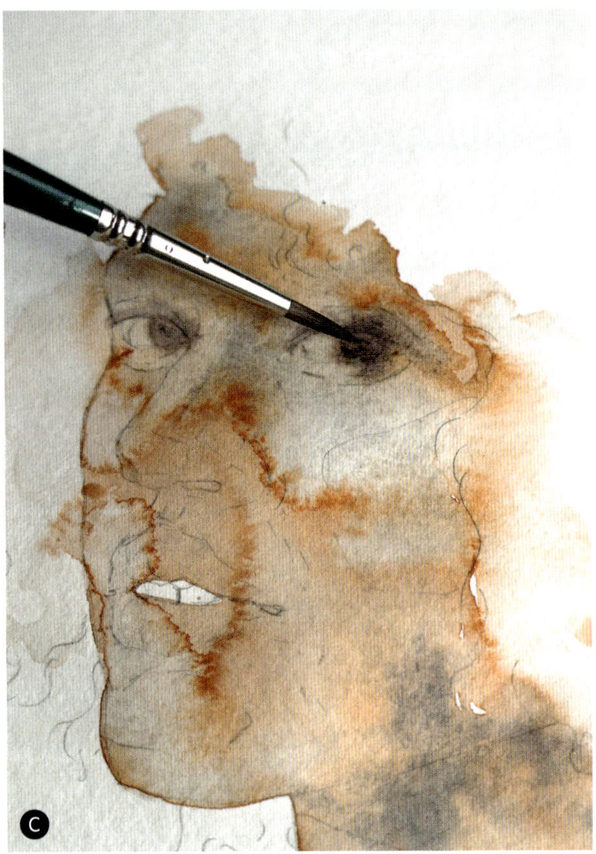

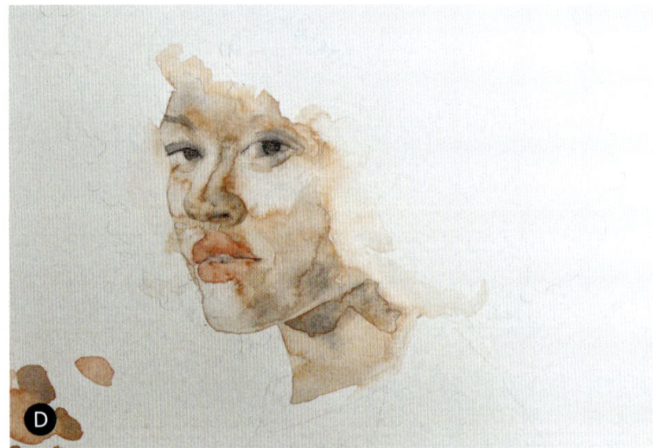

1. Draw the outline of your portrait. (A)
2. Prepare the color for the skin on your palette and apply an even wet layer. Before the layer dries, wet a clean brush with water and apply small strokes to the watercolor layer, allowing the paint and water to freely blend. They will clear areas and form different textures. (B)
3. If the layer is still wet, take the opportunity to apply a second layer of color on some points you want to highlight, such as the eyes or mouth. Don't be afraid to let the paint dance in the water. Let it dry and apply as many layers as you want using the same process. In this case, I wanted something very simple, so I only used one layer. (C, D)

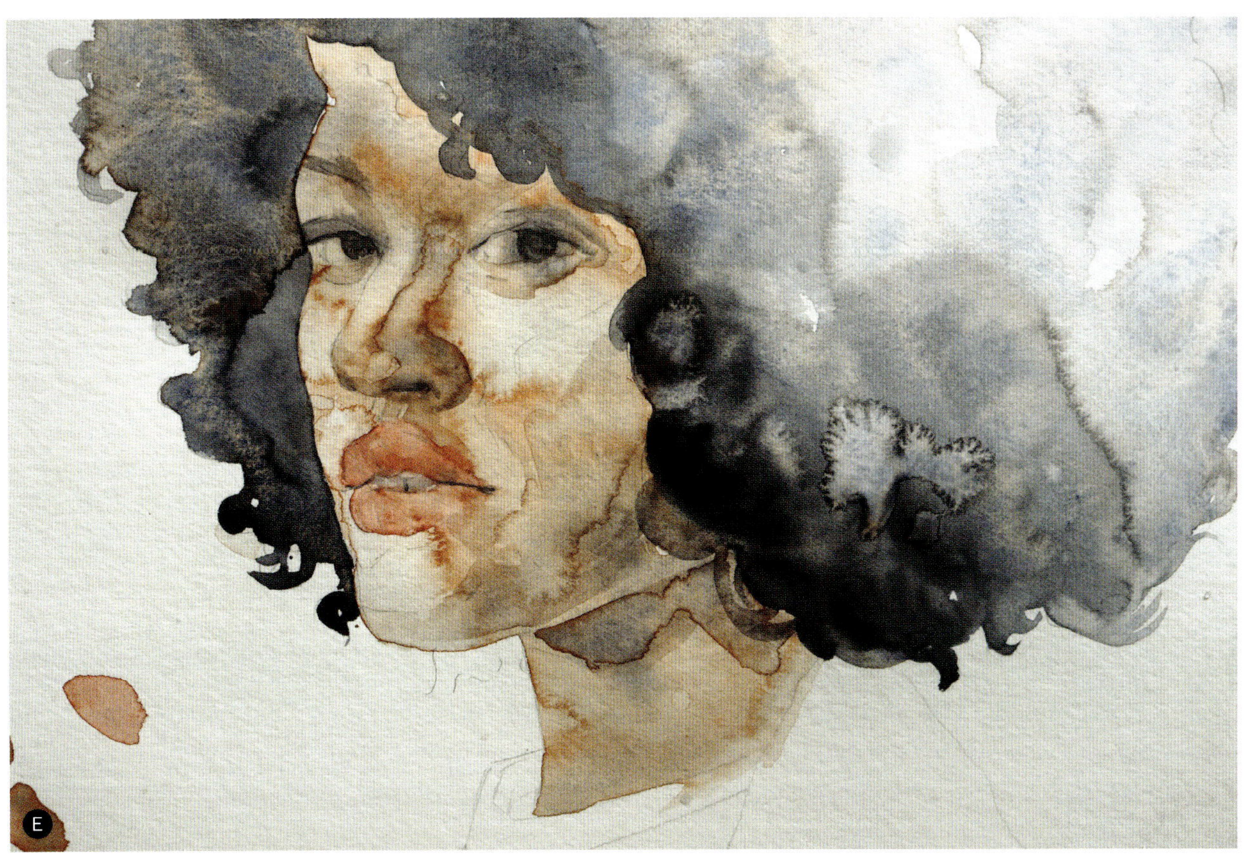

4. Last, I used the same technique for the hair. I used the color Tundra Violet, which adds extra texture. (E)

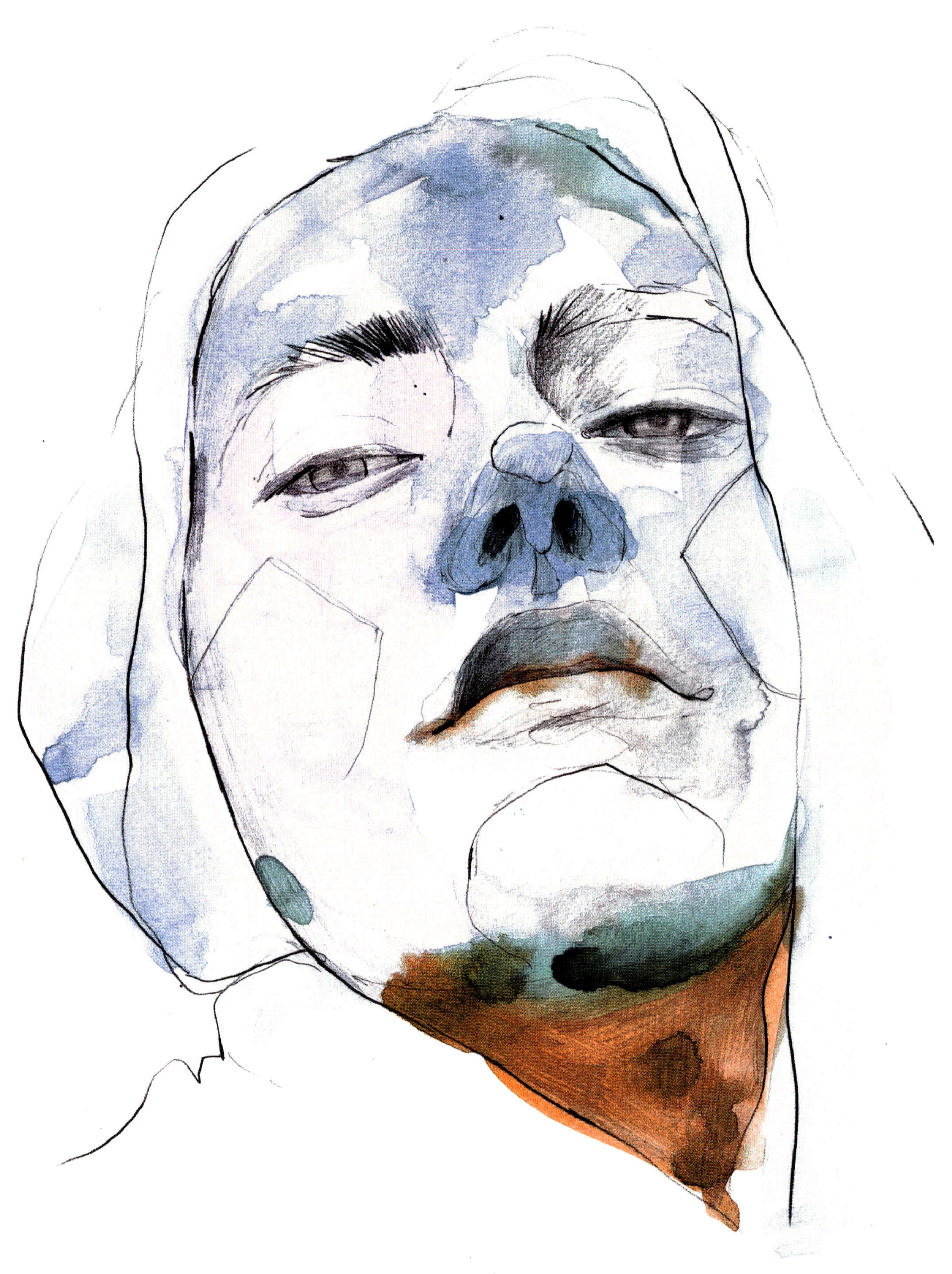

4

CREATIVE PORTRAITS

OTHER APPROACHES

The portrait is a complex subject, and we don't have to always have a realistic approach. Translating reality to paper is always subjective anyway.

In this chapter, we look at other ways to make a portrait. No matter what level you're at, mastering drawing requires a lot of time, patience, and practice! Over time, you'll progress and improve your technique. You'll also increase your dexterity, develop your eye, and expand your innovation.

Drawing is observing, looking, and understanding shape, proportions, and direction. It's stopping to see the details. But it's also having fun, exploring, and playing. It's an act of absolute freedom, and we can pick up a pencil and paper and just draw and start doodling. Drawing isn't simply re-creating reality.

These lessons can help you improve your drawing skills, your imagination, and your creativity.

CONTINUOUS LINE DRAWING

Choose a brush that you like. While you can use any size brush for this portrait, I chose a round No. 6 brush for thinner lines. Using a higher-numbered brush with a fine point will allow you to make long strokes without having to keep adding paint.

1. This exercise is about drawing a continuous line without lifting the brush from the paper. You can use a face from your imagination or look at a model. I find it easier to start with the nose since it is the center of the face and can be used as a guide. (A)
2. You don't need to go over the same lines again. Enjoy the movements and spaces you create and don't be afraid! If you use a reference model, this is a good exercise in observation. I love this type of exercise because it's very relaxing and yields surprising, original results. (B, C)
3. You can end here, but if you want to continue, you can color the spaces you've created. You can add as many as you want. For this project, I limited my palette to three colors: red, pink, and green. I painted some spaces with a wet, transparent strokes. Choose a high-numbered brush for adding color. I left other areas on the paper blank to add brightness to the portrait. (D)

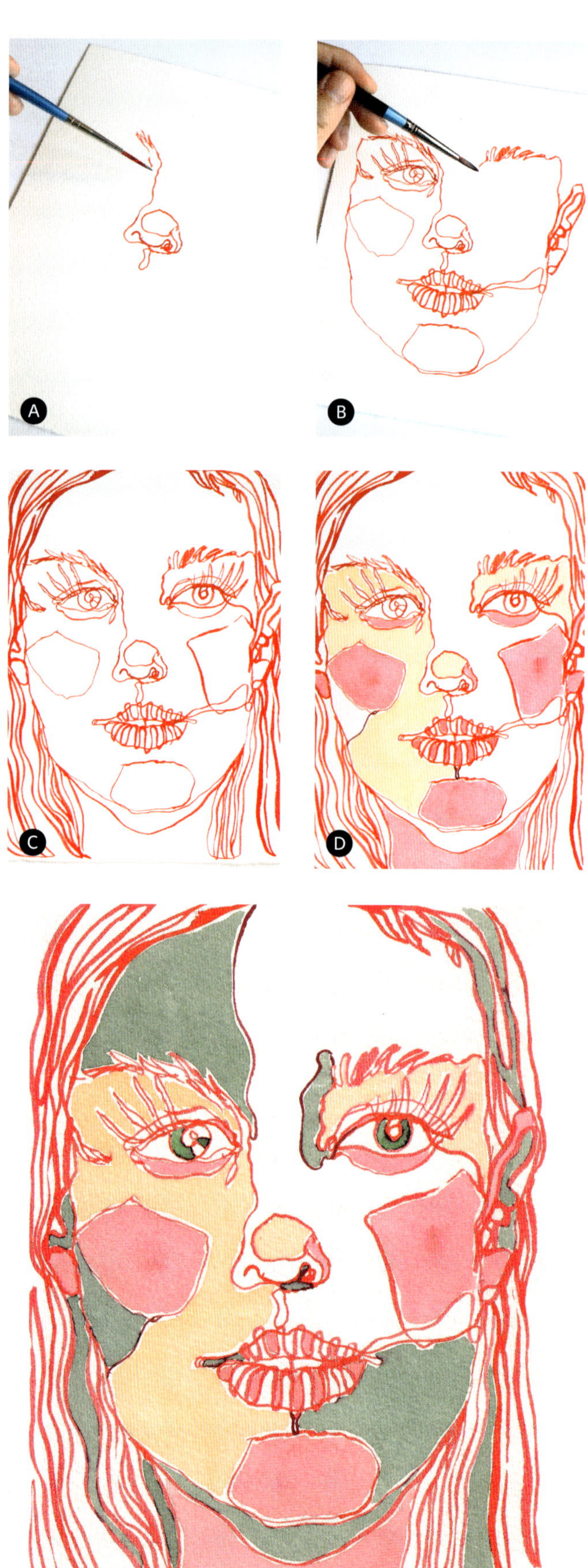
A

B

C

D

CONTOUR DRAWING

For this portrait, you'll keep your eyes on your reference while you're drawing it. It's like drawing with your eyes and transferring the movement to your hand. You can't look at what you're drawing! The result of this exercise is fun and surprising.

You can finish by painting areas in with flat colors, gradients, or patterns. Use your imagination!

Prepare the watercolors on a palette and paint each area with a round tip brush. You can use a No. 12 or No. 20, depending on the size of each section, or feel free to use the brush you're most comfortable with. You can also add more layers of color if you wish using dry-on-dry or dry-on-wet techniques.

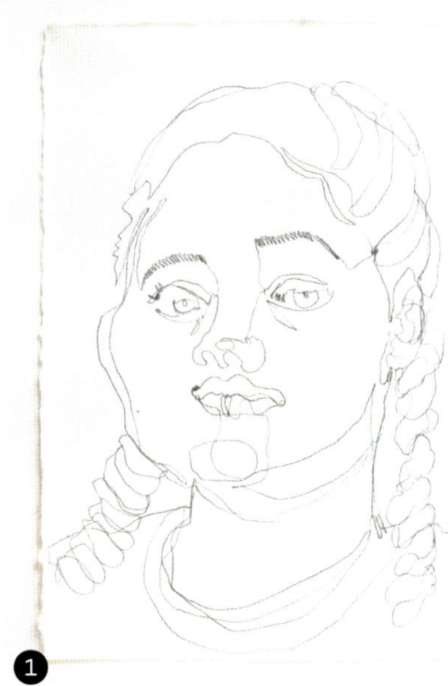

1

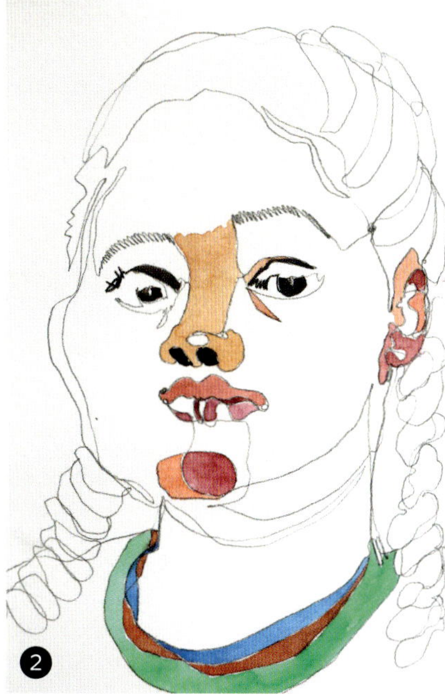

2

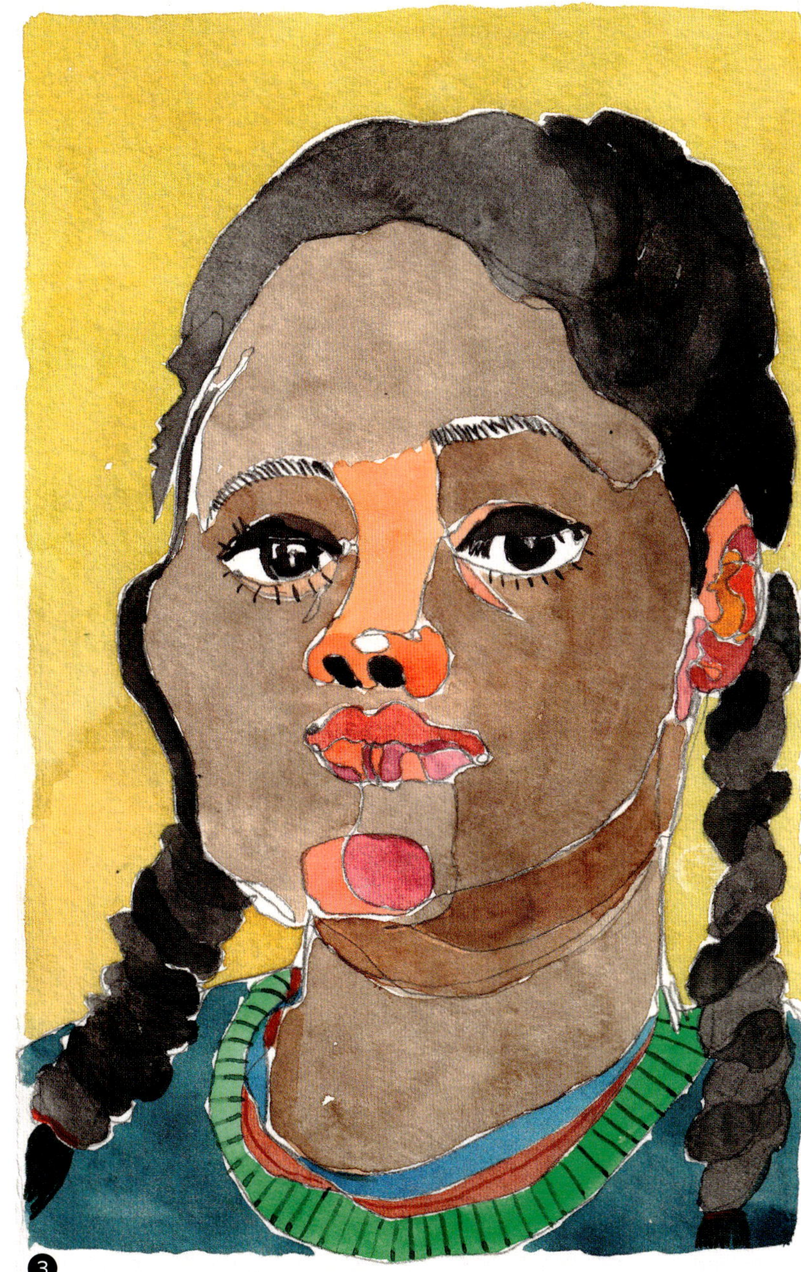

3

DRAWING WITH YOUR NONDOMINANT HAND

Like the previous portrait, you can choose an image from your imagination or use a model. In this case, I chose a model to force myself to try to reproduce what I was seeing.

I like to draw with my left hand when I want a clumsy, fresh result. A drawing made using our nondominant hand is not as neat as one made with our dominant hand.

This is a perfect exercise for finding something natural, genuine, and beautiful in clumsiness.

The degree of difficulty of this exercise will depend on how much you use your nondominant hand. If you don't have practice, it will be even harder. But give yourself a chance and have fun with the result. This is a great way to put the other side of your brain to work.

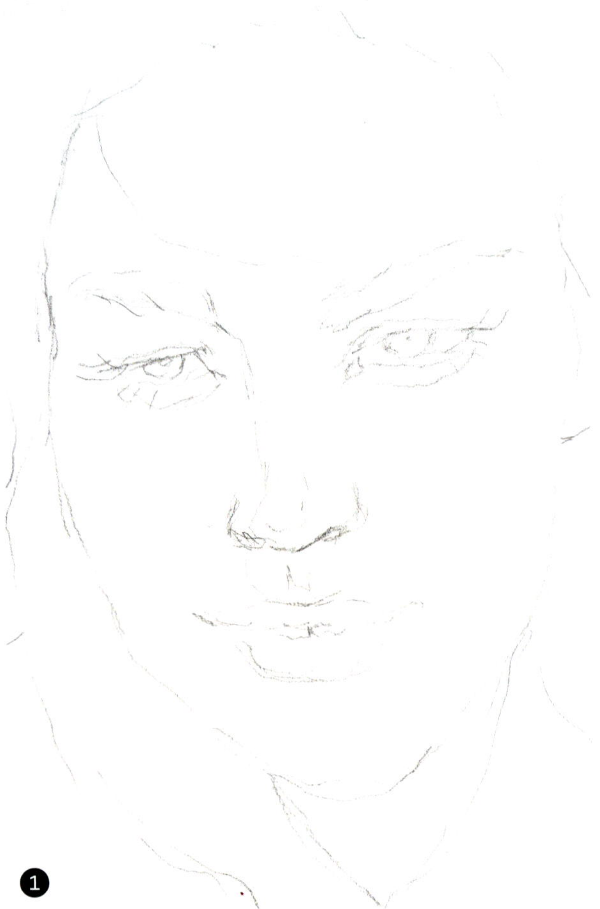

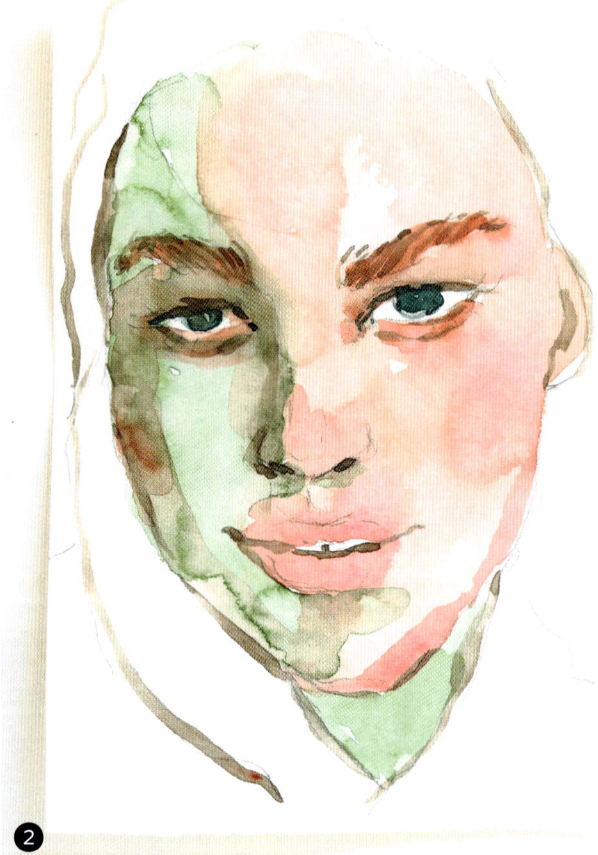

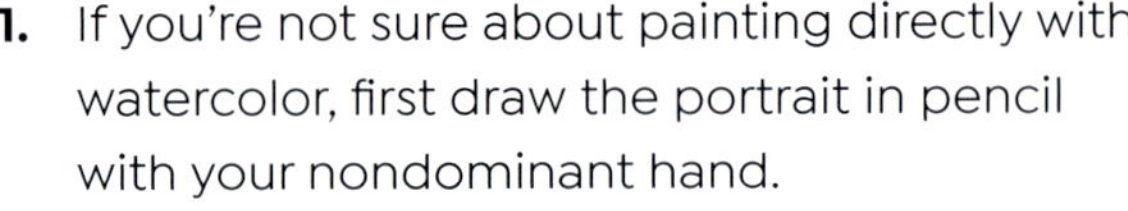

1. If you're not sure about painting directly with watercolor, first draw the portrait in pencil with your nondominant hand.
2. Choose your hues and prepare them in your palette. I chose green for the shadows and a round, wet brush for wide, diluted strokes. Add the first wet, transparent layers.

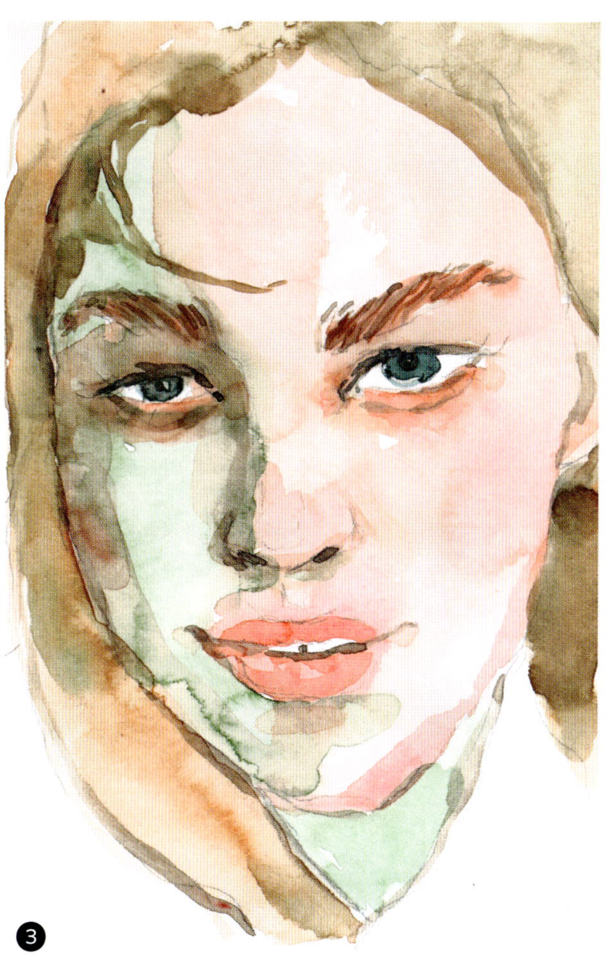

3

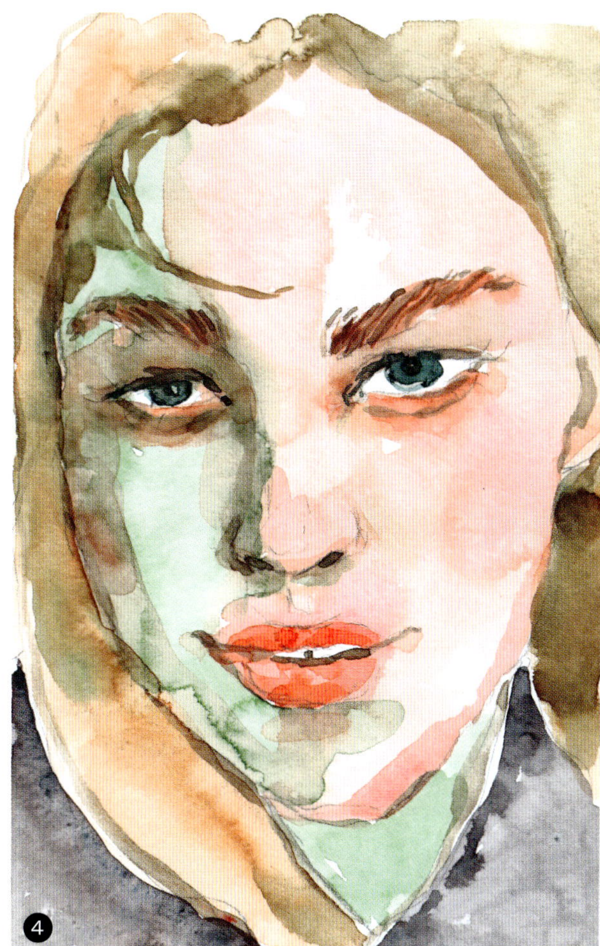

4

3. Every time you add a layer of color, let it dry if you don't want the colors to mix on the paper.
4. Once the first layers dry, add contrast and details to the eyes, eyebrows, nostrils, lips, and so on.

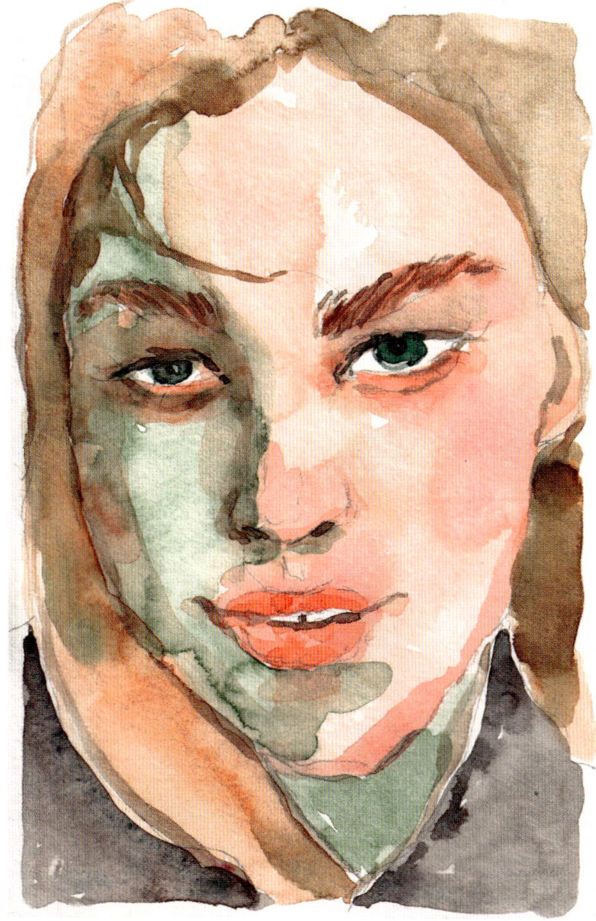

I chose a simple portrait with few layers, but add as many as you think are necessary.

DRAWING UPSIDE DOWN

Choose a photograph and turn it upside down. This will trick your brain, and you won't see the "known" image. You can limit yourself to what you observe. Simply draw upside down and try to reproduce what you're seeing, focusing on the directions of the lines, spaces, and shapes.

This is a fantastic exercise to literally "see" what you are observing and forget about what's "real." The brain becomes used to seeing an image after a while, and when you turn it upside down, the brain breaks up the idea it established, which helps you have new insights about what you're observing.

Many professionals often draw this way to block out drawings.

This is an ideal technique for making corrections. Once you think you've finished your drawing, turn it upside down and compare it to the reference model. Surely, you find faults that you wouldn't have seen otherwise, no matter how hard you looked.

Here's an example:

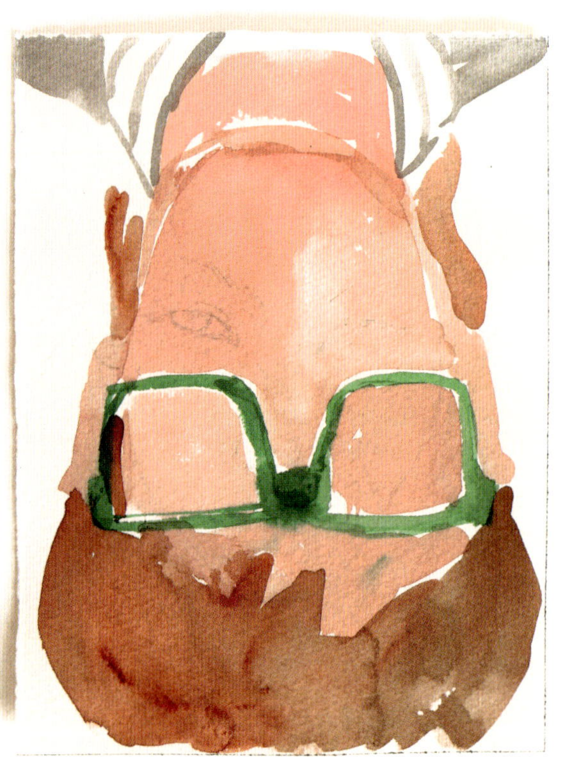

1. I painted directly with watercolors (without sketching in pencil). I painted the general shapes, the main blocks, first. That is, I began by placing the shape of the face and let that layer dry, leaving defined edges. Once dry, I painted the hair, body, and glasses.

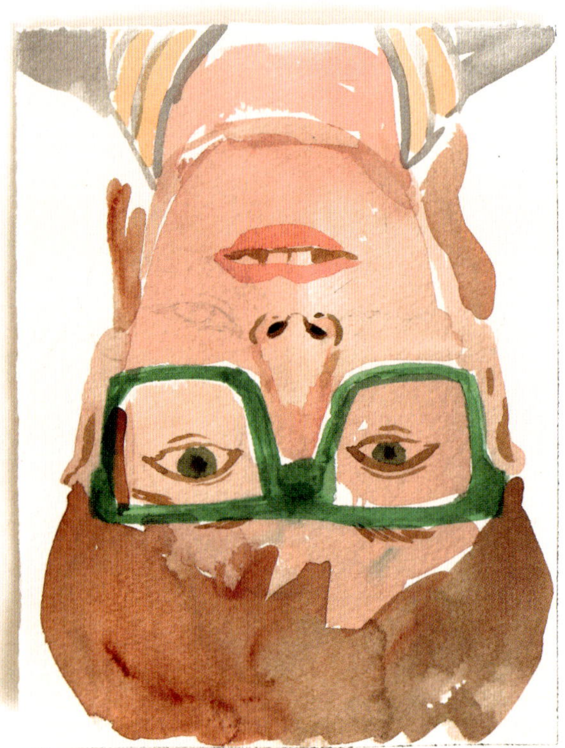

2. Once dry, I added the details: eyes, nose, and mouth. **We're working from the general to the particular, so it's easier to see the shapes and focus on the details later.**

The result will depend on your own effort, patience, and goal. In this portrait, I did a quick and simple exercise, using few layers and looking for a more "childish" result. Sometimes, when you insist on making many layers, you forget that a watercolor with one or two layers can be more than enough.

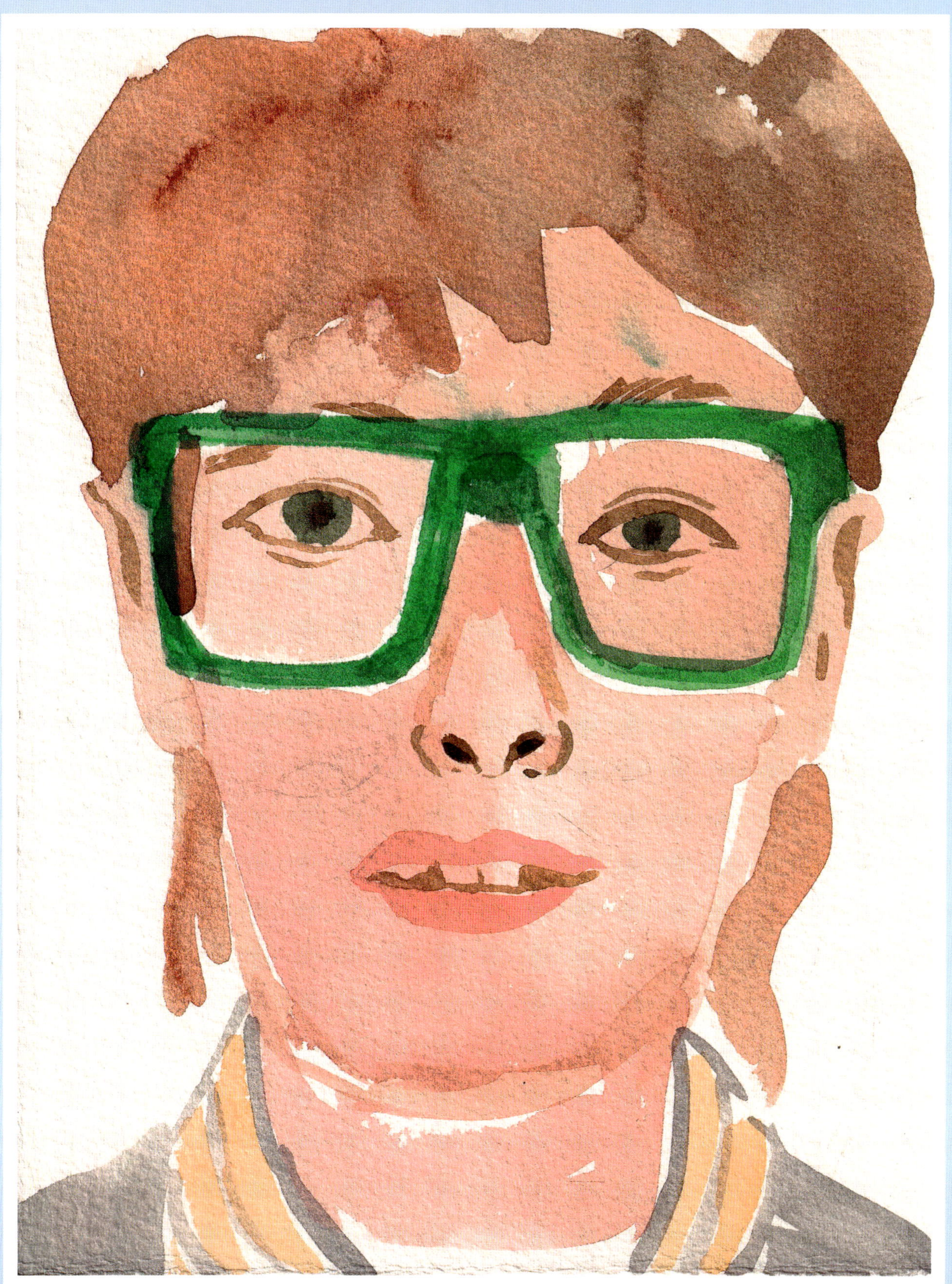

DRAWING FROM MEMORY

Observe an image for one minute and then analyze and remember as many details as possible. Ask questions to better focus on what you're seeing. How long is the hair? If there are glasses, where are the eyebrows located?

Turn over the reference image so you can't see it and try to draw from memory. When you're done, compare the photo to your drawing. How much does your drawing resemble the original? How many details did you manage to memorize?

This portrait is very simple. I chose only two colors: red and pink.

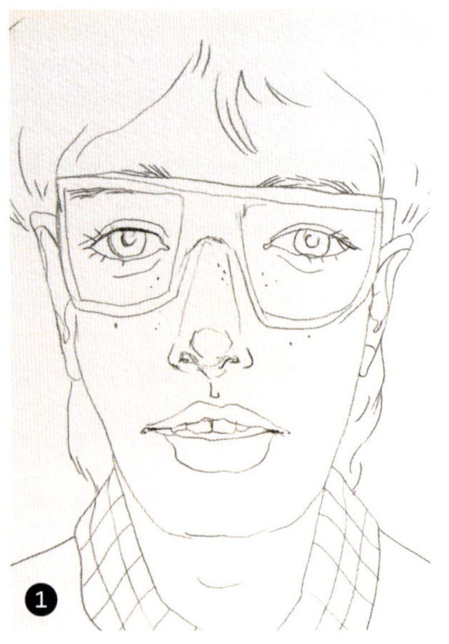
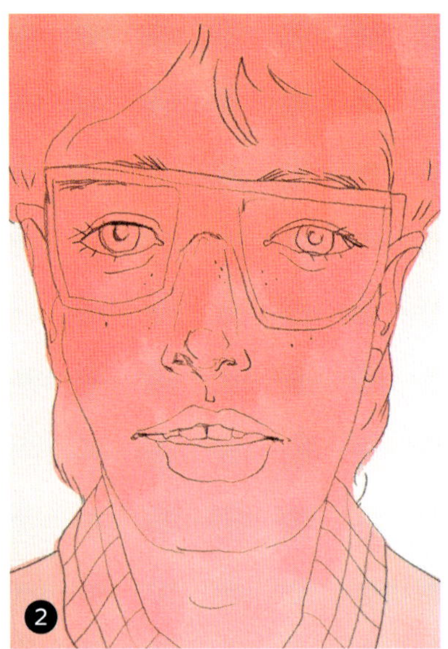
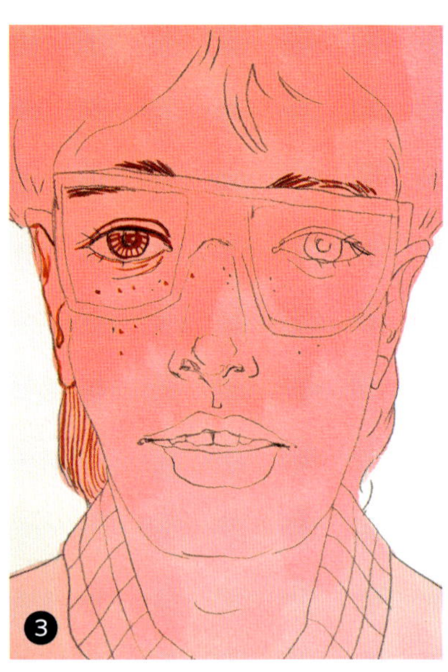

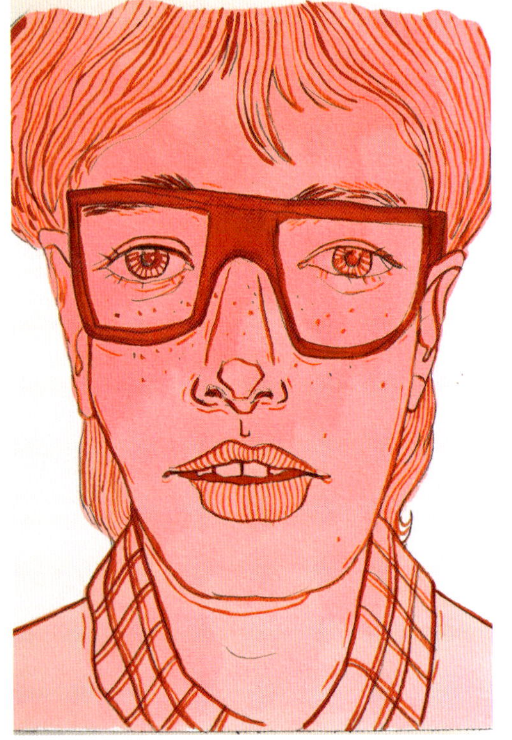

1. The first thing I did was draw with a soft pencil. I opted for a heavy stroke, and the result is a bit "childish."
2. I painted an even, transparent layer of pink and let it dry.
3. Finally, I went over all the lines with an opaque red.

TIMED DRAWINGS

This portrait is all about observation and honing your drawing skills. Set a time limit for yourself. For this exercise, the most important thing is to observe shape and direction. Once you've got those, you can focus on adding detail. This exercise comes in handy to let your hand relax and forget about perfection. Try not to use an eraser so the strokes you applied for the face show through.

Instead of a graphite pencil, I used colored pencils. (A)

After adding details, I added a simple watercolor wash. (B)

The result is a very fresh, spontaneous exercise. I personally love this type of portrait!

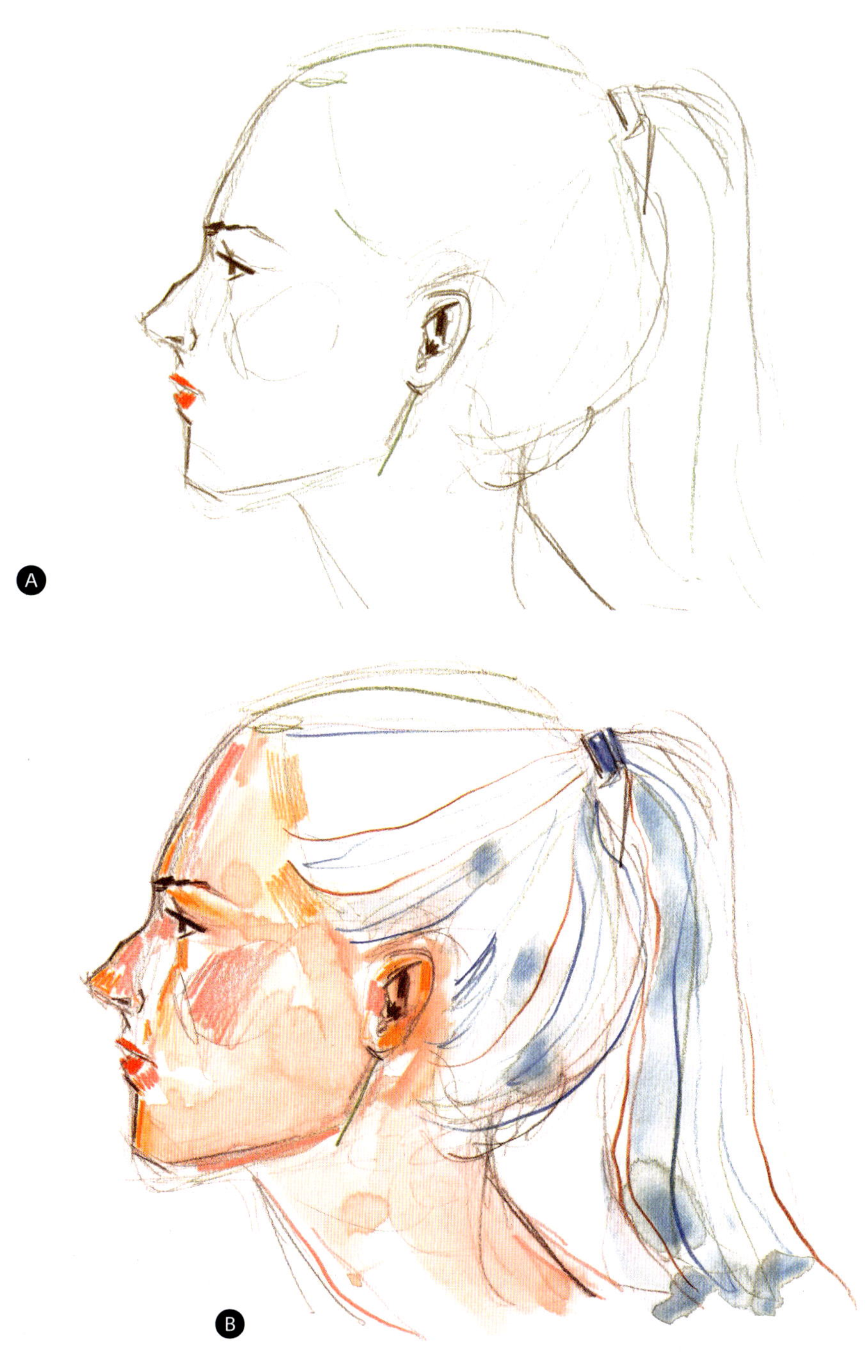

RANDOM SPOTS

Another option is to quickly draw small faces, with varying head shapes and hair. In painting these small faces, you can experiment with different palettes of three or four colors and try different combinations. This exercise is very useful for improving your basic techniques in dry-on-dry, wet-on-dry, wet-on-wet, and so on. The objective of this exercise is to create characters from the shapes created by wet brushstrokes.

Create several random spots and wait for them to dry. Turn the spots around to see all the possible angles and find one that inspires you to create a face. Add in the details—eyes, nose, mouth, ears, and hair—with a fine-tipped brush.

Try using different watercolor techniques: dry-on-dry, dry-on-wet, and transparencies.

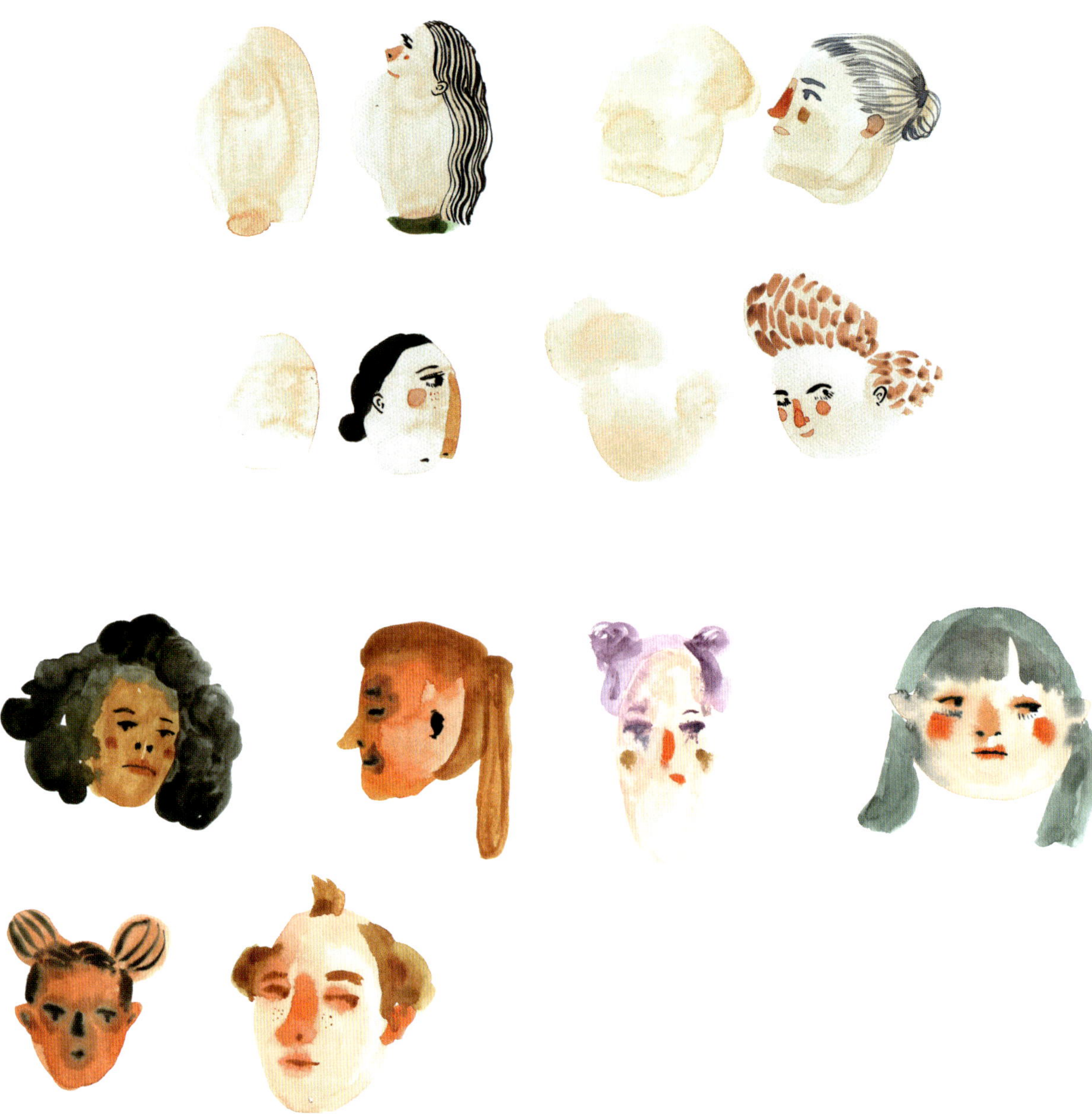

CLOSE-UPS

A close-up is a portrait that exhibits only part of a face. A portrait doesn't have to represent the entire face. Sometimes, it can say a lot about a person to simply observe their hands. Even depicting someone's shoes can be a way to portray someone. In this case, focus on a specific area of the face, or create a different frame, or zoom in.

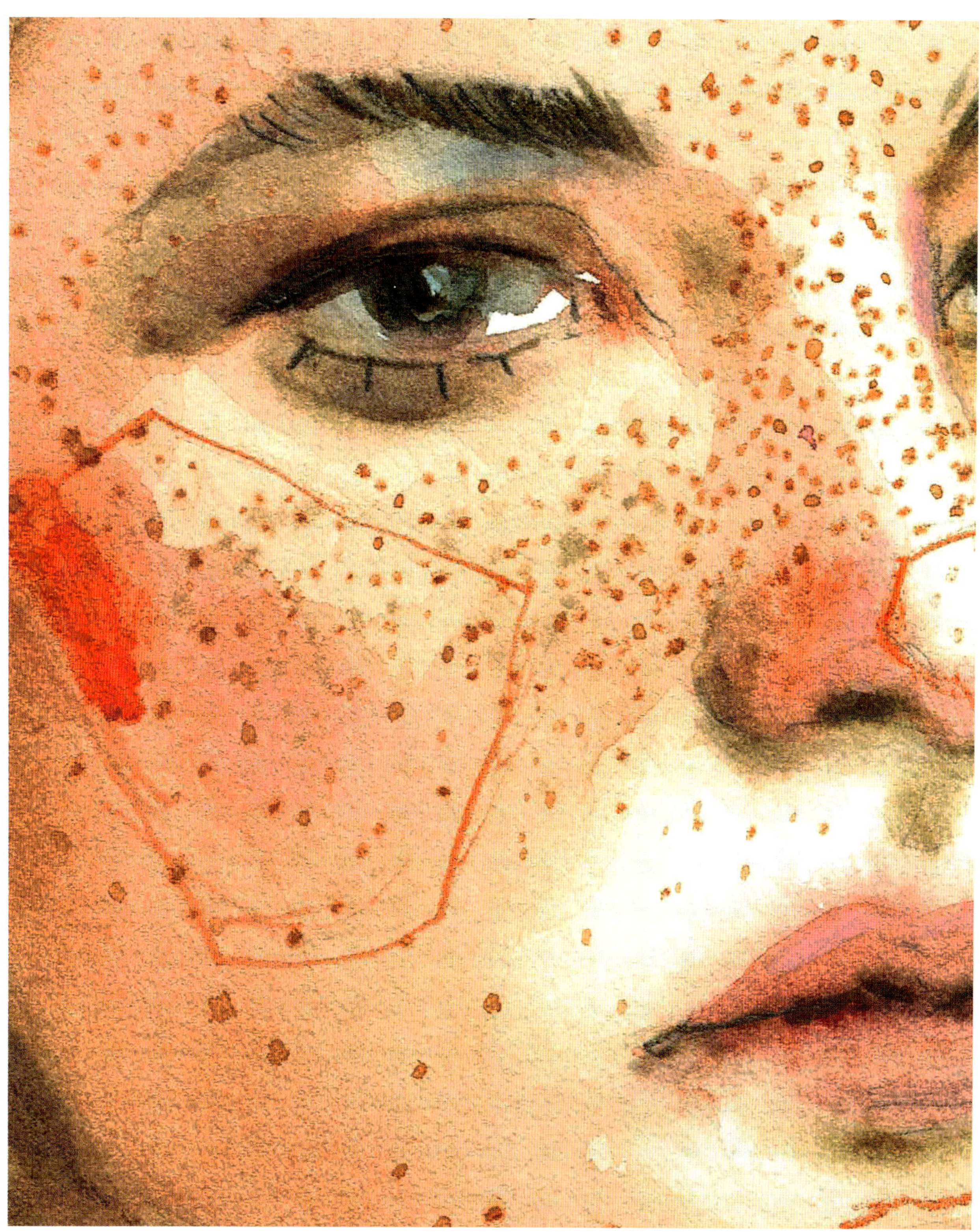

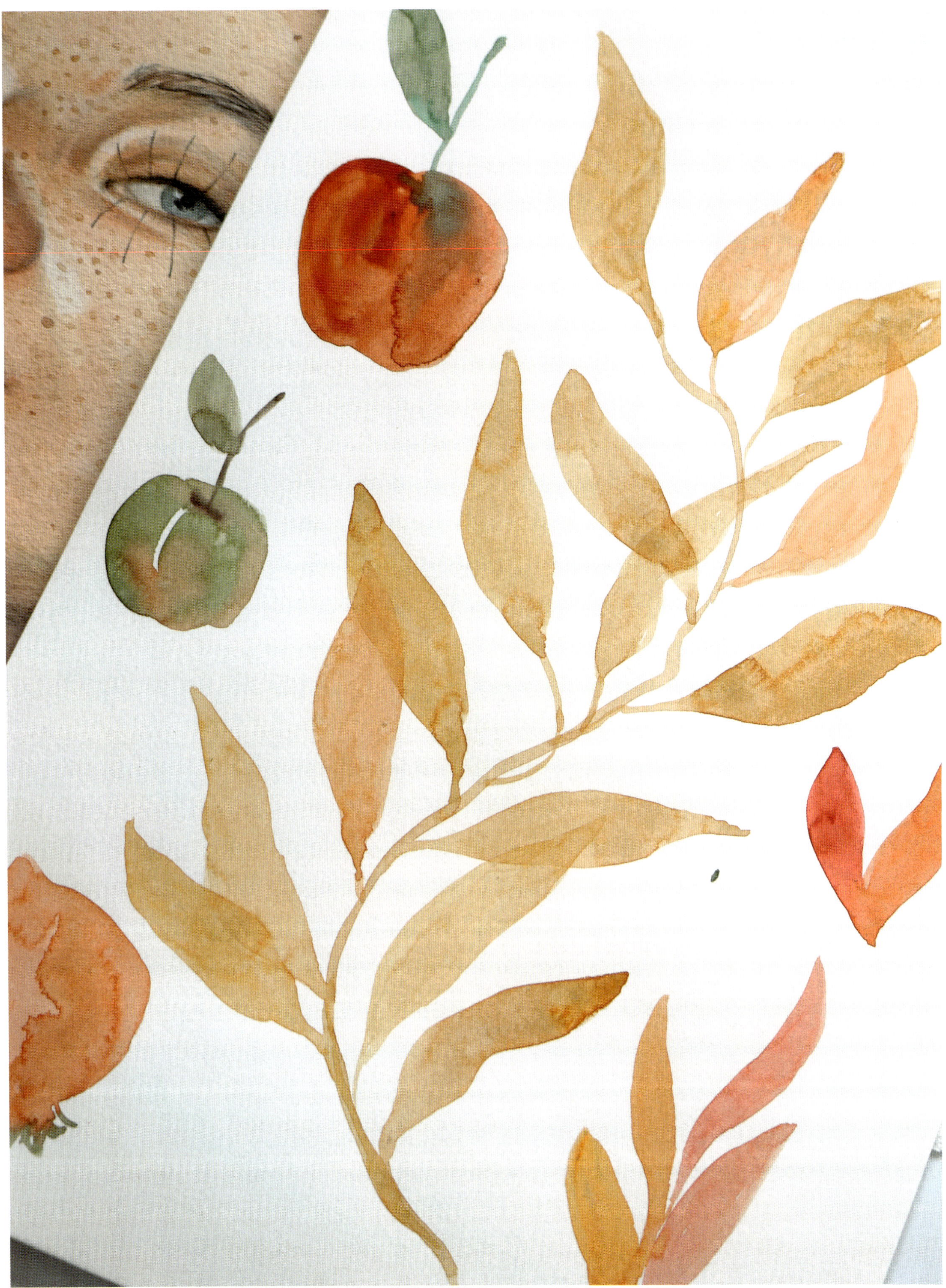

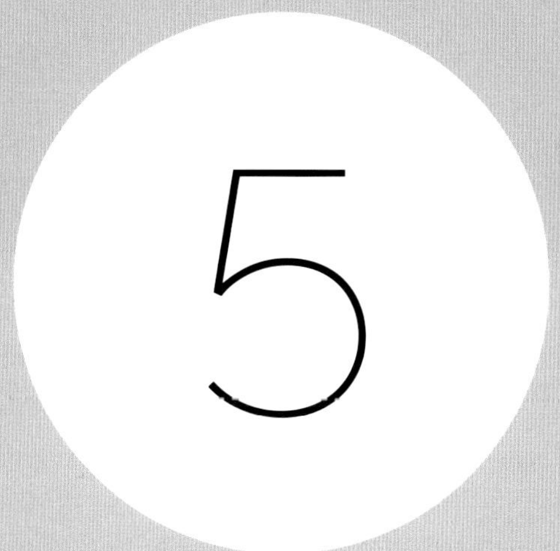

CREATIVE PORTRAITS

WATERCOLOR + DIGITAL

In this chapter, we'll make a digital montage of a portrait combining other motifs of our choice.

To go with the watercolor, I chose pencil and colored pencil, but you can do the lessons with any materials you want. Use the materials you feel most comfortable with and are interested in.

The process in this chapter reflects my own personal style that I developed over time, with much trial and error. I encourage you to not restrict yourself to learning one particular method, but to find your own artistic language, your *own* style, with patience, time, and practice. *Don't limit yourself when it comes to learning and experimenting.*

TRADITIONAL ARTWORK

1. Draw your portrait on the paper of your choice and are most comfortable with. I opted for a fine-grained, glossy paper of 300 grams per square meter (140 pounds).

2. Use a hard pencil (2H) to trace the shapes of the portrait, the outline, and main features. If you want, you can place shadows to help you. I choose not to mark shadows with the pencil so the strokes aren't visible.

3. Place the shadows with a translucent layer in a dark color (blue, green, purple, or an earth tone). Prepare the color with water in your palette, making sure that it's not too opaque. It's best to go from less to more. (A)

If you prefer, you can ignore this step and not place the shadows until the very end. In some previous exercises, we did a general layer and then applied shadows once there was volume. The choice is yours!

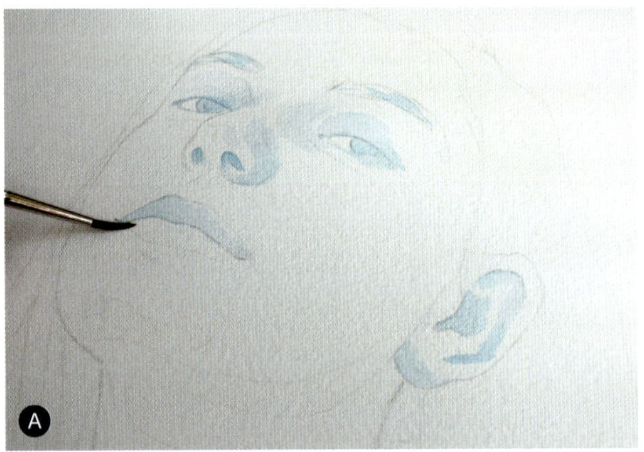

A

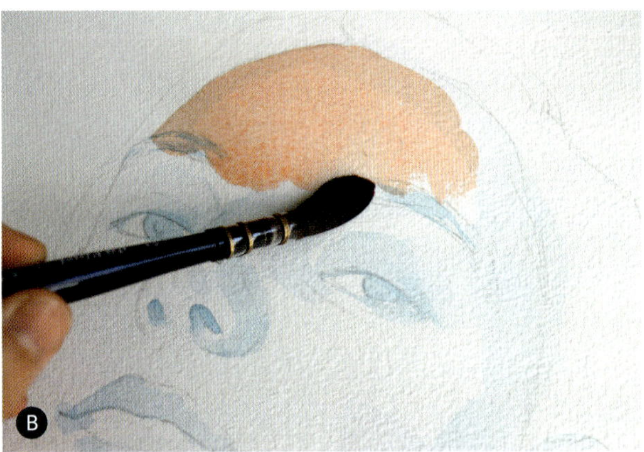

B

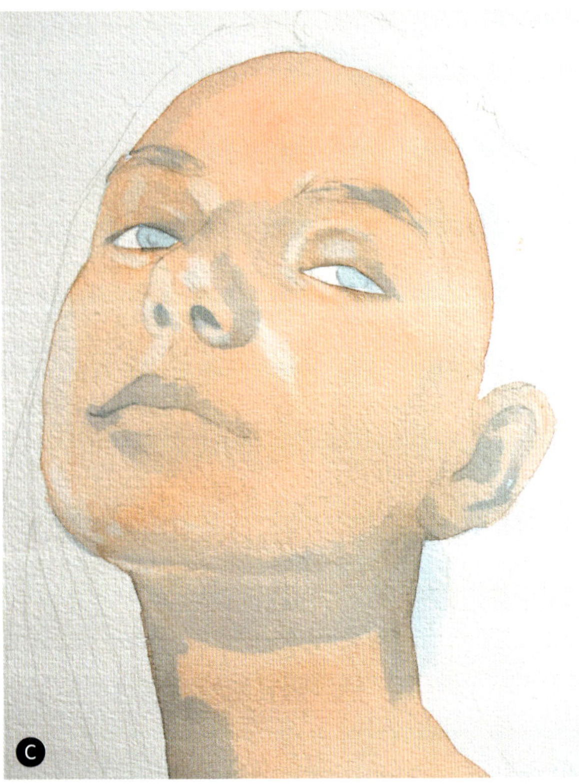

C

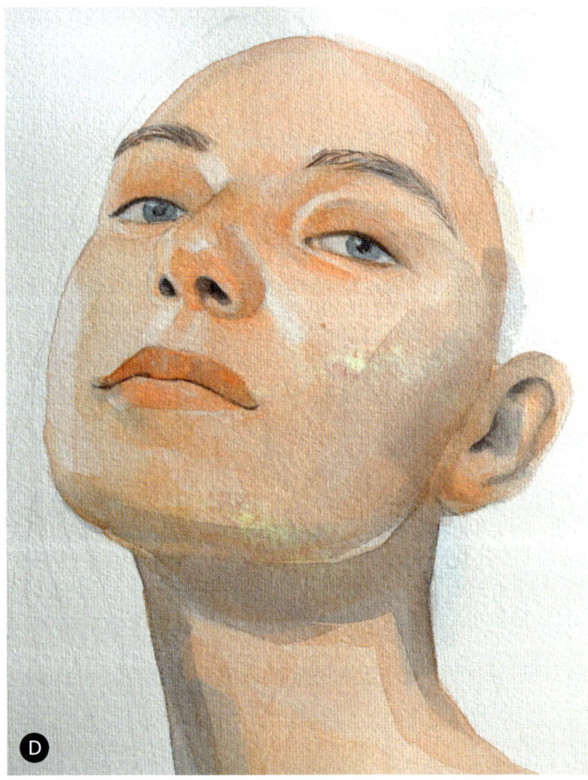

D

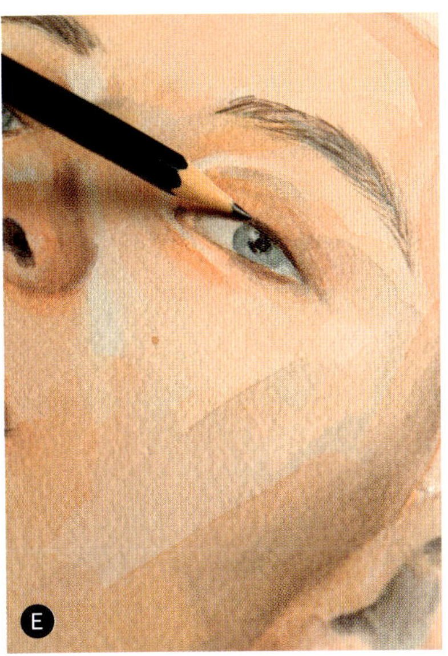

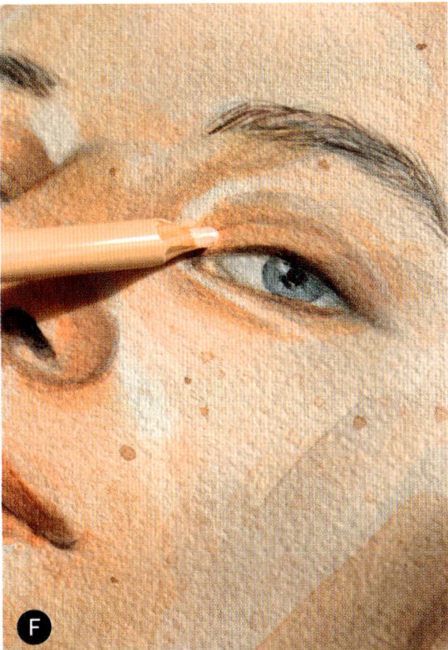

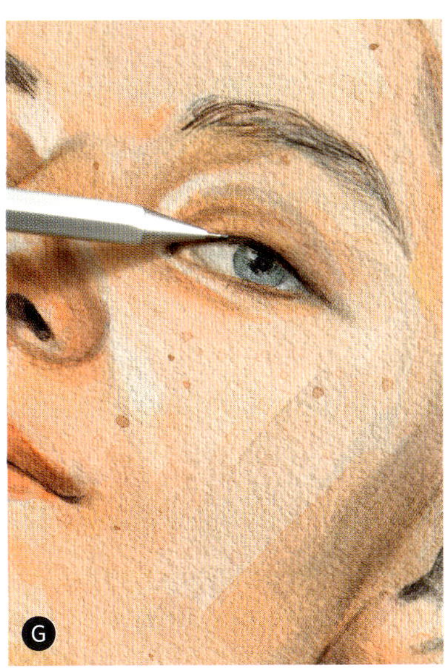

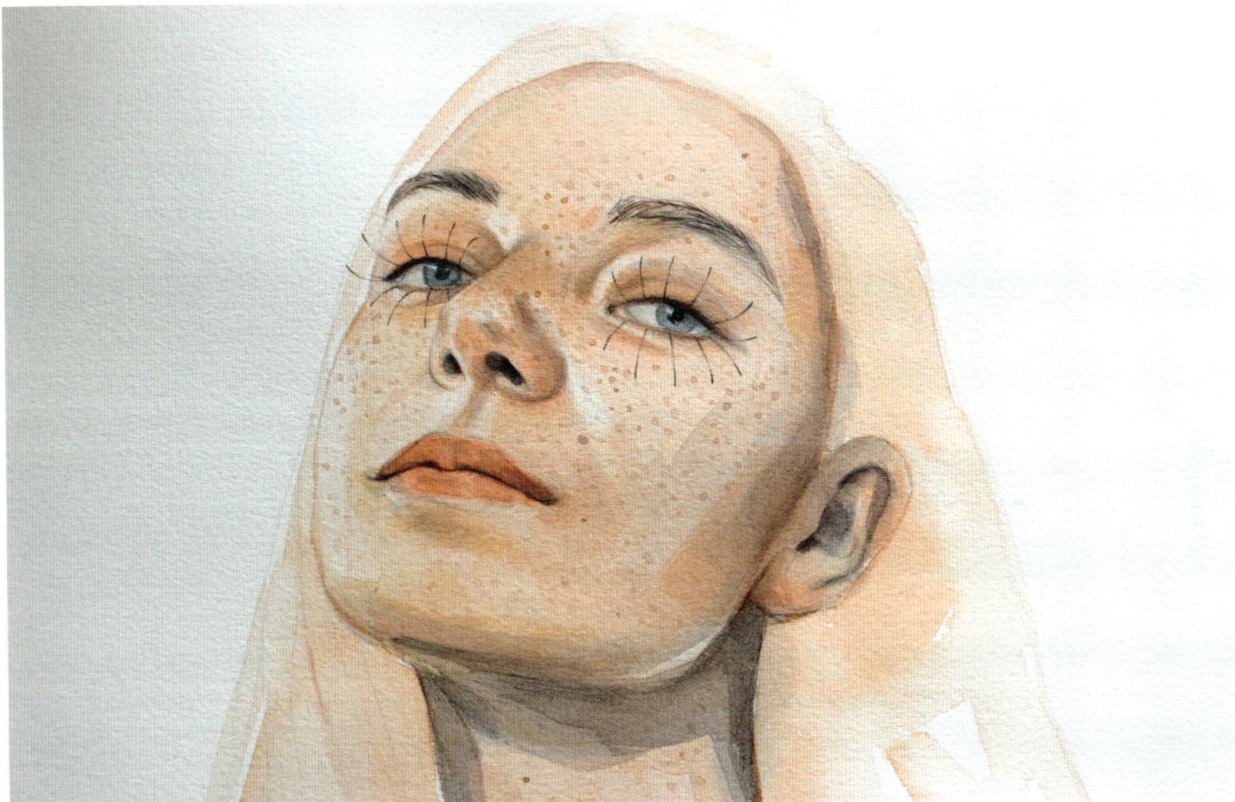

4. When the layer is dry, apply a broad wet layer to the entire face. Before it dries, use a wet brush to absorb and create light areas. (B)

5. Once the layer is dry, you can add details in the eyes, mouth, and ears to build the face. (C)

6. Add the number of layers you need to create volume. If you want the shadows to be precise and controlled, let the work dry between layers. (D)

7. If you'd like, add shading with a hard pencil (2H). I like to add subtle shading in some areas. (E)

8. You can also highlight certain parts of the face with colored pencil. (F)

9. Finally, use a softer pencil (B) to add contrast and define details. (G)

DIGITAL PROCESS

Once you have your watercolor portrait and the main drawings you want to add, it's time to scan. If you want to reproduce your drawings or use them for commercial or editorial purposes, it's a good idea to understand how to edit them.

You need to have a basic idea of how to use Photoshop, which you can easily learn. Photoshop offers an infinite variety of settings. In this case, I'm going to shorten the process to make it as easy and clear as possible.

Be sure to set the scanner to a minimum of 300 dpi (dots per inch) so the image is high resolution and the quality isn't affected. The file will be smaller at 72 dpi, but this configuration is advisable only if you'll use the image online. If you are using it online, be sure to work in RGB (red, blue, and green) colors; and if you're going to print the image, it's best to work in CMYK (four-color model).

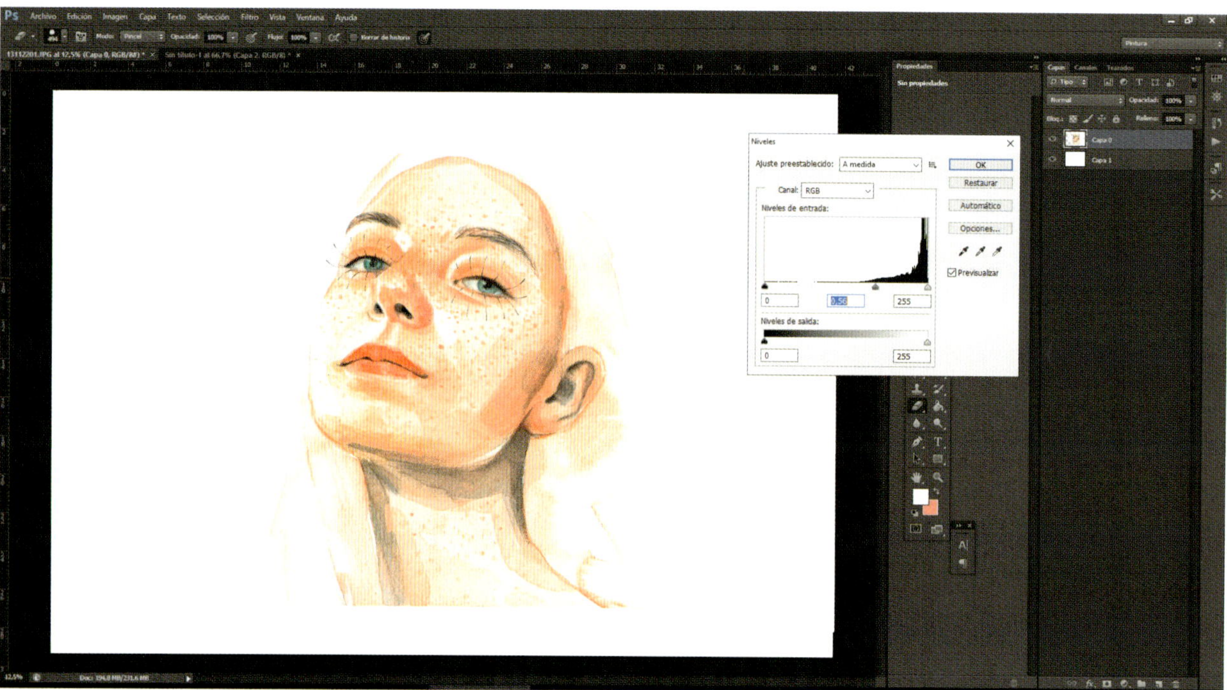

1. We're going to make some adjustments to try to make the image as close to reality as possible. Then, we can vary the tones if we want. Open the scanned file in Photoshop. Depending on your scanner, the colors for the imported image might be off.

The first thing I do to color correct the image is to adjust the levels of shadows and highlights. Go to Image → Adjustments → Levels to make the necessary adjustments to correct the colors. Play around and explore the possibilities that come with each setting. In my case, I always slide the arrow from the left to the center to darken the watercolor because the scanner makes the image seem very bright to me. If there are any unwanted stains, use the Eraser Tool to clean any imperfections.

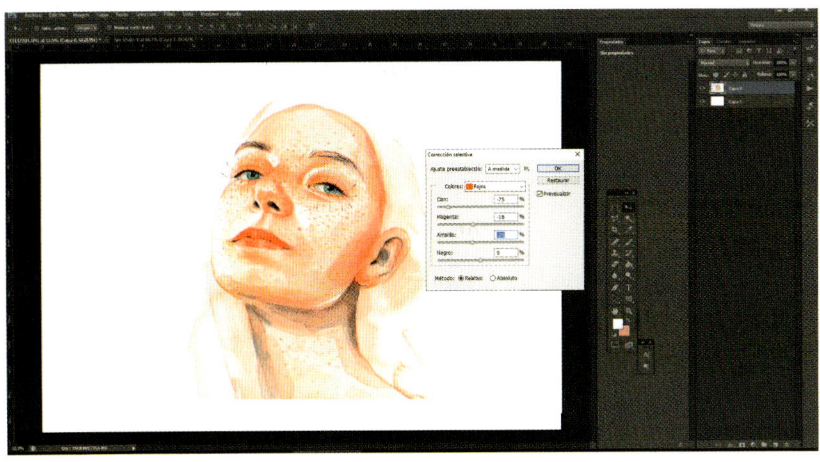

2. Now, let's modify the colors a little. Go to Image → Adjustments → Selective Color. Here, you can adjust the different shades and see which result you like best. I usually do this very intuitively until I am satisfied with the result. If you prefer, you can create a fill layer or adjustment so as not to modify the original. Go to Layers → New Adjustment Layer.

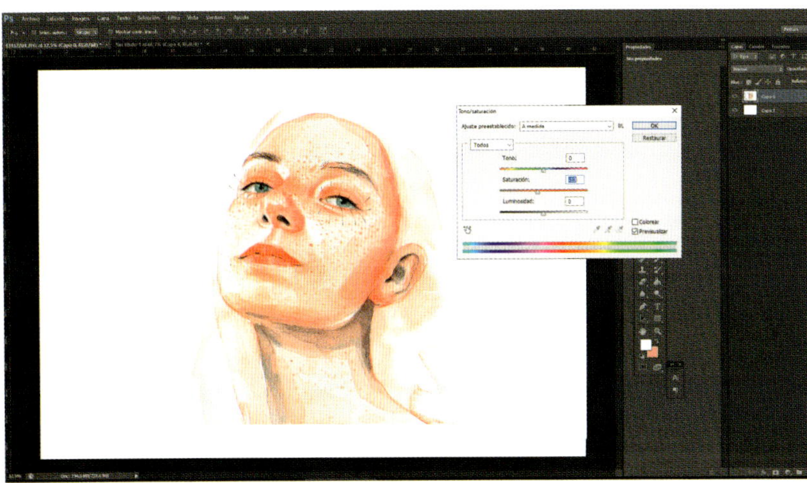

3. Another modification that I usually make is to adjust the saturation. Sometimes, images are scanned with very vivid colors, and I like to lower the saturation a bit. Go to Image → Adjustments → Hue/ Saturation.

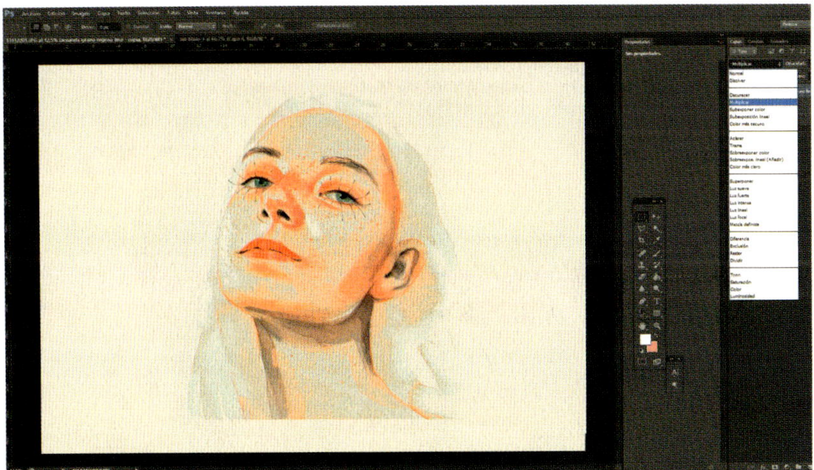

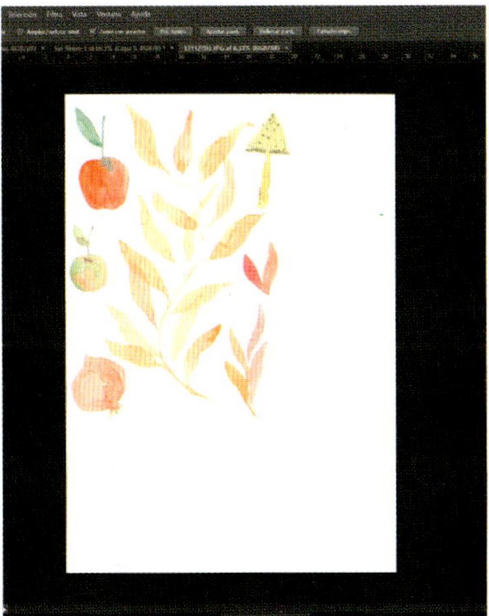

4. One of the steps I like the best is to give a textured effect to a watercolor. You can either scan your own papers or cardboard, explore your own textures, or find them online. If you're going to sell your work, it's advisable to invest in good-quality textures. Open the "Texture" file and copy and paste into the image. Rasterize this layer, converting it into pixels, so you can edit it. Right-click Rasterize Layer. In Layers, move the "Texture" layer to the first place and change the mode from "Normal" to "Multiply." This way, this layer will become translucent. All the layers that fall below it will have that textured effect.

(continued)

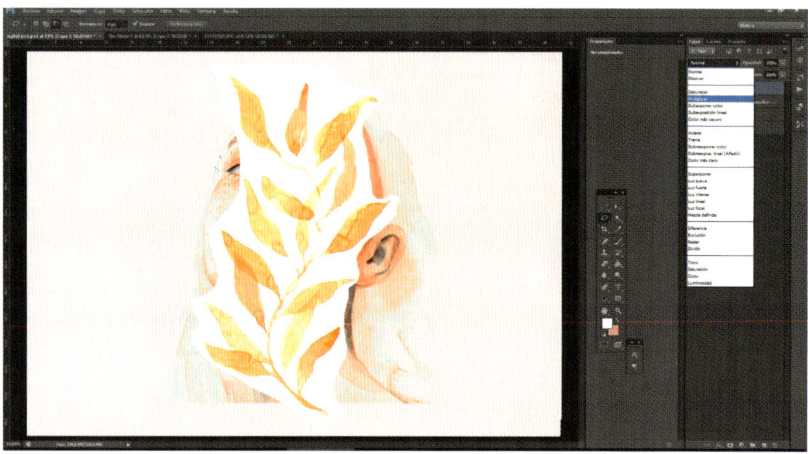

5. Paste another file with the chosen motif. In my case, I scanned a branch with leaves.

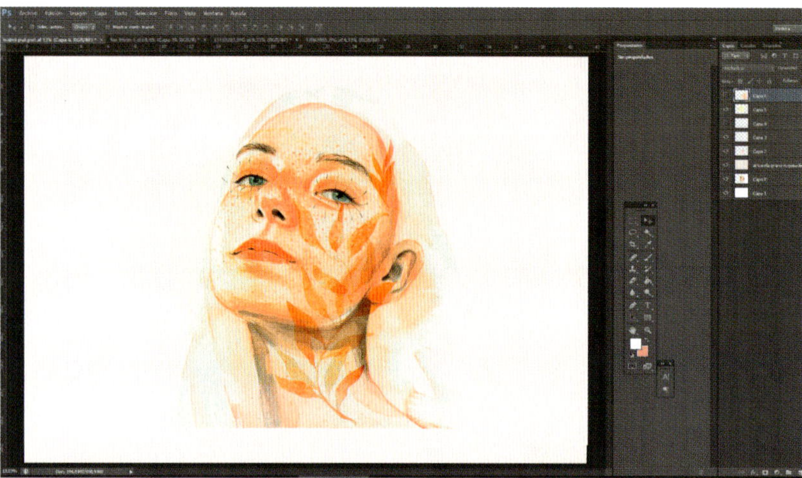

6. Rasterize the layer again so you can edit it to your liking. Repeat the previous step of changing the mode to "Multiply" so that the layer becomes transparent. By going to Edit → Transform → Scale, you can resize it. Use the cursor to move the image and position it the way you want.

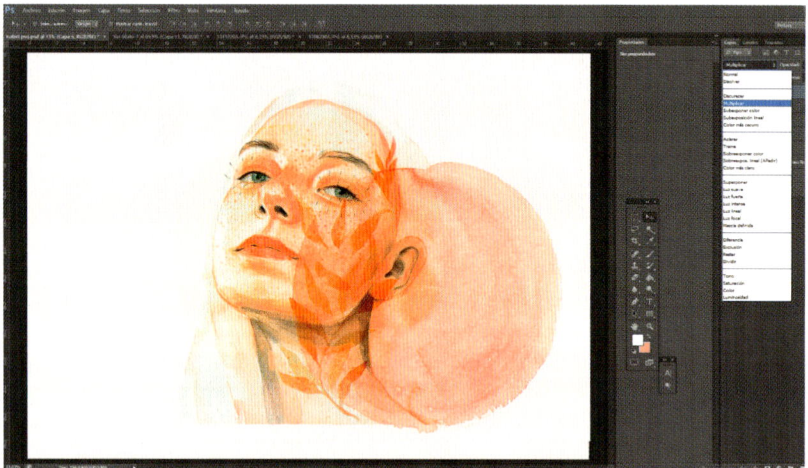

7. Create differently shaped patches with watercolor and scan them if you want to add extra color or texture to the portrait. You can create an image bank of your own watercolor stains and add them to your portraits. In this case, I added a watercolor stain to give more color to the hair and also a slight shadow on the face. As I did earlier, I rasterized the layer and changed the mode to "Multiply." Then, you can make all the color modification adjustments that you think are necessary.

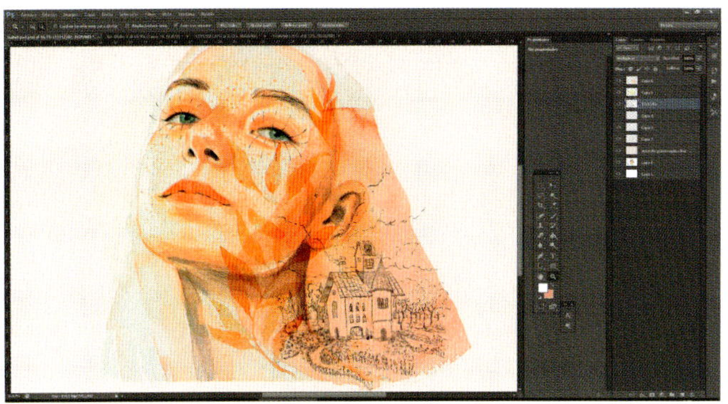

8. Next, I selected the areas I didn't want and carefully deleted them. Again, I added one more drawing that I had previously done in India ink to create an atmosphere and history for the drawing.

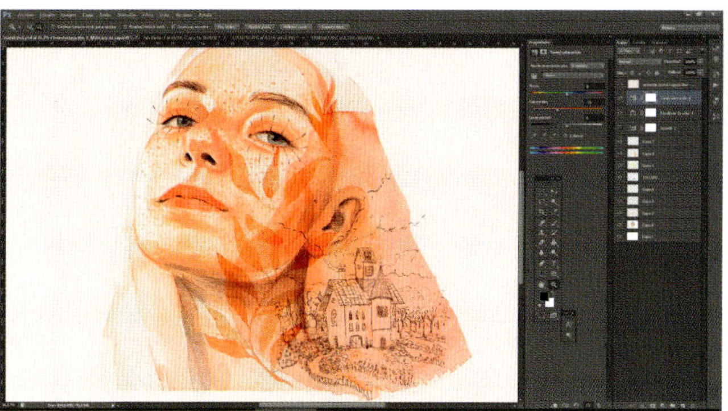

9. Finally, create an adjustment layer to unify all the hues in the portrait, and it's finished! This process has been very simple, but you can create all the layers and modifications you'd like. Really, it's the process itself that's the most fun.

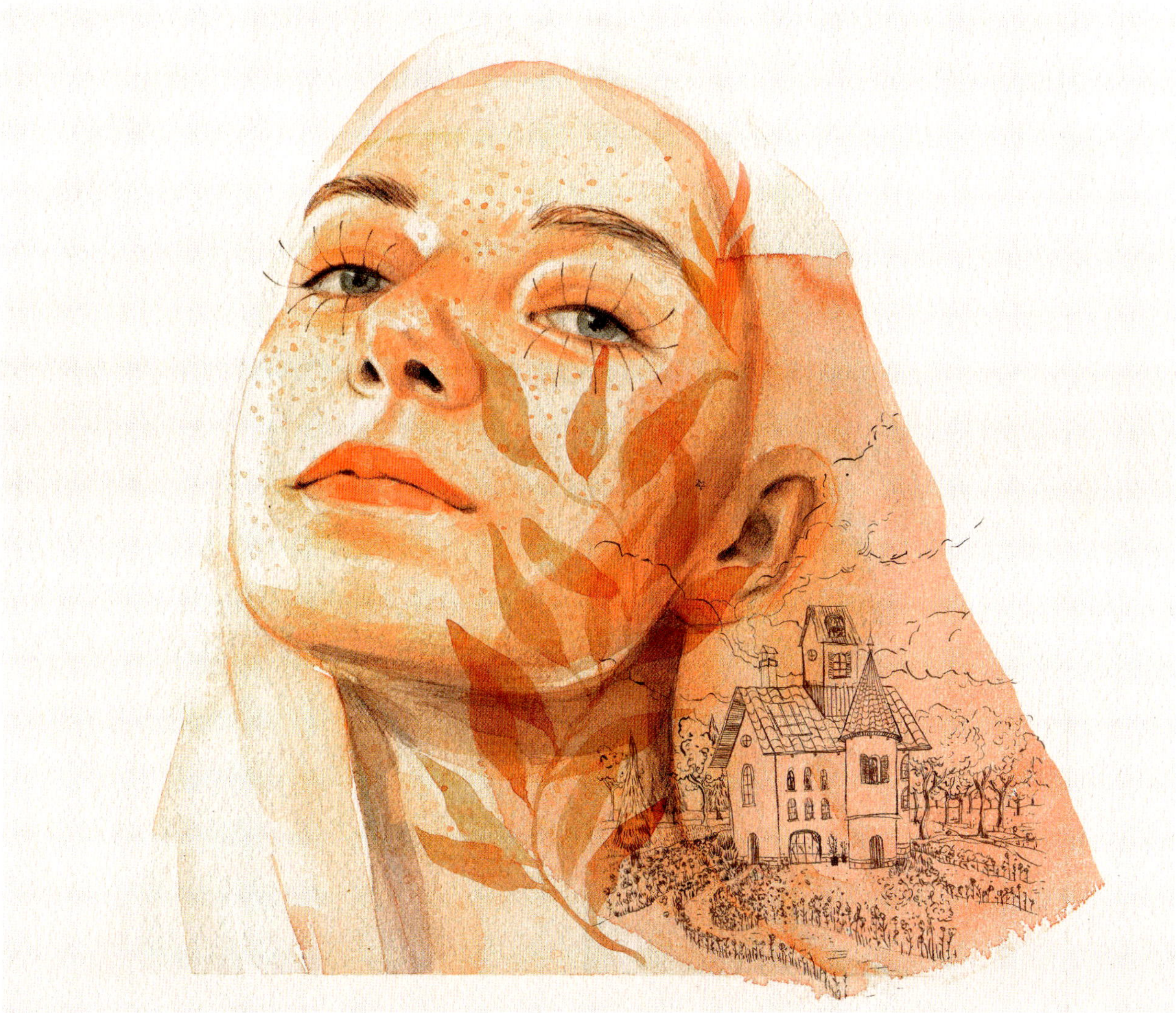

Here's the final portrait.

This doesn't end here. Now it's your turn to keep practicing and exploring! I hope this book has helped you and given you new tools to transform your ideas into reality.

Don't stop showing interest and curiosity to learn new things! Thank you!

ACKNOWLEDGMENTS

I want to thank the entire Quarto team for having confidence in me and showing interest in my work, especially to Joy and Hailey for their kindness and trust. Despite my nerves, I have felt very supported during the process.

To my family, for their unconditional support and for helping me so much from the beginning. To my mother, who always appreciates and values everything I do and made me love drawing without even realizing it since I was a child. Thank you, mom, for teaching me to draw. To my father, for his support and encouragement and for his critiques that make me improve. To my niece, for being so excited about the drawings I make for her, although hers are more exciting for me.

To my closest friends, for heartily rejoicing at the good things that happen to me.

To my former students from the workshop "La Habitación de Lhea," who made me grow both as a person and as a teacher. I have very good memories of that time.

To everyone I don't know personally but who has supported me in one way or another, through social networks, buying and believing in my work, attending courses, and showing interest in what I do, thank you from the bottom of my heart for your love and encouragement. This is also for you.

And to you, reader, who was interested in and purchased this book, thank you very much. I hope you enjoyed it!

ABOUT THE AUTHOR

ANA SANTOS graduated from the University of Salamanca with a degree in Fine Arts, specializing in drawing and graphic design. In addition to her work as an illustrator and designer for a variety of clients, she teaches drawing and painting classes in person as well as on the online teaching platform Domestika. Ana lives in Salamanca, Spain. To learn more, visit anasantosilustracion.com or @anasantos_illustration on Instagram.

INDEX

Quarto.com

First Published in USA in 2023 by Quarry Books,
an imprint of The Quarto Group,
100 Cummings Center, Suite 265-D,
Beverly, MA 01915, USA.
T (978) 282-9590 F (978) 283-2742

Quarry Books titles are also available at discount for retail, wholesale, promotional, and bulk purchase. For details, contact the Special Sales Manager by email at specialsales@quarto.com or by mail at The Quarto Group, Attn: Special Sales Manager, 100 Cummings Center, Suite 265-D, Beverly, MA 01915, USA.

10 9 8 7 6 5 4 3 2

ISBN: 978-0-7603-8242-4

Digital edition published in 2023
eISBN: 978-0-7603-8243-1

Library of Congress Cataloging-in-Publication Data available

Design and page layout: Laura Shaw Design
Cover Image: Ana Santos

Printed in China